AF743365

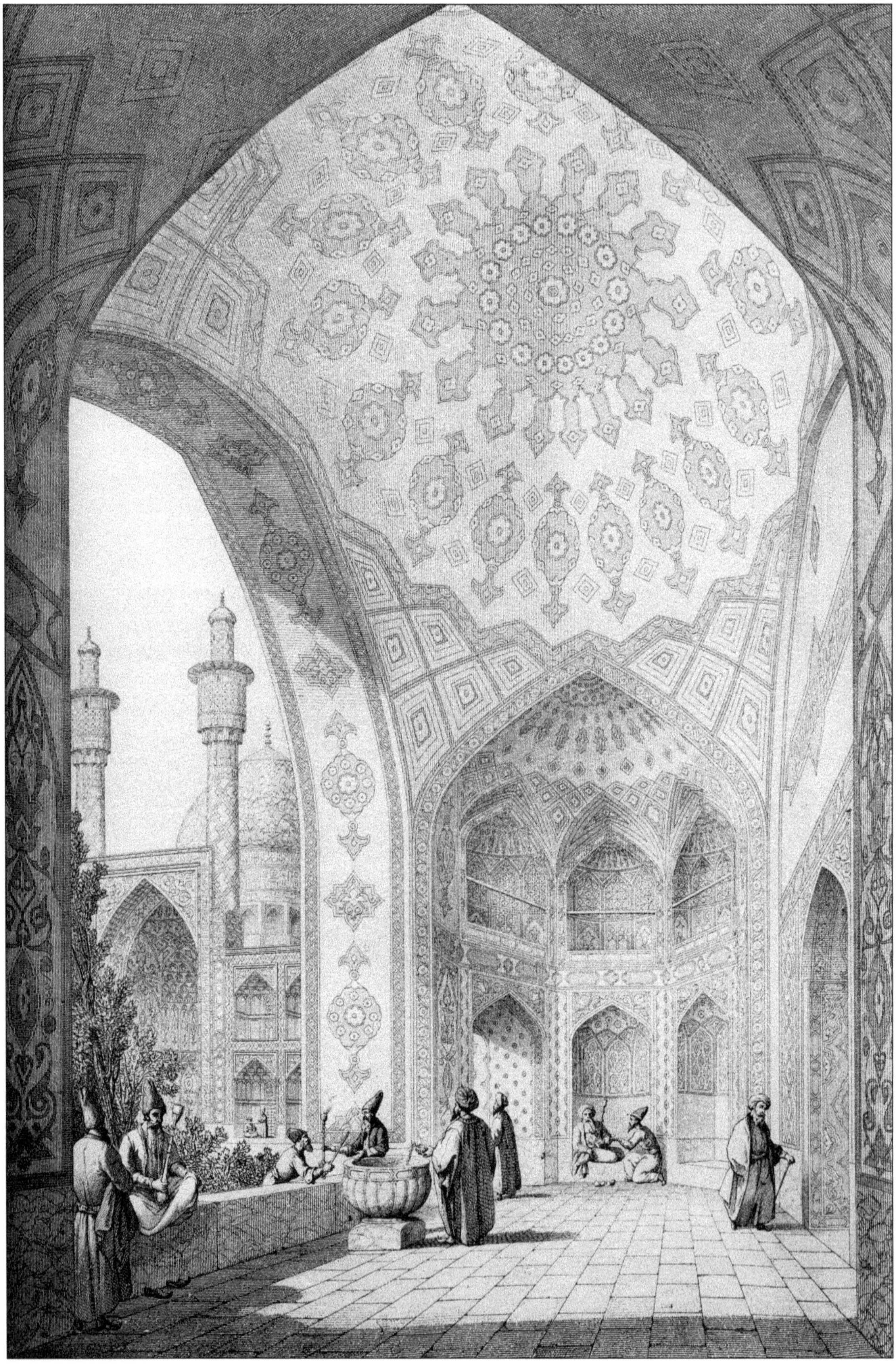

Guilds, Merchants, & Ulama in Nineteenth-Century Iran

WILLEM FLOOR

MAGE
PUBLISHERS

Copyright © 2009 Willem Floor

All rights reserved.
No part of this book may be reproduced
or retransmitted in any manner whatsoever,
except in the form of a review, without the
written permission of the publisher.

Library of Congress Cataloging-in-Publication Data
Floor, Willem M.
Guilds, merchants & ulama in nineteenth-century Iran / by Willem M. Floor.
p. cm.
Includes bibliographical references and index.
ISBN 1-933823-31-3 (pbk. original)
1. Iran--Economic conditions--19th century. 2. Guilds--Iran--History--19th century. 3. Merchants--Iran--History--19th century. 4. Artisans--Iran--History--19th century. 5. Ulama--Iran--History--19th century. 6. Economics--Religious aspects--Islam--History--19th century. 7. Bankers--Iran--History--19th century. 8. Working class--Iran--History--19th century. 9. City and town life--Iran--History--19th century. 10. Iran--History--Qajar dynasty, 1794-1925. I. Title. II. Title: Guilds, merchants, and ulama in nineteenth-century Iran.
HC475.F575 2009
331.0955'09034--dc22
2009006397

Printed and Manufactured in the United States

Paperback Original
ISBN 13: 978-1-933823-31-7
ISBN 10: 1-933823-31-3

Mage books are available at bookstores,
through the internet, or directly from the publisher:
Mage Publishers, 1032 29th Street, NW, Washington, DC 20007
202-342-1642 • as@mage.com • 800-962-0922
visit Mage Publishers online at
www.mage.com

CONTENTS

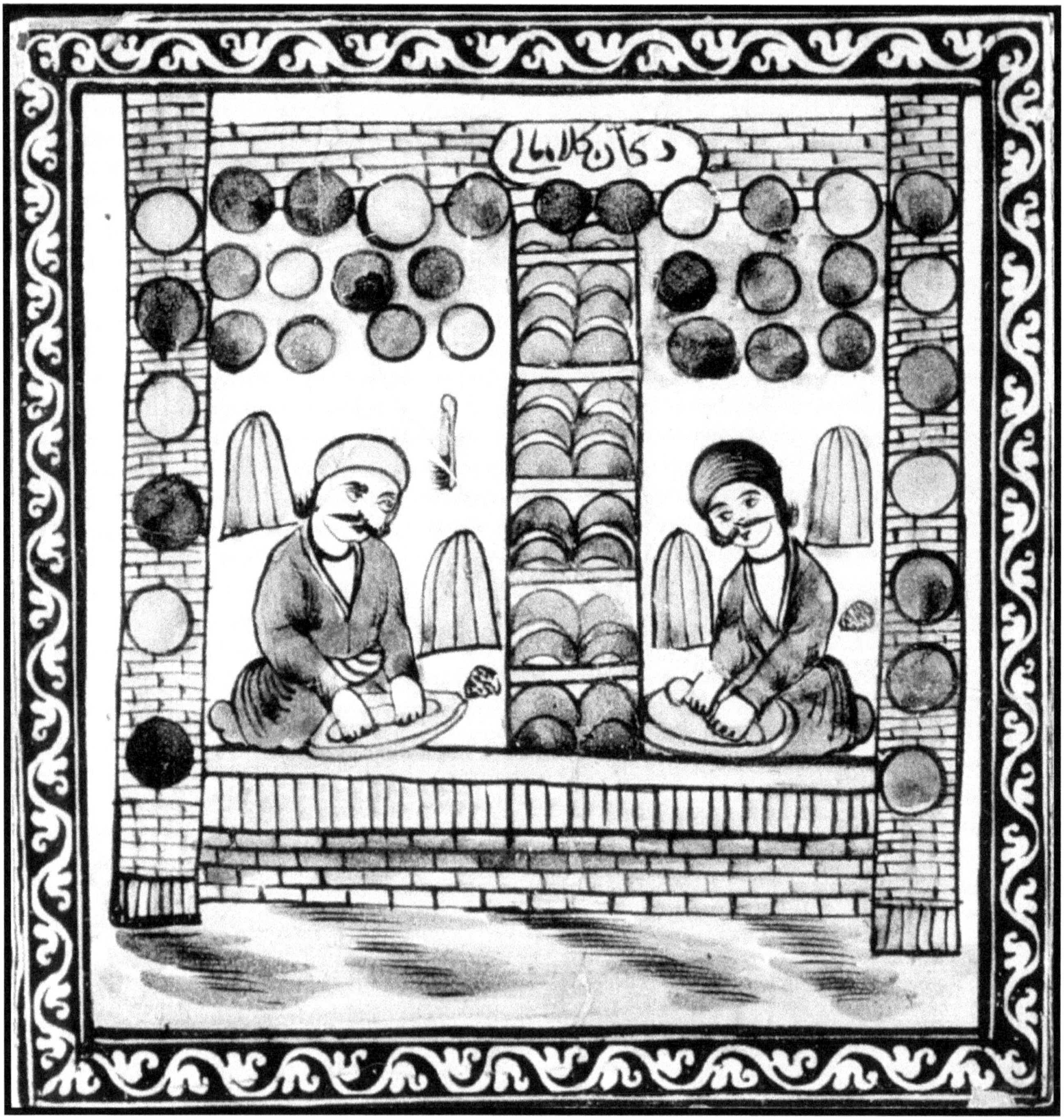

Hat Makers

TABLES

FIGURES

Images in the book on the pages listed below are from the following:

Pages: Cover, 98, Mme Jane Dieulafoy, *La Perse, La Chaldée, et La Susiane* (Paris, 1887).

Pages: 22, 161, 166, 190, 200, S. G. W. Benjamin, *Persia and the Persians* (London, 1887).

Pages: 191, 204, 207, Postcards circa 1900.

Pages: ii, xii, 72, 168, 192, 201, 206, Henri-Rene d'Allemagne, *Du Khorassan au Pays des Backhtoiaris. Trois mois de voyage en Perse* 4 vols. (Paris, 1911), vol. 1.

Page: 51, Iraj Afshar (compiled), *A Treasury of Early Iranian Photographs* (Tehran, 1992)

Pages: x, 162, 165, 170, 199, 208, Jürgen W. Frembgen, *Derwische und Zuckerbäcker* (Munich, 1996).

Pages: viii, 136, 158, 164, 177, 189, 193, 194, 197, 198, 200, Friederike Voigt, *Qadscharische Bildfliesen im Ethnologischen Museum Berlin* (Berlin, 2002).

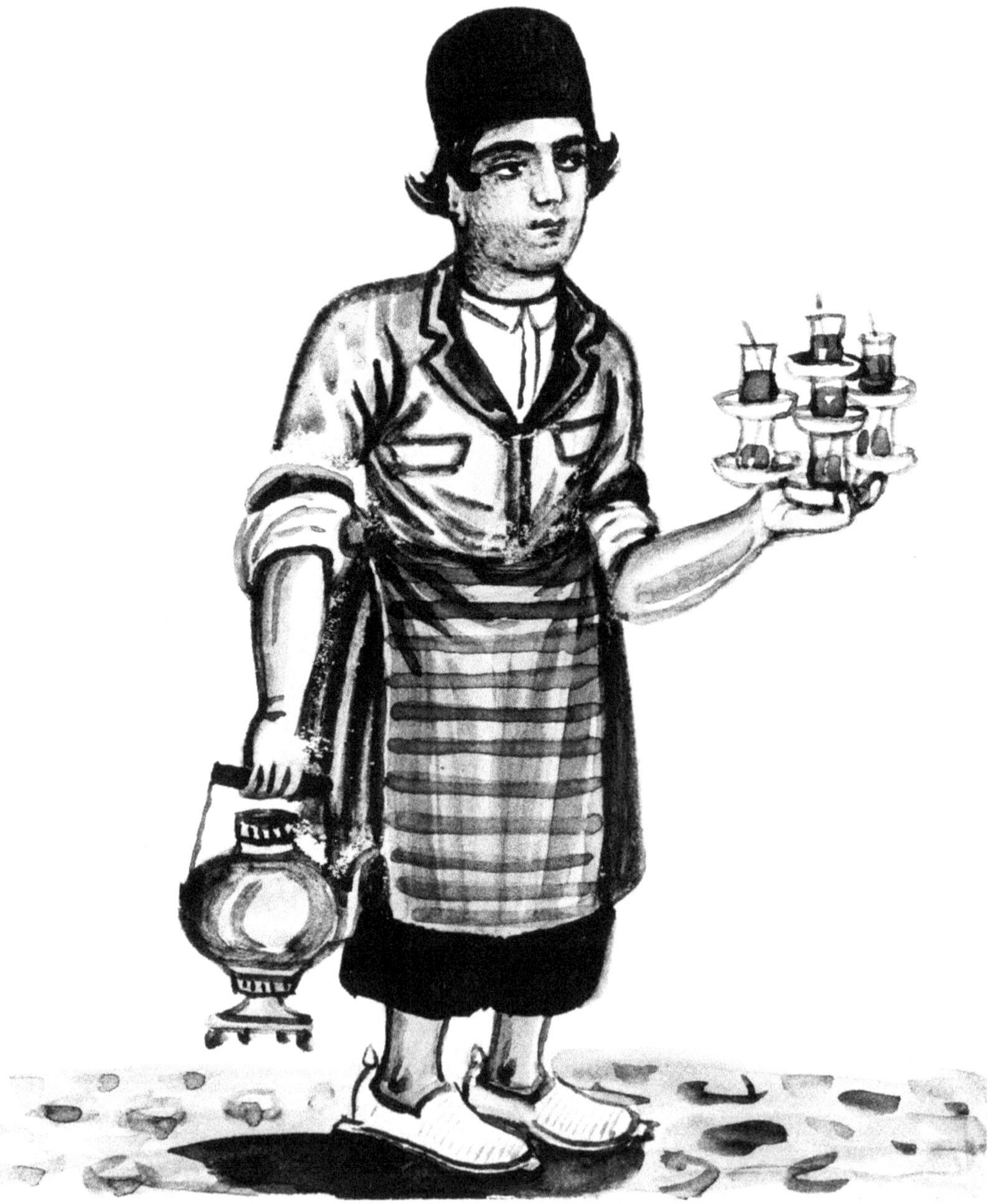

FOREWORD

In this volume I have brought together a number of my articles that deal with those groups that dominated socio-economic and political life in urban Iran during the nineteenth century, to wit: (1) merchants, (2) bankers, and (3) religious professionals. All three articles were previously published in the *Zeitschrift der Morgenländische Gesellschaft* (ZDMG) and I thank the editor of the journal for giving me permission to republish them in this volume.[1] Although I have not changed anything in any of the above mentioned studies, I have occasionally added references to later publications that are relevant; I have also inserted sub-headings. The fourth group that dominated urban life in Iran was that of the traders and craftsmen who were organized into guilds *(asnaf)*. They were the subject of my dissertation, which I publish here for the first time.[2] Because I had not published an article on the labor class in the nineteenth century, I have written a short overview of its main characteristics during the second half of the nineteenth century especially for this publication.[3]

This volume begins with a discussion of the structure of Iranian society in the nineteenth century to provide context and thus a better understanding of the parameters within which these various groups were operating. As the opening chapter of my dissertation, I thought it appropriate to have it also as the opening chapter to this volume of collected studies. I hope that the publication of these related studies in one volume will stimulate further discussion and study of socio-economic conditions in Qajar Iran.

1. See the bibliography for the particulars about where in the *ZDMG* these articles have appeared.

2. This statement is not entirely correct as my study on the guilds has been published earlier in Persian, see Floor 1366.

3. I have published a study on the labor class in the twentieth century in Iran, see Floor 1984 a, which has been republished in the companion volume to this one, Floor 2009a.

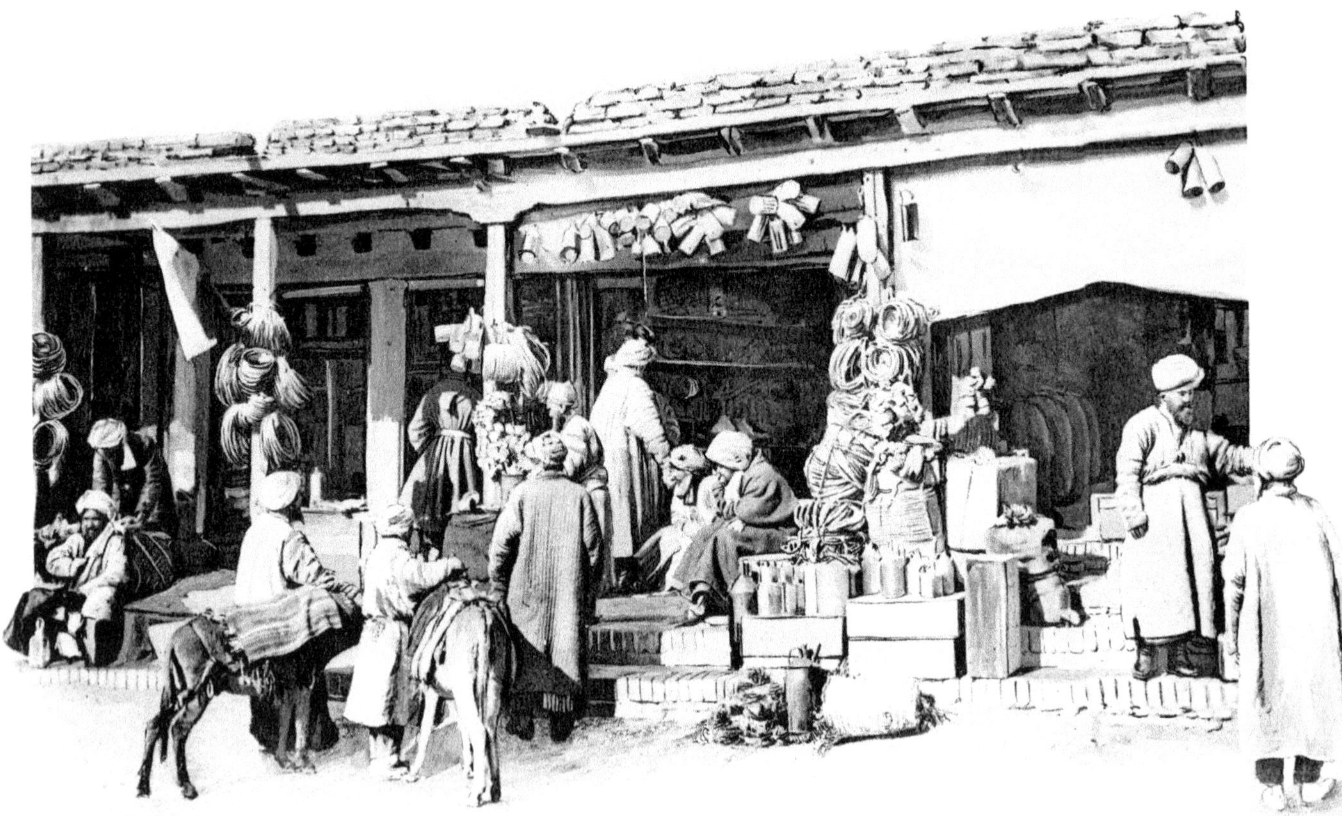

CHAPTER ONE

The Structure of Qajar Society

Before I start discussing the various economic actors and developments in nineteenth century Iran, I'd like to point out a few facts, which usually are neglected in discussions about the country during this period. Qajar Iran was a pre-industrial society with a rather weak central government. The various cities enjoyed self-government to a certain extent, as did many corporate groups, such as tribes, guilds and village communities. The main function of the Iranian bureaucracy was the levying of taxes. As long as the corporate groups paid their taxes and did not try to tilt the balance of power they were allowed to administrate their own internal affairs without too much governmental interference. This policy did not stem from some democratic notion as is clear from the repressive nature of the Iranian police force.[1]

The power elite did not have enough manpower to extend their sphere of influence to all layers of society; and rivalry between factions among the elite undermined their original solidarity. Furthermore the paucity of communications greatly hampered the effectiveness of the central government. All this forced the central government to rely in the outlying provinces on the local elite. This co-operation between the central government and the local influential families enhanced the position of both. The central government was thus assured of local powerful support, which gave a boost to its not infrequently unstable rule. One such local backer was the *kalantar* whose task it was to keep the population happy, so that they would pray for the well-being of the Shah[2] and pay their taxes in time.[3]

Qajar Iran was what is mostly described as a feudal or pre-industrial society.[4] Characteristic of this kind of society is its broad agrarian base and the rule of a small group

---

1. Lambton 1954.
2. Migeod 1990.
3. See Floor 1971 b.
4. I prefer the term pre-industrial to that of feudal society. The term feudal, in particular for the Middle East, offers many problems. On the term pre-industrial society see Sjoberg 1960. On feudalism see Cahen 1960, 2-20; Couldborn 1956.

over a highly illiterate population. The power elite resided in the cities which served as administrative, cultural and commercial centers. Since within this elite the literate group was small and communication between the several parts of the country was bad, the central government had to allow far-reaching decentralization of its patrimonial rule[5] in favor of its supporters at the local level.

At the apex of the ruling elite was the shah, whose power was in principle absolute. By right of his ancestor's conquest, he considered the country to be his personal domain (*dowleh*)[6], and as defender of the faith in his realm, he considered himself to be the Shadow of God. His subjects or *ra`aya* thought of him as the Asylum of the Faith and the Center of the Universe, whose wishes and commands one did not question. Opposition to or rebellion against him was regarded as opposition to God.[7] Thus the shah was the sole source of power, who could appoint and dismiss officials at his pleasure. He was the sole executive; thus officials had no real responsibility[8], they were his [to] sacrifice (*qorban*).

Qajar Iranian society was made up of a conglomerate of corporate structures, each with its own base and influential top. These various corporate groups resembled each other in structure, but each had its own interests and was composed of such groups as a tribe, a clan, a village, a group of ulama, a guild, etc. The central government being unable to appoint the leaders of important groups or to control them completely maintained a sometimes delicate balance by playing them off against one another.[9]

After their conquest of Iran, the Qajars did not establish a new order or start a reorganization of the existing societal structures. Rather they imposed themselves upon the existing situation, putting their own people in positions that had been occupied by members of the previous power elite. On the local level they left the system as it was, as they did with the holders of the offices there. Therefore, Qajar power structure was never secure, for many of the old magnates such as the *beglerbegis* of Tabriz and Shiraz and the tribal chiefs were left in their places and merely 'converted' into supporters of the Qajars.[10]

5. "Princely possessions directly administered as territorial domains have always only constituted part of the ruler's political realm, which in addition embraces other territories which are not regarded as domains proper, but merely as subject to his political authority. Whenever then, a prince organizes his political authority on the basic principles that apply to the exercise of his rule over his domains, we speak of a patrimonial state structure." Weber 1925, 684.

6. "Contemplating Persia neither with the eye of a patriot nor of a father, but rather as a property hold in lease of uncertain duration, his only concern is how to make the most of his incumbency. He treats it as his conquest and not as his country and his aim is to combine the two objects of breaking down the power of all those chiefs who under an able sovereign should form the strength of the empire," Fraser 1834, 309. On the term *dowleh*, Gibb observed for an earlier period: "Note that there is no Arab word for 'state' as general concept. Even for Ibn Khaldun the word dawla often explicitly means and always implies the membership of the ruling family. Similarly, mamlaka combines the concept of 'kingship' and 'kingdom'." Gibb 1966, 46, note 1.

7. Lambton 1958, 43, note 5, 44. Opponents of the shah, however, would justify their actions by pointing out the irreligious and ungodly character of the regime, comparing the shah to Yazid, the murderer of Hoseyn, the second Imam. Keddie 1969, 32, note 2.

8. Lambton 1961, 132.

9. Lambton 1961, 130.

10. Lambton 1961, 130. On the *beglerbegi*s see Floor 1971 b.

The prevailing political system was operated by patronage, which involved a wide system of contractual and personal loyalties based upon the bargaining power of the actors in the political arena. Though patronage (which is a structural principle which underlies asymmetric, personal transactions involving protection and loyalty between two persons or groups of persons) need not imply difference in social power, this generally was the case in Qajar Iran. By virtue of their patron or broker's (*vaseteh*) protection individuals could improve their situation or see justice done. Besides, by belonging to a corporate group (or groups) one could acquire some measure of political and judicial status. It also gave individuals a sense of belonging and recognition and the opportunity to extend their social relationships and economic advantages.

Furthermore, it often provided the only means to effect vertical social mobility or emancipation. Whenever the government took oppressive measures a powerful broker or a group mediated (*tavassot*) on behalf of the oppressed individual or group and would 'bargain'[11] for better conditions. Therefore, in this system everyone was a bargainer, though some were in a better position for bargaining than others. It is not surprising that de Gobineau stated that "all Persians are born bargainers."[12] The principal bargainers in this society, which may be best described as having a spoils system, were first the Qajar clan, followed by the foremost tribal families, the leading religious authorities, and the families who drew their strength mainly from landed estates.[13] Nepotism and inheritance of offices were particular consequences of this state of affairs.

The unstable and often irresponsible[14] rule of the Qajars was caused by this basic insecurity which permeated all layers of society, for even power and wealth only meant relative security. Therefore, the central government concentrated on one task, viz. the collection of taxes, neglecting other functions such as the provision of public services and the maintenance of order, or leaving these functions to the local elite.[15] Government offices were sold to the highest bidders, the collection of taxes was farmed and the royal domains were sold. But not only the wealthy and powerful shared in the spoils. A whole army of clients, relatives and other supporters also profited from their patrons' positions. They often were the executives of their patrons and/or the subtenants of offices and of tax-farming.[16] "The lower classes are thus literally and strictly rayas –flocks- which are kept merely for their fleece; and they are usually shorn as often and closely as greatly to diminish their

11. Binder defines bargaining as: "The technique of achieving cooperation between the independent power structures or of achieving legitimatization and which permeates all phases of political life." Binder 1962, 228. For the concept of *tavassot* see de Gobineau 1907b, 407-11. On the corporate groups see Lambton 1954.

12. de Gobineau 1907b, 379.

13. Lambton 1961, 131. The political and administrative situation was described as follows in 1844. "You observe that this manner of administration resembles passably an organized banditry; it is the realization of the principle of the right of the strongest to its largest extent. It is this spoils system that is adapted and put into practice everywhere." RO 4, 117.

14. 'Responsible' meaning here the pursuance of policies which are prudent and mutually consistent. See Birch 1964, 17-21.

15. See on the tasks of government Sjoberg 1960, 244-52; Keddie 1969, 34; see also Floor 1971 b.

16. Keddie 1969, 34; Lambton 1961, 132-35. "Tehran is a vast bazaar where jobs and favors are sold by auction and almost in public. RO 4, 115.

value and the profit of the owner. So grasping is the hand of avarice that the fowl itself that lays the golden eggs is not frequently killed," wrote Perkins.[17]

For this was the lot and main function of the lower classes, to foot the bill run up by the extravagance of the elite, both local and national. Because tenure of office and one's position in general depended on one's bargaining power, officials were never sure for how long they would be in office. If a patron fell into disfavor his clients were in trouble too. This insecurity often led to oppressive behavior by all officials from high to low. Newly appointed officials or tax-farmers would start their term of office by demanding large sums in advance of the normal date. In 1874, Pelly characterized this state of affairs as follows: "The country is revenued as if the Government were to end with expiry of the governor's lease."[18]

Oppression weighed heavily in the country. Famine, epidemics, raids and high prices already made the population's lot a woeful one, and then the government needed ever more money to pay for the upkeep of the army, the country's administration and the shah's European travels.[19] There were, of course, traditional limits beyond which the elite could not go. This, according to Gordon, "was the ability to pay; as measured by the patience of the sufferers."[20]

Apart from this physical limit there were other means for putting a (temporary) stop to exaction, such as resistance and the seeking of *bast* or sanctuary. The most important device which the lower classes could employ was the seeking of mediation (*tavassot*) of which sanctuary is a special form. Because individuals of the lower classes did not have much bargaining power and had no direct access to the government they could only turn to individual brokers (*vaseteh*) who were accessible to all and had access to all levels of government, viz. the ulama.

The position of the religious leaders or ulama in Qajar Iran was of great importance. Their attitude towards political authority was defined by Twelver Shi'ism, which has as its doctrine that after the occultation of the 12th Imam all worldly activities, especially government ones, were illegitimate. Notwithstanding that the ulama were of the opinion that "there was no true authority, nor the possibility thereof: only power,"[21] the Qajars sought recognition and legitimacy for their regime. They aimed to achieve this, apart from pointing to their alleged descent from the former 'legitimate' Safavid dynasty,[22] by mollifying or bribing the ulama with money, land and influence, so that the ulama, if they would not support the regime outright, would at least acquiesce in the existing political authority. Though the Qajars usually did not make explicit that the ulama should support their rule in return, acceptance of a government appointment or present was considered as recognition of the government by the ulama.

---

17. Perkins 1834, 282.
18. Quoted by Lorini 1900, 278; Lambton 1961, 134-35.
19. Lambton 1953, 151.
20. Gordon 1896, 38.
21. Algar 1969, 4.
22. Asaf 1348/1969, 51, note 1.

Although many of the ulama made common cause with the political authorities, in general they enjoyed more respect and confidence than any other class. Still the extent of this confidence depended on the measure of their integrity and non identification with the government.[23] The power of the ulama was based on the following factors.[24] Firstly, they acted as a buffer between the government and the people, by protecting the people and mediating for them whenever they were oppressed.[25] Secondly, there was the *taqlid* (adherence to an exemplary model), which was the basis of the claim to legitimate power by the ulama. Because the shah was no *mojtahed*, he perforce had to become a *moqalled* (a follower) to a *mojtahed* and uphold his rulings; because the *mojtahed* is regarded as the only authority capable of interpreting the intention of the hidden Imam. Therefore, until his coming "all wordly authority is theoretically bound to consult and defer to the *mojtaheds*; purely temporal authority being only an expedient." The shahs, however, did not want to become the executors of the *mojtaheds*' will and thus alienated themselves from the ulama. Thus by having a legitimate claim to superiority over the secular political authority in the eyes of the people, the ulama became the people's natural leaders.[26] Thirdly, the political authorities often paid the ulama to temper their opposition in the frequent conflicts between the religious leaders and the political authorities, which made the former somewhat dependent on the latter's munificence.

The ties which the ulama had with the tradesmen and artisans were strong ones. The bazaaris were very religious and as the ulama had the virtual monopoly of the knowledge of the Holy Scriptures, they were looked to for spiritual guidance. Besides, commercial transactions, courts of arbitration and the like brought both groups into close contact with each other. In fact, many guild members were mullahs (ordinary cleric) themselves, and in general the ulama had important economic interests to defend. These two factors certainly strengthened their mutual interests.[27]

Many important religious leaders wielded power through their connections with the lower classes in general and the guilds in particular. They used their position and their pulpits to bargain with the government for privileges for their followers and themselves. If their mediation was successful it enhanced their position in the eyes of their followers. We observe that on several occasions the 'clergy' successfully withstood government pressure brought to bear on them, which added to their status and influence. Important landmarks in the competition between political and religious authorities were the combined opposition of the ulama and the population against the Reuter concession (1872), the Tobacco concession (1890-91), and the fight for the Constitution (1905-06).[28] Still, on the whole, the ulama, of whom many came from elite families themselves, gave sanction to the government, or rather showed passive approval.

---

23. Lambton 1958, 49; Algar 1969, 20-21.
24. See e.g. Keddie 1969 and Algar 1969, 11, 21.
25. Algar 1969, 11, 21.
26. Algar 1969, 9-10; Lambton 1958, 49; Lambton 1961, 135-6.
27. Gordon 1896, 24, 30; Algar 1969, 1416; Wills 1886, 45.
28. Keddie 1966.

Within the three-class class structure which may be observed in the cities, guild members belonged to the lower classes.[29] It was unusual for individuals to rise on the social ladder, although exceptions occurred.[30] In general, however, one had to maintain one's proper rank. The three classes could be distinguished by such traits as dress, speech, religion and political power.[31] Only partners of equal social rank were married to each other, which marriages were considered to be a family affair rather than a union between individuals.

The extended family was they key-unit in social life, reciprocal obligations and favors between relatives were more important than any other form of social obligation. Accordingly, duty to the family permeated all institutional activities. Iranians therefore considered nepotism a positive thing, for a man without family ties had little status in society, if any at all.

Economic life was dominated by a small group of influential wholesale merchants. It was on this group that the guilds depended heavily for their supply, capital and credit. The elite only interfered in the economic system by making large profits through the sale of agricultural products, by taxes levied on trade, and by selling monopolies which they had created themselves. Thus in Qajar Iran the economic system was left free to the 'hidden hand' and the rapacity of the few. Consequently the organization of the economy was poor. This was due amongst other things to poor communications (bad roads and slow transportation by mule and camel) and to the lack of organization among the merchants. Distributing techniques were inadequate and trading practices inefficient and costly. This influenced the price system, often to the detriment of the consumer.

29. "The upper classes are composed of officials, military men, ministers etc. The middle classes, of landowners merchants and often money lenders. The lower classes, of servants, traders and artisans. " RMM 33, 77.

30. Lambton 1961, 134.

31. Sjoberg 1960, 123-33; Lambton 1961.

CHAPTER TWO

The Working Class in Iran, 1880-1900

I thought it would be useful to provide a short introduction on the size and composition of the gainfully employed population in nineteenth century Iran, so that the reader has an idea about the relative size and the main characteristics of each of the different socio-economic groups. Because the other chapters deal with groups that may be characterized as employers, I describe in the following pages how the urban poor were employed in the nineteenth century, under what conditions and for what wages.[1] It is good to remember that the urban poor were the people who worked for those groups discussed in chapters three to five.

INCREASE OF URBAN POPULATION

Until recent times Iran was an agrarian subsistence economy. By 1900 it had a population of about 9.8 million. The majority of that population was rural and engaged in agriculture.[2] The urban population had doubled between 1850 (9%) and 1910 (18%), with three towns having more than 100,000 inhabitants: Tehran with about 280,000, Tabriz with 200,000 and Isfahan with 100,000. Four other towns had each 50,000 inhabitants or more.[3] This increase in the urban population was mainly due to rural-urban migration caused by the Great Famine (1870-73) and the large-scale sale of crown lands (*khaleseh*) after 1885.[4] Tehran had a much higher population growth rate (8.6%) during 1873-1910 than the other six towns (1%-4%) due to the large public and development works carried out in the capital and its growing importance as a commercial and services center. As a result of these developments the demand for unskilled labor increased in the 1870s and 1880s. A considerable part of urban casual labor was represented by a flow of rural seasonal labor that descended

1. How the situation of the urban poor developed after 1900 see Floor 2009a.
2. Floor 2003a.
3. Gilbar 1976, 147-49
4. Qazvini 1370, 64, 86; Floor 1999 a.

on the cities each year. As a result, one contemporary social critic remarked that, "Most of the inhabitants of Tehran are *ghoraba-ye motafarraqeh* (dislocated strangers) and *motarde-din* (transients)."[5] There was not only rural-urban migration, but also urban-urban migration. The latter was usually migration from one, even large, town to another, larger town. This held especially for skilled artisans, such as from Isfahan, many of whom migrated to Tehran in search of employment.[6] The same phenomenon could be observed in other towns such as Mashhad and for N. Iran in general, whence many peasants migrated to the Caucasus and Transcaspia.[7]

THE SIZE AND COMPOSITION OF THE WORKING CLASS

The economically active male population over ten years of age was estimated to be 3.9 million around 1910, of which 3.5 million were engaged in agriculture. This means that the active workforce in the urban areas at that time amounted to about 400,000.[8] This figure no doubt was higher, and may be estimated at 450,000 owing to the fact that boys under ten were also employed in handicrafts, services, commerce and manufacturing. Moreover, quite a substantial number of women were engaged in a number of economic activities, especially in carpet and other weaving activities.

Table 2.1: Urban Employment by Sector in Iran (circa 1910)

Type of Activity	Number of Workers
State sector + leisured class	80,000
Trades and Crafts sector (guilds)	90,000
Services sector	120,000
Modern sector	18,000
Day laborers	80,000

Elsewhere I have provided the arguments for the numbers in Table 2.1.[9] Here I only will comment on the state sector and that of the day laborers, respectively, the smallest and largest urban economic sector.

STATE SECTOR

This sector was composed of the administrative and religious class and their support structure, including the army. The administrative and religious class was in charge of the administration of the country. Its function was to: provide security, administer justice, col-

5. Qazvini 1370, 71.
6. Tahvildar 1341, 108, 113.
7. Adamec 1974, vol. 2, 478; Hakimian 1985.
8. Bharier 1971, 3, 27.
9. Floor 1984 b; Floor 1985 a, and Floor 1991; these have been reprinted in Floor 2009a.

lect revenues, provide education, and satisfy spiritual needs. This ruling class maintained its control over the cities, villages and tribes through a hierarchical network of traditional, but officially recognized, self-appointed representatives of these various groups such as town mayors *(kalantar)*, chiefs of city quarters and guilds *(kadkhoda)*, chief merchant *(malek al-tojjar)*, village chiefs *(kadkhoda)*, tribal chiefs *(il-khan)* and an array of religious professionals *(sheikh al-islam, qadi, modarres, naqib)* as well as the lower echelon of support staff. The same class also produced the officer corps that was in charge of the rurally recruited army, part of which was urban based. This part of the urban labor force probably represented some 40,000 men or some 10% of the total.[10] This total included the leisure class that did not have to work for a living, but occasionally also held government functions. The religious establishment that represented 3% of the urban population as well as important merchants is also included among the government officials.[11] I have estimated the part of the army that was urban-based at some 40,000.[12]

SKILLED CRAFTS AND TRADES

Artisans, traders and workers formed the main part of the urban population in the 19th century down to the 20th century.[13] Although we lack reliable statistical data, it would seem that, in the 19th century, about 30 percent of the urban population was gainfully employed in a craft, trade, or some other activity in what we would call to-day the formal sector, i.e., they were organized in guilds.[14] Most of the urban working population consisted of males: boys and adult men, because urban women's economic activities were mainly limited to employment as seamstresses, spinners, darners, sewers, knitters, weavers, maids, midwives, healers, preachers, matchmakers, oil-makers, attendants in public baths and mortuaries, beggars, singers, dancers, and musicians.[15]

The major centers of traditional crafts were: Isfahan, Kashan, Yazd, Kerman, Shiraz, Hamadan, and Tabriz. In addition, secondary towns such as Mashhad, Rasht, and Qom produced certain specific goods. The main craft was the textile industry and its ancillaries, which represented 30 percent of the industrial labor force in many towns.[16] Other important activities were construction, metalworking, leather working and food processing crafts.[17] According to Abdullaev, some 35,000 persons were employed in these crafts.[18] The kind of 'industrial mix' a city displayed was very much determined by its

10. See below chapter six.
11. Floor 2001, 55; see also below chapter five.
12. Based on Migeod 1990, 312ff.
13. Floor, 1984 b, 1985a + b, 1991; see also below chapter six.
14. Kuznetsova 1970, 104; see below chapter five.
15. Höltzer 2535, 22.
16. Floor 1999b, chapter one.
17. Floor 2003b.
18. Abdullaev 1963, 212.

natural resource endowment. "For nowhere as much as in Persia are certain industries as firmly tied to individual towns."[19]

Rural-urban migration had consequences for the occupational composition of the urban population. Whereas in the beginning of the 19th century the formal sector had represented some 30 percent of the urban population, by the 1870s it only represented some 20 percent. In 1870, according to the British consul Thompson, some 10 percent of the population of Tehran was engaged in a formal trade or craft,[20] while his colleague Jones reports in 1871 that "the population of Tabrees is about 200,000 of which the artisan and skilled labor class constitutes 1/12 of the population."[21] In Hamadan, one-eighth of the population was engaged in the tanning industry, its major economic activity.[22] These figures do not include female employment, but women were not part of the urban formal sector. They were engaged in cottage industry activities, part of the putting-out system. If women are included the percentage of the population employed in formal crafts and trades might reach 30 percent.[23] These trade and craftsmen were organized in guilds (*asnaf*). Their organization, characteristics and issues are discussed in chapter six.

SERVICE SECTOR AND DAY LABORERS

A significant share of the urban population was still engaged in agricultural activities such as market gardening and truck farming, which in major towns still held first place in the 1850s.[24] A group peculiar to many Caspian towns was that of the 4,200 fisheries workers, of whom 2,000 were Russian.[25] In addition, there was the group of servants and retainers of all descriptions that served the government and leisure class. In Tehran, they represented some 13% of the total population or about 40 percent of the male population. According to Soltanzadeh, the number of servants and unemployed laborers amounted to 30,000 persons in 1922, or 15 percent of the total population.[26] Moreover, there were those employed in the business of transportation, which by the turn of the 20th century also included wheeled transportation. Porters and dockers in the Northern ports alone numbered 4,000 workers.[27] Finally, this sector included all those who had no regular employment and tried by hook and crook to make a living, or in other word the poor. In total the services sector and day laborers represented about 45 percent of the urban labor force. In the following I discuss how the urban poor were employed.

---

19. Polak 1865, 2, 166.
20. Floor 1987, 1, 36.
21. Jones 1870, 417.
22. DCR 3189, 45.
23. Kuznetsova 1978.
24. Issawi 1971, 286; Floor 2003a.
25. Abdullaev 1963, 212; Floor, 2003 b.
26. Chaqueri 1972, 102.
27. Abdullaev 1963, 212.

DAY LABORERS

As a result of the rural-urban migration after the 1870s, a class of unskilled laborers grew, especially in Tehran, which was known as *kolah-namadi*, "the felt-capped artisans and humble folk of the bazars."[28] This development, combined with the disappearance of many craftsmen, their products being replaced by European imports, increased the services sector considerably.[29] The majority of these newcomers to the urban areas were employed as unskilled laborers, mostly in menial jobs such as porters, charcoal makers, cobblers, sweepers, refuse gatherers (*kannas*), brick-makers and construction workers, in short in all the inferior jobs of the economy.[30] In these informal sector activities casual day laborers were used. During the winter, many of the poor even had to compete with the soldiers for the same jobs, because they also had to eke out a living, because their pay was only for half a year and always in arrears.

Working and other conditions were entirely informal for unskilled laborers. The employers, both the merchants and the masters of the various guilds, drew on the mass of the urban poor, who constituted an important and growing part of the urban population after 1870. However, the demand for unskilled work was not enough to supply everybody with gainful employment. Consequently, streets and bazaars were overcrowded with poor and unemployed persons, ready to sell their labor for a piece of bread after 1870.[31] This source of cheap labor, which initially had been mainly seasonal in nature, settled permanently in the major cities after 1880.

The situation in Tabriz, for example, differed that of Tehran. "With the exception of one or two branches of industry, such as the manufacture of carpets and shawls, there is no demand for skilled labor."[32] In Tabriz, for example, "The laboring classes are nearly all natives of Tabrees, few villagers being found amongst them, except in the capacity of porters or carriers."[33] The lower participation of peasants in the Tabriz population is due to the decrease of its importance as a commercial center and migration from Azerbaijan to Baku and Mashhad.[34] In other cities, the situation was similar to that of Tehran. In Mashhad lived thousands of Hazaras and Barbaris who were the wood cutters and water drawers.[35] According to Qazvini, a contemporary social critic, there "are now 50,000 poor beggars in Tehran, most of which are Kurdish and Turkish tribal women and children. Most of them were driven to poverty by government officials. Most of them come from [privatized] *khaleseh* [crown] land."[36] Although this number is highly exaggerated it nevertheless is an indication of the significance, nature and the perceived size of the problem.

28. Gordon 1896, 73-74; Browne 1889, 116
29. Floor 1991, Ibid., 1999b; Ibid., 2003b.
30. AP 29, 702.
31. Issawi 1971, 48-50; Qazvini 1370, 71-74.
32. Jenner 1870, 396
33. Jenner 1870, 402, 417.
34. Hakimian 1985.
35. Adamec 1974, vol. 2, 478
36. Qazvini 1370, 81.

Because of the irregular income of most casual laborers they used various survival strategies. "Of the workmen who are married, some possess a small piece of land, which helps them to maintain their family; and is some cases the wives and children add a trifle to the family pittance by sewing, or more frequently by carpet-making, or rough weaving."[37] Many urban women and children were engaged in cottage industry activities such as the making of carpets, clothing, embroidering, and knitting of socks.[38] According to Abdullaev, by 1910 some 65,000 people were engaged in the manufacturing of carpets, both men and women.[39] In some towns, economic development provided additional temporal employment, as long as the economic boom lasted. This was the case, for example, in Tabriz and Mashhad at the end of the 1890s. Then there "was scarcely a house or shop which had not put up one or two looms, for not only were the manufacturers gaining money, but the poor class and chiefly boys found employment, whilst the distress which had been prevailing here for so long was somewhat relieved by the fact that parents were helped by their offspring to tide over bad times."[40]

There were, of course, many people who were unable to earn their livelihood, for whatever reason. Given the fact that there was a surplus of labor it was even difficult for able-bodied men to find regular employment or to earn a regular income.

> If a man cannot earn his livelihood he begs it, or steals it, as may be seen most expedient, without attaching any particular blame attaching to either of these proceedings. Should he be caught stealing, and be brought to punishment- both highly problematical cases, he may lose a hand or a foot; but being in that case disqualified from work, he can beg with the certainty of success.[41]

As a result of these developments the British consul Jones concluded, "Notwithstanding the comparative tranquility which the country has enjoyed since the beginning of the present century the inhabitants are apparently poorer and certainly less skillful than formerly."[42]

PROSTITUTION

Many women, girls and boys had to earn money by providing their personal services to those who stood in need of them. Given the extent of poverty in urban areas prostitution was rampant. In Tehran, there was a special city quarter for prostitutes during Fath

37. Jenner 1870, 397.
38. Sayyah 1346, 164; Höltzer 2535, 21-22; Tahvildar 1342, 101; Wills 1883, 118.
39. Abdullaev 1963, 212.
40. DCR 2291, 8; DCR 2533, 7.
41. Jenner 1870, 398.
42. Smith 1870, 402, 421.

`Ali Shah's reign (r. 1798-1834) as was the case in Shiraz.[43] According to Polak, Mohammad Shah (r. 1834-48) closed the quarter of the prostitutes in Tehran. However, the trade was thriving under his son Naser al-Din Shah (r. 1848-96) in the 1850s. The measure, therefore, must have been very short-lived.[44] It was a widespread custom that was practiced in all towns and major caravan halting stations.[45] In Tehran, on a population of some 240,000 people, there were about 5 percent who had to earn their living through prostitution in 1920, according to a municipal survey.[46] The number was lower (less than one percent) in smaller towns. In Yazd in 1879, on an estimated population of 40,000 there reportedly were 500 prostitutes officially registered in the government's fiscal records.[47]

MODERN FACTORY LABOR

According to Abdullaev, the labor force engaged in 'modern industry' was very small, and he qualified only some 6,700 workers as such by 1910. Abdullaev listed 3,000 railway workers and 200 railway employees (45 per cent of total), 2,460 workers (of which 576 foreigners) in the oil industry (37 per cent of total), while 840 factory workers only represent some 12 per cent of this group of 6,700 workers.[48] However, Abdullaev's figure underestimates the workforce in modern establishments, which was larger than he has stated.

Although traditional industrial establishments were mostly small-scale, there also were large-scale craft establishment, which represent a transitional stage between the old craft workshop and the modern factory. Towards the end of the nineteenth century a considerable number of relatively large factories were established in a great many Iranian cities. A very large carpet-making factory in Tabriz, for example, employed up to 1,500 workers in 1899. Most of these large factories were to be found in the carpet industry, but they also existed in other industrial sectors such as leather preparation, preparation of opium, preparation of henna, and in mining. "The larger the workshop the further was the division of labor. The workers received only wages, and controlled neither the raw material nor the finished product."[49] Although modeled after modern factories, these factories did not achieve, in most cases, a complete break with the cottage industries out of which they had emerged, for their level of mechanization was very low and they mainly used manual labor. Moreover, its products were not very satisfactory and its prices as high as its qualities were low. From Table 2.1 it is also clear that the traditional small-scale industries were still very important around 1910. These industries therefore represent an intermediate stage of industrialization. The case of Tabriz (see Table 2.2) is in this respect rather typical for the other 'industrial' centers in Iran such as Tehran, Qazvin, and Rasht. In addition to

43. Polak 1861, 516-17; Waring 1807, 80. On the subject of prostitution in Iran in general see Floor 2008, chapter three.

44. Polak 1861, 517.

45. Moser 1885, 389; Sayyah 1346, 164-65

46. Shahri 1367, vol. 1, 63.

47. Houtum-Schindler 1881, 320-321.

48. Abdullaev 1963, 212.

49. Abdullaev 1963, 116-17.

these factories, there existed in Tabriz, as in the other cities, a great many small traditional workshops, which in Tabriz employed about 23,000 persons.

Table 2.2: Number of Factories and of their Labor Force in Tabriz (1922)[50]

Type of Factory	Number of Employees	Number of Workers	Average Number of Workers
Carpet factories	175	2,625	15
Spinning factory	1	150	150
Weaving mill	2	100	100
Weaving mill	10	100	10
Weaving mill	20	100	5
Weaving factory	30	300	6
Pottery making	10	50	5
Printing	8	120	15
Lithography	7	35	5
Tobacco processing	30	300	10
Cigarette making	5	50	10
Brick-making	5	30	6
Powder-making	3	30	10
Fruit-juice making	20	100	5
Dyeing factories	40	200	5
Soap-making	10	200	5
Iron and gypsum	5	50	10
Total	378	4,485	372

Bharier's statement that modern, large-scale industry, defined as comprising factories with ten or more workers, did not exist in Iran around the turn of the century clearly is wrong.[51] In fact, notwithstanding the many obstacles modern industry had to overcome in Iran - cost of raw materials, high energy and transport rates, no protection against foreign competition, and non-economic factors - industrialization both prior to and after 1900 until World War I was considerable. Between 1900 and 1914 some 30 modern factories were erected in Iran employing 700 people.[52]

Because there was a lack of integration in the economy as a whole, high-lighted by the absence of any government industrialization policy, this pre-1914 development was remarkable. There existed a Ministry of Public Works (*Favayed-e `Ammeh*), which was charged, inter alia, with the management of Iran's industrial affairs. However, its budget of 150,000 to 200,000 *tumans* per year did not even suffice to pay for the salaries of the ministry's staff, and apart from giving out mining leases it did not do much to stimulate

50. Chaqueri 1972, 202.
51. Bharier 1971, 170.
52. Floor 1991; Floor; 2003b.

or regulate industry. The role of government was restricted to a fiscal one in the sense that it tried to get money out of existing industries. The attempt by Muzaffar al-Din Shah to stipulate that foreign investors who wanted to erect factories "to produce cotton, silk, etc."[53] had to acquire a permit from the government also must be seen in this light. Nevertheless, this new measure was in a way an innovation because the usual procedure was to sell concessions to foreign or Iranian investors to stimulate the utilization of the country's natural resources. In exchange for the monopoly of production of a certain commodity or service, the government received badly needed funds, while at the same time modern technology was introduced into the country.[54]

WORKING CONDITIONS

Generally, the poor, engaged in weaving, were in the employ of local investors who owned a small or large number of looms, and who provided them with (colored) yarns, designs and, very important, orders. Many weavers worked in their homes, often apprenticing their own or their neighbor's children, or in a shop in the bazaar, where they worked in rooms that were open to the public view.[55] When such an investor put a number of looms inside a building this was referred to as a manufactory or *karkhaneh*.[56] The easy entrance level to the industry (low investment and low skill level) resulted in a fluctuating labor force, much of which was in the form of self-employed cottage industry. Consul Abbott reports in 1848 about the situation in Kerman as follows: "The manufacture [of woolen fabrics] is carried on in the private dwellings or premises of the people", while in Kashan "the manufactures are carried on in private houses, and factories."[57] Since much production was also carried out in the surrounding villages of the main textile towns it seems likely that this was also operated as a cottage industry. Sock-making was one such cottage industry, in which, amongst others, Armenian women in Jolfa/Isfahan were engaged. They sat outside their houses on warm evenings in groups knitting. "The knitting is a great industry, and a woman can earn 4 s. a month by it, which is enough to live upon."[58] Thus, weaving took place either at people's homes or in special manufactories.[59]

Working conditions in manufacturies (*karkhanehs*) were invariably unhygienic and a danger to the workers' health, but that situation was not much different from their own homes.[60] More often than not the workplace was a dark, damp, and dirty room without windows or ventilation. Weaving manufactories were usually in unhealthy subterraneous spaces, to be protected against the dryness of the air and the dust, which was omnipresent. The workers were thus, half-naked, packed together, at close malodorous proximity, such

53. Floor 1985 a; Floor 2009 d.
54. Floor 1991; Ibid; 2003b.
55. Vaziri 1346, 33-34.
56. Shahri 1367, vol. 2, 1-2.
57. Amanat 1983, pp. 83, 75.
58. Bishop 1891, 272.
59. Floor, 1999b, ch. 1.
60. Floor 2004.

as in Kerman. "I asked why there were no windows to the place, and the skeleton [the foreman] replied that it would be too cold. With these lamps the place was warm enough without clothing. It was just this: glazed windows and clothing were dearer than lamps without either."[61] The situation in the town of Yazd was not different. "In small covered-in-rooms, without pretence of ventilation, the people, men, women, children, from early morning to sunset, and even beyond, work at their trades; and practically live the long day through. It can be imagined, when once an infectious disease attacks the town, how quickly it spreads, and what sad havoc it commits."[62] It would seem that those manufactories visited by Europeans usually consisted of about three rooms; in each room between 10 to 30 people would be working.[63]

WORKING HOURS

Working hours were basically the same irrespective of type of industry or its location. The long days in, for example, Tehran were not different from the working hours in other towns in Iran. Up north, in Tabriz, "the usual hours of labour are from sunrise to sunset less the time occupied by prayers and meals, about two hours. Labourers and journeymen are engaged only by the day. In some trades an additional allowance, generally in bread, is given according to the quantity of work executed."[64] Down south, in Bandar `Abbas, the situation was as follows: "On Fridays no work is ever done, and workmen only receive rations on these days from employers. There are also ten entire holidays in the year on which neither salary nor rations are drawn. The hours of labour are from about one hour after sunrise to noon, when men break off to rest and dine, for about a couple of hours, when they resume till sunset."[65]

Although the days were long productivity was low. Not only was the health and nutritional condition of Iranian workers bad, they also were slow on the job so as to be employed as many days as possible. These workers were hired on a daily basis and therefore had no incentive to finish the job quickly. This phenomenon did not escape European observers. Consul Jones commented: "Being paid by the day, they protract their time as long as possible. Their countrymen appear to prefer cheapness to every other quality. ... The tools they use are all brought from Russia; they are of a bad and cheap description, and would hardly find purchasers in any other part of the world."[66]

61. Floyer 1882, 324; Amanat 1983, 84.
62. DCR 1376, p. 14; see also Gilbar 1978, 197.
63. Goldsmid 1876, vol. 1, 187.
64. Smith 1870, 402; Jones 1870, 418.
65. Smith 1870, 402.
66. Smith 1870, 402; Jones 1870, 420; Issawi 1971, 37; Sykes 1900, 200.

WAGES

Though the available data on wages mainly concern the weaving industry other data confirm that wages were low in all branches of industry, in both the formal and informal sectors. Data on self-employed casual labor are missing, but probably were even lower. "The average wages here are about 9.5 d. a day, or 21*s*. per month." According to the British consul Jenner, the reason why wages were low was because people needed little. "The cost of living upon the pittance which satisfies the Persian workman is so small, and the rate of wages, which is proportionally even smaller."[67] This seems a curious argument given the fact that when a laborer earned more money he also spent more, as one would expect. "The men who earn higher wages possibly wear a better shirt and turban, but nothing more; whatever they save is usually converted into ornaments for their women." Moreover, all hired labor, whether journeymen or apprentices, were only engaged by the day.[68] As a result, if a worker or craftsman did not work one day his family would go hungry that evening, if there was no other source of income or savings.[69] As is clear from Table 2.2 the wages of those emplyed by the guilds were not much higher than unskilled day laborers, in fact they were even lower than the average wages mentioned by Jenner.

Table 2.3: The Rate of Wages for the Chief Handicrafts in Tabriz (1870)[70]

Trade	Daily Wages			
	Masters		Journeymen	
	s.	*d.*	*s.*	*d.*
Butchers	-	-	0	4
Bakers	1	0	0	4
Masons	1	8	0	6
Carpenters	2	6	0	6
Blacksmiths	-	-	0	6
Painters (by job)	-	-	0	6
Weavers (by the yard)	-	-	0	1.5
Dyers	-	-	1	0
Tanners	-	-	0	8
Potters	-	-	0	6
Coppersmiths (same as blacksmiths)	-	-	-	-
Silversmiths	-	-	0	5
Glassworkers	2	0	0	6
Tailors	-	-	0	5
Shoemakers (per pair of shoes)	-	-	0	2

67. Jenner 1870, 397.
68. Smith 1870, 402; Jones 1870, 418; Blau 1858, 101.
69. Qazvini 1370, 71.
70. Jones 1870, 419.

Trade	Daily Wages			
	Masters		Journeymen	
Furriers and hatters	-	-	1	0
Sandlers [sic; saddlers?]	-	-	1	0
Bookbinders	-	-	1	0

The situation was not uniform across Iran, of course. In Bushire and Lengeh, for example, the remuneration was different, as shown in Table 2.4. Also, some craftsmen were paid only when they sold their products. Blacksmiths had to buy their own iron, at about 1 *qran* per 14 lbs., which they sold, depending on the workmanship, for 4 to 8 *qrans*. Goldsmiths charged 2 *qrans* per *methqal* (4.6 g), while sailors did not receive regular pay, but received a certain share in the profits of each voyage.[71]

Table 2.4: Wages in Bushire and Lengeh (1870)[72]

Craft	Daily Wages	Rations	Monthly Total
Carpenters	2 *qrans*	3 meals	7-10 dollars + rations
Head masons	4 *qrans*	3 meals	18 dollars + rations
Porters	0.25 – 0.5 *qrans*		

Unskilled laborers, therefore, were not overpaid, but received enough to make it worth their while, because they needed to bring money home after the four to five months stint in the towns to support their families.

> There is very little skilled labor to be met with amongst them, the utmost they profess to do is to turn up the soil, to dig trenches, and to saw down trees. Their wages are, on average, 3d. a day, but they are entitled to rations and other advantages which, in money value, make up an income of 6d. a day. After four or five months' labour on these conditions they return to their homes, where the snow has smelted and the soil is fit for cultivation. Their savings do not amount to much. From 10s. to 20s. is the utmost that they can put by, and this is usually invested in the purchase of cotton wares for the use of their wives and children, but they have enjoyed a mild winter compared with their own, whereas at home they would have been exposed to all the miseries attending intense cold, and that without occupation.[73]

71. Smith 1870, 402.
72. Smith 1870, 401.
73. AP 29, 702.

Seasonal laborers in Tehran "receive one Kran (9.5 d.) a day as wages and they usually contrive to save about five Tomans, or 16/- a month while they remain in the capital, from 4 to 5 months being the average duration of their stay."[74]

DIET

The diet of the poor was very poor indeed and led to malnutrition among them. It consisted of the barest minimum and of the cheapest foodstuffs. The British consul Jenner summarized the diet of the urban poor as follows: "The winter diet of the workman consists almost entirely of bread, rice and bad cheese, with a small quantity of tea in the form of a decoction, and the summer diet of bread and 'sayfi', or summer produce, i.e. melons, cucumbers, vegetable-marrows, egg-plants, and various forms of edible gourds."[75] Bread was indeed the life staff of the urban poor, because it was eaten in large quantities. People usually ate bread as their staple, with some cheese and some herbs. A porter ate about 2 *cherek* per day or 1.5 kg of bread.[76]

Table 2.5: Prices of Provisions in Tabriz (1870)[77]

Provisions	s.	d.
Bread, per *batman* of 5 lbs.	0	7
Meat, ditto	1	5
Fowls, each	0	4
Eggs, per dozen	0	2.5
Flour, per *batman*	0	9
Rice, ditto	1	4
Tea, per lb.	3	4
Sugar, per *batman*	5	2
Milk, per quart	0	2
Wine, ditto	0	11
Spirits, ditto	1	2
candles, per lb.	3	6
Firewood, per load of 600 lbs.	14	0
Water, annually, for one family	12	3

One *tuman* or 100 *qrans* = 8 *s*. 4.*d*.

74. FO 60/337, report 24/6/1886.

75. Jenner 1870, 397; De Penisse 1867, 102; Schwartz 1942, 35.

76. Olmer 1906, 20.

77. Jones 1870, 420.

In Southern Iran the situation was somewhat different due to other culinary customs. A typical meal for a day laborer in Bushire was "a lump of dates before going to work, some bread (unleavened) and salt fish for dinner [sic; i.e., lunch], and some boiled rice for supper."[78] The cost for life necessities varied, of course, with the seasons, but in the fall of 1870 they were as shown in Table 2.6.

Table 2.6: Prices of Provisions in Lengeh (1870)

Food Item Per *Man* of 9 lbs.	*Qrans*
Wheat, 0.75 *man*	1
Barley, 1.16 *man*	1
Karachi rice, 0.75 *man*	1
Basra rice, 1.24 *man*	1
Clarified butter, 1 *man*	11
Sweet oil, 1 *man*	7
Cocoa-nut oil, 1 *man*	6.5 to 7
Bag of dates, 16 *man*	11
Sugar, 1 *man*	4.25 to 4.5
Coffee, per *man*	6
Mutton, first sort, per *man*	4
Mutton, second sort, per *man*	2
Fish, per *man*	1
Dried salt fish, per 100	12
Firewood, per 100 *man*	5
Tobacco, per *man*	4
Bagar bread, 3.75 lbs.	1
Halva, 3.75 lbs.	7

It was no coincidence that the organization of some kind of bread provisioning in the main cities was established in the 1870s after the Great Famine and the influx of rural unskilled labor into the cities. This was important, because those who were not poor generally did not buy their bread at a bakery. They either baked it themselves at home or had their dough prepared at home and then taken to the bakery for baking.[79] The attempt at price control of the bread price brought some measure of stability in the food market and relief for the poor. However, apart from the recurring 'food corners' aimed to enrich some merchants, government and religious officials (especially after 1890) there was also a tendency to reduce the quality of the bread and thus make more money without changing the price.[80] By confining themselves to the above diet, the workmen in this country can just

78. Smith 1870, 402.

79. Floor 1983 a, 199-227.

80. Floor 1983 a.

manage to keep body and soul together, Jenner concluded.[81] The very urban poor, those without a regular income, thus lived a hard and desperate life.

CONCLUSION

From the above it is clear that the size of the urban labor force that possibly could have developed into a socio-political force was small. Objectively speaking conditions seemed right to stimulate urban workers to congregate, organize themselves, formulate demands, and make their political presence felt. For the lot of the workers in Iran with regard to working hours, health conditions, wages, and social conditions was bad. Therefore, some groups of workers, assisted by some reform-minded spirits from the middle-class, constituted themselves into a small labor movement. However, labor unions were ineffective in bringing about any change in these working conditions. This holds also for the labor legislation that was passed, which was neither the result of, nor in reaction to, demands from labor unions. The fact that these laws did not address the labor force's problems in practice is another issue. If a beneficial development took place it was rather a by-product of other developments, such as the construction of modern factories. Labor had no say in or control over its own destiny, neither about the direction of the course it was on, nor about the pace at which it was to proceed.[82]

81. Jenner 1870, 397.

82. See Floor 2009a.

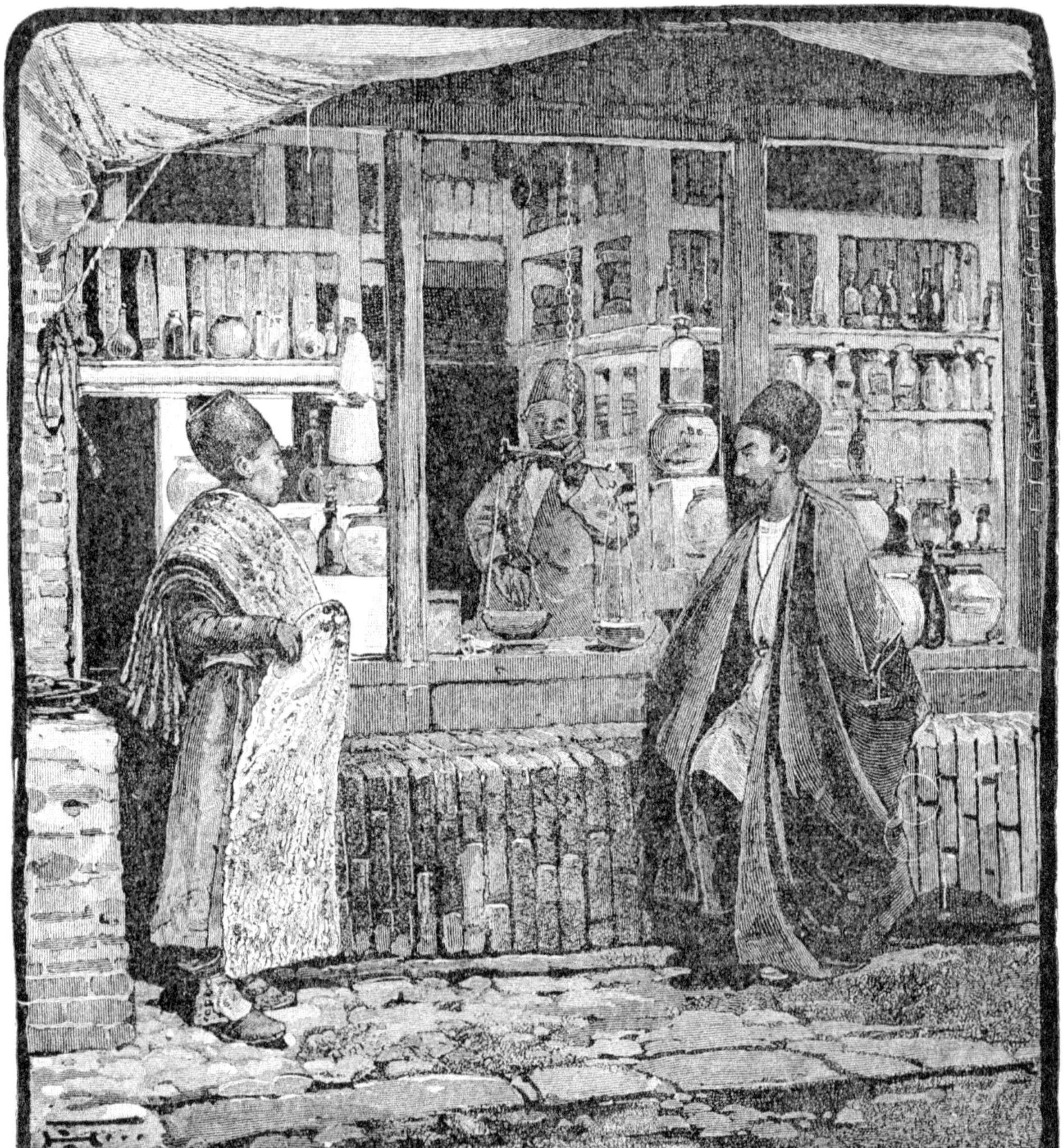

CHAPTER THREE

The Merchants in Qajar Iran

WHAT IS A MERCHANT?

In discussions on the economic history of Iran, authors usually indiscriminately employ the term 'merchant' for all kinds of traders, be they small or large scale traders. In most European languages the term 'merchant' can refer to a great variety of gainfully in trade employed people.

The Persian term, however, *tajer* (pl. *tojjar*) refers to one group only, viz. the wholesale merchants. For other traders a general term like *-forush*, or more special terms like *bazzaz* (draper), *baqqal* (grocer), etc. are used. So as to avoid misunderstanding I shall mark off the *tojjar* from those other groups, which confusingly are called merchants too. Characteristic for those other groups is that they formed guilds (*asnaf*), which the *tojjar* did not. It is true that some authors mention the fact that merchants constitute guilds too, but the confusing term 'merchant' led them into this error. Although there is no denying that there is a corporative aspect to the group of the *tojjar*, this does not make them a guild. In fact, de Rochechouart, who is one of the 19th century sources who mention that the merchants form a corporation, explicitly tells us not to confuse this corporation with a guild.[1]

In chapter six I define a guild as: a group of townspeople engaged in the same trade or craft, who elect their own chief and who pay guild taxes, this group having fiscal and administrative functions.[2] If we apply this definition to the merchants we see that they were a group of townspeople, but who were not all engaged in the same trade. One can, however, make the point that the merchants were all engaged in the wholesale trade, and

1. De Rochechouart 1867, 181; see also de Gobineau 1859, 376; Morier 1812, 237 speaks about "the proper merchant, sodager (*sudagar*) a distinct order," as does Bélanger 1838, vol. 2, 340 (saudaguer).
2. Floor 1975.

thus were all in the same occupation. The difference with the guilds then is that the merchants did not pay guild taxes. As this matter will be discussed hereunder I won't go into it right now.

Having marked off the merchants from the guilds I must define the former. Greenfield, when discussing five groups of businessmen, viz. the *tajer*, the *bonakdar* (market distributor), the *sarraf* (banker), the *dallal* (broker) and the *–forush* (trader) leaves no doubt about it that only the first two belong to the group of the *tojjar*. "As the real merchants rank only those tajirs (merchants), who busy themselves with the export and import trade in one hand for their own account. The wholesale dealers, who act as middlemen between the tajirs and the retail dealers, are called binekdar [sic; *bonakdar*]. They are also to be considered to be tajirs, whilst the retail dealers, like the artisans, are arranged according to their profession in guilds."[3] Thus, the *tojjar* or merchants are wholesale dealers, while all other groups are retail dealers.

Merchants were considered to be more respectable than any other social class.[4] They were considered, in general, to be honest and trustworthy, and were known for their *rastgu'i va dorostkari* (speaking the truth and doing good works).[5] People entrusted great sums of money to them, often without written proof.[6] It is, therefore, no wonder that they were considered notables of the city in which they lived.[7] Every small-scale trader or even a prosperous *sarraf* (banker) wanted to become a *tajer* as soon as possible, for "it was the best occupation there is."[8]

The merchant class as a whole was better educated than the rest of the population, with the exception of the ulama and the ruling class. This is not surprising since they needed to know how to read and write, to be able to draw up contracts and keep note of their sales and purchases, for which they used the *siyaq* notation system.[9] It is for this reason that for instance in Northern Iran more than half, sometimes even 90 percent of the merchants could read and write.[10] Their superior level of education was also to be observed in the more cosmopolitan outlook of most merchants. Europeans found the merchants intelligent people possessing a greater knowledge of the outside world than any other class in Iran. There was nothing strange in this, for merchants were par excellence the class who had contacts with Europe and India, either within or outside Iran. Many of them were widely traveled, and we'll see hereunder that they played an important role in the dissemination of modernist and reformative ideas in Iran. They were also enterprising in accepting new ideas and institutions, adapting themselves very well to new developments and

3. Greenfield 1906, 26: see also Greenfield 1904, 145; Issawi 1971, 106.

4. De Gobineau 1859, 373; de Rochechouart 1867, 168; Polak 1865, vol. 2, 188.

5. Fasa'i 1894-96, vol. 2, 62.

6. De Gobineau 1859, 374, 375; Polak 1865, vol.2, 188

7. Fasa'i 1894-96, vol. 2, 26ff. speaks of the merchants as belonging to the *a'yan* (nobles) of the quarter; Vaziri mentions several merchants belonging to the *a'azem* (notables) of the city. Vaziri 1346, 56, 67, 172; see also Adib al-Molk 1349, 68, 176, 288, 289, 290.

8. Fasa'i 1894-96, vol. 2, 62; Berichte 1910, 353; Polak 1865, vol. 2, 197.

9. Wilson 1896, 281, 327; Rabino 1892, 52ff. For an explanation of the *siyaq* system see Fekete 1955.

10. Issawi 1971, 191, 24.

changes. In 1871 two leading merchants in Yazd, for example, visited general Goldsmid asking whether a telegraph could be constructed between Yazd and Dehbid financed by the merchants of Yazd.[11] Although one would doubt, whether they really wanted to or could pay for such a construction, it at least shows that they realized the possibilities of modern technology for their own business. A few years later the same merchants inquired after the cost of a railway. They were rather dismayed by the cost of such a project.[12] Many merchants were also known for their scholarly activities. Foremost among their studies were religious science, Arabic, poetry, calligraphy, and literature.[13] Many merchants had studied in one of the religious centers, in keeping with the religiosity in general of the merchant class.[14] During Ramazan many merchants were to be seen reading the Koran as they sat before their shops.[15]

The social group with whom the merchants had most in common was the ulama. Apart from the fact that close relations existed between the two classes because of business reasons, the merchants needed them for the legislation of commercial contracts and the like; merchants together with the ulama were the only two powers in Qajar Iranian society which were independent of the government.[16] Moreover the merchants were very religiously minded. Many of them had made the pilgrimage to Mecca, which is shown by the frequent honorific *hajji*. In 1883, thirty of forty-three merchants in Tehran were *hajjis*.[17] In Shiraz almost every one of twenty-six merchants had made the pilgrimage,[18] while in Isfahan we find the same phenomenon.[19] Members of the merchant as well as of the ulama class intermarried. Many a merchant family could boast of a mullah or *mojtahed* among its members and vice-versa.[20] Many sayyed families, a religious important group, were also engaged in trade.[21]

As it was considered to be the duty of the rich to care for the poor it is not surprising that we find many merchants doing good works. In Kerman it was noted that the *Malek al-Tojjar* (chief merchant), though a rich man, whose father and grandfather were well-known for their pious deeds, did not care for the poor.[22] He formed rather an exception, for most merchants, however stingy their reputation, at one time or another contributed to the needs of the community. Many instances are recorded which confirm the mer-

---

11. Goldsmid 1876, vol. 1, 175.
12. Stack 1882, vol. 1, 262.
13. Fasa'i 1894-96, vol. 2, 26, 44, 46, 58, 62, 76, 79, 177; E`temad al-Saltaneh 1306, 215, 220; Forsat 1316, 549, 550. The subjects mentioned are: literature (*adabiyat*), science (*`elm*), humanities (*ensaniyat*), Persian, Arabic, English, logic (*manteq*), philosophy (*kalam*), exegesis (*feqh*), calligraphy, and arithmetic (*`elm-e hesab*).
14. Vaziri 1346, 67; Mostowfi n.d., vol. 2, 238.
15. Smith & Dwight 1834, 341.
16. De Rochechouart 1867, 168.
17. E`temad al-Saltaneh 1298-1300, vol. 3, appendix, 16ff.
18. Forsat 1316, 549.
19. Tahvildar 1342, 92; for other cities Vaziri 1346, 45 (Kerman); Zarrabi 1341, 236 (Kashan).
20. Fasa'i 1894-96, vol. 2, 46, 73, 74, 77, 79, 177.
21. Fasa'i 1894-96, vol. 2, 74, 190, 177, 252.
22. Vaziri 1346, 67.

chants' generosity. Many of them built mosques,[23] or bridges, bazaars, and caravanserais.[24] Hajji Mirza Karim Sarraf spent each year during the holy months of Safar and Moharram hundreds of *tumans* on food and drinks for the poor.[25] The Amin al-Tojjar of Shiraz built some *maktabs* (schools) and paid the expenses of the orphans attending these schools.[26] Furthermore merchants used to organize *ta`ziyehs* (passion-plays),[27] and in general would give alms.[28]

The merchants as a class cultivated the public esteem and kept strictly to a certain way of life. Any merchant deviating from it stood to loose his standing in the merchant community.[29] In general ostentation and contacts with government officials were avoided, and most merchants lived outwardly a very sober, hardworking life. Many a millionaire could not be distinguished from his less lucky fellow merchants, but in their own houses they felt free to spend lavishly on all kinds of luxury.[30] Besides having an honored and prestigious position in society, merchants enjoyed many privileges. For example, they were exempt from military service as well as taxation. The only dues which they paid were customs duties.[31]

In their outward apparel the merchants were hardly different from the religious classes or the prosperous trades people. Important merchants, in general, wore turban of *termeh* shawls, the others wore Bukhara caps. Further an "under cotton shirt and a gown of quilted cotton cloth, velvet, or satin, or silk (*arkhaliq*). In the cold seasons a second gown (the *qaba*) was worn also, made of cloth or *barak*. These two gowns reached half way between knee and ankle, and were secured by a cummerbund (*kamarband*) of cotton or silk, or a leather belt. Very loose trousers were worn of cotton dyed black or blue. Socks and native made leather shoes (*sagheri*) completed the attire. When out walking or visiting the loose *aba* or cloak of cloth, camel-hair cloth, *barak* or Kashmir was thrown over the shoulder."[32] As far as food was concerned, they ate very sparingly and very sober, their midday meal usually consisting only of bread and cheese, although they ate better than most.[33]

---

23. Fasa'i 1894-96, vol. 2, 26, 61; Kasravi 1319-21, vol. 1, 82.

24. Fasa'i 1894-96, vol. 2, 26, 43, 76; Vaziri 1346, 67; Dhabihi 1348, 257; Eastwick 1864, vol. 1, 320.

25. Fasa'i 1894-96, vol. 2, 26.

26. Fasa'i 1894-96, vol. 2, 60.

27. Fasa'i 1894-96, vol. 2, 26; Mostowfi n.d., vol. 1, 281. On these passion plays see Floor 2006, 124-212.

28. Fasa'i 1894-96, vol. 2, 206.

29. Polak 1865, vol. 2, 188; de Rochechouart 1867, 170.

30. De Rochechouart 1867, 170; de Gobineau 1859, 112; Eastwick 1864, vol. 1, 305, 309; Zarrabi 1341, 376; Vaziri 1346, 159.

31. De Gobineau 1859, 374; see on the taxation matter: Floor 1999 a.

32. Zarrabi 1341, 349; DCR 976, 14. In Isfahan merchants wore shoes of native leather, whilst in Bushire they wore imported shoes, Tahvildar 1342, 111; Lorimer 1908, 345. On clothing in Iran in general see Floor 1999 b., chapter two.

33. Zarrabi 1341, 347; Polak 1865, vol. 2, 188; Wills 1883, 172, calls them the most penurious of all Iranians, 188.

Although the merchants had dealings with people of all walks of life, they very much kept to themselves.[34] This resulted in a kind of exclusive class-consciousness and the existence of merchant families. Persian texts, therefore, often speak of someone belonging to the merchant class (*selk-e tojjar, selseleh-ye tojjar, tajerzadeh*).[35]

As social mobility was low in Qajar Iran, and most merchants were *tajerzadehs*, they formed a more or less closed community which kept its own way of life. This trend was reinforced by the fact that one usually married within one's own class.[36] Notwithstanding this low social mobility in Qajar Iran, and the strong clan consciousness among the merchants, members from the lower classes could and did sometimes find a place among them. Not only had many a *sarraf* (banker) become a merchant,[37] but also some people of low origin. In Shiraz, for instance, a well-known merchant Hajji `Ali, known as *chakmeh-duz* (cobbler), was a respected member of the mercantile community.[38] In 1888 in Yazd the Malek al-Tojjar appears to have been of low origin, having gypsy blood in his veins.[39] In Sirjan, Hajji Mohammad Ja`far was Malek al-Tojjar notwithstanding the fact that he was not a *tajerzadeh*, but only a *shaterzadeh* (son of a footman).[40] In Rafsanjan, Hajji Aqa `Ali, was known as `Ali Za`im or peasant.[41]

The exclusive class-consciousness shown by the merchant class was the expression of and furthered by the fact that merchants formed a very small group only, even in the important trading centers. It seems that they did not even constitute 1 percent of the urban population. In Tehran it was about 0.5 percent in 1886, and in Kashan, around 1850, it was about 0.3 percent.[42] In Kerman and Isfahan we find, respectively 250 and 340 merchants in the 1890s, or about the same percentage. For Yazd and Kermanshah the situation was not different, here there were respectively 250 and 200 merchants.[43]

Despite this exclusiveness and the assistance which merchants seemed to have extended to each other,[44] their organizational structure appears to have been vary informal. This was mainly due to the fact that the *tojjar* did not form a homogenous group, in so far that in one city several divisions of the *tojjar* existed. These divisions found their origins in certain trades, religious affiliation, places of origin, and other parochial interests. In Kerman for example we find a distinction made between merchants from Kerman, Tehran, Yazd, Herand, Khorasan, and those of Turkish (from Tabriz), Zoroastrian (Yazd),

34. De Rochechouart 1867, 168.

35. Vaziri 1346, 67; Fasa'i 1894-96, vol. 2, 26, 43-6, 58, 76-8, 97, 131, some families were engaged in trade since Safavid times: 44, 80, 149.

36. De Gobineau, 392; Wills 1883, 64.

37. Fasa'i 1894-96, vol. 2, 26, 58.

38. Fasa'i 1894-96, vol. 2, 161; also a case of a son of *semsar* (dealer in second-hand goods) who became a respected merchant. Ibid., vol. 2, 45.

39. Browne 1889, 407.

40. Vaziri 1346, 159.

41. Vaziri 1346, 172; in Kerman, Hajji Mohammad Sadeq was a respected merchant and son of Aqa Esma`il Churakchi (baker), Ibid., 78.

42. Issawi 1971, 267.

43. DCR 1662, 17; DCR 590, 13,14.

44. De Rochechouart 1867, 177.

and Indian origin.[45] In Kashan a different division existed; here merchants belonged to one of the following groups: Salehabadi, Tabriziha, Rafugarha, Lajvardi, Kuzehkonani, Buneh kalleh, Bazzazha, Darvazeh-ye Isfahani, and the Mohreh-keshha.[46] Similar observations can be made with regard to other cities. The subdivision between the merchants was also to be observed in their geographical distribution in the city where they traded. Each group of merchants occupied its special caravanserai, *timcheh*, or *khan*. Here they had their offices (*hojreh*), and here they did business.[47] In Khuzestan merchants frequently kept their stock at their private homes instead of in their offices in the bazaar.[48]

Apart from this geographical, occupational, and religious division, which may have led to the belief that these groups were different guilds, there was another division. As in every society you have those who pull the strings, while others dance. In Iran we observe that in each city a few merchants dictated economic life. This was due to their economic and political resources, which made them in fact employer of many another merchant and of the guilds.[49] Moreover they were the link between the local authorities and the bazaar community.

THE FUNCTION OF THE MALEK AL-TOJJAR

In most cities, especially in the second half of the 19th century, a Malek al-Tojjar, or chief merchant headed the whole-sale merchants or *tojjar*. This position existed already under the Timurids and the Safavids. In Tehran, the function existed under the first Qajars. In 1807, Gardanne makes mention of this functionary. The Malek al-Tojjar did business in jewels exclusively, selling these to the Shah at a high profit.[50] At about the same time Malcolm writes about 'the first Merchant' which no doubt is the Malek al-Tojjar.[51] In 1801 there seems to have been a Malek al-Tojjar in Bushire, who was in the service of the East India Company, as well as the chief of the Bushire mercantile community.[52] This individual was the same as Hajji Khalil Khan-Kuroghlu Qazvini, Malek al-Tojjar, who was one of the principal merchants of Bushire, and who was appointed ambassador to India by the Iranian government in 1801.[53]

His colleagues chose the Malek al-Tojjar from amongst the most influential merchants in the city. These would propose his candidature to the governor, who had to approve of the elected person.[54] The Malek al-Tojjar was charged with the supervision of

45. Vaziri 1346, 79.

46. Zarrabi 1341, 236, 237.

47. Vaziri 1346, 32; DCR 590, 71-75; Browne 1889, 314; Goldsmid 1876, vol. 1, 189; sometimes merchants occupied the court of an *imamzadeh* like in Bam, Vaziri 1346, 95.

48. Lorimer 1908, 139.

49. De Gobineau 1859, 376; RO 1844, 140.

50. Issawi 1971, 26.

51. Kaye 1921, vol. 2, 38.

52. Lorimer 1908, 186.

53. Fasa'i 1894-96, vol. 1, 311; Lorimer 1908, 1889.

54. Greenfield 1904, 145.

his fellow-merchants, to settle disputes among them, and between them and their clients. In case of bankruptcy he was in charge of the arbitration committee.[55] In some cases the Malek al-Tojjar commanded the bazaar night watchmen, for which purpose he collected a certain fee from the interested parties. Normally, however, this was the *darugheh's* task.[56]

In Tehran, if the Malek al-Tojjar could not assert his authority, or if something unusual turned up, he could apply for help to the Minister of Trade.[57] Furthermore, the Malek al-Tojjar advised the government on economic and financial matters and acted as financial agent for the Shah.[58] Although semi-official sources speak about or imply the granting of a government office (*mansab*) in this connection, this does not necessarily mean that the Malek al-Tojjar was incorporated into the official bureaucratic hierarchy.[59] He was the representative of a professional category which had been allowed certain autonomy to regulate internal affairs, and as such he had an intermediary function only. On the one hand he represented the government before his fellow merchants, with the object of communicating government orders and being responsible for their behavior, while on the other hand he dealt with the government in the name of his fellows to further their interests. Thus, the Malek al-Tojjar was not an absolute chief over his colleagues. In fact, the various divisions among the merchants greatly handicapped the development of such a situation. Because of the informal relationship that existed between the merchants, the Malek al-Tojjar had to act a kind of *primus inter pares*. Moreover, the few big merchants in a city were not subordinate to the Malek al-Tojjar, nor would they have accepted to be. Often one of the powerful opinion leaders among the merchants was the informal leader. In Tabriz, for instance, Aqa Mir Mohammad Isfahani commanded all merchants around 1858. His command made an end to all disputes among the merchants.[60] In the beginning of the 20th century Hajji Mehdi Kuzehkonani played a similar influential role; it was said of him that if he would throw down his hat, the bazaar in Tabriz would be closed.[61] In some cities the Malek al-Tojjar played an important role, such as in Tehran and Bushire as we shall see below.

It appears that up to 1844, only Tehran and Bushire could boast of a Malek al-Tojjar. In that year the number of Malek al-Tojjars was increased. The increase in their number was the direct result of a royal order issued by Mohammad Shah in favor of British merchants, stipulating the necessity of such a functionary in connection with judicial procedures in commercial affairs.[62] It is after that date that the Malek al-Tojjar is often referred to. In 1844 Hajji `Abdol-Mohammad was appointed Malek al-Tojjar of Bushire, in which function he was later succeeded by his brother and his grandson.[63] In 1860 Hajji

55. De Rochechouart 1867, 176; Polak 1865, 189.
56. See on this matter: Floor 1971c.
57. De Rochechouart 1867, 176.
58. Kaye 1921, vol. 2, 38; Molkara 1325, 103.
59. E`temad al-Saltaneh, 1301-03, vol. 3, 4, 25, 120.
60. Adib al-Molk 1349, 190.
61. Hedayat 1344, 213.
62. Floor 1977, 61-76.
63. Fasa'i 1894-96, vol. 2, 205.

Qasem Tehrani was appointed Malek al-Tojjar of Khurasan.[64] In 1862 the Tabriz merchant Hajji Kazem was appointed Malek al-Tojjar of Azerbaijan.[65] In 1870 Aqa Mohammad Kazem appointed Malek al-Tojjar-e Iran after the death of his father Aqa Mehdi Malek al-Tojjar-e Tehran.[66] The number of these functionaries, of whom there were many more,[67] indicates that in all important trading centers the merchants had some kind of organization (however loosely organized), which could be put to their own advantage. It is not true, as has been suggested by Migeod, that these apparently provincial Malek al-Tojjars presided over all their colleagues in one province. The suffixes like Khorasan, Azerbaijan and Iran only refer to the fact that the holders of these titles were representatives of respectively Mashhad, Tabriz, and Tehran.[68] Concomitant with the extension of titles in Qajar Iran in general,[69] influential merchants other than the Malek al-Tojjar also got titles such as: Moshir al-Tojjar, Mo`in al-Tojjar, and Nazem al-Tojjar.[70] It appears that these merchants did not occupy an official position, and did not usurp the Malek al-Tojjar's position.[71] Some of them were asked to give their opinion about economic matters, but the same was asked of non-titled merchants.[72] Like the title Malek al-Tojjar, these other titles were in many cases hereditary.[73] In this way the government no doubt obliged these influential merchants to them.

A functionary with whom the Malek al-Tojjar must not be confused is the *tajer-bashi* as the Malek al-Tojjar was also known in Safavid times.[74] The *tajer-bashis* were representatives and spokesmen for groups of Russian merchants in the cities. The Russians appointed a large number of these worthies in Northern Iran, whom they often had recognized as consular agents. Sometimes there were even two Russian *tajer-bashis* in one city, one for the Christian and one for the Moslem Russian merchants.[75] The Russian merchants in Qajar Iran formed a very close-knitted community. All contacts relating to commercial affairs with the Iranian authorities were in principle taken up by the *tajer-bashi*, who even had some authority over the non-mercantile relatives of the group which he rep-

64. E`temad al-Saltaneh 1294-96, vol. 2, 270.

65. E`temad al-Saltaneh 1294-96, vol. 3, 4.

66. E`temad al-Saltaneh 1294-96, vol. 3, 120.

67. In Shiraz, Kashan (E`temad al-Saltaneh 1294-96, vol. 3, 25), Kerman, Rafsanjan (Vaziri 1346, 67,159), Yazd (note 39).

68. Migeod 1990, 185.

69. Mostowfi n.d., vol. 1, 440.

70. Other titles were Mo`aven al-Tojjar, Tohfat al-Tojjar, Mostashar al-Tojjar, Vakil al-Tojjar, Mo`tamed al-Tojjar, Lesan al-Tojjar, and Amin al-Mada'en, see E`temad al-Saltaneh 1294-96, vol. 2, 270; vol. 3, 5, 33; Vaziri 1346, 69; Fasa'i 1894-96, vol. 2, 236; Kasravi 1319-21, vol. 1, 77; vol. 2, 78; vol. 3, 437.

71. It appears that in Kashan in 1877 the function of Malek al-Tojjar had been usurped by Hajji Hasan Amin al-Tojjar, who was chief of the Salehabadis and all the other merchants. Zarrabi 1341, 236.

72. See below 53-55.

73. See e.g. E`temad al-Saltaneh 1294-96, vol. 3, 5, 120; Fasa'i 1894-96, vol. 2, 205.

74. Asaf 1348, 94, 100.

75. Aubin 1908, 94, note 1; Amir-Khizi 1339, 91, note 1.

resented.[76] It appears that the title *tajer-bashi* was reserved for the representatives of the Russian merchants. For his Turkish counterpart, who had the same task, the title *shahbandar* was used.[77]

MERCHANT-STATE RELATIONS

Contrary to the generally accepted opinion merchants had dealings with the government and its officials. According to most European sources, however, they tried as much as possible to avoid contact with them and to avoid attracting their attention.[78] They appear to have despised government officials, only having dealings with them if they could not help it.[79] This, of course, cannot be a true picture of their relationship. In the first place the government was always in need of the merchants' money, and used the merchants for making payments abroad and at home. In fact, without them, the government could not have functioned, for all the ready money was in the hands of the principal merchants.[80] Merchants, as a security, often took over assignments, monopolies, revenues of real estate, and/or precious stones.[81] They also financed many a candidate governor to buy his governorship. Many leading personalities entrusted them with part of their capital, so that if they should fall in disgrace, the merchant concerned would give their families.[82] Another kind of relationship between the merchants and the political and religious elite was the common cornering of the meat and/or wheat market. They forced prices of meat and wheat to rise and made fortunes.[83] Often the relationship between the ruling class and the merchants would be a commercial one, both parties agreeing to a *mozarebat* (sleeping partnership). This holds for the city based elite, as well as for the tribal elite. In Shushtar, Hajji Mohammad Reza `Azem and Hajji `Abdol-Hamid Papahn did business with part of the capital of the ilkhan of the Bakhtiyari tribe and his family.[84] In this way rich government officials could circumvent the prohibition of the taking of interest. This kind of relationship, in which all government officials, even the Shah, participated no doubt strengthened the position of the merchant class as a whole. Towards the end of the 19th century this relationship

76. Blau 1858, 39.

77. Blau 1858, 26, 28; E`temad al-Saltaneh 1294-96, vol. 1, appendix, 21; vol. 2, appendix, 28; vol. 3, appendix, 26; Hedayat 1344, 214, 216; E'temad al-Saltaneh 1348, 791, however, mentions a *shahbandar-e Rus*; Molkara 1325, 8 mentions a *shahbandar-e Iran* in Baghdad; in the Persian Gulf ports the chief of the customs house was formerly known as *shahbandar.* Sadid al-Saltaneh 1342, 77, and in particular Floor 2006, 267f.

78. Polak 1865, vol. 2, 188; de Rochechouart 1867, 122, 168; Greenfield 1904, 142.

79. De Rochechouart 1867, 168.

80. De Gobineau 1859, 392; Polak 1865, vol. 2, 188.

81. Polak 1865, vol. 2, 188; Curzon 1892, vol. 1, 88.

82. Polak 1865, vol. 1, 188; RO 1844, 115; Kosogovski 1344, 155.

83. Floor 1983.

84. Greenfield 1906, 141; Najm ol-Molk 1341, 30.

appears to have become less usual, because of the more secretive and safer method of putting one's money in European banks and/or enterprises, either within or without Iran.[85]

Apart from the necessary relationship between the authorities and the merchants, a kind of symbiosis dictated by the need for foreign luxuries, money, investments and financial security, there was within the merchant class an urge towards upward mobility. This aspiration expressed itself amongst other things in a search for government posts and titles.[86] In Shiraz in the 1880s Mirza Mohammad Rahim Khan, son of Mohammad Ja`far Khan Nazem al-Tojjar, became *monshi-bashi* (chief clerk) of the provincial government.[87] The Malek al-Tojjar of Mashhad was the *vakil* (representative) of the governor of Khorasan.[88] Hajji Mohammad `Ali, Ra'is al-Tojjar was the personal advisor of the Sheikh of Mohammarah.[89] In Southern Iran Mo`in al-Tojjar played an important role in local government administrating Lark, Hengam, Minab, Khamir, and Hormuz.[90] The Malek al-Tojjar of Bushire was governor of the Gulf Ports in 1886.[91] Many merchants became *kargodhar* or representative of the Ministry of Foreign Affairs.[92] Aqa Esma`il Mohammad (as well as his son after him) became Minister of the Pensions and Allowances Department of Fars province, .[93] In the Southern ports many merchants farmed the customs. While in Tehran, Hajji Mir Sadeq Mo`in al-Tojjar and Hajji Mohammad Hasan were advisors to the Ministry of Customs.[94]

Those merchants aspiring towards a higher place in society had to adapt their way of life to that of the ruling elite, and we can observe that many a merchant copied the leisured class's way of life. One of the most conspicuous aspects of the elite was their interest in landed property. Therefore, an ambitious merchant would buy real estate, stop trading himself and seek a government function. It is in this way that many a 'noble' family in Qajar Iran acquired its exalted position. In Shiraz the Qavam family, in Bam the Behzadi family, and in Kerman the Vaziri family became respectable members of the ruling elite this way.[95] Throughout the early part of the early part of the 19th century we find scattered instances that merchants owned landed property. In 1838, many Tabrizi merchants owned real estate,[96] while Hajji `Ali Isfahani did the same in Tehran.[97] Another early instance, the introduction of a new variety of sugar cane and the opium culture by Aqa Mohammad Mehdi Arbab, one of the leading merchants of Isfahan, shows the continued inter-

85. This development had already begun at the beginning of the 19th century, Eastwick 1864, vol. 1, 309; Naficy 1924, 67.

86. Fasa'i 1894-96, vol. 2, 161; E`temad al-Saltaneh 1306, 102, 106.

87. Fasa'i 1894-96, vol. 2, 58.

88. E`temad al-Saltaneh 1345, 1140.

89. Lorimer 1908, 1744.

90. Sadid al-Saltaneh 1342, 3, 37.

91. Sadid al-Saltaneh 1342, 37.

92. Fasa'i 1894-96, vol. 2, 44, 45, 58.

93. Fasa'i 1894-96, vol. 2, 43, 44, another became vizier of Fars, Ibid., vol. 2, 59.

94. Curzon 1892, vol. 2, 401; E`temad al-Saltaneh 1294-96, vol. 4, appendix, 15.

95. Fasa'i 1894-96, vol. 2, 48; Vaziri 1346, 57, 100.

96. RO 5, 137; Migeod 1990, 191.

97. Migeod 1990, 191.

est for landed property and landlordism on part of the merchants.[98] It appears, however, that notwithstanding this interest, the merchant class as a whole still invested the greater part of their capital in mercantile enterprises in the first part of the 19th century. Later in the century the acquisition of real estate by merchants by merchants increased enormously. This was due to several factors. In the first place, the devastating famine of 1870-73 impoverished a lot of people and made large tracts of land available. In the second place many merchants found the competition with the European companies in Iran unprofitable and sought alternative investments. In Isfahan many people who had met with reverses in trade, had turned to agriculture for their living. They sold their furniture and clothes to get money and enable them to bring the land in cultivation. In this way parts of the city became deserted, while the countryside became more populous.[99] In 1877 it is observed that "of late the important merchants occupy themselves with agriculture and administering their estates."[100] In other parts of the country about the same time this trend was also to be seen. In Kerman province we find many merchants owning real estate and flocks.[101] In Shiraz, many merchants devoted part of their energies to agriculture or became full-time landlords.[102] Of this latter category many invested their money in the cultivation of opium. These merchants were known as *taryakis*.[103] In fact we witness the creation of a new class, the landlords (*molkdars*). The availability of large tracts of landed property, the declining profits in trade and the severe competition with European merchants, turned many a merchant into a landlord. This trend was furthered by the foreign demand for cash crops which turned parts of Iran into production areas of raw materials for the world market. The new products were opium, for which large markets in East Asia were to be found. This cultivation got an impetus by the decline of the silk production. Furthermore, in the North, cultivation of cotton and rice for the Russian market was encouraged.[104] This greatly enhanced the value of landed property. The sale of crown lands (*khaleseh*) towards the end of the 19th century underscored this development. It also promoted the industrialization of agriculture, which led to a greater exploitation of the Iranian farmers, as well as to shortages of food and higher prices.[105]

Copying the elite's way of life meant that one did not trade anymore oneself, but it did not mean that one lost interest altogether in that line of business. This was not the elite's way either. Many a governor or local magnate had large commercial interests, even sometimes commanding a monopoly of certain branches of economic life. The date trade in Khuzestan, for example, was influenced by a prohibition in consequence of which no private owner was allowed to bring his dates on the market until those of the Sheikh of Mohammarah had been cleared off; one result of this rule was that the smaller merchants

98. Najm al-Molk 1341, 177; Tahvildar 1342, 58.
99. Jaberi Ansari 1322, 62.
100. Tahvildar 1342, 92.
101. Vaziri 1346, 67, 100, 158-59, 160, 172.
102. Fasa'i 1894-96, vol. 2, 26, 45, 62, 76, 131.
103. Fasa'i 1894-96, vol. 2, 45.
104. RMM 1910, 618.
105. Keddie 1950, 6-7; see also note 83.

were sometimes obliged to part with their stocks to the Sheikh's broker at a vary low price.[106] In Kerman the lucrative business of exporting wool was the governor's monopoly, as well as the right to produce the finest qualities of carpets and shawls.[107] The *Vali* or governor of Senneh (Kurdestan) had gained the greater part of his wealth in trade, and had money in the hands of many merchants, sometimes demanding high returns.[108] The governor of Bushire in 1838 forced merchants to take his goods at a lower rate "than they possibly can afford, and when any of the stock he has laid by in his granaries is scarce and dear in the bazaar, he forces the merchants to purchase from him at his own price, which is never less than fifty per cent above what they may procure it elsewhere."[109]

Such monopolies and enforced sales were part of the normal pattern of Qajar misrule. No wonder then that according to European sources the fear of unlawful appropriation was very widespread among traders. It seems to me, notwithstanding the examples quoted above, that this fear prevailed specially among the retail dealers and the smaller merchants. As we have seen the leading merchants had to deal continually with the authorities, not only to promote their own personal and business interests and to acquire political backing, but also to do business with them on a grand scale. There even existed friendly relations between many merchants and government officials. The offices of merchants in the bazaar often were meeting places for officials, and they also frequented one another in their respective homes and summerhouses.[110] The principal merchants often were in league with powerful members of the government, for if one wanted to be successful in Iran, one had to seek connections. It was in this way that merchants acquired relative security and great wealth.[111] Very well-known were the ties between Amin al-Zarb, the leading entrepreneur of Iran and Amin al-Soltan, the most influential prime minister in Iran toward the end of the 19th century.[112] In 1838, the Iranian governor of Bushire was chased away by the combined opposition of the merchants and the qadi of the town.[113] Even powerful individuals like Qavam al-Molk had to be careful not to antagonize the merchants. When he did in 1896, by trying to have the Malek al-Tojjar removed, he had to resign after intrigues by a coalition of merchants.[114] In the same city the *Darya-Begi*, who was governor from 1900 till 1903, was but the puppet of the powerful Mo`in al-Tojjar, who financed him. When the governor did not toe line, he had to resign, because of Mo`in al-Tojjar's influence.[115] The Malek al-Tojjar of Bushire also was a very rich and powerful individual, having close contacts with the Imam of Masqat. He acted as go-between for the Imam and the Shah and was expressively mentioned in the treaty about the possession of Ban-

---

106. Lorimer 908, 130.

107. Goldsmid 1876, vol. 2, 99, 101.

108. Rich 1836, vol. 1, 212.

109. Mignan 1839, vol. 2, 141; see also Lorimer 1908, 1855.

110. Tahvildar 1342, 93; Adib al-Molk 1349, 175, 195, 202, 207, 221; E`temad al-Saltaneh 1345, 300, 1016.

111. See e.g. Molkara 1325, 103

112. Dowlatabadi n.d. vol. 1, 95, note 1.

113. Lorimer 1908, 1987.

114. Lorimer 1908, 2060.

115. Lorimer 1908, 2130, 2131, 2140.

dar 'Abbas between the Imam and the Iranian government in 1856.[116] Hajji Mohammad Mehdi, who became Malek al-Tojjar in 1883, had close contacts with Amin al-Soltan and the Sheikh of Mohammarah. In 1888 he even participated in implementing a more aggressive Iranian foreign policy by visiting Jask with Iranian troops and planting the national fag there.[117] Thus one observes many a merchant participating fully in political life, which often brought him great personal gain. In doing so, great risks were taken, for the fear of sequestration was not unfounded. In fact, this insecurity prevailed also among the ruling elite and was a concomitant of life.[118] However, the merchant class was less oppressed than any other class. The authorities could not kill the hen with the golden eggs, for this would have led to a downright refusal from all other merchants to lend money to the government or its officials. As the authorities did not put the squeeze on the merchant class as a whole, and there were ample opportunities to make good losses merchants in general, did not protest en bloc, and accepted their ill-luck resignedly. In some cases, however, they would protest as a group, often with success.[119] Sequestration of property was either induced by political or religious motives. Hajji 'Ali Akbar was harassed by the authorities, having formerly worked for the government. Probably part of his property was gotten out of illegal profits, of which the government wanted its share. Another case is that of Agha Kuchek, who after having been vizier of the province of Fars was squeezed by his successor for an amount of 150.000 *tumans*.[120] A very famous case is the trial of Amin al-Zarb, the director of the mint in Tehran and Iran's leading entrepreneur, in 1896, who was forced by his political opponents to pay a fine of 765.000 *tumans* for illegal practices.[121] Other cases concern persecuted Babi merchants,[122] and forced loans and ransom money from merchants in unruly times.[123] One can say, however, that unlawful appropriation of merchants property was relatively infrequent.

THE NATURE OF THE MERCHANTS' BUSINESS

Before we start discussing the Iranian merchants' reaction towards the European economic onslaught, let us first take a look at the nature of the business carried on by the Iranian merchants. In the beginning of the 19th century most merchants traded for their own account. The Iranian export houses collected the various export products via their agents and sent these abroad, either accompanied by their representative or under the care of the caravan leader.[124] En route the goods were handled by their agents on the spot, as well as

116. Fasa'i 1894-96, vol. 2, 311, 312.

117. Lorimer 1908, 2180, 2067.

118. Lambton 1961, 135.

119. Fraser 1834, 312; E`temad al-Saltaneh 1345, 1096; see, however, Molkara 1325, 104.

120. Fasa'i 1894-96, vol. 2, 45, 49.

121. Hedayat 1344, 100; according to Mostowfi n.d., vol. 2, 11, it amounted to 400,000 *tumans*; according to Sayyah 1346, 494, it was 800,000 *tumans*.

122. Migeod 1990, 187.

123. Kasravi 1319-21, vol. 3, 323; Lambton 1963 b, 80.

124. De Gobineau 1859, 117-119; Greenfield 1906, 79.

in the city of destination. Most Iranian merchants had branch offices abroad, although restricted to a few foreign cities only. Many merchants did extensive business with Istanbul, Moscow, or Bombay, or all three of them. The number of these establishments abroad would increase in the second half of the 19th century when Calcutta, and even London and Paris, but less so, were included in the Iranian merchants' sphere of interest. Considering the long distance the goods had to cover, one can form an idea about the extension of their mercantile network. When the goods were sold the merchant either took the cash-money back home, or he would, as was usual, buy foreign goods in exchange. This combination of both import and export trade in one hand was quite usual, and this was also the case for European houses trading in Iran. Some merchants were only engaged in import trade, paying for goods in cash.[125]

Both European and Iranian merchant did business through a broker (*dallal*). Large trading firms and banking institutions had their own brokers, who were charged with finding customers, arranging business and sale-purchase conditions, and to see to it that safe guarantees for payment were provided for.[126] The brokers were specialized in the various commercial branches, and one can say that almost every branch had its own broker. In Isfahan, around 1877, for example there were four kinds of brokers: cattle brokers (*dallal-e chaharpayan*), fruit brokers (*dallal-e favakeh*), trade brokers (*dallal-e tejarat*), and opium brokers (*dallal-e taryak*).[127] There were differences among them in line of business and in scale; some brokers operated on a more modest scale than others. Although the brokers had formed a guild, having institutions peculiar to them, this organization seems to have fallen into disuse at the end of the 19th century.[128] Leading brokers, such as the chief broker (*dallal-bashi*) of a city, often had government posts and belonged to the city's notables, rather than to the working class.[129]

The brokers mostly had a bad reputation, which was amazing, as their reputation was their only asset.[130] They often were former merchants who had gone bankrupt. The brokers kept a journal in which they noted all transactions as well as the names of both seller and buyer, their city of residence, the price, the quantity, credit terms, etc. The buyer affixed his seal or his fingerprint to this notation in the journal, and the journal was allowed as legal evidence in court. To acquire greater security the broker had both seller and buyer sign or fingerprint an understanding or *qowlnameh*, in which they promised to fulfill the conditions agreed upon. The *qowlnameh* often at the same time was a power of attorney for the broker to conclude a transaction within certain conditions. In Tabriz this document had to be registered by both the consul of the European merchant and the *dabir-e divankhaneh* (clerk of the provincial government) to be allowed as evidence. As the *qowl-*

---

125. Blau 1858, 49, 50; RO 5, 137.

126. Blau 1858, 53; "Should the buyer not be known to the broker he was obliged to find guarantees for his identity and solvency." Commercial Reports 20, 372.

127. Tahvildar 1342,116, 117.

128. Bleibtreu 1895, 125; in 1926 a tax known as *dallali* still was levied.

129. See for example the position of *dallal-bashi* of Bushire. Gleadowe-Newcomen 1905, 39; see also Lorini 1900, 180.

130. "Among the brokers a few honest men may be found, but they are rare exceptions." Wills 1883, 188.

nameh was one of the few documents allowed in the religious courts, a religious authority, who would seal the document, often also legalized it.[131]

According to Moslem law the party who had engaged a broker had to pay him his commission, but according to trade usance, each party would pay half of this due (which amounted to a ½ -2%), unless otherwise had been agreed upon. The broker who mediated the deal supervised the transfer of the merchandise, and he often witnessed the IOU or other documents handed over by the buyer. Although in practice buyers would often pay the seller through his broker, the latter was not entitled to receive such payments according to Moslem law.[132]

The practice in 1872 in Tabriz also prevailed in other Iranian cities. "Each European firm at Tabreez employs a native broker (tallal, sic: *dallal*), who along with the agent treats with the purchasers, fixes the price and conditions of sale, collects the credits when they fall due, and receives for his services 1 % on minor transactions, and ½% when the operations are more considerable. This position is much sought after, as the broker in not held responsible for the payment. He receives his salary without incurring any risk. His interest in retaining his place is supposed to be a sufficient guarantee for faithful service. All merchandise, with some exceptions, are disposed of by the importers to middlemen (binektars, sic: *bonakdar*) who resell them to the shopkeepers or retail dealers (bezas, sic: *bazzaz*) or to purchasers from the interior of the country."[133] It was seldom that large importers sold all their stock to one market distributor (*bonakdar*) only. Even when a few of them associated themselves to get more credit, the importers tended to divide their risks and would sell to several *bonakdars*.[134]

The nature and extent of trade varied per city and per period. It is difficult to find big merchants dealing in only one commodity or being in one line of business, for they dabbled in practically everything, if money could be made. "An intelligent merchant of considerable eminence at Tabreez told me, that if he were about to undertake a speculation to Constantinople, he would carry with him silk, cotton, tobacco, Cashmere shawls, coffee, and money. The coffee he would sell at Erzeroum, without expecting great profit, to pay the expenses of carriage, customs, and other caravan expenses."[135] It was only among the smaller merchants and the market distributors that specialization occurred. As this kind of trade required large financial resources, there were only a few merchants able to trade for their own account. Most merchants were agents or representatives for other bigger merchants or for foreign houses.[136]

---

131. Greenfield 1906, 79, 80; Blau 1858, 53: The fee paid for registration was 2½ *qran*s for the act of registration and 1/10% on the amount involved. "At the present time it is seldom made use of as the advantages do not compensate for the loss of time and money, besides there is a general disinclination to entrust bills, bonds, or any important document to the safeguard of a Persian official." Commercial Reports 20, 273.

132. Greenfield 1906, 79, 80.

133. Commercial Reports 20, 273.

134. RO 5, 137.

135. Fraser 1826, 365; see also Lorini 1900, 351.

136. Blau 1858, 49, 50.

In Bandar `Abbas around the turn of the century there was practically no local trade of importance, though a few Hindu and Moslem traders acted in their own account, mostly with Lar. Most merchants, all strangers from abroad, were commissionaires and forwarding agents for merchants in Kerman, Yazd, Khurasan, Lar, and for Indian houses. They would take care of the customs and consign the goods to partners or agents up country.[137] The bulk of the trade was on indent to agents in Bombay. The Iranian firms usually had a clearing account with Bombay.[138] Hardly any direct orders were sent to Europe, although most of the goods were of British origin.[139] Many of the agents were Indians, the majority being agents of Shikarpur Mahajan firms. In 1890, they numbered about 80,[140] and in 1903 about 50.[141] The Indians did not live permanently there, but were replaced every three years. They normally stayed for the winter only, and did not have their families with them. They had extensive business relations with their compatriots all over Southern Iran.[142] A peculiar feature of trade in Bandar. `Abbas seems to have been the *pish-kerayeh* or forwarding trade, which operation was unique in the Gulf area for Bandar `Abbas. This trade was mainly in the hands of Indians. The *jelowdar* (forwarder) would take care of the customs and would only get his due after the goods had arrived at their destination. When the forwarders needed money, they would loan the *barnameh* (Bill of Lading) for the period of that journey of the goods. The merchants charged 10 percent interest in this case.[143]

In Bushire the situation was not much different from that in Bandar `Abbas. The former was more important, being the main transit port for Iran, especially for the markets of Shiraz and Isfahan. The local trade was unimportant, although it was on the increase.[144] The Iranian traders here were in fact only agents or brokers for foreign firm: no merchant was trading for his own account around 1900. Their real asset was their personal honesty. The Iranian traders consigned their goods to principals or partners in Shiraz and Isfahan. The trade with India was extensive and solid.[145]

Yazd had a considerable trade for local purposes, while it was at the same time the main distribution center for goods destined for markets in Northern Iran. Here the foreign element was almost completely lacking. A number of Shikarpuri Hindus, who were doing a profitable business in the 1890s left the city owing to the hatred of the mullahhs and the impossibility of collecting outstanding claims from the Yazdi debtors.[146] A number of Sunni merchants from Bustak (near Bandar `Abbas) known as Avazees did good

137. Sadid al-Saltaneh 1342, 175; Berichte 1910, 272; MacLean 1904, 54; Gleadowe-Newcomen 1905, 45; Lorimer 1908, 10.

138. MacLean 1904, 54.

139. MacLean 1904, 54.

140. Sadid al-Saltaneh 1342, 168.

141. Gleadowe-Newcomen 1905, 45; see also Lorimer 1908, 10.

142. Gleadowe-Newcomen 1905, 45; Sadid al-Saltaneh 1342, 168.

143. Sadid al-Saltaneh 1342, 175.

144. MacLean 1904, 56; Berichte 1910, 279.

145. Berichte 1910, 279; MacLean 1904, 65; Gleadowe-Newcomen 1905, 62.

146. Their number which had been as much many as 17 in 1866 had dwindled already to 5 in 1871. Curzon 1892, vol. 2, 240; Gleadowe-Newcomen 1905, 55; Goldsmid 1876, vol. 2, 173, 190.

business there; they numbered about 25.[147] In fact, there were only two classes of traders in Yazd: those who imported merchandise from Bombay and the South, and those who bought from the former and sent the goods to Khorasan. A few of the first class of merchants, they numbered 150, had agents in Bombay, while the other group only numbered 75 merchants.[148]

In neighboring Kerman the Hindu element dominated the mercantile scene. Both import and export trade was in the hands of the Shikarpur Indians and of a few Parsis during the second half of the 19th century. The Moslem traders, among them only 40 merchants from Kerman itself, occupied themselves with "trading petty local products or commodities locally purchased." The carpet trade was completely in the hands of Tabrizi merchants though, while in the sugar and tea import trade a few Moslems tried their hand too.[149] Apart from the few Parsis, which group was mostly composed of peddlers,[150] and the Jews, who being too poor to trade were engaged in brokerage,[151] the trade was completely an Indian affair. These, about 25-30 in number,[152] were also moneylenders and bankers, and did business with friends and relatives and agents in Bombay, Sind, and the Punjab.[153] Their business relations were to be found all over Kerman Province, even extending into British Baluchistan. In Rudbar and Jiroft for instance, the trade also was completely an Indian affair, i.e., by Indians who came from Kerman or Bandar `Abbas. All in all Indian merchants numbered about 300 in Southern East Iran. In Kerman they had a caravansary to themselves.[154] In small towns like Bam, Sirjan, and Rafsanjan there were some Iranian Moslem merchants who had agents or partners in Yazd, Bandar `Abbas, Isfahan, Tehran, Mashhad, Tabriz, Istanbul, and Bombay.[155]

Shiraz was the first stop coming from Bushire to the North, and it was from here that the cities more inland were provisioned. The Shirazi merchants bought most of their goods from foreign firms based in Shiraz. Only the principal merchants had direct contacts with Bombay, though hardly any direct contact existed with Europe. Here also the brokers and commissionaires outnumbered those trading for their own account.[156]

The foreign trade of Khuzestan was mainly through Mohammarah. Here the merchants were mainly agents of British or Indian firms.[157] The greater part of the

147. DCR 1662, 24.

148. DCR 1662, 16, 17.

149. Vaziri 1346, 68; Gleadowe-Newcomen 1905, 49, 50; Berichte 1910, 265.

150. DCR 1376, 33; Vaziri 1346, 69 numbers about 50 Parsi merchants, whose names he does not mention, because it would be disrespectful to Moslems and it would take too long.

151. DCR 1671, 2.

152. DCR 1376, 33; see also Curzon 1892, vol. 2, 240 (40 in 1890); Vaziri 1346, 69 states there were 10 Indians in 1876, whose names he does not list, because it does not serve any purpose.

153. DCR 1376, 33; Berichte 1910, 265.

154. DCR 1376, 33; Vaziri 1346, 32; Gleadowe-Newcomen 1905, 55. Their local roots were very strong; some of them had already been in Kerman over 30 years.

155. Vaziri 1346, 100, 158, 159, 172.

156. Berichte 1910, 291; Fasa'i 1894-96, vol. 2, 26, 60, 131.

157. Berichte 1910, 296.

Mohammarah market, however, was in the hands of "small Jew traders, dealing much in odd lots and auctioned goods, which could be placed on the market at low prices."[158]

In Isfahan the situation was not much different from that in Shiraz. Here also a small number of merchants did business with Bombay. The greater part of the Isfahani merchants were commissionaires for Iranian traders in Bushire and Shiraz. Many goods were bought from European firms in Isfahan. Some business was done directly with Bombay on indent to Iranian agents there.[159] In Hamadan Jewish merchants predominated. The import trade, especially from Manchester was mainly in their hands; most of them were from Baghdad. This also explains why most of the Hamadan merchants bought in Baghdad and only some of the goods in Kermanshah.[160] In the latter frontier city at least 80% of the trade was likewise in the hands of Jewish merchants. Because of contacts with Jews in Baghdad and Britain they could import more cheaply than others direct from Manchester, and especially, because they only took small profits.[161] Apart from the Jews, a number of Armenians and Moslems were engaged in wholesale trade.[162] In Kermanshah Province trade was mainly in the hands of Chaldean Christians.[163]

In Tabriz, around 1840, there were only 8 to 10 important merchants on whom the rest of the mercantile community depended. A great number of ambulatory merchants, however, made regular dints in their monopolistic position. Before 1837 Iranian merchants who almost exclusively traded in cotton textiles handled the bulk of trade. Thereafter a great many European firms opened offices in Tabriz, gradually dominating the market. There was still some direct contact with Istanbul and Moscow, but most merchandise was bought locally from foreign firms. In 1859 the greater part of imports was still handled by Iranian merchants, but it decreased more and more.[164]

Apart from the fact that European merchants had a better organization and cheaper production methods at their disposal, they also had larger financial resources than the Iranian merchants. Among the small group of Iranian merchants there were only a few who could compete with European firms, for most of the Iranian merchants did not have large properties. In 1877, Zarrabi considered a merchant having a property of 5,000 *tumans* a man of wealth.[165] This opinion is confirmed by Kasravi, who reports that in 1909 Hajji 'Ali and Hajji Jamshid of Maragheh paid each 2,700 *tumans* to Samad Khan to remain unmolested. This was considered to be a large sum of money. Another merchant Hajji Mirza Hasan was forced to pay 10,000 *tumans*, which he was unable to do. When the demand was lowered to 6,000 *tumans* he had to dispose of all of his property to enable him to pay.[166] In 1893 consul Preece reported of Kerman: "there is not a

158. MacLean 1904, 39.
159. MacLean 1904, 64; Berichte 1910, 302.
160. Berichte 1910, 301; MacLean 1904, 38, 65.
161. MacLean 1904, 38, 61; DCR 4559, 5; Berichte 1910, 296.
162. Berichte 1910, 296.
163. DCR 4365, 9.
164. RO 5, 136-7; Issawi 1971,100, 103, 105; Smith & Dwight 1834, 321.
165. Zarrabi 1341, 447.
166. Kasravi 1319-21, vol. 3, 323.

merchant in it worth 10,000 *tumans*."[167] On the other hand in 1876 Vaziri mentions a merchant in Rafsanjan who owned 100.000 *tumans* in landed property, and the Malek al-Tojjar of Sirjan owned 40 to 50.000 *tumans*, and acted as if he owned more.[168] The Malek al-Tojjar of Tehran was credited to possess 50,000 *tumans* in 1807, while an Isfahani merchant was reputed to have a capital of 1½ million francs.[169] In 1844 there were only 3 to 4 Iranian merchants in Tabriz having a capital of 30 to 40,000 *tumans*, while there were some others who had the same amount, but most of it was invested in real estate and precious stones.[170] In the same town a Russian traveler found that no merchant of the first rank had a capital of over 150,000 silver rubles, and that there were only five such wealthy persons in that city.[171] De Gobineau reports that some merchants in Bushire were millionaires.[172] Around 1860 Hajji Mohammad of Qazvin owned a house for the outlay of which he had spent 190,000 *tumans*.[173] In Astarabad Hajji Mohammad Hasan and Hajji 'Ali Ahmad had a capital of about 110,000 *tumans*.[174] In Yazd, in 1893, the British consul reports that "it has a number of wealthy merchants in the place who have a trading capital of some 2,000,000 *tumans*. This rendered into sterling at the present rate seems but very little, but in a poor country like Persia, it means a great deal and gives security and impetus to trade such as is not enjoyed in all the other centers of the country."[175] In Shiraz the capital of the Iranian merchants was estimated to be over 6,000,000 *tumans* in 1904.[176] In Hamadan the capital of the merchants working in the import trade was not over £ 40,000.[177] In nearby Kermanshah there were in 1897 "6 first class merchants dealing with London-Bombay and Baghdad who have a bazaar credit of over 100,000 £, and who are supposed to have property to an equal amount, another 10 whose credit equals some 25,000 £ deal only with Baghdad and Persia. Besides them are a number of what may be called second class merchants who also deal with Baghdad and Persia in general, but only in a small way, each having a credit to the extent of 1,000 to 2,000 £."[178] As is clear from the above, the rich merchants formed a small number of the mercantile community, and the small and medium scale merchants predominated. The capital of the large merchants did not usually exceed 50 to 100,000 *tumans*.[179]

There were of course, those who possessed a great deal more than that, but these merchants were the exception. Hajji Mohammad Hasan Amin al-Zarb was credited to have a fortune of 25.000.000 *tumans*; he did extensive business abroad, had agents in

---

167. DCR 1376, 35.
168. Vaziri 1346, 159, 172.
169. Issawi 1971, 26-27.
170. RO 5, 137.
171. Issawi 1971, 106.
172. De Gobineau 1859, 122.
173. Eastwick 1864, vol. 1, 305.
174. Stolze & Andreas 1885, 50.
175. DCR 1376, 17.
176. Gleadowe-Newcomen 1905, 57.
177. MacLean 1904, 65.
178. DCR 2260, 26.
179. Issawi 1971, 44.

Europe and China and owned a lot of real estate.[180] Mo`in al-Tojjar made a lot of money in real estate, mining operations and trade with Europe and India. His capital was estimated at 1 to 2,000,000 *tumans*.[181] Other successful tycoons were Hajji Mohammad Esma`il Maghazi Tabrizi, Hajji Mohammad Taqi Shahrudi and the Malek al-Tojjar of Tehran.[182] Of the non-Moslem merchants the Tumaniants brothers (Armenians), whose holdings in Russia alone were estimated at 24,000,000 *qrans* in 1917,[183] and Arbab Jamshid (Zoroastrian) may suffice as examples of successful entrepreneurs.[184]

COMMERCIAL REACTION OF MERCHANTS TO THE RISE OF EUROPEAN INFLUENCE

We have seen that the Iranian merchant's financial position was not very strong and that gradually the greater part of trade was taken over by foreign merchants. The number of Iranian merchants trading for their own account decreased, while the influence of the foreigners grew enormously. One has also witnessed the coming into existence of a great many petty dealers who relied completely on credit, having no capital of their own.[185] In general Iranian merchants lacked the organizational and administrative capabilities as well as the capital necessary to finance and run their affairs on the same scale as the European merchants did. The mercantile community, of course, reacted to this development, sometimes vehemently. In fact we can distinguish two kinds of reactions, in the first place there was a political, and in the second place a commercial one, to which latter we shall turn now.

The commercial reaction was late in coming, for it was only towards the end of the nineteenth century that Iranian merchants, realizing that trading directly with Europe was more profitable than buying from European firms in one's hometown, took the initiative and started buying either through agents or through members of their firms established in Europe directly from the manufacturers. In this way British firms gradually lost the monopoly of the import trade in Isfahan.[186] In Gilan Iranian merchants successfully broke the grip of the Russian Armenian, French, and Italian merchants on the silk trade, by exporting themselves directly to Marseilles and Milan, the two chief markets for silk.[187] It was only in a few cases that Iranian entrepreneurs competed successfully with the foreign merchants, as we have seen above. Europeans were successful because of their financial power and business methods. Therefore, Iranian merchants sought to concentrate their capital to compete more successfully with European merchants. This incentive led to the formation of several large companies. Although there were no legal obstacles against partnerships or larger companies, these were seldom formed, because of lack of

180. Issawi 1971, 43; according to Hedayat 1344, 100 Amin al-Zarb had a capital of only 1,880,000 *tumans*.

181. Issawi 1971, 44; Sadid al-Saltaneh 1342, 3, 6. 37, 212, 343, 350.

182. Issawi 1971, 44.

183. Issawi 1971, 44, 67.

184. Issawi 1971, 44.

185. DCR 1662, 24.

186. DCR 2260, 7.

187. Landor 1900, vol. 1, 60.

confidence.[188] When partnerships occurred it was mostly between relatives, co-religionists and/or fellow citizens.[189] Another reason why companies hardly occurred was the defective and restrictive Shi'ite law in this respect, which only allowed one form of company, viz. the limited liability company (*sharekat al-`anan*).[190] The shortcomings of this law as well as the arbitrary application of justice in Qajar Iran, handicapped the creation of such companies. It was usual for merchants to act in common with each other as far as the purchasing of merchandise and its transportation was concerned.[191] Merchants who traveled from Tabriz to Istanbul to buy merchandise for cash, usually would also carry the capital of some 20 to 40 fellow citizens.[192] It is not known, however, whether their relationship was one of *sharekat* or *morazebeh*. Merchants often had *shoraka* (partners) abroad as well as `*ommal* (agents) and *gomashtehs* (commissionaires).[193] These partners sent merchandise in exchange for goods received from their partner. The agents, whose number was to grow towards the end of the 19th century, were remunerated on a commission basis. These forwarding agents often traded for their own account too. In Erzerum, around 1848, agents received one-third of the commission of the Trebisond agents. The latter, if he was an Iranian, got 100 *paras* or his principal reimbursed, 2½ piastres for every package sent or received from Iran, shipping charges and other expenses. In Erzerum agents did not get a commission for goods from Iran and were merely reimbursed for their expenses.[194] In Bandar `Abbas agents received payment either in produce or in remittance on India.[195]

It was only in the 1880s that large trading companies were found (often with the object to usurp the foreigners' economic position), of which the first appears to have been one created by Hajji Zeyn al-`Abedin Amin al-Tojjar of Shiraz, who bought sailing ships to transport merchandise, and who reinvested his profits to buy steamers. He did extensive business with Bombay.[196] In 1882, the Aminiyeh Company was founded in Tabriz, and it was dissolved in 1892 after the death of the chief director. It then became evident that the books were not well kept, that the other directors had embezzled the company's capital and the result was that neither the shareholders (*sharik*) nor the creditors got one cent.[197] Around 1886 the Commercial Company of Iran was created with a capital of 350,000 *tumans*.[198] In 1890, the Fars Trading Company (Ltd) was founded in Shiraz under the direction of Hajji `Abdol-Rahim; secretary was Mirza `Abdol-Razzaq. Originally founded to thwart the activities of the Imperial Bank of Iran, the company soon devoted its energy to trade only. It had a capital of 500.000 *qrans* in shares of 250 *qrans* each, all of which had been taken up. There were six directors, all resident in Shiraz. The company paid

188. Wilson 1896, 281.

189. Berichte 1910, 351.

190. Greenfield 1906, 59-61.

191. De Rochechouart 1867, 177.

192. RO 5, 137.

193. Vaziri 1346, 7 8, 100, 159, 172.

194. Issawi 1971, 102.

195. MacLean 1904, 54.

196. Fasa'i 1894-96, vol. 2, 60; this company probably existed already before 1878, for it is referred to in a Dutch report: Verslag van bevindingen 1877.

197. Greenfield 1906, 61; Issawi 1971, 44.

198. Issawi 1971, 44.

dividends twice a year, in 1892 amounting to 15%. It had offices in Bombay, Yazd, Isfahan, Bushire and Tehran, and mainly did business in piece goods and sugar. The company had a great deal of confidence of the population, and they did a fair amount of business.[199] In 1892 the Mansuriyeh Company was founded in Yazd,[200] while in Isfahan it was proposed to form a company for the purchase of tobacco under the auspices of Aqa Najafi, the leading religious authority in Isfahan. Its purpose was to obtain the monopoly of the tobacco trade. The capital was to be 2,000,000 *qrans* in shares of 1,000 *qrans* each, and a dividend of 5 percent per year was to be realized. No shareholder with less than 20 shares had the right to interfere with the company's business, and after 7 years the company's capital would be divided among the shareholders. Apparently nothing came of this project since the tobacco trade remained completely in the hands of a Turkish company.[201] About the same time the Naseri Company was formed by Hajji Mohammad Mehdi Malek al-Tojjar (Mo`tamad al-Soltan) and Hajji Aqa Mohammad Mo`in al-Tojjar, both of Bushire. The company was backed by the Sheikh of Mohammarah and Amin al-Soltan, the prime minister, and started a lively competition with Messrs. Lynch for the Karun river transportation. The Naseri Company constructed some buildings at Ahvaz, laid a light horse tramway and had some steamers on the river. Native merchants were discouraged and even prohibited to ship their goods by the Lynch steamers.[202] In 1893 the company discontinued its activities and left the field to the Lynch Brothers. In 1895 a new company was founded known as Shahanshahi by the Sheikh of Mohammarah, and some Shushtar merchants and took over where the Naseri Company had left off. It appears, however, that the Naseri Company came back to life again, for such a company was still in business about 1910.[203] In 1897 the Ettehad Company was formed in Tabriz, which had agents all over Iran and Turkey. In Kerman its representative was in charge of the government treasury. In 1903 the Ettehad Company had to discontinue its operations; all its creditors were paid.[204] In 1898 the Mas`udiyeh Company was formed in Isfahan, doing business in commercial and banking operations.[205] The latter entrepreneurs also founded the Islamiyeh Company in Isfahan about the same time, with a capital of 150,000 *tumans*, which was chiefly financed by the leading ulama of the city. The company manufactured and distributed cotton and woolen cloth, which was of inferior quality, being woven on hand looms. The purpose was to encourage local industries and the wearing of cloth woven in Iran. The company had branches in the provincial capitals and in Najaf. After a good start, the company went

---

199. Forsat 1316, 537; DCR 1376, 44; according to Lorini the Fars Trading Company was a small firm trading in opium. It only became a limited company in 1897 when in Bushire a Trading Company was formed (with a capital of £ 20.000), which issued notes known as *bijaks* (DCR 2346, 5). The Bushire example was followed in Yazd and Isfahan, but here the companies were forbidden by the governor. In Shiraz, however, the Fars Trading Company got an impetus by the participation of important merchants like Mohammad Sadeq, Hajji Sayyed Kazeruni, Mohammad Hoseyn Namazi, Hajii Mirza Bozorg, Hajji Mirza `Ali Shirazi. It was not a real company, but just a bunch of people working together; they paid a dividend of 6 percent, Lorini 1900, 350-51.

200. Issawi 1971, 44.

201. DCR 1376, 66.

202. Curzon 1892, vol. 2, 385-86; Issawi 1971, 172; Fasa'i 1894-96, vol. 2, 60; Lorimer 1908, 1726-7.

203. Lorimer 1908, 1728; Issawi 1971, 172.

204. Issawi 1971, 45; Greenfield 1906, 61; DCR 1671, 9.

205. Issawi 1971, 45.

bankrupt in a bad year, because its financial position had been weakened by embezzlements of its fund by the directors.[206] In 1899 the `Omumi Company was founded in Tehran with a capital of 1,000,000 *tumans* to work in trade and banking operations.[207] In Kerman also existed an `Omumi Company formed by Aqa Mehdi Tabrizi.[208] Other associations of merchants occurred, although most of them were not of lasting influence. A combination of Iranian capitalists in opposition to the Imperial Bank came to nought.[209] In 1911 a group of Isfahani merchants contemplated the revival of the sericulture in Isfahan, but nothing came of it.[210] Most of the above mentioned companies were failures, the most important failure, however, was that of the *Sharekat-e `Omumi-ye Iran*, which according to Greenfield had been the only real company. It was the first company to have its charter validated by the government. This fact and the person of Hajji Kazem Malek al-Tojjar of Tehran, founder of the company, inspired confidence in the general public, which bought up to 1.000.000 *tumans* in shares. The company existed hardly a year, and the directors and the founders started outdoing themselves in getting their hands on the company's capital. The books were falsified and the company could not meet its liabilities. Shareholders and creditors lost their money. None of the defrauders could be brought to justice; Hajji Kazem took sanctuary (*bast*) in the Russian embassy.[211]

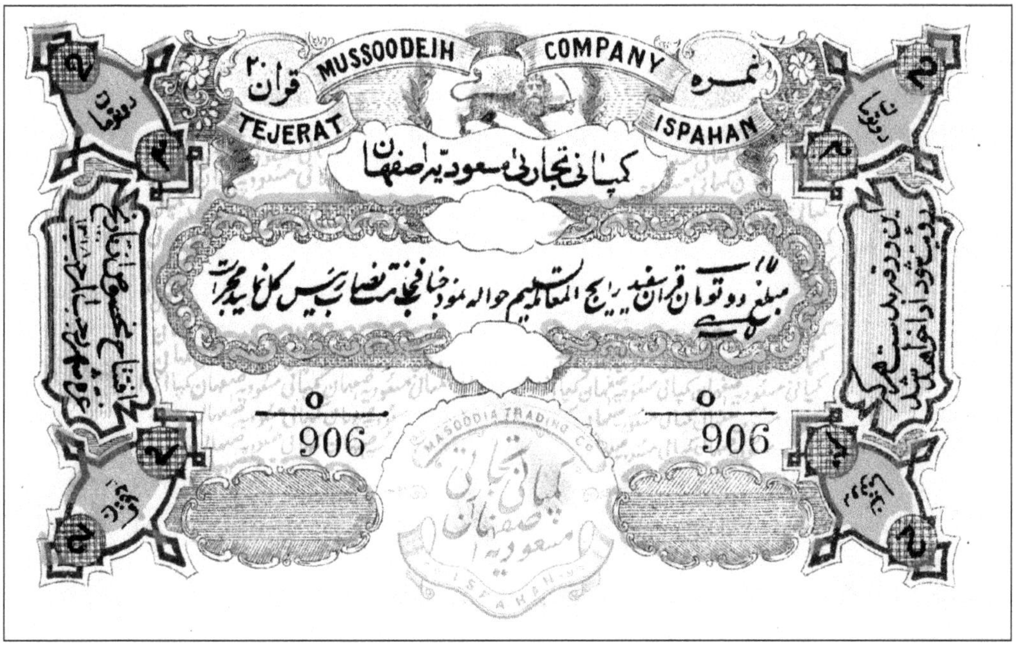

The failure of the Iranian merchant class to compete successfully with the European firms, epitomized by the complete lack of success to establish an independent commercial base to fight the European economic power, led to their dependence on foreign

206. Issawi 1971, 45; DCR 3923, 7; Greenfield 1906, 61; Lambton 1958, 51.
207. Issawi 1971, 45.
208. Vaziri 1346, 68.
209. Issawi 1971, 45; Kosogovski 1344, 24.
210. DCR 4838, 12; DCR 5254, 25.
211. Greenfield 1906, 61-62; Browne 1969, 179, 186.

capital and industry. This and the disrepute which they brought companies (*sharekat*) into, was the only result of the commercial reactions.[212]

POLITICAL REACTION OF MERCHANTS TO THE RISE OF EUROPEAN INFLUENCE

Did they fare any better with their political reaction? In the beginning of the Qajar era trade in Iran was completely in the hands, of Iranian merchants. In foreign trade Armenian and Georgian merchants were largely represented. Trade and industry prospered. The first sign that European influence had penetrated and was resented by the Iranian mercantile community was about 1830, when "the quality of English and Masulipatam, chintzes alarmed the manufacturers so much that they petitioned the King to put a stop to the importation."[213] The Iranian government was not against taking such measures: in fact the British representative reported in 1836 that "the Shah takes every means to check the consumption of European manufacturies and to encourage those of Persia: to effect the latter purpose he has recently advanced money, and offered rewards to the makers of chintz."[214] The turning point in this state of affairs took place in 1837, when European businessmen made their first appearance on the Iranian scene. Up to 1837 the trade in and via Tabriz, then the most important Iranian trading center, with Istanbul had been largely in the hands of Iranian and Armenian merchants. European firms had no direct contact with Iran, but sold their products to Iranian merchants in Istanbul, or to those having agents in Istanbul. Likewise Iranian goods were collected in Tabriz from all over Iran, and from there exported to Europe. However, in 1837, because of many bankruptcies among Iranian merchants and the subsequent decline in credit, some European companies decided to take the trade in their own hands and establish their representatives on the spot to have direct contact with the Tabriz market. When in 1837 the trading house of Ralli opened a branch in Tabriz the first of many protests against European merchants occurred. Seeing their monopolistic position threatened, the leading merchants in Tabriz forbade the market-distributors (*bonakdar*) and brokers (*dallal*) to have anything to do with Ralli, which order was followed strictly. Apart from having political pull these merchants could punish disobedience with withdrawal of credit, the lifeblood of Iranian commerce. The merchants could not hold the *bonakdars* indefinitely so to retain their grip upon them, after one month they allowed them to do business with Ralli.[215] In 1841 a ban on the consumption of tea was issued in Tabriz and Tehran to embarrass the Russian Georgians who completely had this trade in hands.[216] This attempt to break the hold of foreign merchants on a branch of foreign trade proved, however, to be abortive, because the ban was not respected.[217] Three years later merchants in Tehran protested in one body against the

212. Naficy 1924, 83.
213. Fraser 1826, 368.
214. Issawi 1971, 78-79.
215. Issawi 1971, 105, 107, 111; RO 5, 137.
216. Issawi 1971, 76.
217. Issawi 1971, 76.

import of European manufactories, because they were ruined by it. In Kashan a similar vain attempt was made in 1845.[218] In 1864 the merchant body in Tabriz protested against the predominant role of European merchants and manufactories with the same lack of success.[219] Gradually Iranian merchants were losing their hold on the interior market too, and towards the end of the 19th century it was completely dominated by Russian and British merchants. Not only Iranian trade was seriously hurt by the Western impact, but also Iranian industry, which was all but ruined.[220] The actions by merchants not only suffered because of their local nature, but also because of the defective communication system and the lack of a popular response to their plight. The ban on tea, for example, in 1841 did not have any effect because the consumers just ignored it. Although Mohammad Shah had encouraged the trade in Iranian manufactories by giving subsidies, his policy did not find support beyond the circle of the court.[221] The government certainly would have continued such a policy, i.e., before it became subservient to Russia and Britain, if only the population would have responded favorably to such measures, which it did not.[222] Various local authorities exerted themselves to create conditions in which trade could prosper. Unfortunately, these individuals were too few, and the work started by them was not part of a consistent national economic policy. Therefore the work started by them was more often than not discontinued by their successors. The only result of their endeavors often was that their name stuck to the produce which they helped to promote.[223]

GOVERNMENT EFFORTS TO SUPPORT MERCHANTS

Although the government held regular discussions with the merchant community, this did not lead to the formulation of a commercial policy favoring Iranian merchants. Since 1853 the Mo`in al-Tojjar in Tehran presided over deliberations between influential merchants of that city which were held on orders from the government.[224] During these sessions the economic prospects of the country were discussed, and if required economic advice, would be formulated.[225] In the provincial capitals the Malek al-Tojjar and/or the leading merchants seem to have advised the provincial government with regard to commercial affairs. In Tabriz the government discussed the problem of trade bonds with the merchants in 1858.[226] In Shiraz, in 1893, the Malek al-Tojjar attended the governor's council.[227] Regularly the subject of putting a ban on the import of European goods was brought up, also in

---

218. Issawi 1971, 76, 258.
219. Issawi 1971, 103, 114.
220. Ashraf 1970, 322-26; see, however, Issawi 1971, 259.
221. Issawi 1971, 79; see on the ineffective attempts by the Iranian government: Ibid. 292-97, and Mostowfi n.d., vol. 2, 494-96 and in general Floor 2009a.
222. Issawi 1971, 79.
223. Mostowfi n.d., vol. 1, 75; Wills 1883, 395.
224. E`temad al-Saltaneh 1298-1300, vol. 3, 231.
225. E`temad al-Saltaneh 1294-96, vol. 2, 142; Greenfield 1904, 144.
226. Adib al-Molk 1349, 167.
227. Forsat 1316, 281.

meetings between the Shah and the principal merchants of Tehran. At one of these meetings Hajji Mohammad Hasan Amin al-Zarb formulated their powerlessness as follows: "what do we have in terms of manufacturies and industries that we can say: we don't want European commodities."[228]

Even the creation of a Ministry of Trade (*vezarat-e tejarati*) in 1871 as part of the reform policy of the Sepahsalar did not mean that from then on this department furthered the merchants' interests. The ministry was charged with the investigation of complaints by merchants and with running a commercial court (*mahkameh-ye tejarati*). The ministry charged a 10 percent fee for its services (*haqq al-zahmat*).[229] After some years the Minister of Trade created a Trade Council (*majles-e tejarati*), which was presided by the chief-deputy (*na'eb-e avval*) of the ministry. The council was further attended by the Malek al-Tojjar-e Iran, Amin al-Tojjar, Mo`in al-Tojjar, 15 other leading merchants, and three officials from the ministry. This council convened twice a week, on Sunday and Wednesday, to discuss trade results.[230] The place of conference was the Sun palace.[231] This council existed side by side with another commercial council, consisting of officials of the Ministry of Trade. This council convened everyday in the ministry itself, and probably functioned as a kind of preparatory committee. The president of this committee was the *na'eb-e avval*.[232] It appears that the composition of the Trade Council varied, and that the merchants attending, took turns at the meetings.[233] In 1904, Greenfield states that these council meetings had not been held for some years.[234] The last time that the council met probably was in 1893.[235] In December 1896 it was proposed to create a State Council (*shura-ye dowlati*) presided over by the court minister and composed of 24 members, some of whom were to be merchants. It is not clear what its functions should have been, probably it was meant an advisory body to inform the Shah of what was going on in the country. Apparently nothing came of it.[236]

Apart from establishing closer relations with the leading merchants, the government tried to get a better grip on the merchant community through the appointment of a new official, called the Ra'is-e Tojjar, not to be confused with the Malek al-Tojjar, nor with the other titled merchants; he was one of the members of the governor's staff. This official seems to have been appointed in all the provincial capitals, and amongst those who

228. E`temad al-Saltaneh 1345, 395.

229. Mostowfi n.d., vol. 1, 139; it appears, however, that a Ministry of Trade existed already around 1860. Polak 1865, vol. 2, 188 reports that "a few years ago the government appointed a minister of commerce (*vazir-e tejarat*), Mahmud Khan Karaguzlu, who also took over the functions of Malek-e Tojjar. But there were soon so many complaints about oppression and arbitrariness that the old state of things was restored". De Rouchechouart 1867, 176 also mentions the existence of a Minister of Trade around 1860, see also below note 237.

230. E`temad al-Saltaneh 1294-96, vol. 3, appendix, 7; Ibid., 1306, appendix, 47.

231. E`temad al-Saltaneh 1294-96, vol. 3, appendix, 7.

232. E`temad al-Saltaneh 1306, appendix, 47.

233. E`temad al-Saltaneh 1306, appendix, 47; Ibid. 1294-96, vol. 4, appendix, 47.

234. Greenfield 1904, 144.

235. Migeod 1990, 183, note 6.

236. Kosogovski 1344, 158.

filled such a post we find several Malek al-Tojjars and other merchants.[237] In 1881 a Ra'is-e Tojjar was to be found in: Tabriz, Urumiyeh, Khoy, Khamseh, Qazvin, Gilan, Mazandaran, Hamadan, Borujerd, Kermanshah, Kurdistan, Bakhtiyar, Qom, Kashan, Isfahan, Shiraz, Bushire, Yazd, Kerman, Khurasan, Astarabad, Semnan, Damghan, Shahrud, Bistam, and Iranian `Iraq.[238] It was to this official that all differences about merchandise and for instance beatings between merchants, had to be referred or in his absence to the governor.[239] The Ra'is-e Tojjar seems to have sent most cases for judgment to the town's *mojtaheds*. These would judge the case and have their decision executed by the Ra'is-e Tojjar.[240] In case of bankruptcy, especially when Europeans were involved, these latter would apply for help to the Ra'is-e Tojjar.[241]

POLITICAL ACTION BY MERCHANTS

In the meantime the growth of trade gave rise to a growing dependant merchant body. In the North the Russian merchants had about half of the foreign trade in hand, and in the South it was the British merchants who handled "the bulk of the transactions."[242] Because of the Iranian government's failure to support its merchants and industry, and the interference by Russia and Britain on behalf of their mercantile interests, the Iranian merchants became for the greater part dependent on the European firms, not as equal partners, but as agents (*dallal va dastkar*) and hired hands (*mozdur*), whose best asset was their personal honesty.[243] This led to a growing resentment against foreigners and this attitude was reflected in the Iranian commercial relationship with European merchants. The Iranian merchant, who at the beginning of the 19th century had the reputation of a liberal, free-thinking man among a bigoted nation, became a scoundrel in the eyes of the Europeans, whom one could not trust, and whose favorite past time was to-outdo and deceive foreign merchants.[244]

The Iranian merchants had seen that the avalanche of European imports destroyed Iranian industries. They had also witnessed the growing domination over their government by Russia and Britain, which resulted in the granting of concessions to foreigners. This, and the political and social climate which was unfavorable to their interests,

---

237. E`temad al-Saltaneh 1294-96, vol. 3, appendix, 7; Mostowfi n.d., vol. 1, 139, is a very explicit about the date of the creation of the Ministry of Trade, although there already was a *vazir-e tejarat* around 1860. Polak 1865, vol. 2, 188 and de Rochchouart 1867, 176.

238. E`temad al-Saltaneh 1294-96, vol. 3, appendix, 7.

239. Legatie Perzië, Letter January 24, 1891; DCR 590, 13, note.

240. Aubin 1908, 36.

241. Floor 1977, 61-76.

242. Curzon 1892, vol. 2, 573; Issawi 1971, 71, 72.

243. Mostowfi n.d., vol. 1, 496; Ibid. vol. 3, 107 even calls them the *pado-ye dokkan* or errand boy; RMM 1909, 92; the financial situation of the Iranian merchants was such, that in 1907 the *Habl al-Matin* wrote: "our merchants are at their wits end, and do not know where to turn for two or three thousand *tumans*," Browne 1909, 189; according to Nafiçy 1924, 8 the merchants of Tehran were not able to put up 1.000.000 *tuman*s in cash.

244. Avery 1965, 77; Berichte 1910, 279.

damaged their possibilities for expansion, and led to their legitimate demand for change and reform. They wanted a check on foreign penetration as well as on their own absolutist government. The Iranian merchants met with partial success when they found allies in the ulama, who, for their own reasons, wanted to achieve the same ends. The foreigners, in this case the British, provided the occasion. The grant of the tobacco monopoly to a European enterprise affected merchants all over Iran, as well as the ulama, who had large interests in this trade because of vast landed properties.[245] Their concerted action brought this foreign incursion to a halt. The repeal of the Tobacco Regie, however, ironically led to a situation they had wanted to avoid, viz. a greater dependence of Iran on foreign powers, because it was then that Iran incurred her first foreign debt.[246] The anti-government and anti-foreign movement got impetus when the Qajar government became more absolutist, while its power waned. Especially the Iranian merchants abroad, in Istanbul, Baku and Bombay, exerted themselves to disseminate reformist ideas among their compatriots. These merchants had seen what a more democratic and orderly state, where security of property and on the roads was normal, could mean to trade and industry. They wanted to create similar conditions in Iran. The ulama wanted to curb the government's power and to defend the nation's interests.[247] Democracy and nationalism was the road which they took to achieve these ends. Democracy, because it would give them greater access to power, and nationalism, because it would lead to the ouster of foreign domination. It was not so much that the merchants were for democracy (few people in Iran knew what it entailed), but it appealed to them, because it gave them an opportunity to regain lost ground to the detriment of foreigners. Although a few of the leading merchants were against the constitutional movement,[248] the greater part of the merchant body was fervently for it, in its heyday providing the money to sustain its continued efforts and existence, while the ulama provided the moral backing and ideology. The role of the merchants in the first *Majles* was rather influential, taking into consideration that they represented not more than a half to one per cent of the population and were represented by 10 delegates or 15 percent of the total membership.[249] The vice-president of the *Majles* was Amin al-Zarb, who also was a member of the committee which drew up the constitution.[250]

After the fall of Mohammad `Ali Shah (1909), when in the second *Majles* the guilds were completely gone from the political scene, the merchants were still represented but less so.[251] The lack of tradition of participation in politics in a more direct way, the foreign domination and the vagaries of World War I made the merchants acquiesce in this situation. Their national fervor certainly was not spent. In 1915 the Ministry of Trade was merged with the Ministry of Public Works, Trade and Agriculture (*vezarat-e fava'ed-e `ammeh va tejarat va falahat*). The ministry did not function at all, not having an adequate

---

245. Keddie 1966, 65.
246. Keddie 1966, 65.
247. Algar 1969.
248. Kasravi 1319-21, vol. 1, 343, 341; vol. 3, 136; RMM 1908, 693; Ibid., 18 (1912),82, 104.
249. Shaje`i 1344, 185-89; Kasravi 1319-21, vol. 1, 215, 396.
250. Kasravi 1319-21, vol. 1, 233, 302, 308.
251. Shaje`i 1344, 185-89; Dowlatabadi n.d., vol. 3, 151.

budget to pay even its personnel. The settling of disputes between merchants was taken over by the Ministry of Justice. Thereby the Ministry of Trade lost a not inconsiderable source of income. Within the 'new' ministry a so-called *shura-ye `ali-ye tejarat* or High Council of Trade was formed. Six merchants and six government representatives were appointed to this body which had to advise the government on economic affairs. Hajji Mo`in al-Tojjar was its first president, which convened once a week for an hour or so.[252] The trade council did not function very well, but then it could not have, taking into account the miserable and helpless situation the country was in. The council still existed around 1921. During World War I an *ettehad-e tojjar* or union of merchants headed by Amin al-Zarb was formed, which "took part in the political questions of country under the guise of commercial interests."[253] The creation of a Chamber of Commerce (*otaq-e tejarat*) in the 1920s under the supervision of the Ministry of Trade did not serve the interests of the mercantile community, considering its limited and unimportant duties.[254] Nationalism remained a strong force in Iranian politics, also among the merchants. This explains why many of them became supporters of Reza Khan. They hoped to gain by his efforts to unify Iran and bring some order and security to the country. When the petty bazaaris demonstrated against Reza Khan, fearing his secularism, the merchants demonstrated in favor of him.[255]

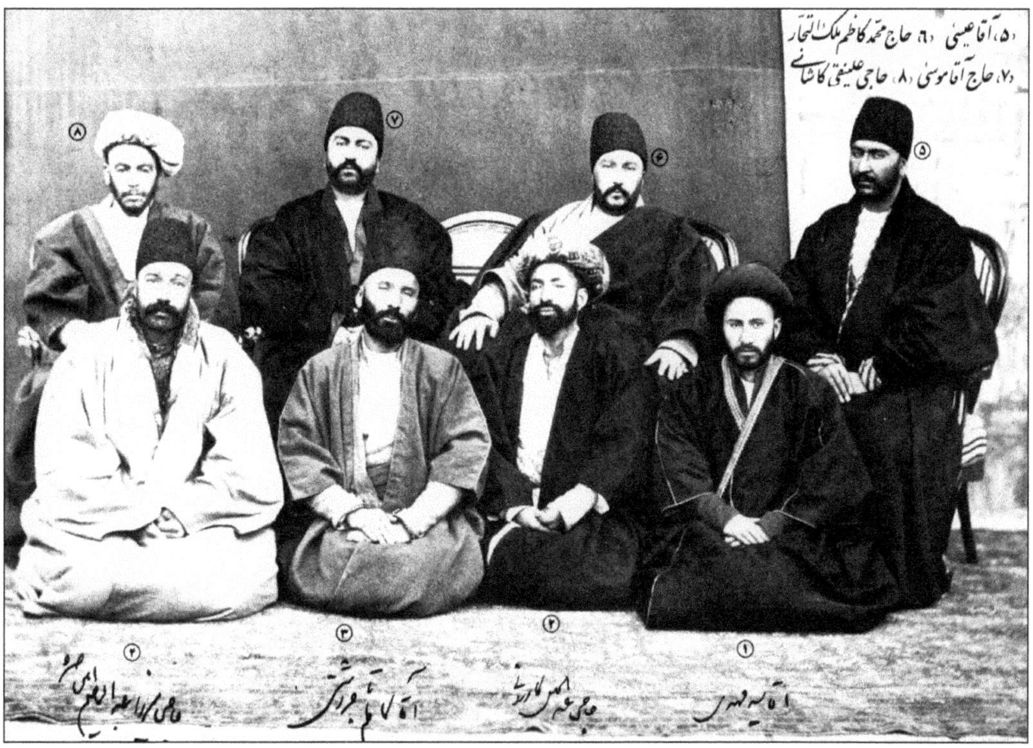

A group of merchants from Tehran during Naser al-Din Shah's reign.

252. Mostowfi n.d., vol. 2, 372-3, 514.
253. Issawi 1971, 45; Mostowfi n.d., vol. 3, 584; Fateh 1926, 82.
254. Fateh 1926, 82.
255. Mostowfi n.d., vol. 3, 594.

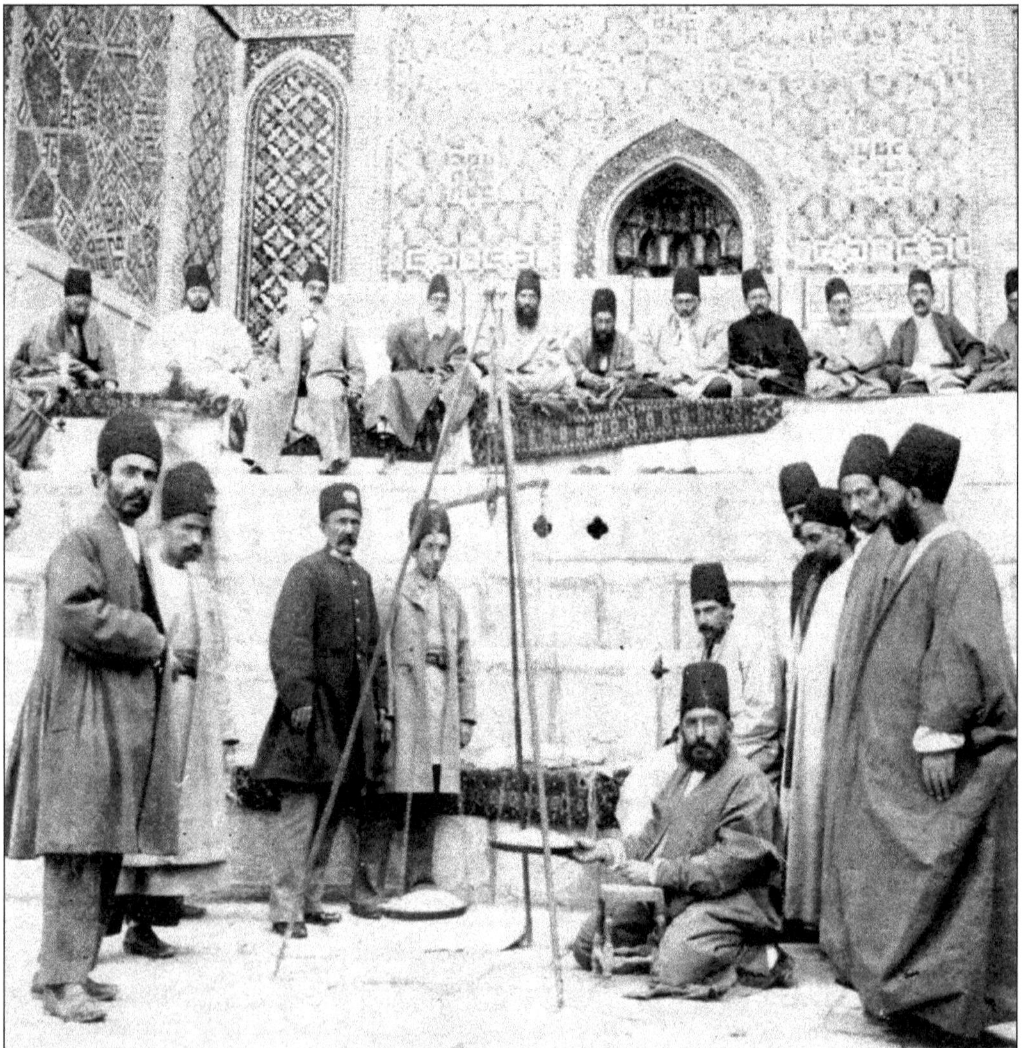

Weighing tax money c. 1906

CHAPTER FOUR

The Bankers (*Sarraf*) in Qajar Iran

AVAILABILITY AND TERMS OF CREDIT

Where public credit did not exist in Qajar Iran, due to the unreliability of the government, private commercial credit was the life force of a brisk trade. As most merchants did not have large capital, business without credit was practically impossible. According to de Rochechouart, to describe the intricacies of business customs in Qajar Iran, one would need to write a big book and need to have 10 years of experience with the subject, reason why he only spent a few pages on the subject and why the present author humbly follows in his steps.[1] Although de Rochechouart was a bit carried away as far as the quick turnover of money was concerned, he rightly gauged the complexity of the Iranian credit system. It was these commercial customs which made it vexatious and unattractive for European merchants to trade with Iran. Foreign consuls and other men with experience in Iran, however, would draw attention to the fact that one could profit handsomely by the existing business opportunities in Iran, if one knew one's way around, or if one had the disposal of a good agent on the spot.[2]

One can say that business without credit did not occur, and that business was done without cash money between European and Iranian merchants, as well as between Iranian merchants. Even when so-called transactions cash down occurred, it meant that at

1. De Rochechouart 1867, 172.
2. DCR 4179, 8.

least 20 to 30 days were allowed before payment took place.[3] The retail trade usually sold for cash, occasionally on book account with good customers.[4]

The terms on which credit was given varied per city or region, per currency, per commodity, and was dependent on such factors as the religion of the client, whether a kinship (or other) relation existed, the solvency and business reputation of the client, the destination of the goods, whether the commodities were in stock or not and, of course, the market.

In Southern Iran and where Hindu or Parsi merchants were concerned the majority of the transactions were concluded on the basis of cash against documents. Payments usually were in bills or produce. The bills were, however, seldom met in time, so allowing traders to pay in drafts drawn on themselves elsewhere at 15 or 30 days' sight; this method extended the period of credit.[5]

In the Kerman region and in Southeast Iran in general goods usually were half paid for in cash or kind, while credit was given for the remainder by handing over bills, at a rate of interest of 24 percent to 120 percent. Credit was allowed from 1 to 12 months, with an average of 4 months. Due payments were either met totally or in ten weekly installments. In the latter case the creditor would charge interest for the whole amount for the period of 10 weeks.[6]

In Central Iran (Isfahan and Yazd) a rather clumsy system credit system was applied to circumvent the interdictions against usury. Here sales were made at fixed prices with long credits, the duration of which fluctuated with the change in the price of the commodities. This did not mean that business in Central Iran usually entailed credit of 20 or even 50 months. In reality the greater part of the transactions were closed in three months.

> To give an account example of how the method works: Tea is selling at a fixed price of krs. 50 per man. 'A' buys tea when credit is 24 months. He pays his debt at the end of the stipulated three months. He gets discount for 21 months, calculated at the rate of 1 % per month compound interest. Tea increases in price before 'A' makes his next purchase. He has now to buy at the rate of krs. 50 per man at a credit of 12 months. He pays at the end of three months and gets a discount at the rate of 1% per month for nine months. He again buys tea when it is very reduced in price, and is selling at krs. 50 per man with 36 months credit. As before he pays his debt at the end of three months. He now gets a discount at the rate of 1% per period of 33 months. It is seen from this that credit is in reality a discount, and the lengthening and shortening of credits only represents the change in price.[7]

3. RO 5, 137. Goods which sold quickly, small quantities and perishable products usually were paid for in cash money towards the end of the 19th century.

4. Gleadowe-Newcomen 1905, 13; "The wholesale dealers issue goods to the shopkeepers, and every Saturday go round to their clients to collect what they can on account". DCR 3885, 3.

5. DCR 3885, 3; Berichte 1910, 297.

6. Berichte 1910, 266, Gleadowe-Newcomen 1905, 13.

7. Gleadowe-Newcomen 1905, 13.

In the earlier part of the nineteenth century Iranian merchants would often finance their operations themselves; the larger ones among them were both importers- and exporters, and would either buy merchandise with the proceeds of their sales, or would take foreign merchandise in barter. The importers would take money with them and pay for the purchases in cash or would sent money with a trusted courier (*chapar*) to their agent. Such a courier would sometimes carry the money of as many as 40 merchants. The risks of this method of remitting money were high and costly. Not only could such a money transport be waylaid, but it also could get lost due to the difficulty of the terrain and the weather in wintertime. Moreover transport of money took a long time and finally payments had to be in gold. Since the export of Iranian gold currency was prohibited merchants had to collect foreign currency for their remittances abroad. The money transports, therefore, consisted mainly of Russian and Hungarian coins in North-Iran, which were difficult to collect in large sums.[8]

This method of payment was rather cumbersome, very risky and expensive. Therefore, when the volume of trade increased and with it the need for credit, which development received impetus by the rapidly growing trade with Europe and Turkey, the trade in drafts and other commercial papers likewise became important.

> If a merchant in Constantinople has to receive a remittance from Persia, through a correspondent in Tabreez or Teheran, for example, in payment of goods supplied, or what not, it is necessary that he should also have or procure an agent in Tiflis, who must draw either upon him or upon his correspondent at Tabreez for the required amount, and then negociate the sale of such bill in Tiflis for Russian bank notes. These Russian bank notes have next to be forwarded to a resident banker in Odessa, who, in his turn, buys bills in Odessa or London or Paris, and forwards these to Constantinople. The inconveniences of this system sautent aux yeux, as the French say; and yet, it must be remembered, it is the modern system, the one found the most practible as things go, and, in fact, the commercial system now generally adopted. In the first place, there is the exceeding loss of time. Instructions to draw take 21 days to reach Tiflis from Tabreez; and it seldom happens, if the sum to be drawn for exceeds £500, that the agent at Tiflis, when he sells the bill, can only realise the amount in Russian notes by installments, in weekly payments perhaps, and so forward them in piecemeal to Odessa. Then, again, it often occurs that Persian houses or agents at Tabreez require bills negotiated at Tiflis, in order to make remittances to Constantinople, or elsewhere in Europe, at a moment when the Tiflis merchants have no actual commercial call for money at Tabreez, and consequently only negotiate the bills as a matter of speculation and profit; the result in which case is - and, indeed, more or less, in all cases - that the rates of exchange on such bills - the discount, in fact, demanded for giving Russian notes for them, - is very high. The drawer, therefore, in addition to loss of time, loses on the high rate of exchange in Tiflis. Again, when

8. RO 5, 142; Blau 1858, 55; Greenfield 1906, 101; de Lacy O'Brien 1873, 72.

> these Russian notes are sent on to buy bills at Odessa, the exchange varies in that city, as elsewhere; and, as a matter of fact, the variation of exchange in Odessa has been against the Persian market for the last four years. Thus, there in the lost of interest on the long time elapsing, the high rates of exchange and commission at Odessa. If a merchant in Constantinople want a remittance from Tabreez of a moderate sum of, say, £2,000 or 3,000. from the time he gives the necessary instructions to his agent in Tabreez until he receives the bills from Odessa, a period of about two months must intervene". This is the usual present mode of remitting from Persia to Constantinople and Western Europe, - via Tabreez, Tiflis, and Odessa." [9]

When an Iranian merchant had a good standing with a merchant in Istanbul, mostly Greek, or when such a Greek merchant wanted money in Iran for buying silk, the latter would accept bills at 3 months' sight on Tabriz. Although this method allowed a merchant to do business on the spot without having to wait for money or drafts from Iran, the costs - 1 to 3 percent commission, up to 5 percent charge for remittance, and a high rate of interest - were as high as the normal manner of remitting money.[10]

Still, drafts were not accepted everywhere or only with heavy discounts up to 20 percent. In commercial centers there were less difficulties than in the cities; more inland, but even in commercial centers in North Iran, for example, bills on Bombay or England were hardly accepted for direct transmission. Sometimes, however, when there was a need or demand in these Northern provinces for drafts on Bombay, e.g., then instead of a discount a profit could be made on the sale of such drafts.[11]

SARRAFS *FACILITATE ACCESS TO CREDIT*

Native bankers or *sarrafs*, who often commanded all the hard cash in a city, acquired a prominent part in trade, because of the growing lack of hard cash, the difficulty of transporting minted silver or specie, and the debasement of money.[12] Thus when someone bought goods from an importer, he would give the latter a draft on the former's banker, -who in turn would give a draft to the importer's banker, who would credit the importer for the amount, settling with bills on e.g. Istanbul, Tiflis or Bombay, depending whether they were in Northern or Southern Iran.[13]

The role of the *sarrafs* was an important one, for they practically conducted all money transactions in Iran. Prior to 1888 the *sarrafs* and the big merchants (*tojjar*) exclusively played this role. For the latter, banking was just one of their many lines of business, for they dabbled in anything in which they could make money. Moreover, in smaller towns

---

9. de Lacy O'Brien 1873,71, 72.
10. de Lacy O'Brien 1873,26, 73.
11. de Lacy O'Brien 1873,42, 44, 45.
12. de Lacy O'Brien 1873, 31; DCR 33,1697.
13. DCR 1671, 9.

there were no *sarrafs* of any significance, and so the *tojjar* financed the local mercantile activities.[14]

The *sarrafs* were organized into a guild (*senf*), their importance differing per city. In the larger commercial centers they played a dominant part. In cities like Mohammara and Hamadan no banking operations of any importance were concluded; if necessary the big merchants would take care of it.[15] In Kermanshah the *sarraf* were merely money-changers with no influence over the market whatsoever. Here the guild of the *sarrafs* paid 60 *qrans* in guild taxes (*asnafiyeh*).[16] In Tehran where the guild of the *sarraf* was important and wealthy, they did not pay taxes at all. Here "the Mustawfi' ul-Mamalik, or Chancellor of the Exchequer, was at the mercy of the five or six leading Sarrafs who inhabit Tehran, and who by a combination among themselves can put any price they like upon specie."[17] In cities like Tabriz, Mashhad and Isfahan the numerous community of the *sarrafs* played a prominent part in the city's trade.[18] In the last city there were two groups of *sarrafs*, each occupying a different bazaar, while the *sarrafs* also had shops in the smaller bazaars of the various city quarters.[19]

Moslem law disapproved of (*makruh*) the banking (*sarf*) business, because of the prohibition to take interest (*reba'*), but trade needed the *sarrafs* to function properly. Although it was supposed to be a reprehensible occupation, many an honorable man made his living in this trade. We even find sayyeds among the *sarrafs*, and some *sarrafs* were mentioned as belonging to the city's notables.[20] The guild of the *sarrafs* acquired two delegates to Parliament (*Majles*) during its first legislative period, which indicates that their occupation was not all that reprehensible. The fact also that they formed a numerous community in many cities indicates that it could not have been a trade of bad repute. The highly respected merchant clan freely intermarried with the sons and daughters of the *sarrafs*.[21]

Notwithstanding the fact that the occupation of *sarrafs* was disapproved of by Moslem law, many Moslems as well as people of other denominations were engaged in it. In Azerbaijan the *sarrafs* were for the greater part Iranian Moslems, in Khorasan Tartars and Russian Armenians. In Western Iran Jews were found among the *sarrafs*, while in

---

14. Berichte 1910, 354; Lorini 1900, 343. *Sarrafs* were often at the same time merchants dealing in such commodities as silk, opium, tobacco, fruit, draperies, silver, etc. Ibid.

15. Berichte 1910, 300, 301; MacLean 1904, 33, 66.

16. DCR 590, 14.

17. Balfour 1922, 152; De Lacey O'Brien 1873, 14.

18. Berichte 1910, 297; Commercial Reports, no. 241, 2. In Tabriz the bankers guild did not pay guild taxes, but gave a present only to the authorities, Greenfield 1904, 142. In fact there were three kinds of *sarrafs* in Tabriz, the difference being the amount of discount they granted, Lorini 1900, 334; see also below note 57.

19. Tahvildar 1342, 103.

20. Greenfield 1906, 29; according to Wills 1883, 192 "the business of the serof (sic) is despised; he cannot be a good Mussulman." On the same page, however, Wills mentions that a few *sarrafs* are respected as good Moslems by their fellow-townsmen; on one of them Hajji Karim see: Fasa'i 1894-96, vol. 2, 26, 58. Still many a *sarraf* would become more respected by being active as a wholesale-dealer.

21. Afshar 1349, vol. 2, 191, 217,219.

Central Iran this position was taken by the Zoroastrians. In the South we find Zoroastrians, Iranian Moslems, Arabs and Indians.[22]

If so many honorable people were engaged in the banking business, why then do we find so many instances relating that banking was a trade of bad repute? The reason cannot have been that non-Moslems only were engaged in this trade, as for example Shamim asserts; a statement which tells us more about the author than about the *sarrafs*.[23] I believe that the taking of interest in crucial to this question and that those who were taking usurious interest were despised by most people. That this may be the case is indicated by the *Joghrafiya-ye Isfahan* which states with regard to the group of usurers (*morabeheh karan*) "this sort of people are very few now, and those who are still there, only have a small capital at their disposal. They demand high profits and take (therefore) high rates of interest. Those who are owing them money are always having disputes with them. That is the reason why there is such a lot of misery among the population."[24]

WHAT KIND OF TRANSACTIONS WERE SARRAFS *INVOLVED IN?*

This statement may also indicate that there were more kinds of *sarrafs* than just one; in fact there probably were three kinds. In the first place there were the usurers (*morabeheh karan*) as a group per se. In the second place there were the small time *sarrafs*, their range of activities often overlapped with that of the first group. They were referred to as the *sarraf-dowrehgerd* (ambulatory banker), who carried his purse on his shoulder going about the streets in search of customers.[25] They also were called the *sarraf-e rah neshin* (side-walk banker). Soldiers, who devoted a great part of their time to lending money, charging very high interests, mainly formed this group of small time *sarrafs*.[26]

The 'real' and big time bankers, who were socially accepted members of society, had their shops in the bazaar, often only small stalls "at which are exposed old bracelets, gold, silver, and copper coin, and jewels always full of flaws. A few bankers have offices in the caravanserais, and are in the position of merchants, but there are no mahogany counters, no row of clerks; a couple of scribes and a black slave often comprise the whole staff, but the bankers manage to do all that is needfull with this small assistance."[27]

Most bankers did not have a capital larger than a few thousands *tumans*, while only a few commanded a capital of about 100.000 *tumans*, which was a very considerable amount. Curzon reports that in 1889 he found "144 private bankers or usurers in Mashhad, with a united capital of 931,000 *tumans*, or 266,000£. Two only of these had a capital

22. Berichte 1910, 353; Gleadowe-Newcomen 1905, 14.
23. Shamim 1342, 307, note 1.
24. Tahvildar 1342, 92.
25. Mostowfi n.d., vol. 2, 370.
26. Amin al-Dowleh 1349, 196; De Rochechouart 1857, 175.
27. Wills 1883, 192; Wilson 1896, 181-82.

of 100,000 *tumans* (28,570£); three a capital of 50,000 *tumans* (14,285£); and two a capital of 30,000 *tumans* (8,570£) each. The rest were petty money dealers."[28]

Most banking operations consisted in the buying and selling of bills on foreign trading centers such as Bombay, London, Tiflis, Odessa, Baghdad, and Trabson. Further in remitting money to other cities, in trading local drafts, in discounting mercantile paper, making advances to respectable buyers in current amount or for short fixed periods, and to respectable private persons for periods not exceeding six months with guarantees or to landowners against crops. A few of them were also engaged in financing a nobleman's purchase of an office or remitting money for the government.

Advances on crops played in most parts of the country an important role, which was quite natural, Iran being an agricultural country. The advances concerned mainly cash crops such as: opium, tobacco, wheat, rice, cotton, and silk cocoons. In Gilan advances were made up to 4 to 6 months. Sometimes credit was given to nearly the full value of the crop, even before the delivery date of the cocoons.[29] In the rice trade the Russian bank made advances against consignments to be sold on commission.[30] In Mashhad large advances were given in the wool trade, which was completely in the hands of the Armenians. Here wholesale buyers of the wool gave advances to the sheep owners up to 5 to 6 months, other buyers would pay cash. Often the buyers would buy the whole clip. These in turn were advanced money by the exporters at 12 percent for periods of 2 to 3 months. In this way exporters were assured of a fixed quota in the market.[31] In cotton likewise the buyers would make advances of 5 to 6 months.[32] In Isfahan the advances to opium cultivators were very considerable.[33] Leading merchants in Shiraz also made advances. When the crop was bought several months before the harvest a fixed price was agreed upon. The landowner often drew a bill on the merchant after date, which, after acceptance, he discounted or paid away to a third party against claims on himself.[34] In Kerman advances to farmers were given at interest rates of 100 to 150 percent.[35] It was in this kind of business that *sarrafs* had large interests since most crops had to be paid for in cash. There were only a few firms, mostly European, who could finance these operations independently. For most importers-exporters had to finance their other activities too, and during harvest time these agricultural transactions often commanded all the hard cash in the region. This resulted in a slack time for normal trading activities, which in adverse years would lead to many failures, people unable to buy and the retail dealer unable to meet his obligations.

Loans to individuals were only given against guarantee, often a mortgage was taken on landed property. As repayment of loans was often tardy and the risks high inter-

---

28. Curzon 1892, vol. 1, 167; Berichte 1910, 254; Kasravi 1319-21, vol. 1, 205; see also de Lacey O'Brien 1873, 73.
29. MacLean 1904, 63.
30. MacLean 1904, 63.
31. MacLean 1904, 63, 64; DCR 976, 6.
32. MacLean 1904, 64.
33. Berichte 1910, 305.
34. DCR 1474, 5.
35. Berichte 1910, 265.

ests were very high.[36] In Kerman merchants of good repute had to pay 24 percent interest, while lesser-known or small merchants had to pay more than double this amount. The Imperial Bank advanced only money to solid persons at a rate of 18 percent.[37] In general one can say that the rate of interest depended on a person's reputation and his repayment capability. Although Moslem law forbade the charging of interest as much as 100 percent and even more was demanded and obtained.[38] "The principal offenders against the Sharia were the Mullahs themselves who reap large benefits from such illegal financial operations."[39]

A very risky business was the financing of the sale of offices. Many an impecuniary nobleman borrowed money at high rates, for which the *sarrafs* issued promissory notes (*fateh-e talabha-ye tejarati*) to the prospective holder a governorship drawn on themselves. The debtor in his turn would transfer these notes to the treasury as the necessary *pishkesh*. If, however, the debtor was dismissed from office before his period of tenure was over, the *sarraf* had to be content with the nominal sum, sometimes even less so. A few of such gambles could lead to his ruin. In this way a *sarraf* starting out with a small capital could in a very short time double or treble his capital. The risks, however, were accordingly high.[40]

WHAT KIND OF COMMERCIAL PAPER EXISTED?

Before we start discussing the draft trade we first take a look at what kind of credit documents were used in Qajar Iran. We discuss the *tamassok*, the *barat*, and the *havaleh*.

The *tamassok* is the simple I.O.U. The *tamassok* was used for loans and sales on credit. Clearings with this document were not usual. The *sarrafs* hardly ever and the European banker only in some cases would give discounts for the *tamassok*. In such cases the transfers were according to Moslem law either a *havaleh* or a forced sale. In the former case this would mean that the debtor's permission was necessary and in both cases there was no claim of redress against the endorsee.[41]

The real draft was the *barat*. This document normally contained the date, the city of issue, the residence and the name of the drawee, the date of payment, the amount, to whom must be paid, the claim to confirm the receipt of payment, and the assurance that the drawer will confirm the debt and pay the drawee. Often the currency was stated too.[42]

The *havaleh* was a kind of cheque. It was a money-order on a third party, with whom one had a bank balance or who granted credit. The rules of Moslem law for the

---

36. Mortgaging of landed property could be very risky. When water was scarce these lands became practically valueless, because nobody would offer to buy them. Arbab Jamshid went bankrupt because he could not meet his liabilities, and though he owned large tracts of land, nobody would buy them, because at that time water was scarce.

37. Berichte 1910, 265.

38. De Rochechouart 1857, 174.

39. Landor 1902, vol. 1, 124.

40. Mostowfi n.d., vol. 1, 622, R0 5, 142; Kosogovski 1344, 155, 156.

41. Greenfield 1906,100. The *tamassok* was also called *hojjat*.

42. Greenfield 1906,100.

havaleh contract were applicable in these cases. Formerly the *havaleh* was contracted orally, one told one's banker to pay a third party. This meant that the *havaleh* was only used in local trade. It was, especially the written *barat*, also known as *bijak*, which was the object of a very lively trade.[43]

The *tamassok* when transferred became a *havaleh*, and because the written *havaleh* often was called *barat*, the confusion was complete. Iranian jurists only considered documents as *havaleh* "when they are drawn against money held by the drawee on account of the drawer. Other bills are called '*barat*'. In common usage the distinction is not made, and bills are indifferently called '*havaleh*' or '*barat*', and transactions with them are settled with the customary law."[44] As is clear from the above, there was ample opportunity for a bad debtor to get the better of a European creditor by appealing to a religious court, which would apply the religious law leading to the verdict that some *havaleh*s were not legal.

The written *havaleh* (also called *barat* or *bijak*) played an important part in the State finances. Practically all creditors of the State were paid with a *barat*. The *barat*s were drawn on, for instance, a province, with the command to the governor of that province to pay. As these officials only paid those who could force them to pay, people often had to wait for years before they got their money, if they were lucky. And then only because they settled for a partial payment of what was due to them. There were even merchants who specialized in buying these *barat*s against reduced prices. The governors to pay the central government in Tehran for the nominal value then used these cheap barats.[45]

HOW DID THE CREDIT SYSTEM WITH DRAFTS FUNCTION?

Most payments in trade were facilitated because payments by *havaleh* from one *sarraf* to another were usual. The stipulations of Moslem law made it difficult to develop a real stable Bill of Exchange. Although secular courts, applying customary law, considered the *barat* to be a draft, as in European law, the religious courts applying religious law ruled that once the *barat* was accepted by the drawee, the drawer was not further liable. The Iranian government tried to make this ruling into a law. Two circulars of the Ministry of Foreign Affairs and Commerce, of November 1893 and of July 1902, declared the acceptance of bills binding. The European merchants refused to accept this; for once a bill was accepted the drawee normally would pay. But if he, for whatever reason could not or would not pay, he could not be forced to do so. If this would happen on a large scale the European

---

43. Greenfield 1906, 102,103, see also 57, 58; according to Lorini the *havaleh* was neither a check nor a payment-order, but rather a promise to pay, an availability of funds, Lorini 1900, 336.

44. Rabino 1892, 52.

45. The situation in 1840 was described by Layard 1894, 192, as follows: "The usual method of settling claims by individuals upon the royal treasury was by giving the claiments drafts upon villages, tribal chiefs, or wealthy notables, and leaving them to get them cashed as debt they could. The bearers of these documents, which were frequently sold by the original possessors with a very large discount, generally quartered themselves upon the persons upon whom they were drawn, and remained for many months - even years - until the sum for which they were given was paid." These people were called *baratdar*s. In 1911 and 1920 this situation had not yet changed, see Balfour 1922, 152 and Shuster 1968, 42, 43, 311. Greenfield 1906, 103.

merchants would "have to refrain from buying paper as means of remittance, which would, in a country, where all the flow of coin is to the capital, be a source of great loss to them."[46] In fact they would not be able to do business any more. Although the secular courts ruled otherwise, and the Ministry of Justice also applied customary law, this did not mean that, according to European merchants, justice was administered in a satisfactory manner.[47]

The transfer by endorsement for local *barat*s was not very usual. When the creditor was not able to present the *barat* personally to the drawee, he usually would give the document to a specialized firm or agent who would cash the *barat*. By signing a *fehrest* the encasher promised the creditor to present the *barat* after the date due and either to pay the creditor or return the *barat* when this was not paid or refused. The trade in these *fehrest*s seems to have been considerable, because when in 1907 the *sarrafs* refused to do business any longer, the government owed them 6 million *tumans* in *fehrests*.[48]

The creditor could demand payment any moment after the date due. There was no surannuation. If on the date due the bill was not paid one usually allowed a certain period of grace. Iranians considered it their right not to pay on the day agreed upon and resented any change in this practice. Only Europeans protested when after the period of grace the bills were still not paid. In Shiraz it was customary to hold unpaid bills over for 15 days after maturity, Iranian firms allowed one month or even longer periods.[49] In Tabriz unpaid bills had to be protested within a period of ten days after the date due.[50]

Towards the end of the 19th century the *bijak* trade became a very lively one, accounting for about 60 percent of the volume of the bazaar trade.[51] A creditor, in stead of cashing drafts given to him in payment, would endorse these to one of his own creditors, and so on.[52] The *sarrafs* favored this intricate system of payments charging an agio for each transfer. The agio would, under normal circumstances, amount from 0.1 percent to 2 percent, but during periods when money was very scarce the *sarrafs* might take advantage of their position as holders at the cash money, sometimes charging an agio as high as 22.5 percent. But these conditions seem to have been the exception rather than the rule. A report from Bushire over a period of five years shows that even when money was scarce the agio remained within reasonable bounds.[53]

1903-04	0.75 percent
1904-05	1.0 percent
1905-06	2.0 percent
1906-07	1.50 percent
1907-08	2.75 percent

46. DCR 4397, 6; DCR 1953, 10; Greenfield 1906, 101; Rabino 1892, 51-52.
47. Rabino 1892, 51-52.
48. Greenfield 1906, 102; Legatie Perzië II, letter August 17, 1907.
49. DCR 1474, 4.
50. Blau 1858, 54.
51. Lorini 1900, 336.
52. DCR 241, 2; de Lacey O'Brien 1873, 67.
53. DCR 4179, 8.

This apparent reticence on part of the *sarrafs* may be explained by the fact that after protests by the merchants, governors took steps to stop the charging of high agios and punished the offenders. Another reason was the establishment of European banks, with whom the *sarrafs* had to compete.

In Tabriz a monetary system characteristic for that city was developed. "This system was born out of necessity, since Persian bookkeeping does not lend itself to changes of interest on daily balances, consequently when cash was scarce in the bazaars the banker, instead of altering his rate of interest, made a distinction between book transfers and cash payments, charging an agio on the latter."[54] The agio rates differed per article, often even per banker. For example the agio for German yarn was 16 percent and for English white shirting 4 percent. According to MacLean, the Stamboulchis only used this form of quotation. British and Continental piece-goods were often quoted on the basis of *havaleh-ye sarraf*, or only 4 percent discount, while Russian goods were quoted in *qrans*. Silk and woolen goods were quoted in *choruk* money (see below). In fact the agio system was charged on all manufactories, but metals and sugar were paid for in cash. Somewhere in the 1880's the agio was fixed at 7 percent for cash money versus *choruk* money, and later another 4 percent was added. At the end of the 1890s a further 4% under the heading of banker's transfer (*havaleh-ye sarraf*) was added.[55]

This intricate system of calculation was used to fix the prices, which were paid for with *havaleh* at 10 to 15 days' sight, with the amount of value cash at due date. The *sarraf* received no cash guarantee from the drawee, but he in turn was paid with the drawee's *havalehs* on smaller traders, and the banker would charge an agio on paying the *havaleh* in cash money. This method held for both book transfers and cash payments.

An example will illustrate how the system worked:

The cash price for an article sold at 200 *qrans choruk* money is:[56]

I 1200 x 7% = 1400/107 = 13.1

II another 4% is added. 200 – 13.1 = 186,9 x 4% = 747,6/104 = 7.1

III a third agio of 4% is added. 186.9 – 7.1 = 179.8

179.8 x 4% 719.2/104 = 6.9

179.8 – 6.9 = 172.9 *qrans*

This means that a book money price of 200 *qrans*, when paid for in cash amounted to 172.9 *qrans* only. This shows how intricate the system was, a system which in fact was even more intricate than just shown here. We have seen that there were two kinds of

54. MacLean 1904, 61.
55. MacLean 1904, 61; Berichte 1910, 314.
56. Berichte 1910, 314; MacLean 1904, 61.

money, book money and cash money, but in fact the book money was again subdivided in three different monies, differing in discount only.[57]

> 1. 'Raidj divan' [*rayej-e divan*] or government rate by which 15 pieces of 20 c. plus 2 shahees are the countervalue for a toman. This rate is used in paying the army, official salaries, pensions; also in payments to custom house, telegraph, and pensions.
>
> 2. 'Raidj bazaar' [*rayej-e bazar*] or market rate by which 15 pieces of 20 c. we equal to 1 toman, three pieces of 20 c. making 2 krans. Servant's wages, bazaar purchases, household expenses, &c., are paid at this rate.
>
> 3. Lastly, 'Raidj toojar' [*rayej-e tojjar*] or merchants' rate, adopted in mercantile transactions, by which 15 pieces of 20 c. are equivalent to 1 toman and 10 shahees. Money paid at this rate is termed 'Poul tchourouk' [*pul-e choruk*] or rotten money (litt. filthy lucre) in contradiction to 'Poul saf' [*pul-e saf*] or pure money, which is another name for 'Raidj divan'.

INTRODUCTION OF MODERN EUROPEAN BANKING METHODS AND INSTITUTIONS

The monopolistic position of the *sarrafs* was challenged by the introduction of modern European banking in Iran. This was the result of the growing economic penetration by European business of the Iranian market, which wanted to secure its financial interests.

It was not, however, Europeans who urged the establishment of a bank after European model, but an Iranian, namely Mirza Malkom Khan. He, in his treatise *Ketabcheh-ye Gheybi* "submitted to Naser al-Din Shah, proposed the establishment of a national bank with an initial capita of one million *tumans* to be obtained by selling a portion of the royal lands (*khalisa*)."[58] Although Malkom Khan did not get a favorable response to this or to his other proposals, the idea apparently took hold, for in 1866 the Shah opened negotiations with the French house Erlanger to establish a bank in Tehran. Nothing came of it, however, since the Iranian government declined to guarantee the inviolability of deposits against arbitrary seizure by authorities.[59] After a few other attempts to introduce European banking in Iran,[60] it was the New Oriental Bank Corporation (*bank-e jadid-e sharq*) which founded the first European bank in Iran in 1888.[61]

Although the traditional banking system of *sarrafs* and merchants (*tojjar*) was an encumbrance to economic development both by its high price for its services and its

57. DCR 445, 4; Lorini 1900, 334; see also Wilson 1896, 282.

58. Algar 1969, 32.

59. Ronall 1969, 257.

60. In 1872 Naser al-Din Shah granted a concession to Baron de Reuter which included the formation of a national bank. In the same year the concession was annulled by the Shah. In 1879, Amin al-Zarb suggested the establishment of a national bank with private and public capital, but nothing came of it. Ronall 1969, 257; Issawi 1971, 346.

61. Ronall 1969, 257.

non-susceptibility to government interference, it responded to the needs of the traditional Iranian business community. Men like Amin al-Zarb, Iran's leading entrepreneur, who realized that modern banking could provide Iran with a sound economic base, could not change this. The European banks certainly satisfied the needs of European firms, who in view of the growing volume of trade felt handicapped by the Iranian system and found it "increasingly difficult to remit funds abroad, or even to effect speedy payments within Iran."[62] In 1890 the Imperial Bank of Persia was founded as a sort of pars pro toto settlement of the Reuter claim. The operations of these banks were greatly resented by the *sarrafs* who together with the ulama and merchants led the opposition against these symbols of European penetration.[63]

The establishment of the Imperial Bank surprisingly led to the formation of trading houses which also performed banking operations. Although these trading-banking firms represented a sort of concerted effort on the part of the Iranian business community to oppose and thwart European influence, they failed in their objective, because apart from concentrating capital in their hands, they did not change their methods. In fact they were but *sarrafs* on a larger scale, although they did not become modern bankers.[64]

The Imperial Bank, which had the sole right to issue banknotes, soon was challenged by the New Oriental Bank, which issued "papers designated as 'Cashier Orders' which pass from hand to hand and are taken as cash in the bazaars."[65] After an official protest a compromise was reached and the Imperial Bank bought the assets of the New Oriental Bank.[66]

Although the New Oriental Bank set the tone of the opposition, the sequence was a completely Iranian affair. The notes which were issued by the Imperial Bank[67] were either refused or more usually accepted at a discount when the owners were willing, but the *sarrafs* retailed them at a premium when opportunity arose.[68] According to Lorini the *sarrafs* paid the following rates:[69]

normal rate for a 100 *tuman* banknote =	100 *tuman* silver, old
	99.5 *tuman* silver, new
the *sarrafs* paid =	95-98 *tuman* silver, old
	69-70 *tuman* silver, new

62. Ronall 1969, 257; see also Rabino 1892.

63. See for the reaction of the merchants Floor 1976.

64. Floor 1976, 126-28; see also Issawi 1971, 45-46.

65. FO 60/517, letter March 17, 1890.

66. Ronall 1969, 259.

67. When in 1883 Russian paper rubles appeared in Iran, the Shah forbade people to use these banknotes as currency, and decreed "the people are very foolish who take dirty pieces of paper for gold and silver, and in future all Russian ruble notes will be confiscated." The decree, however, remained a dead letter, see Curzon 1892, vol. 1, 478.

68. DCR 976, 11; Lorini 1900, 348.

69. Lorini 1900, 348-9.

Another method used to oppose the Imperial Bank was to organize a run on one of the branches of the bank. The merchants and *sarrafs* would collect a great amount of money in banknotes and send these by post to a provincial town with a branch office of the Imperial Bank, and offer these notes in exchange for silver money. The branch office would not have enough money and transportation of silver took some time. This would result in a run on the bank, "and the bank had to take recourse to the sale of drafts below the real value, and to the transaction of expensive loans with agents of the wily *sarrafs* who had sent the banknotes and had perpetrated the crisis. Meanwhile in the mosques the ulama vilified the infidel foreigners and had to be quieted with presents. The local governor, of course, also took care at such occasions to got his *madakhil* by politely apologizing for the troubles in the bazaar; one was prepared to use one's influence with the ulama to calm the population; there were always rowdies who caused *ekhteshash*, the Iranian population were still so ignorant, they did not understand the solidity of the Bank, one should not resent their actions, they were so poor that they even fear a small loss, but the governor would make things all right (*eslah*), they could be sure of that. It just happened that the governor needed a remittance to Tehran, may be the Bank etc."[70]

The biggest run, which could have resulted in the closing down of the Imperial Bank, took place in 1899 and was engineered by a combine of merchants and *sarrafs* such as the Tumaniants brothers, Hajji Lotf `Ali, the Ettehadiyeh Company, Hajji Baqer, Malek al-Tojjar and others.[71]

Thereafter the bank took care that a great deal of cash money was available and that the banknotes were issued, not only by the central office, but also by the branch offices, which could only be exchanged at the central office, so as to hamper prospective runners.[72]

Finally, merchant-bankers, in imitation of the New Oriental Bank, issued themselves banknotes, which looked like the Imperial Bank notes and which were money orders on the company which issued them. The Fars Trading Company for example issued notes of 1, 5, 10, 25, and 50 *tumans*, which had to be filled in by hand. Everybody accepted these notes, except of course the Imperial Bank. The Fars Trading Company issued in this fashion paper-money to the value of 300,000 *tumans*.[73] The Russian Bank also used this practice at several occasions to challenge the position of the Imperial Bank.[74]

These notes, known as *bijaks*, became very important in trade transactions, because of the lack of cash money. Apart from the decrease of capital among Iranian merchants there was the growing insecurity on the roads, which led to the losses for many merchants. The insecurity also led to the falling off of trade; the continuous depreciation of silver led to a diminishing purchasing power and made the position of the Iranian merchant very uncertain. It was, therefore, that individual merchants also started issuing

70. Dunlop 1912, 419.

71. Dunlop 1912, 419; Kosogovski 1344, 179 ff.; Entner 1965, 4.

72. Dunlop 1912, 419; Ronall 1969, 259.

73. Berichte 1910, 358.

74. Ronall 1910, 260, so-called *bons de caisse* were circulated by the Russian Bank in 1903. This Bank started to operate in Iran in 1891.

bijaks, in this way raising money which they did not have. This was done either to stay in business or by those merchants "who have no other means of employing their funds buying long-date paper, which they hold for the greater put of its term and resell when short usance prevails."[75] Although the issuance of *bijaks* had been forbidden, the issuers got away with these illegal practices by putting pressure on the bazaar and by manipulation of both the local and central authorities.[76] Had the earlier issues of *bijaks* been backed by solid companies, around 1906 and later many of the *bijaks* were raised on credit granted or rather on the interest of debts. Since the issuance of *bijaks* brought an average profit of 12 percent, while trade in goods did not show such good results, it is easy to understand that many indulged in *barat-bazi* or *kolah-bazi* (issuing accommodation paper).[77]

This, of course, created a very unstable market situation, and trade as well as credit would come to a standstill when the *barat-bazi* game broke down. The bankruptcy of one of the big issuers of *bijaks* would result in a run on all *bijaks*, leading to the inability of the other issuers to pay. This led to a temporary clean up of this abnormal situation.

SARRAFS *MAINTAIN MARKET PRESENCE*

Notwithstanding the failure of the *sarrafs* and merchants to thwart the activities of the Imperial Bank, and despite the success of European banks in Iran, the *sarrafs* continued to play an important role in economic life in Iran. Ronall mistakenly contends "that with the establishment of the Imperial Bank of Persia in 1889, none of these small banking houses survived."[78] Not only were these companies created after the establishment of the Imperial Bank, but some of them survived and prospered for as many as 20 years. Although most of these companies disappeared after a few years,[79] the *sarrafs* continued to hold their important place for several reasons.

In the first place the *sarrafs* had a better understanding of the local conditions and needs than any European bank, which moreover only serviced the modern sector of the economy.

In the second place, even when Iranian banks were established later on, the *sarrafs* continued to hold their place in the economy, although they lost the relative advantage of a better knowledge of the market. This was because the *sarraf* was not just another lending institution, but he was a business friend. The business relationship between *sarraf* and client was of a personal nature. One can say that there was not a merchant, a tradesman, or

75. DCR 3748, 10; Already in 1898 the British consul in Bushire doubted whether the Bushire Trading Company could redeem all the *bijaks* it had issued, DCR 2346, 5.

76. "The central authorities were induced to issue ambiguous orders of which due use was made", DCR 5048, 50.

77. DCR 3748, 10; DCR 3923, 13; Landor, vol. 2, 98; "There are in Birjand several native merchants having fair amounts of capital at their disposal, but it appears that the prices which they are willing to pay are so low and the credit required so long, that it is most difficult to do business with them. The retail trade is, therefore, more profitable than the wholesale".

78. Ronall 1969, 268.

79. See Floor 1976, 126f.

a man of property who did not have his own *sarraf*.[80] If the client needed money no questions were asked why he needed the money and how he could repay it. The purpose of the loan did not interest the *sarraf*. More important was the reputation of the borrower, his reputed repaying capability.

In the third place the *sarraf* serviced an important part of the economy which the modem banks considered to be too risky and not interesting enough as far as profits were concerned in view of the relatively small amounts of money which the *sarrafs'* clients demanded, The modern banks did business mainly with the modern sector of the economy, while not bothering with the traditional or informal sector. Thus the *sarrafs* were the only financial resource for farmers, small-scale industrialists and traders.[81]

In the fourth place the *sarrafs* formed a convenient outlet of savings which one did not want to advertise. For the *sarrafs* not only used their own capital but also funds of third parties which could be set out with them at monthly, weekly or even daily interest. These funds were drawn by the offer of high returns, which resulted in greater cost to the borrower than with a modern bank, but then the bank probably would not lend money to this borrower and the *sarraf* asked no questions.[82]

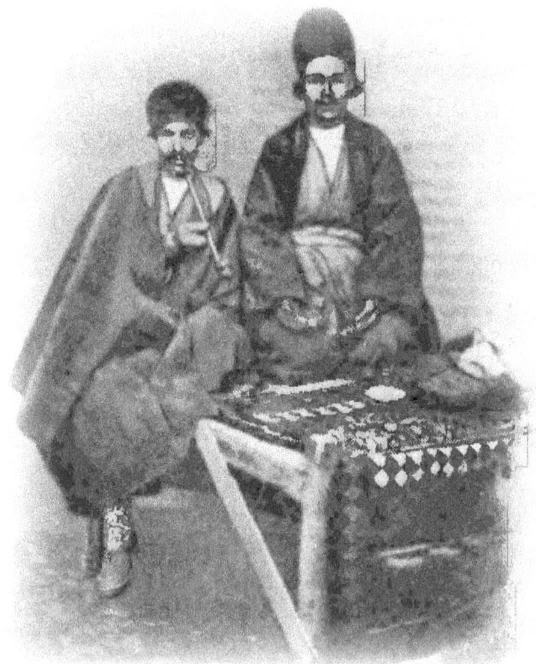

80. Lorini 1900, 334.

81. Greenfield 1906, 27.

82. FO 601354; Issawi 1971, 77; de Lacey O'Brien 1873, 45.

CHAPTER FIVE

The Economic Role of the Ulama in Qajar Iran

The focus of this article is on the role of the religious class, in particular its leading proponents, the ulama, in the economy of 19th century Iran. I begin by describing the context in which the religious class functioned as well as the estimated size of this class. In the first section, those groups that made up the religious class are identified and discussed. In the second section, the alleged financial independence of the religious class and, in the third section, their main sources of income are reviewed. In the last section, the economic role of the religious class is assessed and some conclusions are drawn.

INTRODUCTION

To understand the role, economic or otherwise, of the religious class in Qajar Iran, it is necessary to understand the nature of the society they were a part of. Although their role as preservers and guardians of religious values gave them a clearly, though narrowly defined role, the manner in which they carried it out was to a great extent determined by the society of which they figured prominently. Since they lived in a society of believers, most of them, by the very nature of their function, were respected by the populace. As private individuals rather than as members of an official priestly hierarchy (though Shi`ite hierocratic organization came close to that) they used that respect to advance their own private interests as well as their religious cause.

The scope of their activities was further determined by the fact that Qajar Iran was a pre-industrial state which was divided along regional, ethnic, and linguistic lines. Such societies are dominated by a small power elite who supply most of the political, administrative, military, and religious leaders. The role of the religious professionals was not only to promote Shi`a Islam, but also to provide legitimacy to the political system. Because of the legitimization of power through religion, the latter's values and norms, including economic ones, reflected those of the body politic. Moreover, religion provided most of the formal legal structure. It also meant that the religious leaders influenced the limits of the state's power through their broad legal, social, and educational functions. Therefore, any opposition to the existing political order was opposition to the religious order. The conflicts between the political and religious elite were never about the need to fundamentally change the political or economic basis of the existing system or how it should be managed, but always about who should manage it!

Although Qajar Iran in the formal sense was a centrally governed state, in actual practice local elite families and governors administered the outlying regions as they saw fit. As long as they paid taxes and kept law and order, the center (shah) did not interfere. So-called antigovernment activities by ulama, therefore, were but jockeying for a larger share of the political and economic pie. This also meant that most ulama, as the most learned of the religious class were known and about whom the data are more abundant than on other members of the religious class, played a local or regional role, and only very few played a national role or were known nationally. Further, local differences between leading ulama were very important, and these personal and/or doctrinal differences were often couched in political and social slogans to rouse their adherents. Factionalism, financial needs, and the pursuit of private gain determined the role of the religious class in the economy.

Although the religious professionals sought income and wealth, they did not need those resources to propagate obedience to God and the Shi`a faith, for every Shi`a Moslem in Qajar Iran practiced this belief on a daily basis. Therefore, funds were needed mainly to (a) sustain that achievement, both spiritually (with education) and physically (by means religious ritual and buildings) and especially (b) to increase the percentage of Shi`ite believers in the particular point of view held by a religious leader, one that did not even necessarily needed to be doctrinal. For example, when somebody died without heirs his, or her, property had to be disposed of in accordance with the verdict of a religious judge. Such a case in Qazvin in the 1890s, led to a battle between the partisans of the two leading religious professionals there: Aqa Sayyed Jamal and Aqa Sayyed Ebrahim Tonkabuni. Aqa Sayyed Jamal won the battle because he had more troops.[1] Thus, leading religious leaders literally fought rival colleagues for control in their towns. The ulama on opposite sides of the Tobacco Régie issue even went so far as to call one another "infidel."[2] To sustain this factionalism required financing. Thus, the medium acquired as much importance as the religious message, if not more. In modern marketing jargon this is called "market share" and "brand name recognition," and that is what many leading ulama fought and paid for.

Qajar Iran was also a subsistence economy, which meant that it was a poor country. Changes in the weather that adversely affected the harvest, and sickness that diminished the human and/or animal population, had a devastating impact on the quality of life and disposable income, which were generally minimal for the majority of the population. Such adversities made these largely illiterate people credulous in the extreme as well as hopeful for improvement of their lives. They suffered from arbitrary rule, tyranny, and wickedness at the hands of most of their self-appointed superiors, secular or otherwise.

---

1. Greenfield 1904, 133. On the factional, mostly nonreligious but political, strife between the leading religious professionals and their use of *lutis* and other criminal elements, see Floor 1981 and Floor 1979.

2. Majd al-Eslam 1351, 144.

In fact, the poor populace wanted to be saved and looked to the religious professionals for the road towards salvation, for which they were willing to pay. The fact that most people (more than 90 percent) could not read, write, or calculate occasioned respect for those who had mastered those skills, in particular those who could read the Qur'an, of course. Those who belonged to the class of the literati often had achieved this in the pursuit of religious studies.

THE SIZE OF THE RELIGIOUS CLASS

The religious class consisted mainly of those who made their living by providing religious guidance and practicing various kinds of ritual; if they were independently wealthy, they engaged in religious affairs as part of a family tradition and usually held important local religious positions. It would be wrong, of course, to assume that all these religious professionals were only driven by financial gain and not by religious conviction. These two considerations did and do not exclude one another, and, after all, religious professionals and their families also have to live.

Typically, the class of religious professionals represented about one to 3 percent of the population in large towns towards the end of the 19th century, though in some cases this number was higher. For example, in 1301/1880, the religious class in Tehran[3] represented 3 percent of the total population (i.e., households); its composition is shown in Table 1.

Table 4-1: Number of Religious Professionals in Tehran in 1880

`alem	108	*pishnamaz*	103
modarres	18	*talebeh*	210
va'ez	90	*rowzeh-khvan*	391
maddah	107	*nowheh-khvan*	85
qabr kon	25	*talqin-khvan*	16
qari	92	*mordeh-shuy mard*	8
mordeh-shuy zan	6	*motavalli + khadameh*	180

Shahri, vol. 1, p. 86.

However, in cities whose business was religion, such as centers of pilgrimage like Mashhad, the religious class and their dependents may have represented as much as 25

3. Shahri 1367, vol. 1, 86.

to 30 percent of the city's population.[4] A census taken by the ward chiefs (*kadkhoda*) of Qazvin in 1298-9/1878-9 at the instruction of the Naser al-Din Shah (r. 1848-1896), showed that the religious class was the second largest group (9% of households) after that of the general population of workers (83%). They were followed by the group of notables and administrators (4%) and merchants (3%).[5] However, Greenfield reports that Qazvin province (city plus 700 villages) around 1900 boasted only of 60 high-ranking religious professionals.[6] It may be that Greenfield did not count the sayyeds, who could constitute a significant percentage of the population in certain areas.[7] One could argue that the size of the religious class would be reduced if one considered that it consisted only of religious scholars, or ulama, about whom more is known. However, I prefer to take the broader view and consider all those for whom religion was their major source of income. This, of course, comprises a much larger, more diverse, and more representative group.

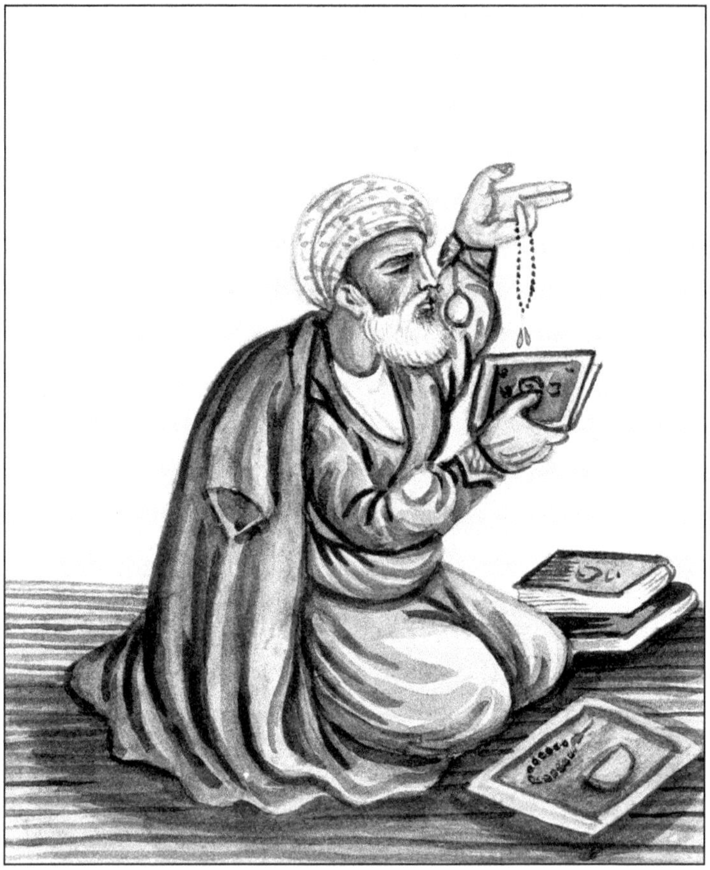

A mullah makes an augury, *estekhareh*.

4. Curzon 1892, vol. 1, 163; E`temad al-Saltaneh 1301-03, vol. 2, 31.

5. Golriz 1337, 402-03.

6. Greenfield 1904, 127.

7. According to Polak, the sayyeds as a group represented as much as two percent of the entire population. Polak 1865, vol. 1, 38. Another nineteenth century source estimates their number even higher, viz., at 20 percent of the urban population, which cannot be right, but indicates that the impression existed that sayyeds were omnipresent and were a hard-to-avoid urban phenomenon. Greenfield 1904, 121.

The available data for smaller towns shows that the number of religious professionals, aside from the sayyeds, was very low and usually less than 1 percent. In each of the towns of Bam, Sirjan, Shahr-e Babak, and Rasanjan in Kerman province, for example, the main religious professionals numbered three, in addition to some lower ranking mullahs.[8] More data are reported by the Russian traveller Shopen in 1852: that in Ordubad, a small town with about 3,500 inhabitants, the high ranking ulama represented 1 percent, the mullahs 2 percent, and sayyeds 31 percent of the population. In Erevan, a town of 11,500 inhabitants, there was a mullah for every 100 Moslems. There were 50 mullah and 39 sayyed families, thus representing less than 1 percent of the population.[9]

There were very few ulama in the rural areas. However, in Akda, a village of 1200 inhabitants, the British frontier commission received a visit of the five principal men of the place- four of which were sayyeds, out of 100 in the village.[10] Some villages consisted almost entirely of sayyeds, but these were exception to the rule that the number of the religious class living in villages were few.[11] In the tribal areas very few religious professionals were found. Tribal chiefs might have a mullah in their entourage, "who acted as secretary and chaplain."[12]

WHO WERE THESE RELIGIOUS PROFESSIONALS?

The upper echelon, or leaders of the religious professionals, were the *mojtaheds*, the *sheikh al-islams*, the *buyuk-akhunds*, the *imam-jom`ehs*, the *motavalli-bashis*, the qadis, the *molla-bashis*, and the *modarreses* (chief professors). Thus, with the exception of the *mojtaheds*, these were all holders of important positions that were bestowed by the state. Except for the last two, most of the other well-paid functions were usually hereditary. All these functions were highly respected by the community of believers.[13]

"The priesthood of Persia are almost all Syuds," Malcolm reports.[14] Polak goes even farther, stating that you can only become a *mojtahed, sheikh al-islam*, or *imam-jom`eh*, "if you are a sayyed."[15] Indeed it would seem that sayyeds dominated those functions throughout the nineteenth century in Qajar Iran as they did the ranks of the ulama (35%) in the shrine cities of Najaf and Karbala.[16] Their number was probably higher among the ulama in Iran itself, because the religious community in the shrine cities constituted

---

8. Vaziri 1346, 97, 158, 167, 172-73.

9. Kuznetsova 1358, 84.

10. Goldsmid 1876, vol. 2, 170.

11. E`temad al-Saltaneh 1301-03, vol. 1, 159; Polak 1865, vol. 1, 38; Afzal al-Molk Kermani 1396, 242, 244.

12. Layard 1894, p. 152.

13. Malcolm 1820, vol. 2, 443-45, 574; Sheil 1856, 170; Southgate 1840, vol. 2, 23; Drouville 1819, vol. 1, 117-18; Höltzer 1354, 19; Adamiyat 1351, 60-61; Polak 1865, vol. 1, 325; Afzal al-Molk Kermani 1396, 65-67.

14. Malcom 1820, vol. 2, 573.

15. Polak 1865, vol. 1, 325.

16. Litvak 1990, 45-46.

a more open system. The *sadat-e 'ali*, or first-rank sayyeds, occupied the leading religious functions, in particular those granted by the state and the well-paid functions in the shrines. The lower-class sayyeds had to fend for themselves in the market, as we will see.

Each city had a number of clans who for generations had monopolized the local religious functions, the appointment to which was controlled by the government.[17] These clans not only supplied religious functionaries but also exercised political, social, and economic influence that the governor, and even the shah, had to consider. Similar secular clans, dominating the local administrative and economic functions, existed at the same time. Members of these clans intermarried and jockeyed for more power and influence to advance their clan's position.[18]

Nevertheless, the ulama were a much more open group than any other social class. Also, they were more inclined to reward piety and scholarly excellence than family ties. Litvak has shown that non-clerical origins dominated among ulama who immigrated to the shrine cities, as opposed to those born there. On the other hand, many who held "hereditary" religious functions often did not study in the Iraqi shrine cities, but in Iran itself, thus maintaining a more closed system.[19]

After the *mojtaheds* and the holders of important religious functions, who, as we have seen, were often sayyeds hailing from the professional and hereditary religious clans, there were the middle and lower echelons. These were the preachers, or *akhunds*, and mullahs, who taught and preached, and for the most part enjoyed a good reputation. This middle group consisted of less educated religious professionals who served the first group as aides, aspiring to attain the rank of their masters. Further, this group included teachers at the intermediary level of the local madrasas, clerks at the religious courts, and the various middle-class religious of the small towns.[20]

In smaller towns the number of middle-echelon religious professionals was limited, but like their high-level professional model in the city, they had under them a number of mullahs, who were in charge of religious rites, circumcision, marriage, and burial. The *akhunds* supervised them and undertook these same functions for the notables who paid them annual stipends in return.[21] The mullahs "conduct the services in the mosques, teach and recite the Koran, preach, visit the sick and write letters, and in the villages their fees are paid in kind."[22]

The working-class religious professionals included the rural mullahs, the managers of small shrines, mosques, and madrasas (seminaries), and further, low-level teachers at the madrasas and the Qur'anic schools (*maktab*), the pulpit preachers and reciters of panegyrics, seminarians (*tollab*), and the lower-class sayyeds. All these were financially and otherwise dependent on their masters. They served as their eyes and ears as well as conduits for propaganda to the public at large and even as shock troops to fight competing

17. Greenfield 1904, 130.
18. Amanat 1989, 38-39 with references to various towns.
19. Litvak 1990, 43, 58.
20. Fraser 1842, 256; Höltzer 1354, 19.
21. Drouville 1819, vol. 1, 118.
22. Sykes 1910, 135-36; Adams 1906, 386; Malcolm 1820, vol. 2, 445; Shakeri 1346, 133.

religious professionals. For the important ulama kept a large retinue to serve them in all their endeavors, both religious and otherwise.[23] In villages they had seldom more than an inferior mullah, who sometimes doubled as the local government administrator.[24]

WHY THE LABEL "MULLAH" DOES NOT ALWAYS STICK

Not every mullah or sayyed was engaged in the pursuit of religious affairs as a profession, however. Sayyeds, whose siblings exercised important functions in the religious establishment and who were members of important professional religious families, were engaged in trade and other economic pursuits, while literate members of the artisan class were often referred to as "mullah" because of their religious or literary education.[25]

However, all who went to the madrasa did not necessarily want to become a religious professional. According to Sir John Malcolm, "there are a number of persons in Persia who pursue their studies till they are entitled to the name of Moollah, and to all the honours of a Persian college, without classing themselves with the priesthood."[26] Consequently, many of the students showed a less than religious attitude and behavior in life. In the 1870s, half of the students in Isfahan were considered to be without religion by the leading religious leader of that city.[27] According to Malcolm, this was due to "the facility with which a Persian can obtain a certain degree of education at the colleges in the principal cities, and that indulgence to which the usages of these seminaries invite, produces a swarm of students, who pass their useless lives in indolence and poverty."[28] In fact, in the rural, and especially the tribal areas, "mullah" meant only a man who could write and read the Qur'an.[29]

THE DESCENDANTS OF THE PROPHET OR SAYYEDS

The sayyeds, as part of the religious class, constituted a separate category. They are a hereditary class of nobility. There are several kinds of sayyeds. The most important ones are descended from Fatima, the prophet's daughter, and her husband `Ali b. Abu Taleb, the prophet's cousin. They had two sons, Hasan and Hoseyn, and consequently there are Hasani and Hoseyni Sayyeds. The Razavis, or descendants of Imam Reza, enjoyed special privileges in Mashhad, where Imam Reza is buried, and "comparatively few of them appar-

---

23. Brugsch 1862-63, vol. 2, 95; Ussher 1865, 59.

24. Malcolm 1820, vol. 2, 445; Brydges-Jones 1834, 305; Forbes 1844, p. 152.

25. For a few examples see Amanat 1989, 356; Fraser 1826, 119; Ferrier 1857, 121 n; see also chapter three supra.

26. Malcolm 1820, vol. 2, 575. Many merchants, e.g., had studied at the religious seminaries. Vaziri 1346, 67; Mostowfi n.d., 2, 238, which was in line with religiosity of this group. See also chapter two supra.

27. Höltzer 2535, 19.

28. Malcolm 1820, vol. 2, 580.

29. Bird 1891, vol. 2, 7.

ently work for their living."[30] Descendants of `Ali through his offspring from other women are called `Alavi Sayyeds. Although it all started with a woman, Fatima, sayyeds who were descended from a male sayyed were known as *sharif* and ranked higher than those who were descended from a sayyeda mother only. Because of their descent, sayyeds enjoyed general respect and immunity from normal state regulations. Therefore, a chief sayyed was responsible for the behavior of the sayyeds, for only a sayyed could judge another sayyed. In the past such a chief sayyed was called *naqib al-ashraf* or *naqib al-mamalek*, but in Qajar times this official was generally referred to as *ra 'is-e sadat*. The *naqib* was the overseer of all dervish groups.[31]

As among the rest of society, among sayyeds also there were prominent families, such as the Tabataba'is, whose credentials were well-known and acknowledged. However, it was also a well-known fact that many sayyeds had no claim to such distinction. These fake sayyeds took advantage of the reverence and the pecuniary benefits paid to sayyeds by presenting themselves as a legitimate sayyed in communities that did not know them. It was sufficient to put on a green belt or turban, for even to question the validity of the claim to sayyedship was considered to be blasphemy. Whereas the Tabataba'is have a recognized family tree, these self-made sayyeds had such family trees fabricated in the Shi`ite shrine cities in Iraq, in particular from Samarra, and were therefore referred to as Samarra sayyeds.[32] In fact, according to Dieulafoy, only four families in Iran were recognized as having a legitimate—though even there on disputable grounds—claim of descent from `Ali.[33] This was also reflected in the large number of *imamzadehs*, or tombs of alleged descendants of the Shi`ite Imams. The chief professor of the madrasa at Qazvin told the Dieulofoys, for example, that he was quite aware that in Iran alone there were more than 20 *imamzadehs* claiming to house the ashes of the same sayyed, in addition to those in the country where the sayyed had or even had not lived at all. However, the point was, according to this scholar, one did not really need the ashes of the *imamzadeh* to dedicate a tomb in his honor and pray to him.[34]

As a consequence, the number of sayyeds was large. "Persia swarms with Saiyids, a lazy, worthless set of men as a rule, who do-not work and expect to be fed by others, and the Turkoman Khojah is the same," according to Yate.[35] Other contemporary European observers concurred with Yate's opinion. According to Polak, the sayyeds as a group represented as many as 2 percent of the entire population.[36] Another nineteenth-century source estimates their number even higher, that is, at 20 percent of the urban population, which cannot be right, but indicates that the impression existed that sayyeds were omnipresent,

30. Yate 1900, 333-34.
31. Greenfield 1904, 121.
32. Polak 1865, vol. 1, 38; Greenfield 1904, 121
33. Dieulafoy 1887, 77.
34. Dieulafoy 1887, 116.
35. Yate 1900, 267.
36. Polak 1865, vol. 1, 38.

a hard-to-avoid urban phenomenon.[37] In rural areas sayyeds sometimes dominated a village's population, as, for example, in the Khabujan area in Khorasan.[38]

THE FINANCIAL DEPENDENCE OF THE ULAMA

During the interregnum, between 1722 and 1797, a separation of political and religious hierocratic domination had occurred, due to the breakdown of the Safavid state in 1722, and thus of state control over the religious class through the Safavid's centralized hierocratic system under the *sadr*. The *mojtaheds* therefore overthrew the *sadrs* "without possessing their revenues."[39] Thus, "freedom from the state" for the religious class came at a price. For endowments and stipends, which formed the backbone of their revenues, were not available to them anymore. Because of this breakdown, the religious professionals had to find ways to survive economically.

The financial ruin of the Shi`ite religious professionals was completed by the 25-year misrule of Afghan Sunnis (1722-30) and the ecumenical Nader Shah (1732-47). The latter had discontinued most of these stipends and had usurped most of the religious endowments around 1740 and had converted these into crown lands, thus bankrupting the religious class. His successors did not improve the financial situation of the religious establishment. The Zand rulers, for example, only showed some largesse to a few high-ranking ulama.[40] This situation, combined with a major displacement of religious scholars from Iran, led to some measure of financial autonomy of the religious leaders who were in the Iraqi shrine cities. This was possible through the collection of the *khoms* and *zakat* (religious taxes) paid by the Shi`ite believers, which now had become the exclusive domain of the *mojtaheds* after the abolition of the function of *sadr*. Also, their appropriation of extensive judiciary functions that were independent of state control brought in sorely needed revenues. These sources of income sustained the religious Shi`ite leaders in the Iraqi shrine cities throughout the late 1700s and formed the basis of their financial independence to pursue their religious and scholarly objectives.[41]

With the end to state-controlled religion through the *sadr* and his provincial network of agents, combined with the religious legitimacy of the Safavid sayyed kings as upholders of the Imamate, the Shi`ite religious scholars had been seeking new ways to position themselves in the religious market. During the unsettled times of the second half of the eighteenth century, migrant ulama from Iran had brought Usulism to the Iraqi shrine cities and had developed new structures independent of the state. When the Qajars established their hold over Iran in the 1790s, they needed legitimacy. They obtained it by espousing the cause of Usuli orthodoxy and acquiescing to the termination of formal state control over religion in the persons of the *sadr* and *molla-bashi*. At the same time, the Usuli

37. Greenfield 1904, 121.

38. E`temad al-Saltaneh 1301-03, vol. 1, 59; Greenfield 1904, 121; Polak 1865, vol. 1, 38; Afzal al-Molk 1396, 242, 244.

39. Fraser 1842, 255.

40. Cole 1985, 22.

41. Cole 1985, 3-34; Algar 1969.

leaders of the religious class acquired greater power and autonomy through the active political and financial support from the new Qajar government. In exchange, the Usuli leadership extended their support for the legitimacy of Qajar rule.[42]

It therefore comes as no surprise that the religious professionals during the early Qajar period depended very much on the state, because they relied on royal grants and religious endowments, a custom that, moreover, around 1810, "seems to have become nearly obsolete."[43] Brydges argued that the shah therefore had great power over the religious. Whereas a mullah was held in great esteem in Turkey, "in Persia the person holding the same station, and possessing the same qualities, is laughed at, and is almost a proverbial joke."[44] However, as with modern-day politicians, people may have had little respect for mullahs as a class, but they certainly were quite satisfied with their "own" local mullah.

Very rich *mojtaheds* could afford to snub the shah and even refuse his money to help build a mosque. Others, however, gladly accepted the state's bounty, especially those who had been appointed by the shah to remunerative functions. Association with the state was to their best interest.[45]

This begs the question whether the ulama were really that independent from the state, as some scholars have suggested. If they had their own funds, why then did they have to compete with one another for the state's largesse? To answer that question we need a better understanding of the size and nature of the financial resources that the religious class could count on.

SOURCES OF INCOME

The sources of income that were necessary for the religious professionals to sustain themselves and their families, and for the leading ulama to maintain and expand market share among the mass of believers, consisted of the following. In the first place, there was personal wealth through inheritance or income from gainful employment or remunerative economic activity in which a religious professional might be engaged. Second, there were pensions, stipends, grants, gifts, and paid administrative offices that the shah bestowed on religious leaders as a form of government employment. Third, there was judicial income as well as the *khoms* and *zakat* taxes, canonical taxes that were paid to the religious class. Fourth and last, there were endowments, from which the ulama, either as *motavalli* (manager) or as *nazer* (trustee), derived an income, while, in addition, these same endowments often had as their main purpose the financing of stipends for students and teachers as well as the maintenance of buildings (school, mosque, shrine, etc.).

---

42. Algar 1969. Usulis considered the collectivity of *mojtaheds* as a souce of emulation for Sh`ite laymen.

43. Brydges 1834, 406.

44. Brydges 1834, 407; Malcolm 1820, vol 2, 573; Gordon 1895, 28; Ferrier 1857, 30; Benjamin 1887, 343; Tahvildar 1342, 86.

45. Algar 1969, 49; Seystani 1369, 2, 558; E`temad al-Saltaneh 1349, 109.

PERSONAL WEALTH

Contemporary observers have created the impression that the ulama were rich and belonged to the country's economic and power elite. This certainly held true for the leaders of the religious class, who only constituted a small number. However, the majority of the religious class was not rich, and many of them were poor. As Sir John Malcolm wrote, "The lower ranks of priesthood ... are exposed to great temptation; and receive, with their office, but a very limited income. They therefore are often corrupt and bigoted."[46]

Nevertheless, the rich were very wealthy. According to Fraser, "the ecclesiastical body, which includes the expounders of the written law, is very numerous, wealthy, and powerful."[47] Indeed, many contemporary observers believed that the largest fortunes had been derived from religious service. Some *mojtaheds* were believed to be as rich as the shah.[48] The concentration of wealth among the religious professionals was, of course, most evident in the large towns. According to Edward Stirling, "The moolahs and priests, which amount here [Mashhad] to about two thousand, are the most wealthy individuals. They enjoy many privileges and perquisites and gifts which are often very rich and high. . - The Mujtahyd and the Mutawalle [mutavalli] are people of large fortune, the former is said to be worth two or three crores of rupees; his son possesses sixty lacs or more."[49]

Among this group the *imam-jom`eh* of Isfahan, Mir Sayyed Mohammad Baqer Shafti Hojjat al-Islam, stood out. He came from a very poor family. The source of his vast wealth is unknown, His contemporaries believed that through alchemy he could transform paper into money or that he had found an ancient treasure hoard. A more likely source of his start-up capital is less sensational. His piety was rewarded by the khan of his village of Shaft, who gave him money to invest in trade and property. The proceeds he had to divide between charitable purposes and his own expenditures. Sayyed Mohammad Baqer was able to earn great wealth from real estate deals and owned four hundred caravanserais and two thousand shops in Isfahan alone, and many villages all over Iran. From his villages in Borujerd alone, he had an annual income of 6,000 *tumans*. Shafti paid 17,000 *tumans* in taxes on his villages in the Isfahan area. His total wealth was estimated at 200,000 *tumans*. The mystery of his wealth was part of his success as a religious leader. It is alleged that he was, if not the richest man of his time, certainly the richest religious leader, much richer than the super-rich religious professionals such as Hajj Mohammad Karim Khan Qajar or Hajj Mullah `Ali Kani. Most of the landed property in Isfahan was either his or belonged to the Sadr family, who had been engaged in religious service for several generations.[50] His

46. Malcolm 1820, vol. 2, 446. "The greater number, however, are poor, and disappointed with the world and their callings." Bassett 1887, 308. "There are in every city, ... a crowd of mullahs, who live by their wits ... and contrive by these means to prolong a miserable existence." Fraser 1842, 256.

47. Fraser 1842, 255.

48. Kuznetsova 1358, 76.

49. Stirling 1991, 169-71; Eastwick 1864, vol. 2, 197, 207; Adams 100, 386; Basset 1887, 308; Stack 1886, vol. 2, 272.

50. Eqbal 1327, 27-35; Tonkabuni 1304, 104-05, 135; Algar 1969, 60-61; Ussher 1865, 590f; Vambery 1867, 176; Brugsch 1862-63, vol. 2, 95, 233; Sepsis 1844, 100; Vazir 1346, 45-46.

wealth and greed grew so much that after the death of the powerful governor of Isfahan, Mo`tamad al-Dowleh, the sayyed tried to become the dominant political force in the city. His bands of *lutis* terrorized the population and forced people to sign over property to the sayyed which he turned into a *vaqf* (religious trust) for the people. When Mohammad Shah (r. 1834-48) put an end to the reign of terror in 1842, he at the same time took the misappropriated property back but did not return it to the original owners. Instead, he turned them into *khaleseh*, or crown property.[51]

Others, usually landowners and proprietors of lucrative urban property, were less wealthy, but still well-off. However, those specified as well-off were invariably first-echelon members of the religious class such as *imam-jom`ehs* and *mojtaheds*.[52]

Aqa Najafi, another powerful religious leader in Isfahan in the 1880-90s, also started out in life very poor and became very rich. Aqa Najafi, his brothers, and their sons, who were as much as 14,000 *tumans* in debt and possessed one village after their father's death, owned 5 million *tumans* twenty-five years later. Aqa Najafi was called Na'eb-e Imam by his *tollab*. He also tried to leave his mark on Isfahan through his *lutis*, or thugs. The regular taxes on his property alone amounted to 60,000 *tumans*, while the irregular ones were still almost 30,000 *tumans*.[53]

Some *mojtaheds*, such as Mohammad Baqer Shafti of Isfahan, the Baraghanis of Qazvin, and Mirza Aqa Javadi of Tabriz, derived their authority and power both from their economic power and from their piety and erudition advantage, the former as much as, if not more than the latter. In fact, Shafti's rise from the status of poor student to that of one of the richest men in Iran in itself was interpreted as a sign of divine grace that one might attain just by associating with him. The wealth of the high-ranking religious professionals gave them enormous latitude in their dealings with both the government and society at large.

Nevertheless, the myth of poverty of the *mojtaheds* was part of the image building that took place and that even a *mojtahed* could not avoid.[54] For, according to Malcolm, "their occupation enjoins plainness of dress, and forbids the vanity and display to which other persons in this country are so much attached."[55] However, these religious leaders, who indeed may have had hardly any personal wealth, nevertheless controlled vast financial resources through their custodianship of endowments and monies that were received from believers in the form of *zakat*, *khoms*, and gifts. The offspring, or *aqa-zadehha*, of these religious leaders did quite well for themselves after the death of their parent.

---

51. Fashahi 2536, 38; Jaberi-Ansari 1321, 47.

52. Sani` ol-Dawleh 1307, 137; Majd al-Islam 1351, 170-71; Stack 1886, vol. 2, 262, 272f.; Golzari 2535, 110-11; Afzal al-Molk Kermani 1396, 190, 196, 199, 200; Goldsmid 1876, vol. 2, 189; Vaziri 1346, 47-50; E`temad al-Saltaneh 1301-03, vol. 3, 188, 340; Lambton 1953, 268; Houtum-Schindler 1896, 78; Greenfield 1904, 156. The wealth of the leading religious professionals increased after the 1873 famine. Lambton 1953, 261; Pavlovich 1910, 618.

53. Yaghma'i 1363, 53; Majd al-Islam 1350, vol. 2, 335; Ibid. 1351, 170-71.

54. Brugsch 1862-63, vol. 2, 100; Franck 1926, 186, 192.

55. Malcolm 1820, vol. 2, 573.

INCOME FROM ADMINISTRATIVE FUNCTIONS

Part of the wealth of the leading ulama was obtained through their religious affiliation and judicial activities, part through secular economic activities such as management of agricultural properties, commercial enterprise, and money lending. The religious professionals had close contacts with the bazaar community. This was of course logical in view of their role in drawing up contracts, acting as notary public, and the like. Each section of the bazaar, therefore, was under the jurisdiction of a mullah, who oversaw and advised merchants, traders and artisans on all commercial and other transactions. This relationship held in particular for the guilds. According to de Gobineau, "it is clear that these organized cooperations are backed on the one hand by the merchants for whom they work and on the other by the mullahs who, their prestige requiring that they be surrounded by the masses, are glad to take up the interests of apprentices, craftsmen (artisans), and even master craftsmen."[56]

Religious professionals were also directly involved in many business transactions, often as silent partners. In addition, members of important religious clans were heavily engaged in commerce as well as in real estate.[57] It was not exceptional for a *mojtahed* or lower ranking religious professionals to be landlord to artisans or other urban dwellers.[58] Also, as managers of endowments with extensive property in the bazaar or of agricultural lands cultivated with cash crops, the religious professionals came into close contact with the trading and financial community.

As holders of large amounts of cash, either as personal property or as managers of religious endowments and gifts, the religious professionals were sought after in an economy where money was scarce. This scarcity was partly due to the hoarding of a large part of their cash revenues by these same religious professionals. According to Stirling, "the system of hoarding is carried to a prodigious extent and not the least among the moolahs. The rate of interest is very high and never less than thirty percent and often as high as fifty percent, and money is only granted on deposits to twice or four times the value of the loan, which if not redeemed in a given time, is liable to be sold and disposed of. The Mussalmen are prohibited from lending money on interest and the whole of the transactions are carried on with secrecy."[59] Or, if not involved directly in money lending, religious professionals put their money in the banks on interest-bearing accounts. This even happened with money from the Imam Reza shrine.[60]

---

56. De Gobineau 1923, 2, 133.

57. Sepsis 1844, 101; Eqbal 1327, 34. For a discussion of a religious family which boasted of familial relations with Shafti, who made their money in trade and real estate and members of which continued to be involved in these activities see Amanat 1989, 340-43.

58. For example, the *mojtahed* of Kerman rented a caravansaray to the Hindus in Kerman for 120 *tuman*s/year. Goldsmid 1876, vol. 2, 189. In Tehran some mollahs rented out some shops. Sa`dvandiyan and Nezam-Mafi 1368.

59. Stirling 1991, 169. For similar remarks, in particular on money lending by religious professionals see Sepsis 1844, 101; Ferrier 1857, 127; Polak 1865, vol. 1, 325, 336, 345.

60. Majd al-Islam 1350, vol. 1, 67.

A particularly immoral activity, in addition to money lending, was the organization of prostitution, in which especially the lower-class mullahs and seminarians (*tollab*) were engaged.[61] In fact, these lower-class religious professionals were heavily involved in providing a legalistic veneer to prostitution—for a fee, of course. The women involved in this trade had a saying, *halal bekun, hazar bekun* (make it legal, make a buck), which basically summed up their position.[62] Hajj Sayyah, the nineteenth century reformer, fulminated against the mullahs who made their living by exploiting poor women and immoral behavior.[63]

Some merchants became very critical of the involvement of some *mojtaheds* in economic life as competitors and controllers. Through direct investment, usurpation as well as inappropriate use of endowment funds, these religious leaders had accumulated substantial funds that needed an outlet. These funds, they invested in trade among other things, allying themselves with one or more trading partner. Merchants who had no backing from a religious professional were in a very precarious position, for they either paid for protection or they would suffer severely in court cases. The protection awarded by the ulama to bankrupt and dishonest merchants was a constant cause for complaint by European merchants.[64] Such shady practices also upset some Iranian merchants, who, for example in Qazvin, protested the biased verdicts by Mullah Mohammad Taqi Baraghani.[65] Amanat strongly suggests that the religious influence in economic life at a time when there was an economic downturn may have contributed to the appeal of Babism among the merchant class and others.[66]

JUDICIAL INCOME

Another important economic activity and source of income was the judiciary. No dispute could be resolved and no commercial transaction would go ahead without the ulama's seal of approval. In case of litigation, both parties paid and/or bribed the religious judge. Although religious judges were not entitled to fees, they received presents or plain bribes to sway their opinion. In fact, judges and their staff acquired a reputation of venality, which increased toward the end of the nineteenth century.[67] Nevertheless, the state-appointed judges were paid high salaries. The *sheikh al-islam* enjoyed a state salary. Around 1810, the judges of Isfahan and Shiraz had salaries of 2,000 *tumans*. The qadi of Marand received 140 *tumans* per month in 1860, an amount that had just been reduced by one-fourth.[68] The small clerks in the judiciary earned an irregular pittance, however.[69]

61. Curzon 1892, vol. 2, 164-65; Polak 1865, 1, 208.
62. Shahri 1357, vol. 1, 259-61.
63. Sayyah 1346, 164-65.
64. Floor 1977; Ibid., 1983.
65. Tonkabuni 1364, 24, 32-33.
66. Amanat 1989, 348-49, 352-55.
67. Sykes 1915, vol. 2, 385; Polak 1865, vol. 1, 325-26.
68. Malcolm 1820, vol. 2, 472; Fraser 1842, 256; Eastwick 1864, vol. 1, 175.
69. Curzon 1892, vol. 1, 164; Malcolm vol. 2, 445.

Because many *mojtaheds* and other high-ranking ulama often considered the function of judge below their standing and referred many cases to mullahs who stood in a client relationship to them, any ignoramus with some meters of black or white textile on his head could become a qadi (religious judge), according to Mostowfi.[70] The judiciary, therefore, provided excellent opportunity for clerical patrons to get their clients employment. Some social critics stated that the judicial cases dragged on for too long because of the personal gain that the religious judge derived from this. Often, therefore, both parties agreed to arbitration to avoid the high cost of litigation.[71] E`temad al-Saltaneh, who had a dispute with Adib al-Molk, his uncle, about his father's inheritance, referred the case to a leading religious scholar, Aqa Sayyed Saleh `Arab, for whom he had not much respect. However, he knew that the Aqa was against Sheikhis and his uncle was a Sheikhi. As a result, E`temad al-Saltaneh won his case "as had been my purpose," he dryly remarks.[72] The ulama also were engaged as notaries public for legal and personal documents, but their willingness to falsify documents did much to invalidate this system. In view of the lucrative opportunities offered by the judiciary, the ulama opposed modernization and increased transparency of the judicial system.[73]

STATE ENDOWMENTS: STIPENDS, PENSIONS, AND FUNCTIONS

Important ulama and sayyeds received stipends and pensions as well as money and other during festivals.[74] These government contributions to the important ulama were insignificant when compared to the flow of funds controlled by the ulama themselves.[75] According to Sheil, the estimated total revenue in 1850 was 3,177,000 *tumans*. Of this some 800,000 *tumans* was for salaries, of which only 4,110 *tumans* was spent on ulama, sayyeds, etc., a quarter of what was spent by the shah on poets and physicians, or on the administrative class.[76] An estimate made in 1868, by the British consul Thomson, indicates that the total state expenditures were 8.5 crores of *tumans* or 1.7 million pounds. Of this amount 0.5 crore of *tumans* or 100,000 pounds was spent on pensions for "the priesthood and syeds," or less than 4 percent of total state expenditures,[77] while Andreas estimated it at 6.7 percent in the early 1880s.[78]

In addition to endowments the state controlled the appointment of many religious functions (*sheikh al-islam, molla-bashi, imam-jom`eh*). It also granted stipends and pensions,

---

70. Mostowfi n.d., vol. 2, 375; see also Kasrasvi 1323, 145, 148; Rushdiyeh 1362, 15. In general see Floor 1983, 113-47.

71. Greenfield 1904, 261; Polak 1865, 1, 326; Floor 1983 b and c; see also chapter two supra.

72. E`temad al-Sataneh 1357, 279; see also Majd al-Islam 1350, vol. 2, 382-89, 422.

73. de Rochechouart 1867, 63; Greenfield 1904, 260; Polak 1865, vol 1, 325-26)

74. Hommaire 1856, vol. 2, 74; E`temad al-Saltaneh 1294-96, vol. 1, 570; Ibid., 1300, vol. 1, 25; Binning 1857, vol. 1, 397.

75. De Rochechouart 1867, 114.

76. Sheil 1856, 388-89.

77. Issawi 1971, 32.

78. Migeod 1990, 153; Brugsch 1886, 182 gives a higher figure of 8 percent for the mid-1880s.

or bestowed gifts on "deserving" religious professionals. The high-ranking ulama purposefully moved to get hold of those public functions (education, judiciary) that gave them control over society as well as access to funds, Both these functions and funds they used to further their cause. It enabled them to control the *vox populi* through the education system and the mosques, while through the courts as judges, and through actively participating in trade and real estate deals and money lending, they had considerable influence with merchants and landlords as agents, partners, competitors, and financiers. With all this power, they could hold out against government demands, strengthen their bargaining position, and gain more from the government than did most others.

RELIGIOUS ALMS AND GIFTS

The leading ulama received large amounts of tithes, alms, and gifts from the believers. The amount of these payments was substantial. Sayyed Mohammad Baqer Shafti received tithes and alms as the Imam's share from India, the Caucasus, and Turkestan, part of which he gave to the poor, while the rest he kept for himself.[79] The tithes from the believers also reached Sheikh Mohammad Hasan Isfahani, who for years was recognized as the leader (*marja`-ye taqlid*), and he used these funds to enable students to study and for the propagation of knowledge in general. He also spent 80,000 *tumans* on a water supply canal from the Tigris. One of his students was Sheikh Mortaza Ansari, who became his successor and to whom the community gave each year about 200,000 *tumans* in the 1870s.[80] Ansari's successor, Mohammad Hasan Shirazi, received the same amount in alms and voluntary contributions.[81]

Many of the religious professionals, particularly sayyeds, begged or, rather, demanded alms, on the ground of their holy character.[82] The demanding behavior, termed *molla-bazi*, was not limited to the lower levels of the religious class.[83] In Isfahan the ulama demanded, and obtained by force if need be, one-third of the property if somebody died. The ulama did this in their own quarter, and the *imam-jom`eh* all over town (asking *yak-hasht*, or one-eighth). The *imam-jom`eh* would send an agent who would seal all rooms in a house, even going so far as delaying the burial preparations. The justification for this behavior was that they claimed that the deceased during his life had not paid the *khoms* and *zakat* tax and/or the *sahm-e Imam* (the Imam's share).[84] There were also religious scholars, such as Mohammad Mehdi Naraqi, who criticized the hereditary sayyed class for their assumption that piety is an innate quality obtained through lineage.[85]

---

79. Eqbal 1327, 34.

80. E`temad al-Saltaneh 1306, 136-37.

81. Houtum-Schindler 1895, 197.

82. Macolm 1820, vol. 2, 573; Drouville 1819, vol. 1, 119, 121; Adams 1900, 387-88; Ferrier 1857, 41, 56; Sykes 1910, 134.

83. Litvak 1990, 44 n. 40; Hume-Griffith 1909, 114; Polak 1865, vol. 1, 327.

84. Majd al-Islam 1350, vol. 1, 101-05; Ibid., 1351, 165. Elsewhere, this one-third was demanded by the state. Majd al-Islam 1350, vol. 1, 101.

85. Cole 1989, 26.

Such behavior was not lost on the public, either, which in various theatrical, literary, and other art forms criticized this mercenary attitude by ridiculing it. Members of the religious class sometimes fell foul of officials who knew if a person had no protection. Instead of paying in this instance, they made him pay - a role reversal that was almost theatrical, and certainly ironic.[86]

The sayyeds drew so much attention to themselves because they were a kind of religious hereditary nobility, and entitled to part of the *khoms* tax under Shi`i law. Consequently, "it is an act of greater savab (act of merit) to give to a drunken seyid than to the most deserving beggar."[87] Dieulafoy reported that by 1880 this custom had largely fallen into disuse, though in the large towns, such as Isfahan, where sayyeds were numerous they continued to exert much influence and impose themselves in particular on small shopkeepers who did not have the clout to oppose them.[88] Sayyeds therefore enjoyed prestige and this led to a proliferation of sayyeds (fabricated or not) because of the material reward this position offered. Many true believers cheated the Imam out of his share by conniving with his descendants, who, for a fair remuneration, would hand out a signed statement that the religious obligatory payment had been truly effected.[89] To increase their fair share, many people also would dress up their children and/or relatives as beggars and would grant these fake poor their share of the bounty for the poor. If they were religious professionals they could keep the rest for themselves.[90] Sometimes rich persons, including religious professionals, did not pay their full contribution either.[91]

Sayyeds also demanded that the notables pay for their upkeep. There was not a notable who had not a sayyed or two on his payroll. After the harvest the lower ranking sayyeds would go into the villages of the jurisdiction where they lived. "They go to the village chief who considers their visit a great honor. He sends criers into the village to announce that the sayyids have arrived and that they submit themselves to their charity. They will not forget them when they meet Muhammad. The peasants hasten to bring presents to the village chief's house where everything is gathered. These presents normally consist of wheat, barley, straw, cheese, mostala, cream, fowls, cotton etc., and also some silver coins. The sayyids then have dinner with the chief and grey-beards and the chief humbly asks them to accept their gifts, which they gravely do. The next day they leave and go to the next village. These illustrious beggars thus are assured of a comfortable living for only showing up once a year. This takes them two months per year, during which they collect produce to the value of 700 to 800 *tumans*. Entering gatherings of the great, they did not hesitate to ask for a contribution and nobody refuses; they even accepted my money

86. Malcolm 1820, vol. 2, 573; Tahvildar 1342, 86; Brydges-Jones 1836, 407; Ferrier 1857, 30, 35; Hume-Griffith 1909, 115.

87. Sykes 1910, 134.

88. Dieulafoy 1887, 310-11.

89. Greenfield 1904, 136; Polak 1865, vol. 1, 336.

90. Greenfield 1904, 137.

91. Sirjani 1361, 642.

though I was an infidel."[92] The dervishes behaved in a similar manner and paid their dervish chief.[93]

At the *sartip*'s house, "I found several Syuds with him, who were doing their best to talk him out of some money, and, unless one has witnessed the fact, it is impossible to conceive the impudence of these descendants of the Prophet; they are the veriest bloodsuckers of the people, who are obliged to keep them at their own expense. Nothing can equal their ignorance, but, generally speaking, they are afraid to refuse their demands, intolerable as they may be."[94]

Among the Yamut Turkomans, sayyeds enjoyed an extraordinary position. When Yamut raiders had taken sheep they believed belonged to the Goklan tribe, they soon found out this was not the case. The sheep belonged to a *khojah* or sayyed, who came to the chiefs tent the next day and demanded restitution of his sheep. The chief Morad Khan, "at once gave back his share of the sheep, with many cries of 'Taubah, Taubah' (repentance, or remorse). The dread that the Turkoman have for the Khojahs is a curious one. It is dread pure and simple that makes them restore property stolen from Saiyids in the way they do, sooner than incur the wrath or the curse of the owner."[95]

A sayyed also might organize a pilgrimage. According to Ferrier, "For two months previously to his intended departure [the sayyed] scours the towns and villages, inviting the faithful to join his green standard, and undertake a pilgrimage to the holy places. A sufficient number being collected, he passes them in review, and, raising the wind from each to the extent of 4 or 5 sahebkrans a head, promises to conduct them in safety" to the shrines. "He promises also to halt at the best and the cheapest stations, to preserve them from the effects of the evil eye, the temptations of the devil, the machinations of the bad genii, to consult the stars, to leave on propitious days—in a word, he promises to make this pilgrimage the happiest and most acceptable to God that was ever made."[96]

Sayyeds were also hired hands for those who wanted to create a riot or a nuisance.[97] For example, creditors would use sayyeds as servers of bills or as collecting agents, because they would not be beaten by the debtor's servants due to the inviolability of their person. Their behavior was often so obnoxious that Mozaffar al-Din Mirza, as governor of Tabriz, forbade sayyeds "to frequent bazaars and thoroughfares in large bands. Merchants in whose employ they are must not depute them to settle pecuniary claims."[98]

There were, of course, also sayyeds who worked for a living as farmers, artisans, merchants, government officials, soldiers, muleteers (*charvadars*), and as religious professionals. In government service, either as military or civil servant, they were, however,

92. Drouville 1819, vol. 1, 119, 121; see also Adams 1900, 387-88.

93. Drouville 1819, vol. 1, 122-24.

94. Ferrier 1857, 41, also for further impolite behavior; Cole 1989, 26.

95. Yate 1900, 246-47.

96. Ferrier 1857, 56; Adams 1900, 388; Dieulafoy 1887, 67.

97. Dieulafoy 1887, 239, 314.

98. Floor 1977.

not allowed to wear the sayyed turban, only a green belt.[99] There were also sayyeds who were not xenophobic and fanatic, but in fact were quite humanistic in their outlook on life and behavior. Such was the case with Sayyed Mohammad Hoseyn of Isfahan, who saved Eugene Boré as he was about to be set upon, if not worse, by irate Armenians because he wanted to convert them to Roman Catholicism, and spirited the misguided Frenchman away from Jolfa, hid him in his house in Isfahan and then took him in person to Kashan, so that he could escape via Enzeli.[100]

ENDOWMENTS

Endowments were a very important source of income for ulama either as *motavallis* (managers) or as *nazers* (trustees), and, in addition, they often had as their main purpose the financing of stipends for students and teachers as well as the maintenance of buildings (school, mosque, shrine, etc.). Around 1900 Majd al-Islam estimated that one- third of all cultivated land in Iran comprised religiously endowed lands or *owqaf*, and he was certain that the figure was at least 15 percent.[101] Grollman estimated the income from endowments in the 1860s at 2 million *tumans*.[102] Around the 1890s, the income reportedly was 4 million *tumans*, of which the state only directly controlled 12 percent or 0.5 million *tumans*.[103]

In some areas, endowments were large, such as in the Sabzavar area, where over 10 percent of the villages were endowments.[104] In the cities many of the bazaar shops, houses, baths, and caravanserais were also endowments, The Sepahsalar Mosque in Tehran, for example, which included a madrasa, a *maktab*, a hospital, a bathhouse, and nine villages, two baths, and 53 shops in the Tehran bazaar.[105] Endowments were not only villages and/or shops but often included, among other things, water shares, a share in a garden, a share in a water mill, and a share in a bathhouse. The uses of the endowments were various, including expenditures for the upkeep of pilgrims going to the Iraqi shrine cities and Mashhad; for *rowzeh-khvani* on the tenth of Moharram and/or on Friday nights; for the repair and illumination of a shrine or Hoseyniyeh on specific days; for tea and sugar for the audience of passion-play (*ta`ziyeh*) performances; for the construction of a bathhouse or its repair; for an ice house for the shrine's *hospitium*; or for the repair of a tomb.[106]

99. Greenfield 1904, 121; Gasteiger Chan 1881, 19; Dieulafoy 1888, 333. Sayyeds were also governors. Layard 1894, 201, 205; Polak 1865, vol. 1, 38; Dieulafoy 1888, 63.

100. Dieulafoy 1887, 309-10.

101. Majd al-Islam 1351, 169.

102. Von Grollman 1893, 213.

103. FO 60/581, Memorandum Sir Mortimer Durand (December 1895, Confi 6704), 26-27; Sheikholeslami 1975, 282; Migeod 1990, 152-53.

104. Greenfield 1904, 137.

105. E`temad al-Saltaneh 1306, 83.

106. Mehrabadi 1367, vol. 3, 645-46, 649, 651-52, 654.

Sometimes endowments benefited an entire group, such as one clan of Isfahani sayyeds, who had an income of 3,000 *tumans* per year from property in the Jarquyeh district.[107]

Of course, endowments dominated those areas where important shrines were located, such as Mashhad. Here, as in other centers of pilgrimage, the religious professionals managed the main economic activity of those towns, which was religion. In Mashhad, for example, in 1860 some 50,000 pilgrims visited the city, which was more than the entire city's population. This number of pilgrims, which had been consistent each year, was reduced by half in 1873 due to famine. However, by 1890 it is reported that the number of annual pilgrims had reached the 100,000 mark.[108] Other cities were not affected in the same way, but many less important centers of pilgrimage were also dominated by the economics of religion. This held true for Qom and to a lesser extent for smaller shrines such as in Shiraz (Shah-e Cheragh), Torbat-e Heydari, and Qazvin.[109] But wherever an important or less important *imam-zadeh* was buried, that site also had its share of visitors. Because the number of shrines in many parts of Iran are impressive, and the guardians of these shrines received gifts from the many local visitors, the total amount of money channeled to the religious class this way was significant. The situation in Baluchistan, where the people "are extremely superstitious, and resort largely to *ziyarat*s or shrines, and the custodians of such places derive no small profit from their visitors"[110] was typical for the rest of Qajar Iran.

These visitors gained spiritual satisfaction and in return left something tangible. Many brought votive offerings, which, if donated by the rich, could be very precious indeed.[111] Although many pilgrims ate at the shrine's public kitchen, most could afford to eat in town where they also sought lodging. The financial infusion was considerable, and much found its way directly to the shrine. Another source of large income came from deceased believers who wanted to be in good company at the time of resurrection and paid heavily for the privilege of being buried within the shrine's area. The price per grave varied from 20 to 200 or more *tumans*, "which is one of the perquisites of the motavalli."[112]

Not only dead religious leaders attracted visitors; the living ones also received throngs of visitors who either wanted to bask in their glory or wanted something more tangible. "The offerings in return for the oracular responses given by the Imam to the anxious enquiries of numerous pilgrims, form no small part of the perquisites of the attendant *mujtahid*s and mullas."[113]

107. E`temad al-Saltaneh 1357, 91.

108. Curzon 1892, vol. 1, 162-63; E`temad al-Saltaneh 1301-03, vol. 2, 31. For the situation in the 1960s see Maria Paola Pagnini Alberti, *Strutture Commerciale di una Citta di Pelligrinaggio: Mashhad* (Udine 1971)

109. Fraser 1825, 141. For example, the shrine at the village of Mashhad (Qom), the resting place of the *imam-zadeh* `Ali b. Baqer, had only 150 families. Nevertheless, the shrine had a *khadem-bashi* and the *panj-keshik* just like the shrine of Fatima in Qom itself, who were remunerated out of the endowments attached to the small shrine. Kermani 1396, 242.

110. Tate 1910, 228.

111. See for example in the case of Mashhad Mo'taman 1348, 341-57.

112. Fraser 1825, 455-56. The cost of a grave ranged from 1,000 *tuman*s in the *haram* proper to 2 *tuman*s at the gate of the new court yard, in addition to administrative fees. Gurney 1983, 140.

113. Adamec 1974, vol. 2, 475-76; for similar remarks see Goldsmid 1876, vol. 2, 364.

WHAT WAS THE MONEY WAS SPENT ON?

Though it is difficult to estimate the total financial power of the ulama, it has been estimated that around 1860 they disposed of 2 million *tumans* per year when the state budget was estimated at some 4 million *tumans*. Most of these funds (75 percent) were revenues from their own landed properties. When we add to this the transfer payments by the government and the mass of believers in the form of tithes, alms, and gifts, the total financial flow controlled by the ulama could be as high as 2.4 million *tumans* per year.[114]

It is impossible to estimate how much was spent on the personal establishments of the religious professionals and how much on religious activities *strictu sensu*. We lack a breakdown of such expenditures that would allow us to analyze the available data, and the flows to private households of ulama may also have been spent partly on religious activities rather than purely on everyday concerns. We therefore focus on the budget of the Imam Reza shrine at Mashhad to illustrate how the religious class distributed its revenues (Table 4.2).

According to the manager of the Imam Reza shrine, the revenues and expenditures in 1306/1885 were, respectively, 59,260 and 52,140 *tumans*. His non-aggregated, non-audited budget is conservative, because it does not show income, for example, from rice, vegetable oil, nuts, beans, and so on.[115] The expenditure pattern shows that salaries constituted the highest expense category (46%), followed by the costs of lighting, the kitchen, and the library (34%).

As to expenditures on personnel, the shrine of Imam Reza employed as many as 2,000 persons in 1889,[116] of which there were "some 20 mojtaheds or chief priests, and the same number of superior Shrine officials.[117] The largest share of the revenue went to these 40 people, for most of the rank-and-file servants either received no pay, or received very little money, or only grain for their support.[118]

Table 4.2. Income and Expenditures of the Imam Reza Shrine (in *riyals*)

Barley (*kharvar*)	Wheat (*kharvar*)	Cash (*riyal*)	Income or Expenditure
Income			
2,726	5,452	131,970	Agricultural property (23.7 percent)
7	15	102,144	Real estate (19.1 percent)
272	944	74,416	Khorasan *vaqf*s (14.0 percent)

114. Migeod 1990, 153 n. 9.

115. Mo'taman 1348, 364; the tax of 1,000 *tumans* levied on the endowments of the Mashhad shrine probably is the same as the expenditure for the robes of honor that were sent to court. Curzon 1892, vol. 2, 489.

116. Curzon 1892, vol. 1, 163; for the staffing of the Qom shrine see Fraser 1825, 456; for Mashhad-e Qali near Qom see Houtum-Schindler 1896, 88 n.

117. Adamec 1974, 2, 476.

118. Fraser 1825, 141.

Barley (*kharvar*)	**Wheat** (*kharvar*)	**Cash** (*riyal*)	**Income or Expenditure**
2	2	30,063	Iraq, Fars, Dar al-Marz *vaqfs* (5.5 percent)
		49,890	Burial fees, gifts (9.3 percent)
706	1,492	76,887	Special *vaqfs* (14.2 percent)
392	975	76,235	Last year's saldo (14.2 percent)
4,105	8,880	541,605	Total income (100 percent)
Expenditures			
		45,395	Cash purchases (8.8 percent)
		420	Cleaning
53	418	43,995	Gifts to ulama, pilgrims, poor (8.5 percent)
	387	177,931	Lighting, kitchen, hospital, library (34.2 percent)
816	1,710	95,652	Salaries for *motavallis*, *nazer*, cost of transportation grain (18.4 percent)
		12,964	Robes of honor for shah, crown prince, and others (2.4 percent)
606	3,513	127,656	Wages for staff (24.4 percent)
52	330	17,393	Pensions and stipends (3.3 percent)
1,527	6,358	521,406	Total expenditures (100 percent)

A large part of the salaries to staff, including the leading ulama, was represented by those hired to officiate over religious ceremonies and to teach at the shrine and its affiliated madrasas. In Mashhad, in the 1820s, there were 14 madrasas, each with its sources of funding, supporting between 15 to 90 mullahs each, for education was a major sector of economic activity that the religious professionals claimed as their own, a major source of income for them.[119] Higher education was funded mainly through legacies in which the donators had stipulated that a share of the endowment had to be used for stipends for students and professors or the upkeep of educational buildings. Primary education was usually financed through contributions from the parents and guardians of the children.

Controlling access to and the substance of education was a prime target of the religious establishment. The *Usuli* group of ulama had been able to gain control over "state religion" in Qajar Iran by exercising control over the teaching circles through the maintenance of a kind of oligopoly to influence the thinking of students as well as steer the *ejazeh* or authority to exercise *ejtehad* on those who thought the same way. Also, instructing their students to spread out over Iran and attain positions for themselves to advance the cause of *Usuli* orthodoxy further strengthened their religious and economic position. For these students, turned teachers, would locally dominate the school curriculum and religious

119. Fraser 1825, 456-59.

life and thus attract more funding that enabled them to better their position and that of orthodoxy.[120] This was one of the reasons why many conservative religious professionals opposed educational and judicial reforms; it affected them economically.[121]

Because the religious class depended on voluntary contributions, most of which went to leading ulama, the rank-and-file mullahs had to seek a patron who would be willing to give them support, business, and gainful employment. This implied, given scarce resources, that teaching and other jobs were not well paid. However, they hoped to supply better compensation in the future. "The elder moollahs receive no fixed pay from the medressas to which they are attached, and many receive nothing at all. Those who can afford it maintain themselves, and do the duty of giving instruction for the sake of the faith they profess, or rather gaining a name, [and] disciples and followers, and the consequent respect and riches to which they all aspire. The poorer moollahs, who cannot support themselves, have sometimes a small allowance from the extra revenues of the medressa, when the moolwullee, or director, can prevail upon himself to part with so much for the purpose. Pecuniary remuneration for tuition is seldom expected or received; but when a moollah has educated the children of a rich or a noble family, a provision of some description is generally made for him."[122]

The function of head professor or *modarres* of the most important madrasas, on the contrary, was very well endowed and bestowed upon important ulama.[123] Wealth, therefore, was the lifeblood of success for a teacher, for he then could attract a large number of students whom he provided with stipends. Also, given the competitive nature of religion, it provided him with a large following and allowed him to hire thugs or *luti*s, to protect his neighborhood and ward off strong-arm dissent. Both groups were used to send the scholar's message to those who unwilling to hear it.[124]

Therefore, in all major, and even in many smaller towns, there were seminaries (madrasa), which in many cases were well endowed with legacies and had established, remunerated teaching positions.[125] Because "a teacher is paid as much as a waiter,"[126] in some cases the wives of the mullahs also earned money by teaching female members of households.[127] Typically, these teaching positions were also endowed with funds to provide for the upkeep of students.[128]

120. Cole 1985; Amanat 1989, 39.

121. Majd al-Islam 1351, 166-67; in general, see Roshdiyeh 1362.

122. Fraser 1825, 464-65.

123. Tahvildar 1342, 66-67.

124. Floor 1981.

125. Fraser 1826, 85; Bassett 1887, 310; de Rochechouart 1867, 107; Häntzsche 1869, 440; Majd al-Islam 1351, 169-70; Binning 1857, 1, 283; E`temad al-Saltaneh 1294-96, vol. 1, 345; Adams 1900, 143; Brugsch 1862-63, 1, 217.

126. Sykes 1902, 205.

127. Brugsch 1862-63, vol. 1, 270.

128. In Tehran, half of the students of the Madraseh-ye Marvi received stipends to the annual amount of 464 *tuman*s. Rochechouart 1867, 111; see also Curzon 192, vol. 1, 493; E`temad al-Saltaneh 1301-03, vol. 2, 31; Ibid., vol. 3, 268; Polak 1865, vol. 1, 289; Binning 1857, vol. 1, 282; Frank 1926, 182, 189; Fasa'i 1314, vol. 2, 162; Höltzer 1354, 19; Bassett 1887, 310.

Apart from teaching, expenditures were also incurred for other spiritual activities such as various kinds of panegyrics (*rowzeh-khvani, nowheh-khvani, talqin-khvani*, and *maddahi*). This held for the big and small shrines as well as for the more commonplace religious locations. It was not exceptional to see "the experienced moollahs who are employed as stage managers hurrying through the town on their mules, going from one takeah to another to give the benefit of their experience."[129] The shrine of Torbat, for example, just like the larger Mashhad one, was richly endowed for the maintenance of the mullahs, who day and night performed religious services beside the shrine. Kakh, near Torbat, had a shrine to the brother of Imam Reza, and a number of mullahs were employed to read the Qur'an near it.[130]

In addition to these spiritual activities, much of the expenditure was aimed at maintaining the physical aspects of religion. Fraser, in the 1820s, observed that one of the expenses was lights, which in the case of the Imam Reza shrine were paid from the revenues of a caravanserai.[131] The believers also needed physical sustenance, for many of them were poor and when on pilgrimage literally spent their life savings. To assist the poor, donators had granted endowments that had been set aside specifically for that purpose, in the form of public kitchens, and these probably existed in all centers of pilgrimage, both small and large, minor and major.[132]

The numbers of people fed in important religious centers such as the shrine of Imam Reza in Mashhad varied between 300 to 800 persons per day.[133] In 1860, Eastwick records the following description: "The public kitchen, supported by the revenues of the Imam's shrine, is in the avenue of Bala Khiyaban. Eight hundred persons are fed at this kitchen daily. I saw the dinner served up—there was a goodly mess for every two persons, that is, four breads, four chops, and a platter of rice. Any stranger may dine for twenty days."[134]

The ulama also fed the poor during periods of scarcity such as famine. Eastwick says that Hajji Mullah Rafi` distributed 2 *tumans* "to each individual of several thousand people in 1861 during the famine. He did not, however, tell me that this was money collected at his instance from the rich, and that he himself only gave his influence."[135] During the famine of 1873, some 500 persons were fed daily, which represents 1 percent of the population of Mashhad and was far below the percentage represented by the poor in that town.[136] Hajji Mohammad Baqer during the 1840s reportedly distributed about 240,000 *tumans*, but this was during a period when he tried to have political control over Isfahan.[137]

---

129. Watson 1866, 21.
130. Forbes 1844, 150 n, 153.
131. Fraser 1825, 141.
132. Brugsch 1862-63, vol. 1, 376 (*imamzadeh* in Hamadan).
133. Chanykov 1862, 99; Bassett 1887, 226; Vambery 1867, 323; Goldsmid 1876, vol. 2, 364.
134. Eastwick 1864, vol. 2, 213.
135. Eastwick 1864, vol. 1, 333.
136. Goldsmid 1876, vol. 1, 364.
137. Denis 1840, 140; Tonkabuni 1364, 109.

Religious festivals were another occasion to feed the poor, especially during the month of Moharram. Public representations of the passion plays (*ta`ziyeh*) were staged, at which, according to Wills, "the crowd are often regaled with sherbets by the personage at whose cost the tazzia is given, also pipes, and even coffee; and the amount expended in pipes, coffee, tea, etc. to the numerous guests is very considerable indeed."[138]

Some shrines also maintained hospitals for the poor. Eastwick visited "the new hospital, built by the Mashir [the Mashhad shrine's manager] for eighty sick persons. It is in a fine large garden, and the Mashir told me he intended to endow it with funds."[139] According to Abbot a hospital also existed at the shrine at Qom. "A small annual allowance was formerly made from the revenues of the country for the maintenance of this establishment," Abbot continues, "but at present, beyond the accommodation afforded by the bare apartments, there is no provision for distress and sickness."[140]

IN PURSUIT OF ECONOMIC GAIN

The religious class controlled significant financial resources that represented about 40 percent of the state's annual budget. This amount was high enough to enable the ulama to make a difference in the economy. In the following section we explore whether this occurred.

Given that the ulama had both political and economic influence, did they use it to improve the lot of their adherents, or did they behave as the secular elite did? One could argue that their role as champions of the poor had already distinguished them from the rest of society. However, first, the ulama were never a monolithic bloc that acted as a united group working for a common social cause. Second, many ulama defended the government's position. Third, many ulama used the respect and influence accorded to them to further benefit their own personal financial interests.[141] This was facilitated by their access to the highest levels of government, which enabled them to protect their own and their relatives' property. For example, during the border delineation of Seistan, "the Saiads and the priestly families had not only been able to hold on to their property but even enlarge it. The superstitious fears of the rival Baluch claimants for supremacy enriched both of these classes."[142]

It is for these reasons that Hajj Sayyah, a late-nineteenth-century reformer, accused the ulama of stealing from the poor to get rich themselves.[143] Also, the author of Ibrahim Beg accused them of cheating the people, just as the governors did, and claimed

138. Wills 1882, 283. At *ta`ziyehs* "food is provided for the crowd by the patron of the Takeeah. The provision consists of large quantities of boiled rice." Bassett 1887, 306.

139. Eastwick 1864, vol. 2, 213; it still exists today, see Adamec 1974 2, 486; Mo'taman 1348, 404-14.

140. Eastwick 1864, vol. 2, 213; Abbott 1855, 9.

141. This influence could even take very banal forms like claiming exclusive rights on fish. Ferrier 1857, 111-12.

142. Tate 1909, 22.

143. Sayyah 1346, 21-22.

that they respected wealth more than piety and true learning, for they were only engaged in casuistry.[144] Greenfield also notes that wealthy religious professionals usurped the rights of the co-proprietors of villages and neighboring lands along with other abuse of authority, for personal gain.[145]

The growing burden on the population was *inter alia* due to the growth of the number of high-ranking ulama. For this meant an intensified competition for the same amount of money that did not necessarily grow. Whereas in the first decade of the nineteenth century,[146] Malcolm knew of only five *mojtaheds*, there were hundreds by the end of the century. This fierce competition for scarce funds, which had grown over time, was reinforced by high inflation after 1880 and the depreciation of the Iranian currency and consequently the erosion of everybody's purchasing power, including that of the religious class. After 1871 the gold-silver ratio changed dramatically and dropped 30 percent between 1871 and 1889, and a further 50 percent by 1898, when it stabilized. As a result Iran's trade, population, and currency suffered.[147]

That the ulama were not reluctant at all to associate themselves with the court also evidenced their need for money. They gladly accepted high sounding titles, participated in New Year's and other official ceremonies, and high ranking ulama paid their respect to the shah when visiting Tehran.[148] In general, the ulama flocked to receive high-ranking government officials - this is clear, for example, in Nezam Mafi's memoirs. In fact, Mafi mentions very few who refused to associate at all with them, such as Mullah Qorban `Ali *mojtahed* in Kashan. The usual phrase he uses is "all the ulama" or "groups of ulama," the mullahs and others, who came to welcome him.[149] Also, in other ways, the religious professionals tried to improve their financial position. They were willing, for a price, to support government policy or to be silent when others criticized the government. A number of ulama in 1321/1903 each received 250 to 500 *tumans* to remain quiet.[150] There were also religious professionals who were accused of having accepted money from the British to advance their cause in Iran.[151] The ulama, to make money, at times would declare an important government official an infidel, and then, for a big payoff, would repeal their judgment and even visit his home.[152]

The religious class controlled vast landed properties. However, the peasants on these lands were not better treated than on land owned by secular landlords. According to Forbes, "this village is now the property of the Hazrat Imam [the shrine of the Imam Riza

144. Ibrahim Beg 1903, 182-84, 230, 237; see also Adamiyat 1363, 39; Majd al-Islam 1351, 169-70.

145. Greenfield 1904, 130.

146. Arjomand 1984, 246; Tahvildar 1342, 66; Dowlatabadi 1336, vol. 1, 23-24.

147. Lorini 1900.

148. Sheikholeslami 1975, 123.

149. Mafi 1361, vol. 1, 16, 23-24, 71-72, 82, 87, 112, 144, 153, 155, 233, 245, 275-76, 284; Ibid., vol. 2, 402; Sirjani 1361, 787; Ghaffari, 25, 27, 37, 43. Many accepted titles and gifts from the shah. Afzal al-Molk 1361, 433; Sirjani 1361, 39, 42, 49, 159, 269, 270, 285, 425, 521.

150. Moghith al-Saltaneh 1362, 83; E`temad al-Saltaneh 1345, 1002.

151. Ra'in 2536, 48-49, 96, 100, 103, 180; Adamiyat 1334, 421-22.

152. E`temad al-Saltaneh 1357, 280; Mafi 1361, vol. 1, 204.

in Mashhad], but the rapacity of the priesthood is more ruinous than the violence of their temporal proprietors."[153] Despite the fact that the ulama pretended to be independent of the government, when they needed the state to protect their own landed interests they exerted their influence to do so.[154] The same held for the usurpation of property by religious professionals, often in league with government officials.[155]

Rich religious professionals were also in league with other wealthy landowners, especially government officials and merchants, who like them had invested heavily in land, to speculate with the price of bread or meat in the cities.[156] A particularly well known case was the bread ring organized by one of the leading religious professionals in Tabriz, the well-known and very wealthy *mojtahed* Nezam al-Ulama. The governor who could not break this bread ring, because of the influence of the ulama involved, organized a bread riot that resulted in an attack on the Nezam al-Ulama's house on August 24, 1898. The mob plundered his house and that of five sayyeds, who had killed a few people defending the Nezam al-Ulama's house. The *mojtahed* had to flee the city, which despite all this still had to wait some time before the price of bread dropped.[157] According to the British Consulate in Ishahan, the mullahs' role in bread rings was facilitated when locusts arrived and the Iranian peasant, "led by his Moollahs, who are chiefly the great holders of the stores of grain in the place, and do not regard this advent of the locust as an unmixed evil, says it is the Divine will, and that Providence will provide the remedy."[158] Mirza Javad Aqa, the *mojtahed* of Tabriz, who was not only rich, but also greedy, persisted in pursuing his private interests.[159] When the Russian road from Rasht to Tehran was planned, he publicly agitated against it in 1895. According to Gordon, "He saw that the new road was likely to draw away some of the Tabriz traffic, he set himself the task of stirring up the Moullas of Resht to resent, on religious grounds, the extended intrusion of Europeans into their town. The pretence of zeal in the cause was poor, because the Resht Moullas are themselves interested in local prosperity, and the agitation failed."[160]

Malversation was another way through which members of the religious class enriched themselves. Some observers argue that the endowment revenues were rarely used for their dedicated purpose, which is borne out by the many instances of abuse of endowment funds. The perpetrators all went scot-free because of their social position. As a result

---

153. Forbes 1844, 149-50.

154. Brydges-Jones 1836, 304.

155. Sirjani 1361, 548, 577; Majd al-Islam 1350, vol. 1, 55; Tonkabuni 1364,20; Nader Mirza 1323, 118; sometimes the state opposed these activities for local political reasons. E`temad al-Saltaneh 1345, 1001-02.

156. Polak 1865, vol. 1, 325-26; Greenfield 1904, 130-31; see chapter two supra. On the formation of bread and meat rings see Floor 1983 a, 199-227.

157. Greenfield 1904, 131; Gordon 1895, 24; Floor 1983 a. In 1905, there was a grain ring once again in Tabriz, the leaders of which were the *Imam-Jom`eh* and Sa`d al-Molk, the mayor, while it was believed that the crown prince was their sleeping partner. Bratislaw 1923, p. 53.

158. DCR 1662, 6.

159. E`temad al-Saltaneh 1345, 1001.

160. Gordon 1895, 24.

shrines and mosques were not repaired and *tollab* did not get their stipends.[161] Another contemporary observer writes about property of an owner who died without heirs that such property "according to law goes to the poor, but unfortunately it has to be done through a medium, and that medium is the mullah. He promptly pockets the property and gives it supposed value (valued, mark you, by himself) to the poor. We can imagine what a large percentage the poor receive of that property."[162] Finally, when they could, the important ulama, among whom was Aqa Najafi, one of the richest men in Iran, paid either no taxes or hardly any at all.[163]

DISCUSSION

Should we conclude from this that all ulama were mercenary and only bent on personal gain? Majd al-Islam, who is critical of many leading ulama, points out that there were many sincere and pious religious leaders.[164] I agree, but have to conclude that the pious ulama were not active in trying to improve the lot of the population. In general, the economic behavior of the ulama did not differ significantly from that of the secular elite. Religious professionals were not the only ones who usurped landed property, exploited the poor, and misused or usurped other people's property. If anything, the religious class was representative of the society in which it lived. However, what I also emphasize is that the ulama had no special economic agenda. They, as a class, were not interested in changing the inequity that existed in Iran, because they were neither revolutionaries nor social reformers. They saw their economic role as limited to the prevention of some forms of oppression—either high taxation or unjust official behavior, They never questioned their own role and behavior as landlords, *motavallis*, real estate owners, taxpayers, or moneylenders as symptoms of the existing inequities.

This ignorance of the link between the level of taxation and their own demand for money proceeded from their strong belief that whatever the ulama did was good, because it was guided by religion or motivated by religious purposes. This ironic dilemma is nicely captured by an event in 1884 when taxes were raised and the Minister of Finance inquired what the "people" [ulama] thought about this. One of the replies from the tax official in Semnan was: "Still some banal and insipid ulama, seeking the support of the feebleminded multitude, consider tax collection haram [unlawful], although it is only thanks to the shah's charity, may we be sacrificed to him, that their lives, properties and honors are safe and secure. The taxes collected are spent on their own allowances, pensions, and comfort, and yet they consider the Shah an oppressing tyrant and the property and honor of great men of the state as common property. They never paid the original taxes without much complaining save now that the taxes are in creased."[165]

161. Sirjani 1361, 705; Majd al-Islam 1351, 169-70; Curzon 1892, vol. 2, 163; Forbes 1844, 153; Hume-Griffith 1909, 114; Mehrabadi 1367, vol. 3, 643-44, 646.

162. Hume-Griffith 1909, 114; Polak 1865, vol. 1, 325-26.

163. Sirjani 1361, 527-28, 531-32; Majd al-Islam 1350, vol. 2, 335.

164. Majd al-Islam 1351, 171.

165. Sheikholeslami 1975, 119.

For similar reasons the religious professionals had neither a positive nor a consistent economic policy message. The cultivation of tobacco is a case in point. Whatever the ulama's reason for opposing the Tobacco Regie, it was not necessarily in the economic interest of the tobacco-cultivating peasant. Their opposition, which was by no means universal,[166] was for many ulama more a knee-jerk xenophobic reaction than a rational economic one, though some believed it would hurt their own economic interests. Once the Tobacco Regie had been repealed in 1891 and the country had become indebted to foreigners (the exact opposite of what the ulama had wanted), the right to export tobacco was sold to a Turkish company. And when this company reduced its annual payment to the shah in 1894, the latter immediately placed a tax of 4 *qrans* per bag on the cultivator, to make up for his loss. The peasants, stating that it would not pay them to sow tobacco, appealed to the ulama, but they were not interested to interfere.[167] The reason was the personal interest of some of the ulama. Gordon explains that the *Société de Tombac* had "bought the monopoly of tobacco export had trouble with a Persian combination, who want to buy from cultivators and sell to the foreign agents. A prominent mullah was involved in this business, which was at variance with the principles on which the ulama had declared the original concession to be unlawful."[168] In 1895 and 1896, the ulama interfered when purchasers of the *Société* did not want to buy old tobacco that was unfit for export. They, without inquiry, ordered that all tobacco had to be bought and ordered all the workshops and storehouses closed. The agent of the Turkish company was beaten up. As a result, the *Société* agreed to buy more of the unfit tobacco but ended up being forced to buy it all. The government then stepped in and caused the ulama to rescind their orders.[169] This interference by the ulama, in Isfahan in particular, continued, though it was contrary to what they had claimed to stand for. However, it served their short-term financial interests. Forcing the *Société* to buy their inferior tobacco, however, would only hurt the long-term market prospects of the Iranian commodity in the world market.

Thus, the interventions of the ulama, which were motivated partly out of concern for the Iranian peasant, artisan, and merchant, did not help them and actually often hurt them. The ulama may have been superior religious scholars, but they had neither a comparative advantage in the field of trade nor a long-term economic program. They behaved in the same way in the pursuit of their own commercial and/or financial interests, which focused on short-term gain; moral conviction may have been enough justification for them. The leading ulama who interfered in the market were not personally affected by the results of their behavior. Not only did they and their dependents have sufficient wealth to weather negative reactions by the international market, but they also could recoup themselves, just like the secular elite, through political means to make up for economic loss. What they did not want, but could not realize, was that their flock, whom they wanted to protect, had to foot the bill of their costly, ill-advised, and irrelevant economic interventions. Also, interference was intermittent and incidental, reactive rather than pro-active, because the reli-

166. See, e.g., Majd al-Islam 1351, 143-44 (Isfahan); Stroeva 1963, 171-74 (Tabriz, Mashhad).

167. DCR 1662 (1894-95), 9.

168. Gordon 1895, 29-30.

169. DCR 2260 (1897-99), 9; DCR 1953 (1895-96), 5.

gious professionals, as a group, had neither a policy nor a strategy to deal with economic problems. Beyond that, as a group, the religious professionals shared little beyond religion, and even in that area there was sometimes fierce local infighting. The ulama were too insular and ignorant of the modern and fast-changing world to be effective and helpful agents of change. They were convinced, incorrectly, that by identifying the problem and giving their verdict, the problem would be solved.

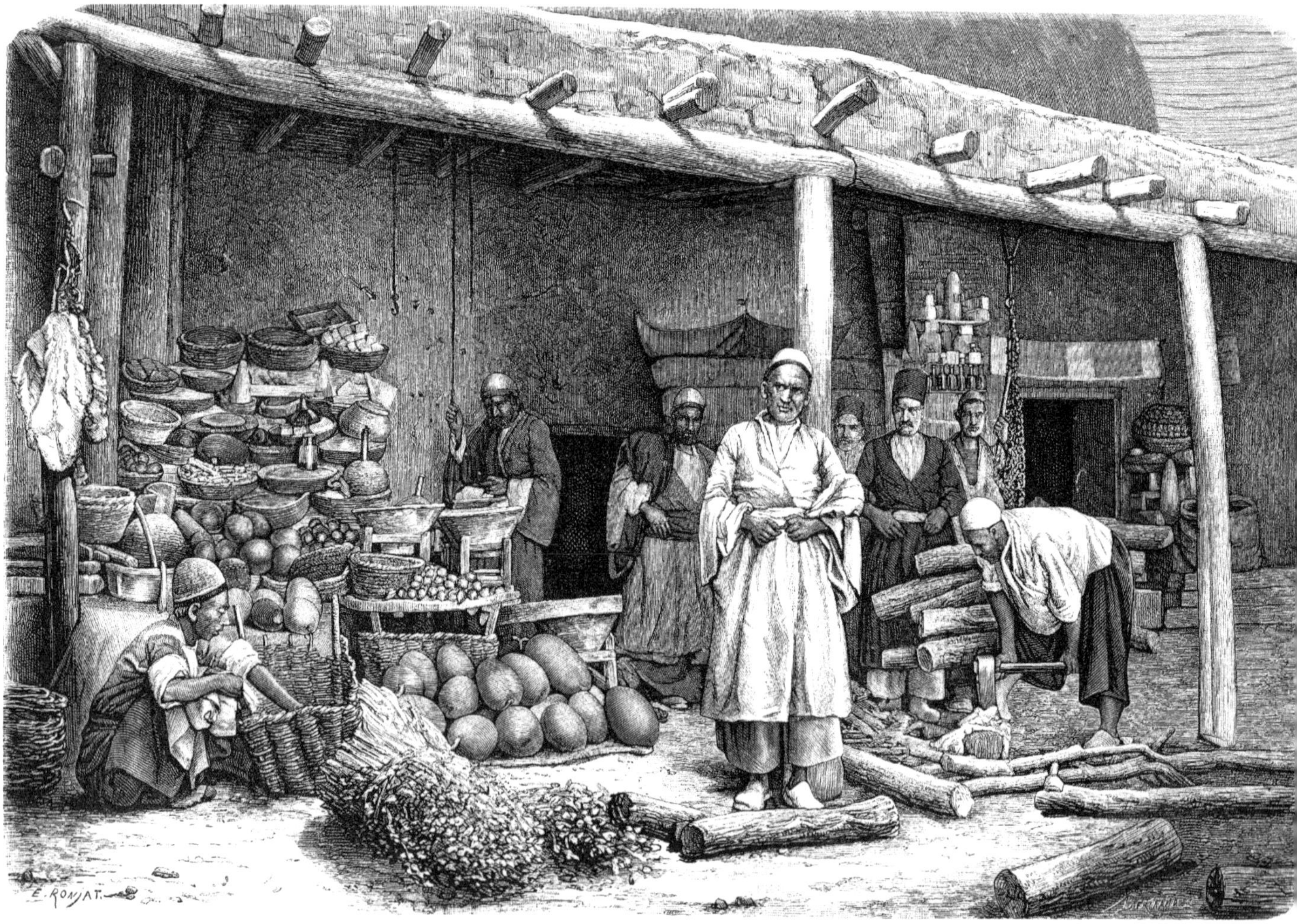

CHAPTER SIX

The Guilds in Qajar Iran

I. INTRODUCTION

Traditional artisanal industry formed the major component in Iran's urban economic life throughout its history down to the 20th century.[1] The major centers of traditional Iranian industry were: Isfahan, Kashan, Yazd, Kerman, Shiraz, Hamadan, and Tabriz. In addition, secondary towns such as Mashhad, Rasht, and Qom produced certain specific goods.[2] The main industry was the textile industry and its ancillaries, which represented 20-30 percent of the industrial labor force in many towns.[3] Other important activities were construction, metalworking, leather working and food processing crafts. The kind of 'industrial mix' a city displayed was very much determined by its natural resource endowment. "For nowhere as much as in Persia are certain industries as firmly tied to individual towns."[4] Due to bad road network transport was mainly limited to high unit value products. This meant that most raw materials rarely were transported over long distances, silk and cotton being major exceptions.[5]

Industrial activities were technically organized along different lines. Most activities took place in enterprises employing less than 10 persons both in terms of employment as well as output.[6] These were family operated shops, crafts and trades where one master employs a few journeymen and boys. As Braudel has pointed out the Bourgin model for

---

1. Floor 1984 b; Floor 1985 a; Floor 1991.
2. Abbot 1855, 1-78; FO 60/165; Polak vol. 2, 186; AP 30 (2896) LXIII 1859, 60-61.
3. Floor 1999 b, chapter one.
4. Polak, vol. 2, p. 166.
5. About transportation cost see Clawson 1993.
6. These small establishments still employ most of the labor force to-day. Karshenas, Massoud. *Oil, state and industrialization in Iran.* (Cambridge 1990), p. 178-9, 270-5; see also ILO, *Employment and Income Policies for Iran.* (Geneva 1973), p. 51, table 7.

the classification of pre-industrial activities is also applicable outside Europe. This model distinguishes four types of 'industrial' activities, to wit:

a. the small, mostly, family operated workshop which was the most frequent industrial activity that one found in Qajar Iranian cities. These workshops usually had one master with 2-3 journeymen and some young unskilled helpers. There was neither division of labor nor specialization in process. All parts of a product were made inside the workshop and put together to make a final product. Often the workshop was not only the site of production, but also the location of sale of the product. In Isfahan, in the 1850s, there were many hundreds of workshops located in the covered bazaars, the total length of which was 3 miles.

b. scattered, but interconnected, workshops. Here there was specialization of process, and one artisan produced only an intermediate product, for another artisan, the last one in the production line would make the final product. The textile industry is a good example of this type of workshop. After the wool (or cotton or silk) had been purchased, it was carded, then it was spun, then it was washed, then it was dyed, then it was woven. Finally, the cloth would get a final processing such as printing or tailoring.

c. concentrated manufactories were less prevailing in Iran. This type of manufacture was basically a large building where all parts of the production process and its labor force was brought together. This allowed an increase of productivity and better quality control. Also, the use of mechanical devices such as water or animal operated mills/machinery was possible. This applied, for example, to the leather industry where all processes were as a rule carried out in the same workshops.

d. finally, factories that were equipped with machinery, that allowed even higher productivity and better quality control than the previous industrial categories. In fact, it allowed, comparatively speaking, mass production of the final product. As of the 1850s we see that a number of such factories were established in Qajar Iran.[7]

These four types of industrial categories occurred simultaneously in Qajar Iran, although the first two were the oldest forms and the fourth category represented a very recent innovation as of the 1850s. The technologies used by these workshops and manufactories, in general, were primitive and did not require major training or skills. This, on the one hand, explained the low wage level in these industries, which impeded the substitution of labor by capital. On the other hand, it facilitated the use of the large pool of

7. Gilbar 1983, 197; Issawi 1971, 298-99, 303; Floor 1991; Floor 2009 a.

unskilled and casual labor that was available in most Iranian cities. Because the skill levels did not differ that much from that available in the rural areas rural labor in search of extra seasonal income could easily fit in these industrial activities. Because of these conditions (low investment level, low skills level) investors were quick to finance in profitable activities such as weaving, if the market prospects were right, but they as easily disinvested when the market was in a slump.[8]

The middle-class, i.e., the trade and craftsmen, who were organized in guilds (*asnaf*), lived close to the bazaar, the place of their daily work. The guilds, which served as the mechanism for solving inter- and intra-guild problems, as a buffer against and bargaining instrument with the government, as well as a revenue raising body for the state. A number of local officials, such as the *kalantar* (city mayor), the *darugheh* (head of market police), and the *mohtaseb* (market inspector) exercised some measure of control over the guilds and economic life in general.[9] The mix of functions that such guilds could acquire varied with time and per guild. Price-fixing, quality control, controlling of weights and measures generally were not roles that guilds performed. Entry into the market was an area that was controlled, however, by the guilds. They were taxed as one body, and it was one of the tasks of the guild chief to distribute this fiscal burden in an equitable manner.[10]

But what were the guilds? Can we transpose this W. European term and concept to Iran, as has been done by many authors? Lambton, in her stimulating inaugural address "Islamic Society in Persia" sketched amongst other things the organization of the guilds in Iran. Although she made some interesting observations on the subject of guilds, these were but of a general nature.[11] Similarly, Migeod provides us with many details on artisans and traders in Qajar Iran in his very detailed dissertation, but he failed to put these data in their socio-historical context.[12] This is due to the fact that for his theoretical orientation Migeod had to rely on one-sided studies on Islamic guilds, studies which according to Baer "have not yet progressed beyond the initial stages."[13]

The same holds for the study of the guilds in Iran, which has hardly begun. Only a few studies have been published as yet on this subject, not all of which are satisfactory. There is a great need for further study, for there are many *lacunea* in our knowledge and some accounts are inaccurate. An example is Issawi's inclusion of part of a study by Kuznetsova in her "Economic History of Iran." This study indiscriminately uses material from the 17th and 19th century, as well as sources on Armenian, Georgian and Moslem guilds in the Russian Caucusus to present a picture of the guilds in Iran. The result is an unbalanced view, which does not present a picture of the guilds in Iran in the 19th century, as Issawi suggests.[14]

8. Vaziri 1346, 158, 168-9.
9. Floor 1971 a, 253-68; Ibid. 1971 b, 212-29; Ibid. 1980; Ibid. 1985 b, pp. 53-74.
10. See part V of this chapter.
11. Lambton 1954.
12. Migeod 1990.
13. Baer 1964, 1.
14. Issawi 1971, 285-92.

Many authors who write about Iran tell us that traders and artisans form guilds. They, however, always fail to define what they mean by this term, and implicitly assume that the reader knows what they mean. Even when authors feel the need for a definition, they do not formulate one themselves, but use what is known, for instance, about European guilds as a yardstick to establish the fact whether one has to do with a guild or not. In fact, whenever an author suspects the existence of some kind of corporate association[s] he designates it with the pass-partout term 'guild'. And even when, for example, Lambton divines that a certain group is not a guild, she still speaks of such a group as having a guild-organization.[15] It is unnecessary to say that defining our starting point is necessary.

The identification of *fotovvat* orders, which were spiritual organizations, with guilds, which were professional organizations, muddled the thinking of many scholars and obscured the issue.[16] A fine example is to be found in Meier's introduction to his translation of Mahjub's article on *sokhanvari* (rethorics). Meier states that the rhetoricians' guild "is a special guild, which seems to have originally been a kind of training center for 17 (according to others 44) professional guilds."[17] As I discuss this matter in detail in part V of this chapter, I will not discuss his statement here.

Finally, because scholars were too much pre-occupied with the uniqueness of Moslem patterns, they only saw the differences between Moslem guilds and those occurring outside the Moslem area, while ignoring those traits which both areas had in common.[18]

Although looking for differences between guilds in Europe and similar organizations in Islamic countries is a valid method (did not Pieter Geyl say: "it is the differences which matter"), I think that looking for which functions of guilds featured in all cultures and periods, and whether these are to be found in one's particular country or period of interest, is more promising. For, "strictly speaking, the unique can be established only in contrast to predetermined universal reference points."[19] Comparative sociology provides us with an important lead for such an approach. Sjoberg contends that pre-industrial society "everywhere display strikingly similar social and ecological structures; not necessarily in specific cultural content, but certainly in basic form,"[20] and the same holds for the guilds in those societies. He distinguishes the following functions of guilds, which he found are universal. Guilds in the first place have the monopoly of their particular occupation. Secondly, they have rules for the selection of membership. Thirdly, it is only by the guilds that personnel in their occupation are trained. Fourthly, they see to it that members maintain a certain standard of workmanship. Fifthly, guilds are an important channel to voice political demands of the artisans. Sixthly, guild members may assist each other in economic

15. Lambton 1954, 19.

16. Thorning 1913 was one of the first to have done so. Since then others have fallen into the same error, the foremost among them being Massignon 1920.

17. Meier and Gramlich 1961.

18. Lewis 1937, 20-37; Massignon 1927. See the excellent article by Stern 1970, 45-6, which debunks these earlier studies.

19. Sjoberg 1960, 5.

20. Sjoberg 1960, 5.

life by pooling resources. Seventhly, amongst guild members the idea of mutual welfare is strong. Eighthly, guilds have a religious and ceremonial function.[21]

Apart from these functions guilds display a few more aspects which are peculiar to them. I mean the election of their officers by their members; belonging to one branch of the urban economy; being taxed by the government as a corporate body. Taking this structural view of the guild phenomenon gives us a better possibility to determine what guilds in different cultural areas had in common, where they differed, or whether guilds were special for some historical periods only. To make this view operational I would like to define a guild as: a group of towns people engaged in the same occupation, who elect their own chief and officers, who pay guild taxes, this group having fiscal and administrative functions. These I contend are the minimum factors which determine whether we have to do with a guild or not. In addition this group may have social, economic, political and religious functions. The fiscal and administrative functions are ascribed functions; the other functions are acquired ones.

As I said above, guilds function in pre-industrial societies. Such a society is ruled by a small urban elite, and has a large illiterate agricultural mass and a small urban population. The government concerns itself mainly with (i) the maintenance of social-political control and the enforcement of law and order; (ii) the provision of a limited number public services, and (iii) the collection of taxes to be able to (i) and (ii).[22] In the economic sphere this means that the government had to interfere in economic life for several reasons. To carry out public services and construct public buildings, the government provided the planning and organizations, often also the money by way of taxation, while it demanded the population to provide the manpower. This mostly resulted in corvées, which were also a kind of taxation. Further to maintain order and security and to strengthen the stability of its rule the government had to head off social unrest by insuring such important economic facilities as the sufficiency of bread, fuel, meat, fodder, and the like. The government based its right to obedience and the legitimacy of its rule on the fact that it reigned in accordance with the divine laws and the fact that it maintained justice and order. Therefore, on the moral side of its rule the government had to guard the rights of the poor against the wiles of the rich. In Islamic Iran, the symbol of government's role in this respect was the overseer of the markets and public morals, the *mohtaseb*.[23] It cannot be too often stressed that according to Moslem law and tradition it was the government's right and duty to guard and guide the people's interests, also in economic life.

Because of the lack of literate and other trained persons among the elite, the latter had to fall back on qualified persons among the non-elite part of the population. Handbooks on market supervision sometimes recommend the appointment of a "reliable, trustworthy man from their own profession."[24] That such recommendations were only given for some crafts does not mean that such practices were restricted. For these books only refer to a theoretical situation, while the actual practice was quite different. To stream-

21. Sjoberg 1960, 244-52.
22. Sjoberg 1960, 190-94.
23. On the *mohtaseb* see Floor 1971 c, 222; Floor 1980; Floor 1985 b.
24. Stern 1970, 42-43, especially note 27.

line the administration and get an efficient execution of its rules, the government had to get the population or groups to co-operate with it. The best way to do this was to single out groups among the population, which could be clearly distinguished from other groups, and which had problems and interests characteristic for one group only. The government treated these groups each as a corporate body, i.e., the government did not treat with individuals of such a group in fiscal and other matters, but with the leaders of this group only. While setting certain limitations the government allowed these groups to regulate their own internal affairs, without relinquishing its legitimate rights to interfere in, or control these activities. This could well mean that a guild was controlled by a government overseer, while at the same time the internal matters were completely their own affair. For example, even though police handbooks do not mention rigid rules on apprenticeship and admission to guilds, this does not mean that such rules did not exist.[25] The fact that police handbooks are not concerned with these matters is significant too. For it means that the government either left these matters to the guilds on purpose, or was not interested in these matters, as is clear in later periods. As far as the government was concerned goods had to have a certain standard for which it had laid down rules; it was up to the guilds to make their products according to these rules. The government in the person of the *mohtaseb* and other overseers controlled the execution of these rules. Thus it is the government rather than the artisans and traders which brings the guilds into being. The tendency of pre-industrial government to foster occupational groups accorded with the special interests of these groups, and thus their formation was facilitated.

Guilds then grew out of corporate bodies of craftsmen, created by the government for fiscal and administrative purposes. These corporate bodies of artisans gradually began to distinguish themselves from other similar corporate groups. In fact, they differed already from such groups as tribes and villagers by the fact that they were a branch of the urban economy. In addition to the fact that they choose their own chief and officers, the artisinal corporate bodies were taxed in a different way from all other economic groups in the city. They were the only ones who paid guild taxes, i.e., were taxed as a group. Other groups, such as the whole-sale merchants (*tojjar*), were not, neither were such groups as ulama and entertainers.[26] It is only when corporate bodies of urban economic groups elect their own officers and pay taxes, not as individuals, but as a group, that we may speak about such a group being a guild. These are, as I have mentioned above, the minimum factors which mark off guilds from other corporate groups. Apart from these minimum factors guilds could acquire a certain set of functions which made them into full-fledged guilds. It is easy to imagine that the common interests, the common deliberations about taxes, mostly in their own habitual coffee-houses (*patuq*), and the concentration in the same part of the bazaar, created a kind of social bond. The strongest social spirit was to be found among those parts of guilds which were composed of an (ethnic) group. Here probably, the mutual assistance prevailed stronger than among other guilds. It is also likely that when a strong social bond amongst guild members existed, this could lead to common action for higher prices and to restrictions towards newcomers.

25. Goitein 1966, 267ff.

26. Floor 1999 a. chapter nine. On the entertainers see Floor 1971 a and in particular Floor 2005.

Occupation with the height of the taxes and prices had to lead towards some sort of political action. For were these not subject to, sometimes lengthy, negotiations with the local government? It was then the bargaining power of the guilds, in other words their political power, which decided the issues in their favor or not. The fact that we do not always find all these functions represented by Moslem guilds did not mean that these were not guilds. For these functions one might acquire, and some did not. The number of these functions varied per guild and per period, likewise the importance and the intensity of these functions. One could say that the increase in the number of acquired functions is an indication for the strength and vitality of a guild. I contend that terms like *senf* or *hirfah* may be translated as guild, if the groups denoted by these terms satisfy the criteria of the minimum factors mentioned above. The fact that "the powers of the medieval guilds in Europe in controlling the industry were much wider than those of Islamic corporations," as Gibb has it[27] is not a very convincing reason not to do so. Nobody is going to call the trade unions of the 19th century something else than trade union, just because their powers of controlling industry were much less than those of the 20th century trade unions! One might, however, contend that when European guilds acquired a certain degree of autonomy vis à vis the government, and even wielded the power of city government, these groups ceased to be guilds and became a category apart. But then the two, Islamic guilds and European municipal institution, cannot be compared anymore.

Guilds then are the natural outcome of pre-industrial society's structure. It is, therefore, my opinion that such theories as "guilds in Islamic Iran are of Sassanian origin, or of Carmatian or `*aqila* system origin" are spurious and not based on facts. The evidence adduced to prove that guilds existed in Sassanian Iran is only guess work. For nothing is said about the functions of the chiefs of trades and crafts who are mentioned in the texts. These officers were most likely government officials.[28] The theories of Massignon have been dealt with by several authors so there is no need to repeat their criticism.[29] As Lambton did not put forward her idea of the `*aqila* system being the origin of Islamic guilds very seriously, we leave it that way.[30]

As to Islamic Iran we have no evidence that guilds existed before the 14th century. Nezam al-Molk mentions a chief of the bakers in the 11th century, but he unfortunately gives no indication of the function of this chief. It is interesting to read though, that this chief was trampled to death by elephants, because the bakers in Ghazna wanted to fix higher prices for bread. This means that we have here a good example of an articulated group interest, for which the representative of that group was put to death as an example to and punishment of the group as a whole.[31] Although very tempting, the evidence is not conclusive to say that we really have a guild here.

It appears that on the eve of the Mongol invasion certain crafts in Samarqand, Isfidjab, and Merv practiced the idea of mutual assistance (*nusra, yatanasaruna*). However,

27. Gibb & Bowen 1956, vol. 1, 281, note 5.
28. Pigulevskaia 1346, vol. 1, 141-144.
29. Stern 1970; Cahen 1970.
30. Lambton 1954, 20.
31. Nizam al-Molk 1960, 48.

beyond this fact nothing is known about this institution.[32] It seems that during the Middle Ages artisan life flourished in Iran, for a great body of literature, known as *shahr-e ashub*, praises the traders and craftsmen. The first of these poems date from the 13th century.[33] But although we get interesting information on the existence of a great many crafts and trades, the existence of such a diversity of occupations does not necessarily mean the presence of guilds.[34]

In the 13th century Ghazan Khan appointed overseers (*amin*) over certain crafts, who were obliged to deliver certain quotum of arms.[35] This information is not without interest. It shows that at least certain crafts were not just amorphous bodies of craftsmen, but formed clearly separate, and from each other distinguishable groups. Moreover, having been singled out by the government, this means that these groups had at least the ascribed functions of the guilds already. In discussions about guilds this fact is often dismissed as not to the point, but I think that this either means that we have here the beginnings of a guild or that these groups already formed guilds, having some of the acquired functions. The fact that certain guilds had government overseers did not mean that these groups did not form guilds, as is clear from the situation in 17th century Iran. So in this and similar cases the same may have been the case. Yet, we do not have other facts to substantiate this supposition, and it is on facts rather than on conjecture that we have to base our views.

Ibn Battutta, in the 14th century, leaves no doubt about the fact that guilds existed in Iran, flourishing in Isfahan and Shiraz. The corporations knew a spirited social life, for each guild or individual member tried to outdo the other in prowess and pomp.

> The sultan Abu Ishaq had at one time conceived the ambition to build a vaulted palace like the Aywan Kisra and ordered the inhabitants of Shiraz to undertake the digging of its foundations. They set to work on this, each corporation of artisans rivaling every other, and carried their rivalry to such lengths that they made baskets of leather to carry the earth and covered them with lengths of embroidered silk. They did the same with panniers and sacks on the donkeys, and some made mattock of silver and lit quantities of candles. When they were digging they would put on their best garments and fasten silk aprons around their waists, while the sultan would watch their work from a balcony he had (there).[36]

It is true that we still do not know a great many things about these groups, but we know that they were subject to corvées, an important feature of guilds. Moreover Ibn Battutta mentions that in Isfahan: "the members of each craft appoint one of their members

32. Cahen 1970, 59.

33. Ma`ani 1347/1968.

34. This body of literature has been studied by Dr. Reza Qasemi for material on artisans and craftsmen. I have been unable to consult his unpublished dissertation *Pisheh va Pishehvaran dar Iran*. Tehran University 1347/1968, literary faculty.

35. Rashid al-Din 1940, 336-39.

36. Ibn Battutta 1962, vol. 2, 310.

as headman over them, whom they call kilu."[37] Here we have another feature of the guilds, the chief elected by the guild members. Therefore, we may assume that here we have to do with guilds, of which we only know that they had a strong social function, served as fiscal units, and that they elected their own chief. However, we are not informed about their internal organization, and what the function of the *kilu* exactly entailed.

Information on the guilds in the 16-18th century is somewhat more copious. Under the Safavids each trade formed a guild headed by a chief elected by the guild members. The guild heads did not have a shop themselves, but received a salary paid by the guild. Ideally one of the oldest and trust-worthiest masters of the guild would be chosen as guild head, in practice, however, this function was often hereditary. The guild head was confirmed in his function by the *kalantar*, who drew up a *ta`liqeh* (certificate) and gave him a robe of honor after the guild head had presented himself with his official election document, which was legalized by the *naqib*, the assistant of the *kalantar*.[38] Guild leaders had some judicial powers in guild matters, especially if these concerned disputes among guild members. Complaints by clients could also be taken up with the guild leader. This field, however, was also controlled by the *mohtaseb*. The guild leaders in those guilds who were subject to corvées were more powerful than others, for they decided who and to what extent had to contribute to the corvées. Opposition was punished by contribution to imaginary corvées.[39] Everyone wishing to start a shop addressed himself to the guild leader, stating his name and address, which were registered. If no objections existed against the candidate he was allowed to start working in exchange for the payment of a small sum. The only limitation which could be made was that in several trades a certain distance had to be kept between the shops, outside the area exclusively occupied by the guild.[40]

As to fiscal purposes the guilds were put under the orders of the *kalantar* and *naqib* and for the corvées under the *nazer-e boyutat* (steward of the royal household). Each year the *kalantar* appointed someone to convene all guild leaders in the house of the *naqib*. Here they discussed the *bonicheh* or quota to be paid by each guild. This procedure, called *bonicheh bandi*, took place every first quarter of the year. When the quotas were fixed the *naqib* wrote these on a roll, sealed it and entrusted it to the *kalantar*'s charge, whose duty it was to collect the guild taxes. It was he who decided the installments in which the *bonicheh* had to be paid. The *bonicheh* having been fixed the guild members assembled to allot to each master (*ostad*) his share of the burden. As base for the contribution the annual income was taken. However, ample opportunity existed for favoritism and fraud, especially in those guilds which had to do corvées. Those guilds as the shoemakers and leather makers, who were exempt from corvées, had to pay a lump sum in stead, known as *kharj-e padeshah*. It appears that some guilds were exclusively subject to corvées and did

37. Ibn Battutta 1962, vol. 2, 295. In Shiraz the head of the coppersmiths (*saffar*) was also called *kelu*. Ebn Bazzaz 1373, 803.

38. Tadhkirat al-Muluk 1943, 81, 83; Chardin 1811, vol. 6, 119.

39. Chardin 1811, vol. 6, 119-124.

40. Chardin 1811, vol. 4, 93.

not pay other taxes. All the same the tax burden weighed heavier on these guilds than for those who paid in money.[41]

If the shah wanted some work done it was the *nazer-e boyutat* who ordered the leaders of the guilds concerned to do the job. Corvées were an oppressive burden, in particular for the masons. The guild leaders together with the guild elders (*rish safid*) decided who had to contribute to the corvées. Those guilds who did not want to do the corvées could buy off this obligation for a year with the payment of a lump sum.[42]

In addition to the guild tax and the corvées guilds had to pay the expenses incurred by visits of ambassadors of foreign nations. This extra burden was known as *havadeth*.[43] The revenue from the guilds in Isfahan (guild tax and *havadeth*) yielded 3,000 *tumans* yearly.[44]

Under the Safavids the ascribed functions of the guilds appear to have received special attention. The strict supervision over taxation by the *kalantar*, over corvées by the *nazer*, was the result of a strong government policy. Outside the guilds a group of privileged artisans worked in the 32 royal workshops, which each had their own chief. These chiefs (*-bashi*), along with other court officials, were put in charge of a certain number of guilds. For example, the *zargar-bashi* (chief of the gold-smiths) controlled all jewelers and goldsmiths of Isfahan.[45] Thus it appears that a certain number, may be 32, of main guilds existed.[46]

The acquired functions of the guilds in Safavid Iran were weakly developed. In fact, the guilds were loosely organized. It appears that they only assembled a few times per year, once to fix the *bonicheh*, the other times to discuss problems pertaining to their other interests. Chardin, however, asserts that the guilds never convened.[47] This indicates that guild life was very inconspicuous, for else this shrewd observer certainly would have noticed it. That the guilds were not powerful is indicated by their inability to fix minimum prices for their products, by the fact that they did not control the standard of workmanship of their members, nor had a rigid apprenticeship system. The period of apprenticeship differed per guild; in fact no system existed. Someone eager to learn a trade was apprenticed by his parents to a master, who paid him a salary which rose as his experience increased. Both sides could make an end to their relationship, for no contractual obligations existed between master and apprentice.[48]

As far as prices were concerned the guild leaders, convened by the *mohtaseb*, would draw up a price list (*tas`ir-e ajnas*) together with the *mohtaseb* at the beginning of each month. Public criers (*jarchi*) would make public the new list; the *mohtaseb* supervised the

---

41. Chardin 1811, vol. 4, 95; vol. 5, 405; Tadhkirat al-Muluk 1943, 81-83.
42. Tadhkirat al-Muluk 1943, 48, 181; Chardin 1811, vol. 6, 120.
43. Du Mans 1890, 30.
44. Tadhkirat al-Muluk 1943, 65.
45. Tadhkirat al-Muluk 1943, 129, see also 88, 89, 90, 96, 100.
46. See below part IV.
47. Chardin 1811, vol. 4, 93, see, however, Tadhkirat al-Muluk 1943, 81.
48. Chardin 1811, vol. 4, 94-95.

execution of the list and punished defaulters.[49] Another session convened by the *nazer-e boyutat* (steward of the royal palace) was attended by the guild leaders, the vizier the workshops, the *mohtaseb* and the *mostowfi* of Isfahan to fix prices of goods which were bought by the chiefs of the royal workshops. This was done once a year; the prices were fixed in conformity with the interests of the *divan* (administration).

Although the above description is based on material which is valid only for the situation in Isfahan, we may assume that in other cities similar conditions prevailed. For it seems that in the provinces, in cities like Kashan and Kerman, guilds existed too.[50]

In the next sections I will query whether the characteristics which I have identified for guilds were also present in Qajar Iran.[51]

II. GENERAL ASPECTS OF THE GUILDS

"Amongst the merchants, artisans and shopkeepers in Persia it is customary for each trade to form a separate corporation under Ked Khoda, or chief, selected by themselves." This statement, made by a British Consul in 1886 is corroborated by many other sources.[52] The common term for guilds in the 19th and 20th century is *senf* (pl. *asnaf*), which is used both by Iranian and European sources.[53] Other terms which are used to denote the same group, such as *san`at, pisheh* and *hirfeh,* only mean craft.[54]

Now I have to define precisely what a guild is, for as we have seen above, many authors mistakenly call other groups than those of traders and craftsmen 'guilds' too. So as to avoid misunderstanding I state at the outset, that it is my thesis that other groups than traders and craftsmen do not form guilds.

I have now restricted the use of the term guilds to the groups of craftsmen and traders. But to prevent ambiguity over the meaning of "craftsmen and traders" I narrow down the possibilities by stating as my second thesis that merchants (*tojjar*) do not belong to this group.

Merchants form a group apart and do not constitute guilds, though one cannot deny a similar corporate element in their group. It is striking that merchants are nearly always mentioned apart from the guilds. During the royal audience (*Salam*) on *Nowruz* (New Year's day), for instance we find both groups making their appearance separately.[55]

This does not mean that trade guilds did not exist. On the contrary, a large percentage of the guilds were accounted for by traders. The solution of these contradictory

49. Chardin 1811, vol. 4, 79-80; Tadhkirat al-Muluk 1943, 66, 67, 83, 150.

50. Tadhkirat al-Muluk 1943, 48.

51. Tadhkirat al-Muluk 1943, 66.

52. FO 60-337, report of June 24, 1886; Orsolle 1885, 303. Bleibtreu 1894, 125, Greenfield 1904, 144, de Rochechouart 1867, 180, de Gobineau 1907b, 376. A French source, however, denies the existence of guilds in Qajar Iran. "There is no cooperation among artisans in Persia, because there are no guilds". de Fournoux 1887, 10.

53. De Gobineau 1907b, 376; Tahvildar 1342, 92 ff.; Zarrabi 1342, 242.

54. Forsat 1316, 499-501.

55. Zarrabi 1342, 242.

statements is more logical and self evident than would appear at first sight. The problem is really more a linguistic than a factual one. The merchants were not members of the guilds, but the traders (*-forush*), who form a great part of the guilds, were not merchants (*tojjar*).[56]

In the following I shall define what both merchants and traders are, to prevent confusion. Greenfield has most succinctly defined who merchants are and who are not. "As the real merchants rank only those *tajers* (businessmen), who busy themselves with export and import trade or with internal wholesale trade. They mostly unite both import and export trade in one hand and trade for their own account. The wholesale dealers, who act as middlemen between the *tajers* and the retail dealers are called *binekdar*. They are also considered to be *tajers*, whilst the retail dealers, like the artisans, are arranged according to their profession in guilds."[57] Thus only the big businessmen, the tycoons as we would call them to-day, and the middlemen who likewise trade on a large scale are *tojjar* and do not form guilds. All other businessmen are traders (*-forush*).

Although I have defined guilds in a negative sense, it is incumbent on me to define what a guild is in a positive sense. Most authors who have written on this subject assumed that the readers knew what a guild was. Baer was one of the few who defined what he understood by the term guild, but his definition is not satisfactory[58]: "a group of towns-people engaged in the same occupation and headed by a shaykh". This definition includes all kinds of groups which in fact do not constitute guilds at all. Baer was led astray by his own definition, when he wrote at the end of his first chapter that "one may say that every town dweller in Egypt had his guild."[59]

The fact that he and other authors did not realize that feudal or pre-industrial societies had a corporate structure marred their understanding of the guild. This, taken together with the failure to define precisely what is understood by a guild, led them to identify all corporate bodies with guilds. But, as we want to describe guilds in Qajar Iran and not corporate bodies in general, it is the difference between them that matters. Socially and economically guilds fulfilled another role than groups of musicians, doctors, mullahs, etc. Even the group with which guild members had most in common, the merchants, differed in a great many aspects from them.[60]

Therefore each of the components of my definition has to emphasize the differentiating characteristics of the guilds rather than the ones they have in common with other groups in Iranian society. Guilds are an urban phenomenon and do not occur outside the cities. Although manufacturing was done in the villages, especially weaving and pottery, this has never led to the formation of guilds. The first part of my definition is the same as the first part of Baer's. But then our views diverge. One of the main differences between guilds in the strict sense of the word and the group of musicians, etc., is that the latter did

56. There is no evidence for Lambton's contention that: "merchant guilds as distinct from craft guilds were, however, a late growth in Persia and not widely found until the late nineteenth century", Lambton 1954, 10; see also Issawi 1971, 285.

57. Greenfield 1906, 26.

58. Baer 1964, 18.

59. Baer 1964, 48.

60. See on the role of the merchants, Floor 1976.

not have a chief elected by themselves, while the guilds did choose their own leaders from their midst. By the inclusion of a self elected chief in my definition I have excluded all low-status occupations, those supervised by state officers.[61]

I now still have to exclude such groups as merchants, ulama and the like from my definition. Because guilds are taxed in quite a different way from all other groups in Iran[62] it seems justified to add this final criterion to my definition. The criteria named above preclude any ambiguity as to which groups belong to the guilds and which do not. It seems to me that I may now proceed and define what a guild is.

> A guild (*senf* - pl. *asnaf*) is: A group of townspeople[63] engaged in the same trade or craft, who elect their own chief and who pay guild taxes; this group having economical, social, fiscal and political functions.

It is a widespread misconception that all crafts and trades in Iran were limited to a certain area in the bazaar.[64] For this system of aggregation of the guilds in the bazaar only refers to certain trades.[65] The *Joghrafiya-ye Esfahan* gives evidence that guilds were concentrated in the central bazaar, had shops in the smaller bazaars in the *mahallehs* (city districts), or were spread out all over the city. For individual guilds the combination of these three possibilities was common. In almost all large towns the division of trades in the bazaars and city districts, was in accordance with Fraser's description: "Each class for the most part is keeping to their respective quarters, so that smiths, braziers, shoemakers, saddlers, potters, cloth and chintz sellers, tailors and other hand craftsmen may generally be found together; but confectioners, cooks, apothecaries, bakers, fruiters end greensellers are dispersed in various places."[66] Thus the geographical division of the guilds was less uniform than it was until now believed to be.

Additionally, one can observe the differences between a pre-industrial and an industrial society by the "specialization that occurs in the product and not in the process" as in an industrial society.[67] In general, a craftsman in Qajar Iran would make all parts of an object and assemble them himself. This striking difference was already observed by the author of the *Joghrafiya-ye Esfahan* who wrote that each European gun hammer-smith made a different part, while in Iran all parts were made by one man.[68]

Even throughout the country product specialization can be seen. The guilds of different towns were not connected and we see that many towns specialized in a certain

---

61. Floor 1971a.

62. "Wholesale exporters and importers are exempt from these [guild] taxes, on the ground that they pay their proportion of the general taxation in customs duty. Men engaged in professions, such as doctors, lawyers, and the priestly class generally, are also excluded." Issawi 1971, 285.

63. On the difference between a town and village, see Greenfield 1904, 253 and Floor 2003 b.

64. See e.g. Curzon 1892, vol. 1, 330; Adams 1900, 161, 162.

65. Wills 1886, 224.

66. Fraser 1843, 33; see also Bleibtreu 1894, 57.

67. Sjoberg 1960, 197.

68. Tahvildar 1342, 108.

products which were not produced elsewhere or if imitated were of inferior quality.[69] The *moqannis* (*qanat* diggers) of Yazd, for instance, were said to be better *moqannis* than those of other towns,[70] likewise the opium worker's from Yazd spread out over Iran because their technique was also better.[71] Yet another difference was the craftsmen's simultaneous production, and retailing in their shops. Accordingly a coppersmith not only made copper vessels but also sold them.

Guilds were non-existent in the villages and even in the small towns there were only a few. In Semnan, for instance, a town of 3,000 to 4,000 inhabitants in 1822, there was no regular butcher, nor a saddler. Only the most common and essential trades were found by Fraser.[72] The larger the size of a city the greater the number of guilds would be, of which many produce for markets outside the city itself.

Unfortunately statistics about guilds in Iran are few in number, incomplete and unreliable. Although all important production and trading centers could boast of a great number of guilds, information on them is not proportional to their important economic role. Whereas there is a long list of guilds and a description of their work for Isfahan, there is no information on the actual number of their members. Our curiosity must therefore be satisfied by the incidental observations of European and Iranian authors.

Even these, however, give only piece-meal information, hardly serving as material for an analysis of their importance, for information which only tells us that in 1886 in Tabriz there were 3,922 shops and 166 caravansarais does not indicate those guilds which were the most important.[73] The greater part of the information available is of the same kind. Around 1893, Mashhad, for example, had about 650 silk looms and 320 shawl looms,[74] while around 1850, Isfahan could boast of 1,800 silk-weaving factories, employing some 9,000 laborers; this industry, however, was ruined some twenty years later.[75] In 1871 there were 28 caravansarais in Kerman, 120 shawl factories and 80 cotton factories.[76] In 1907, Urumiyeh had 30 caravansarais and 1500 shops,[77] and Hamadan had 150 tannery shops in 1921.[78]

These date are not very satisfactory, the only notable thing about them is that they tell us that in many Iranian cities the weaving industry, in comparison with the other guilds, was important. In Isfahan the members of the weavers' guild (*nassaj*) formed at least 10% of all guilds in the city. Taking into account that a great number of other weaving crafts prevailed in Isfahan this percentage no doubt was much higher for all weaving

69. "Almost every town of any size can boast of its specialty, which it is impossible to procure elsewhere." Curzon 1892, vol.2, 523.

70. Polak 1865, vol. 1, 117.

71. Wills 1886, 235.

72. Fraser 1825, 301.

73. Wilson 1896, 59. For a list of guilds and the number of masters in Tabriz in 1869 see Javadi 1350, 227-29.

74. Curzon 1892, vol. 1, 167.

75. Curzon 1892, vol. 2, 242.

76. Curzon 1892, vol. 2, 245.

77. Aubin 1908, 66.

78. RMM 43, 222.

(textile) guilds.[79] Tehran, as far as statistics are concerned, is relatively well documented. Unfortunately, these data have as yet not been analyzed, and to do so would require a separate study.[80]

In 1870, Thomson, the British Consul, estimated the entire population of Tehran at 100,000 inhabitants, not including the garrison. Women and children were estimated to constitute nearly three fourths of the whole population. The remaining 29,000 souls were divided by Thomson as follows:[81]

If we leave aside all justified criticism as to the reliability of these data and accept them as a fairly good indication of the relative positions of the several social groups *vis à vis* each other, we can conclude the following.

High functionaries, such as ministers, generals, mustoufees etc.	250
Government employes, such as petty magistrates and court officials	1,000
Meerzas, ferrashes and servants employed at the palace.	2,000
Persons of independent means having no profession or employment	100
Influential merchants	100
Shopkeepers and dealers in manufactured goods of all kinds	3,000
Shopkeepers and dealers in products "en nature" such as grain, fruits, provisions, drugs and spices, bakers and butchers, and keepers of eating houses	2,000
Shopkeepers being artisans, such as carpenters, gunsmiths, saddlers, tailors, watchmakers, bookbinders, glaziers, coppersmiths, blacksmiths, dyers, printers, cotton spinners, goldsmiths, furriers, painters, farriers, etc.	5,000
Workmen including masons laborers etc.	2,500
Servants and retainers of all descriptions	13,000
Total	28,950

Groups 6, 7, 8 and 10 may be identified with the guilds and together number 12,500 men or 12.5 percent of the whole population, or about 40 percent of the male adult population. These percentages are rather deflated, however, for they do not include the number of women who are also part of the working population, and who were especially engaged in the various weaving crafts. In Isfahan, e.g., about five percent of the widows in the city were working in the weaving guild (*nassaj*).[82] Moreover we observe that in Tehran, the craft guilds and trade guilds equaled each other in number. If, however, the group of workmen is added to that of the artisans, the craft guilds are only half as numerous.

Thomson also reproduced a division of the group of the artisans, which is indeed fortunate, since data on the number of guild members are even fewer than those on the number of guilds. The following list shows the number of artisans employed in Tehran and the occupations which they follow.

79. Tahvildar 1342, 101.

80. I refer to Tehran Municipality 1310; Keyvan 1311; Pakdaman, 1353, 324-347, and *Amar* 1368.

81. FO 60-337, report June 24, 1886.

82. Tahvildar 1342, 101.

Table 6.1: Number of Artisans and their Employment in Tehran (1886)[83]

Occupations	Oostads or Skilled Workmen	Shahgirds or Apprentices	Total	Remarks
Goldsmiths	150	300	450	Experienced workmen receive from 3 Krans (2s.-4d.) to 5 Krans (3 s.-10d.) a day and apprentices from half a Kran (5 d.) to 2.5 Krans (2 s.) as a general rule. Those employed as seal engravers, watchmakers, goldsmiths and printers receive one or two Krans more.
Blacksmiths	52	156	297	
Coppersmiths	40	80	120	
Stonecutters	57	114	171	
Dyers	96	192	288	
Carpenters	86	415	498	
Gunsmiths	30	78	108	
Shoemakers	170	500	670	
Tailors	150	700	850	
Hatters	160	300	460	
Furriers	40	80	120	
Watchmakers	12	24	36	
Nail makers	12	25	36	
Tallow chandlers	25	50	75	
Haircloth makers	35	70	105	
Saddlers	30	90	120	
Bookbinders	36	30	66	
Makers of women's shoes	36	70	106	
Carvers in wood	18	72	90	
Seal engravers	18	34	52	
Glaziers	5	10	15	
Makers of inlaid ivory and other boxes	13	27	40	
Printers	6	60	66	
Glass blowers	3	15	18	
Cotton spinners	12	24	36	
Farriers	70	-	70	
Painters	30	-	30	
	-	-	4,914	

We must be careful, however, to draw conclusions from these data about Tehran which would have a wider significance than for the situation in Tehran only, for each of the

83. FO 60-337, report June 24, 1886

cities had its own peculiarities. Important commercial centers such as Tabriz and Isfahan will of course show a different picture from servicing centers like Tehran and Bandar `Abbas. In 1890, in Bandar `Abbas the ratio between the various guilds was quite different from that in Tehran. The total number of guild members was 412. Here the craft guilds numbered only 4%, while the dealers in produce "en nature" made up about 60% of the total number of guild members.[84]

Table 6.2: Number of Artisans and their Employment in Bandar Abbas (ca. 1900)

Dealers in Manufactured Goods	
drapers	121
haberdashers	24
	145
Dealers in Products "En Nature"	
grocers	104
hucksters	21
tobacco sellers	4
coffee shopkeepers	5
confectioners	6
corn chandlers	52
druggists	5
fish sellers	16
bakers	16
pear sellers	1
cooks and others	21
	251
Artisans	
tailors	3
watchmakers	1
dyers	1
goldsmiths	6
cobblers	5
	16
Total	412

These data present a different picture from the situation in Tehran in 1886 and may be explained by the fact that Bandar `Abbas was a transit port only, offering no industry of importance.

84. Sadid al-Saltaneh 1342, 55.

Data from the early 1920s about the number of guilds and the people employed by them indicate that the situation in Tehran had not significantly changed with that of 1886 as to the nature of the economic activities guilds were engaged in. Leaving aside the fact that the number of guilds appeared to be much higher, the guilds still were traditional in nature. I.e., they still were mainly engaged in the same traditional trades and crafts and their greater number was only due to the increase of Tehran's population. Craft guilds, for example, had not as yet transformed themselves into modernizing manufacturies, and thus only did more of the same, even though some new economic activities had been added to the skills-mix. For example, there were new guilds such as of that of the mechanics and bicycle repairmen, but they worked in the traditional way rather than trying to engage in technical and economic innovation. Although the latter took place, it was not spear-headed by guilds, but rather by the state and mercantile interests.[85]

Table 6.3: Number of Guilds, Shops, Masters, Workers and Boys in Tehran (1922).[86]

Main Groups	No. of Guilds	No. of Shops	No. of Masters	No. of Workers	No. of Boys
Merchants	14	822	734	876	134
Shopkeepers	89	9,589	7,498	6,179	1,538
Artisans	99	4,988	5,035	7,128	2,631
Total	202	15,399	13,267	14,201	4,303

A similar situation existed in other large cities in Iran at that time such as in Isfahan, around 1920, where 9,555 masters were engaged in various industrial activities.[87] Unfortunately, the number of skilled workers and apprentices employed by these Isfahani masters is unknown.

Since about 98% of the Iranian population is Moslem it is not surprising that most guilds had a Moslem membership. Whereas only 2% of the population professed other creeds than Islam, the percentage of non-Moslem membership of the guilds was probably higher than this 2%. Although no data are available to prove this contention, it is plausible, nevertheless, because non-Moslem groups were for the greater part concentrated in the urban centers, where they constituted a higher percentage of the urban population than is indicated by the national average. With few exceptions there is no proof for the existence of a causal relationship between religion and/or ethnic origin and the exercise of a craft of trade as is the case for instance in Egypt.[88] It is true that many occupations were barred to non-Moslems, whilst others were exercised only by non-Moslem groups. The latter occupations were considered religiously unclean, while the former could not be exercised by religiously unclean persons. For example the occupations which had to do with foodstuffs appear to have been a strictly Moslem affair. For "there are no Christian bakers, butchers

85. Floor 1984 b; Floor 1991, Floor 2009 a.
86. Keyhan 1311, vol. 3, 328-33.
87. Janab 1303, 77-79.
88. Baer 1964, 29 ff.

or fruit dealers in Persian cities, because in the case of vegetables, meat or anything that is moist, and sometimes in the case of dry articles of food, a Christian is not permitted to trade them," Wilson reports in 1896.[89]

On the other hand certain occupations were monopolized by the Christians and Jews, such as that of goldsmith, gunsmith and carpenter. In particular the production and sale of wine, which trades were contrary to Islamic Law, were a Christian and Jewish business.[90] The remainder of occupations, the greater part, was open to people of all denominations.

Notwithstanding the fact that non-Moslems were allowed to join Moslems guilds (except for those occupations cited above) generally speaking they were engaged in professions to which no great respect was attached,[91] in line with the discrimination which non-Moslem groups generally suffered from the Moslem population and governments. Especially the group of Jews were badly treated and "when anything filthy is to be done a Jew is sent for."[92] In many cities the minority groups were not even allowed to have shops in the bazaar, which, of course, put them to great economic disadvantage *vis à vis* their Moslem colleagues.[93] Although conditions varied from place to place and guild to guild, members of minority groups experienced great difficulties in attaining leading mercantile positions. Even in those cities where they occupied a relatively better status than elsewhere in Iran, they were subject to many kinds of socio-economic restrictions.[94]

It appears that in many cases Jews, Armenians and Zoroastrians were treated differently from Moslem guild members, namely as a group. In 1870 the Armenians of Isfahan petitioned the British Government to exert its influence in their favor with the Iranian government after their wine jars had been destroyed by the local authorities. "They wished the corn chandler business to be given to them or else money for their houses so that they could leave the country."[95] In Kashan, Lambton writes: "So far as Jews belonged to the guilds they were under the Moslem *ra'is* but had their quarters in separate bazaars."[96] Most clearly this attitude toward the minority groups is shown by the action of the provincial *anjoman* (council) of Isfahan in 1906, who forced the leaders of the Jewish community of Isfahan "to sign an ordinance that in future no Jew would (i) sell wine or spirits to a Muslim, or (ii) hawk goods for sale within a radius of eight miles of Isfahan."[97] Apart from the serious act of discrimination on the part of the authorities against the Jews,[98] it shows that the local authorities did not deal with the heads of the guilds. Whether or not this

89. Wilson 1896, 280; Adams 1906, 162, 163."This debars the Christians from the following the trades of masons, tanners, painters, bakers, butchers, &c." Jones 1870, 417.

90. Jones 1870, 417; Wills 1883, 74.

91. Curzon 1892, vol. 1, 510.

92. Wills 1883, 74, Kosogovski 1344, 85; Gordon 1896, 19.

93. Curzon 1892, vol. 1, 510; Fischel 1950, 125.

94. Fischel 1950, 125.

95. FO 60-327, letter September 22, 1870.

96. Lambton 1954, 23.

97. Lambton 1963 b, 52, 53.

98. "A large number of the small travelling merchants in the Isfahan neighbourhood were Jews." Lambton 1963 b, 52.

was a general rule is uncertain. Similar proceedings were probably followed when the guild tax was fixed. The guild headman, then, probably would also refer himself to the leaders of the Jewish community instead of referring himself directly to individual Jewish guild members.

Hardly anything is known about the ethnic composition of the guilds. It appears that people belonging to the same ethnic category or having a common place of origin, remained together and that they formed a sub-group within the guilds. For instance, among the butcher's guild in Tehran, the Kurmis, who were Afghan subjects, took a common stand on certain issues. Moreover, they appear to have worked mainly for the British embassy.[99] The members of the baker's guild in Tehran seem to have been from Mashhad for a considerable part.[100] Besides, people from the same city or region tended to meet each other in their own habitual cafes or *patuq*.[101] Another feature specific of Iranian guilds was the existence of a kind of master-organization or head-guilds, in which all guilds of a city were united. That is to say that, though scores of guilds could exist in a city, the actual number of head-guilds in the seventeenth century was only 32 according to one source, 33 according to another. In the divan of Khaki Khorasani (16th century), the guilds are said to be 33 in number[102] and this number corresponds with the figure given for the Royal workshops in the Safavid period.[103] About 1650, however, Chardin puts this number at only 32.[104] Each of the 32 or 33 department chiefs of the royal workshops supervised these guilds.[105] Thus under its aegis one head-guild united several related guilds. This particular feature is of great interest for this study, because a similar configuration occurred in Qajar Iran. Namely, the guilds in the first *Majles* (Parliament 1906-1909) were represented by 32 delegates. Each delegate was a representative for several guilds, closely related to or dependent upon each other.[106] Whether the Royal workshops still numbered 32 departments in the Qajar period is not known. It is possible that this number 32 or 33 is used symbolically and that it referred to a Sufi (spiritual) conceptual tradition. This, however, seems unlikely, for it has been reported regarding several guilds in Qajar Iran, that they were a sub-division of a (head) guild. The engravers for example were supervised by the *naqqash-bashi*, the head of the painters guild.[107] The *tonki-duzan* (the trouser makers for wrestlers or *pahlavans*) were a sub-division of the saddlers or *sarraj*.[108] These examples amongst other things indicate, that this division of guilds existed prior to the advent of the Iranian parliament and that the number of guild representatives therein was the result of an existing administrative structure.

---

99. Mostowfi n.d., vol. 1, 310.
100. Mostowfi n.d., vol. 1, 400.
101. Benjamin 1887, 90.
102. Ivanov 1933, 12.
103. Tadhkirat al-Muluk 1943, 30.
104. Chardin 1811, vol. 5, 499.
105. Tadhkirat al-Muluk 1943, 29, 30.
106. RMM 1, 414-6.
107. Benjamin 1887, 321.
108. Beyza'i 1337, 85.

In yet another division of Iranian guilds, perhaps identical to the one described above, I find support for the existence of a number of head-guilds. E`temad al-Saltaneh reports that in Tehran in 1880 the cow slaughterers (*gav-kosh*) were in charge of Amin al-Soltan. The money changers (*sarraf*), the drapers (*bazzaz*), the grocers (*baqqal*), and the common laborers (*kasabeh-ye `omumi*) were supervised by `Ezzat al-Dowleh and the *keshikchi-bashi* (chief of the guard) of the governor of Tehran respectively.[109] What their exact relationship was is not clear, however. Amin al-Soltan had the right to say when and how many cattle would be slaughtered; no other government official could interfere in this matter.[110] From this meager information one may conclude that the nature of the relationship between these officials and the guilds was a fiscal one, although this relationship had nothing to do with the collection of guild taxes.

As is clear from the *Joghrafiya-ye Esfahan* there were several fiscal categories in Isfahan, some of which concerned guilds. These tax categories were not assessed for the annual guild tax, but were to pay certain fixed duties on their daily activities. Although these Isfahani tax categories were not supervised by courtiers as in Tehran (they were in charge of government officials) there is a structural similarity with the division prevailing in Tehran.[111] Accordingly it becomes tempting to consider these fiscal categories as a partial continuation of the Safavid practice to have a number of guilds under the supervision of a state official.[112]

Not to be overlooked is the internal gradation of status of the urban lower classes, of which the outcast position of the above mentioned minorities is a typical example. Baer, in his illuminating study on Egyptian guilds, devotes considerable space to the stratification of the guilds.[113] However, no trace whatsoever is to be found of such elaborate social classification of the Iranian guilds. This does not mean that among Iranian traders and artisans there did not exist a set of ideas about the social status of occupations. On the contrary, for although these ideas have not been articulated, there are several indications that some professions were despised, whilst others were esteemed. Unfortunately, as far is known to me, these ideas have not found their way into written guild-lore as they did in Egypt. Although a conceptual system for social stratification of the guilds did not exist it is known that for instance *lutis* (rowdies)[114] would never work as flayers (*hallaj*), masseurs (*dallak*), *qanat* diggers (*moqanni*), refuse collectors (*kannas*), or as porters (*hammal*); they preferred the profession of selling fruit or edibles, particularly that of dried fruit seller (*ajil-forush*) and seller of *firni* (*firni-forush*).[115]

109. E`temad al-Saltaneh 1345, 1040.
110. E`temad al-Saltaneh 1345, 1040.
111. Tahvildar 1342, 122-25. see Appendix I
112. Compare Tadhkirat al-Muluk 1943, 95-100.
113. Baer 1964, 33-45.
114. For the meaning of this word see Floor 1971a.
115. Mostowfi n.d., vol. 1, 304.

III. ORGANIZATION OF THE GUILDS

The organization of the guilds in Qajar Iran is one of the least documented aspects of our study. Although it would be exaggerated to say that we are completely in the dark about this subject, we have next to nothing compared with the extensive material available from Egypt and Turkey.[116]

The choice of a profession in Qajar Iran was a free one, limited only by family and/or financial considerations.[117] There were indeed a great number of families who traditionally pursued certain crafts but this was not because of guild compulsion in the European sense of the word.[118] Entrance into a guild was obligatory and posed no problem for those Iranians who wanted to earn their living in craft or trade; their main task was to find employment with some master. Guild membership was prerequisite for the practice of any occupation. Entrance into a guild was governed by particularistic criteria.[119]

Migeod contends that entrance into the guilds was not obligatory. He admits, however, that no trace of artisans working outside the guilds is to be found.[120] Each guild, as far as the government was concerned, constituted a fiscal category. Nobody who pursued a trade or craft, therefore, was allowed by the government to be in business outside the guilds. This regulation was applied very consistently. Thus it was for fiscal reasons that the Iranian government wanted to incorporate the European retail traders and craftsmen working in Iran into the guilds.[121]

Although no guild compulsion existed, many of the newcomers to the guilds were of course sons or relatives of guild members, being trained by their kin, to eventually take their place. Consequently, this practice promoted the traditional pursuit of a craft or trade in certain families.[122] Moreover, this development was furthered by a lack of money which prevented an artisan from buying new tools and equipment for starting his son in a craft other than his own. About 1878 we find that in Abadeh several families of spoon carvers (*qashoq-tarash*) had been carrying on their craft for three generations.[123] A similar situation existed in Ardakan for a number of carpenters (*najjar*).[124] In Isfahan we also find a few family monopolies, such as for the engravers and the lentil cooks.[125] The hereditary character of jobs has probably been very strong among the baker's and butchers' guilds because

116. Baer 1964; Gibb & Bowen 1963, vol. 1, part I, chapter VI.

117. Migeod 1990, 199; Häntzsche 1869, 434; Greenfield 1904, 144.

118. Greenfield 1904, 144; Häntzsche 1869, 434.

119. By particularistic criteria I mean that (for purposes of recruitment) 'who one is' is more important than what 'one can do'; it is the autonym of universalistic criteria. For these terms see Sjoberg 1960, 191.

120. Migeod 1990, 199.

121. See below part V and appendix III

122. "Generally the apprentice is a relation, for in Persia many families keep to a particular trade." Wills 1883, 225.

123. Migeod 1990, 204

124. Migeod 1990, 204.

125. Wills 1883, 332 ; Tahvildar 1342, 120.

of their special organization. We shall, however, return to this later. In 1912 at least, the sons of the leaders of the baker's guild followed in their fathers' foot-steps.[126]

Most guild members had no formal education,[127] due to the fact that they would start as a jack-of-all-work or *pado* at an early age to earn money and to learn the craft. The *pados*, mostly children,[128] were trained in the workshops and used for all kinds of jobs ranging from simple techniques of the craft to running errands and serving tea to the customers, just as they are doing to-day.[129] At what stage a *pado* became an assistant or *shagerd* and whether qualifications were required for this is not known. The only other thing we learn about this position is that he was paid less than the *shagerd*.[130]

A great many guilds required a period of apprenticeship, although we do not know how long the time of apprenticeship lasted. It certainly did not last "a few months only" as Polak asserts,[131] but it probably varied in accordance with the nature of the craft, the ability of the *shagerd*, and the willingness of the master.[132] Lorini writes that apprentices had to serve for a very long period, during which they had a hard and tough life.[133] Many of the accomplished assistants or *shagerd* remained with their masters (*ostad*) because they could not afford to start their own shop.[134]

To become a master and have one's own shop was the hope of every *shagerd*. If an assistant had adequate means it was relatively easy for him to become a master in most guilds. In many guilds such as the grocers' guild (*baqqal*), a master's certificate, subject to approval by the *kalantar* (mayor of the city) was needed.[135] In practice, however, things seem to have been much easier. The candidate would request permission from the head of his guild. After he had received a sum of money or a present, the head of the guild would

126. Mostowfi n.d., vol. 2, 398.

127. Of the 32 representatives of the guilds in the first *Majles* (Parliament) only 7 had received some kind of formal education. Four delegates had received an elementary school training (*mota`aref*), 2 delegates had received a superficial old fashioned training (*qadim hodud-e sath*). Only one delegate, a physician, had received an advanced training. On this subject see the interesting study on the background of the members of the Majles by Shaje`i, 1344/1965, part 2, chapter 2 and part 3.

128. "Some trades accepted boys at nine years of age, others not until they were twelve or more," Arasteh 1962, 8.

129. "The youngest in the team, the baker's boy (pado), does all the odd jobs such as getting water and meal to the trough, fuel to the oven, and so forth." Wulff 1966, 294, see also Arasteh 1962, 8.

130. "At the beginning the youth received a very low wage, or nothing at all if he worked with the silversmiths", Arasteh 1962, 8. For a description of a shoemaker's training from *pado* to full-fledged master, see Ibid, 8, 9.

131. Polak 1865, vol. 2, 185. According to Arasteh, "the actuel apprenticeship lasted many years," Arasteh 1962, 8.

132. De Rochechouart 1867, 180 f., Arasteh 1962, 9.

133. Lorini 1900, 244. "Apprentices commence to learn their trade at 11 years old, and remain with their masters until the reach man's estate." Jones 1870, 418.

134. According to Arasteh, "some youths preferred to stay on with the master and eventually manage his shop, " Arasteh 1962, 9; Lorini 1900, 244 ; Adams 1900, 162.

135. According to de Gobineau 1907b, 367, a master's certificate was needed for all guilds. De Rochechouart 1867, 180f.

permit him to carry out his profession in a certain neighborhood without checking his credentials or skill.[136]

The *haqq-e bonicheh*, as the right to set up a shop was known, was characteristic of a few guilds. To guarantee each member of the guild a fair share of the available trade, the number of shops in every quarter had been fixed in accordance with the number of inhabitants and houses. This fixed number could not be increased and the opening of new shops could only occur outside the original area, i.e., when the city expanded, and then only with the permission of the Government.[137] The holders of the *haqq-e bonicheh* could sell their rights. The sale, however, was valid only when the buyer satisfied the qualifications required by the guild, such as a master's certificate and the consent of the other members of the guild.[138] Among the butchers guild the *haqq-e bonicheh* was known as *pa-chub*.[139]

In Isfahan the *haqq-e bonicheh* existed among the *orusi-duzan* (makers of a shoe called *orusi*), the *qannad* (confectioners) and the *qassab* (butchers). In Tehran this institution is only known to have existed among the bakers (*khabbaz*) and the butchers. The revocation of the Tobacco concession in 1891 kept the tobacco sellers guild from acquiring a similar organization, for the concession defined that: "Permission for sale, &c., of tootoon, tobacco, cigars, cigarettes, snuff, & c., is the absolute right of the concessionaires. The Guilds of the sellers of tobacco and tootoon who are engaged in this trade will remain permanent in their local trade and transactions, on condition of possessing permits which will be given to them by the concessionaires."[140]

In 1866, according to de Rochechouart, the number of bakers' and butchers' shops in Tehran was 100 and 70 respectively which number, he reports, had remained unchanged since the days of Fath `Ali Shah (1801-1834) when it had been fixed.[141] Whether or not these figures are correct for 1830, they are certainly wrong for the situation in 1866. A list of shops, drawn up for Naser al-Din Shah (1848-1896) in 1852/53 gives the number of bakers' and butchers' shops as 201 and 93 respectively.[142]

The *shagerd* who wanted to become a master depended on the goodwill of the established masters, whose willingness to allow a new competitor to set up his shop depended on such considerations as family ties, money, etc.[143] Furthermore, a period of apprenticeship was required, which one had to finish satisfactorily. Whether the master's certificate required by these guilds, which had to bear the signature of the *shagerd*'s master (*ostad*) and the *kalantar*, was conferred on a *shagerd* at the end of his period of apprenticeship or only later on request, is not known.[144] Whenever the master of a *shagerd* in the bak-

136. Greenfield 1904, 144. See, however, de Rochechouart 1867, 182.

137. Lambton 1954, 24; Kosogovski 1344, 46.

138. De Rochechouart 1867, 180; Lambton 1954, 24.

139. Kosogovski 1344, 46. The word *pa-chub* referred to two wooden poles and one girder upon them. The two poles held iron hooks, and on these the meat was hung. Gradually it became synonymous with the butchers shop itself.

140. Lambton 1954, 24; Kosogovski 1344, 46 ; Hurewitz 1956, vol. 1, 205.

141. De Rochechouart 1867, 180.

142. Migeod 1990, 200, n. 2.

143. Lambton 1954, 23, 25.

144. De Rochechouart 1867, 180.

ers' build refused to sign the master's certificate, the signature of two other master bakers was sufficient proof of his skill for the *kalantar,* who would then sign too and thus make the certificate valid.[145]

It is a moot question whether in former times these regulations existed among a greater number or even all of the guilds. The fact that the term *bonicheh* was used for guild-tax in Shiraz and Tabriz[146] and that the procession during the `*Eyd-e Qorban* (Feast of Sacrifice) in Isfahan was grouped according to the 'old *bonicheh*'[147] are not conclusive evidence to support such a hypothesis. When one takes into account that the term *bonicheh* was used to denote other forms of taxation as well,[148] it seems best not to think of any but the literal meaning of the word, 'group assessment,' in the cases cited above. We do find the term *bonicheh* used in the 17th century in which it refers to all guilds, but there its fiscal aspects is also meant.[149]

Besides the *haqq-e bonicheh* there were other means to guarantee the guild member a reasonable share of the trade. For in some guilds the number of shops was not fixed, but a newcomer had to set up his shop at a distance of at least seven other shops from that of his colleague.[150] Of course, this rule did not refer to the bazaar. Since a craft or trade was restricted to a special part of the bazaar, the number of shops available to newcomers was limited or nil. Therefore in many cases newcomers had to open a shop outside the bazaar in the various quarters. Yet another variation of the restrictive measures taken by the guilds existed. Greenfield mentions that outside the bazaar area the guild members had their own territory or *godhar* where they would not allow others of the same guild to settle.[151] That this new regulation was not a recent variation of the 'fixed number' theme is indicated by the tact that this rule already existed in the 17th century.[152]

The internal organization of each guild was in the hands of the head of the guild together with the most influential *ostads*, who were known as *rish safid* or greybeards, although this did not necessarily mean that they were old. They formed the governing body of the guilds, which met regularly.[153] Here guild affairs were discussed and decided upon. When there were disputes to be settled or misdeeds to be punished, this governing body constituted the guild court which would try these cases. "Disputes between gilds were settled by a joint court. In Shiraz in the early twentieth century four persona of either gild would assemble in an appointed place and try the case. In the period immediately following the establishment of a modern police administration in Shiraz the findings of the gild court were referred to the police (*nazmiyeh*) or the municipality (*baladiyeh*) for

145. De Rochechouart 1867, 180.
146. See part V.
147. See Appendix II
148. Stack 1882, vol. 1, 259; Mostowfi n.d., vol. 1, 69.
149. Du Mans 1890, 31, 32.
150. De Rochechouart 1867, 182.
151. Greenfield 1904, 145.
152. Chardin 1811 vol. 4, 93.
153. Lambton 1954, 22, De Gobineau 1907, 376.

execution."[154] The head of the guild, acting as president of the Court, was variously known as *kadkhoda, bozorg, ra'is, (ostad)-bashi, rish safid*, or *vastaji-e senf*.[155] The *ostad-bashi* was chosen by the guild masters out of their midst, but this nomination had to be approved by the governor of the city.[156] The approval by the governor, may have led the British consul-general in Tabriz to write that "The carpenters, masons, and silversmiths are each under their own chief, who is usually in the employment of the Governor and nominated by him."[157] It is not known in what way such a guild election was organized, but it probably occurred at a plenary meeting of the guild.[158] It seems doubtful whether originally the oldest guild member was chosen, as Greenfield contends,[159] for not age but influence and wealth were required for this function. The office of *ostad-bashi* was hereditary in most guilds.[160] In this respect the situation in the 19th century did neither differ from that in the 17th century, nor from that of all official functions in Qajar Iran.[161] Presumably elections were held even when somebody succeeded his kinsman as head of the guild.

The task of the *ostad-bashi* was not restricted to representing the guild before the Government; consumers for instance referred to the *ostad-bashi* in case of complaints about the quality of a master's work or delayed delivery.[162] These complaints were investigated and tried by the *ostad-bashi* and the *rish safid*. In case of disputes among guild-members themselves, the matter was also referred to the *ostad-bashi*.[163] I do not agree with Lambton's contention that "it was no doubt partly the shortcomings of Islamic law which encouraged the gilds to carry out certain judicial functions. The limitations of the *shari`a* (Islamic law) made it difficult to take cognizance of many trading disputes. These were, thus, in the first instance referred to the guilds."[164] I do agree with Lambton that limitations were the cause of the fact that guilds dealt with judicial affairs, but these were not the limitations of Islamic law, but restrictions inherent to pre-industrial society. As has been shown in chapter one, the bureaucracy in pre-industrial societies lacked skilled personnel. It was for this reason that the government had to allow a great many groups a considerable amount of self-government.

This is closely bound up with the far-reaching decentralization of the patrimonial rule. Therefore the function of the *ostad-bashi* was a rather hybrid and Janus headed one. On the one hand he was appointed by his fellow guild members to represent and promote

154. Lambton 1954, 22.

155. Binning 1857, vol. 1, 278. Brugsch 1862, vol. 1, 222 ; Greenfield 1904, 144. Bleibtreu 1894, 125.

156. A guild headman was seldom dismissed, except on ground of objections against him from his electors; even they had to prove his negligence or criminal practices. Bleibtreu 1894, 125 ; Lambton 1954, 144, Häntzsche 1869, 434 ; Greenfield 1904, 144, Bleibtreu 1894, 156; Orsolle 1885, 303.

157. Jones 1870, 421.

158. Lambton 1954, 22.

159. Greenfield 1904, 144, Migeod 1990, 195.

160. Greenfield 1904, 144.

161. Lambton 1954.

162. Lambton 1954, 28. Greenfield 1904, 144.

163. Greenfield 1904, 144.

164. Lambton 1954, 21.

their interests before the government, while on the other hand the authorities expected him "to keep the men under their charge in order and through them to bring home responsibility for misdemeanors and fraudulent actions."[165] This schizoid task of the guild headmen was not restricted only to the guilds. A similar situation existed among other corporate groups in Qajar Iran. The wardens (*kadkhoda*) of the city quarters and the village headmen all fulfilled this double role.[166]

To maintain the rules laid down by the government the guild headmen had the power to punish offenders. Formerly, when the heads of guilds were much more powerful, they had the right to give the bastinado or to fine offending guild members. But, as in the case of the city wardens (*kadkhoda*), their powers had been curtailed towards the end of the 19th century, which were probably taken over by the *darugheh* (chief of the market police).[167]

But the heads of guilds were not only links or mediators between the government and the guild. A great deal of their prestige and influence was derived from the fact that they could restrain a too demanding governor. Their success in doing so depended on their 'bargaining power' with the authorities.[168] This influence added to their strength of position *vis à vis* the guild members; for although the judicial powers of a guild headman were limited, the members of his guild would not wish to add his opposition to their other troubles.

In 1912 the bakers in Tehran only deviated from the rules laid down by the *nanva-bashi* (head of the bakers' guild) because they were sure that the responsible authorities would not back their superior.[169] Moreover the *ostad-bashi*s were made responsible for the payment of the guild tax of members of their guild. This rule worked in two ways. Firstly, it gave the government a hold on the *ostad-bashi* and, secondly it strengthened the position of the *ostad-bashi vis à vis* the guild members.[170]

Although the guild headman was chosen by the guild members, he was a representative of the government rather than a representative of his guild before the government. Thus the government disposed of reliable and influential members of the guild, who were held responsible for the conduct of their group. In this way, the lack of qualified administrators was solved. The heads of guilds, although having limited judicial powers, could always use their influence with the authorities and their powers in guild affairs as a lever to force obedience of the members of their guild. Therefore many guilds did not benefit at all from their corporateness, since "their organization resembled rather a police regulation than a privilege."[171]

---

165. Lambton 1954, 21.

166. Lambton 1954, 10, 11 ; Lambton 1953, 337, 338.

167. Greenfield 1904, 145. On the weakened position of the guild headsmen, see also Bleibtreu 1894, 156, and below part VI.

168. See chapter one and below part VI. "Any disputes among the members are submitted to his [the chief's] decison, from which there is no appeal." Jones 1870, 421.

169. Mostowfi n.d., vol. 2, 398.

170. See part V.

171. De Rochechouart 1867, 183.

Only in few cases, when guilds had a good organization, were the guild headmen in a position to further the guilds' interest. The other function of the *ostad-bashi*s tended to recede into the background. This did not mean, however, that they did not try to further their guilds' interests.[172]

IV. THE SOCIAL FUNCTION OF THE GUILDS AND FOTOVVAT

I now deal with a subject which can tell us much about the importance of the guilds for its members, viz. its social function. Notwithstanding the rather loose organization of many guilds, there were conditions which favored a development towards an 'esprit de corps.' The fact that guilds had their own bazaars and that in some cases their economic life was strictly regulated to their common weal, "no doubt strengthened their sense of corporate life."[173] Moreover, like other corporate groups many, if not all, guilds had their own habitual coffee-houses or *patuq*, where they met after working hours. Here they chatted, did business; here day laborers were paid by their employers and here they probably held their guild assemblies too.[174]

But this sense of togetherness did not necessarily lead to cooperativeness among them. It certainly is an overestimation on Lambton's part when she contends that "guilds provided for mutual assistance in difficulties."[175] Her contention is not confirmed by the available evidence; on the contrary, Thomson, the British Consul in Tehran, states: "this system of association is not adopted with a view to render assistance to such of its members as may be in difficulties or distress owing to sickness or other unforseen misfortune."[176]

In one case only do we find a guild acting as a kind of welfare agency. The bakers' guild in Tehran, according to de Rochechouart, had a guild fund with the aim "to help those of the colleagues, whose business is doing badly; in that case the debtor is obliged to redeem his debt out of his profit; on the other hand when a colleague was in business trouble because of his own fault and bad conduct, the guild would force him either to sell his business or to accept a manager being put in charge of his shop."[177]

This practice, however, seems to have been an exception to the rule observed by Thomson. De Rochechouart states explicitly that such guild funds did not occur among any other guild.[178] The common practice in cases of bankruptcy, for example, was that relatives and friends helped the bankrupt.[179]

---

172. Bleibtreu 1894, 125.

173. Lambton 1954, 20. According to Arasteh the apprentices' training was also aimed at fostering a kind of 'esprit de corps'. "The master expected them to observe daily prayers, attend the mosque and participate in religious ceremonies, often with fellow guild members." Arasteh 1962, 8.

174. Meier 1961, 291; Benjamin 1887, 90; Mostowfi n.d., vol. 1, 279.

175. Lambton 1954, 26.

176. FO 60/337, report June 24, 1886.

177. De Rochechouart 1867, 180.

178. De Rochechouart 1867, 181f.

179. Basset 1887, 284.

The absence of a similar institution among the other guilds does not warrant the impression we get from Lambton's contention that a strong social bond prevailed among the guilds. It is true that two other authors mention that the guilds had a communal fund. De Gobineau even mentions that the guilds had a treasurer. But nothing is said about the purpose of this fund. The only thing de Gobineau and Orsolle report is, that the money levied by the guilds from their members were kept in this fund. Therefore, it is justified to assume that the main purpose of this fund was to collect the tax quota due by the individual guild members, and to pay the guild tax out of it to the authorities. It may also have served to provide money for ceremonies in which guilds participated.[180]

However, we do not have any written sources that give us a better insight into this matter. Therefore, we have to take resource to the more circumscribed aspects of guild life such as public ceremonies and the like. The guilds best demonstrated their existence when they participated in public ceremonies, of which the *Moharram*[181] and the *`Eyd-e Qorban*[182] processions were the most important part. The material available is not copious and I cannot say after Baer "public events and festivals is certainly the most fully documented aspect of guild activities, even the most superficial of observers generally had something to say about them."[183] As I already have said, it is strange that in contrast to Europeans traveling in other Moslem countries, those traveling in Iran hardly ever mentioned the existence of guilds. Even when they did, they described them in general and non-committal terms.

According to Lambton, "in Tehran certain craft guilds had their own places according to tradition in the procession which took place on the occasion of the `id-i qurban, and the right to represent the gild in the procession was hereditary in certain families."[184] The participation of the guilds in this procession is corroborated by other sources, although these do not agree in detail. In 1852, Brugsch reports that "according to ancient custom the various parts of the camel are divided among the guilds, the smiths receive the legs, the tailors the head and other guilds the other parts until the camel is divided among all guilds."[185] It seems hardly possible that the camel was divided among all guilds as he asserts, since even a camel is not big enough for that purpose. It is more likely that only a few guilds received a share, as is borne out by another source, which states that in Tehran the camel was divided among six guilds only.[186]

---

180. De Gobineau 1907b, 376; Orsolle 1885, 303.

181. On the 10th of Moharram in 680, Hoseyn, the son of `Ali b. Abu b. Taleb, the fourth caliph, died fighting against the troops of the caliph Yazid. Therefore, this is a great day of mourning for the Shi`ahs, to whom Hoseyn is their second Imam. In Qajar Iran, apart from processions and mourning sessions, passion plays played the most important part during that month. For more information see Floor 2005, chapter four.

182. The *`Eyd-e Qorban*, the festival of sacrifice, is celebrated on the 10th of Dhu'l-Hijjah. It is obligatory on every free Moslem who can afford it to sacrifice an animal. Shah `Abbas I started the custom that on that occasion in the large cities a camel was slaughtered. Various groups had a traditional right to a different part of the camel.

183. Baer 1964, 116.

184. Lambton 1954, 26.

185. Brugsch 1862, vol. 1, 258.

186. Aubin 1908, 146.

The ceremony as it was performed in Isfahan showed the same pattern as in Tehran. In the procession, however, the various groups did not represent the guilds, but a town quarter, that either belonged to the *Heydari* or the *Ne`mati* order. Guilds participated in the procession, but as part of the town quarter and not as an independent body. Moreover, the representatives, who received part of the camel's body on behalf of their group and whose function was hereditary, represented either the *Heydari* or the *Ne`mati* order.[187] In Tehran the custom of *`Eyd-e Qorban* was still current in 1918. Balfour mentioned that after killing the camel "it is dismembered by the heads of the various trade guilds, each using an instrument of his calling."[188] In 1930, however, Reza Shah forbade this festival.

Several guilds also participated in the *Moharram* processions. In 1893, according to Knobel, the Dutch Consul-General, the core of that procession consisted of the following groups:

1. Sayyeds
2. Hajjis
3. Important merchants
    (a) older persons
    (b) younger persons
4. Arabs
5. Several guilds, not in a strict order

"This order is not strictly adhered to, irregularity prevails. The procession consists of groups (*dasteh*) of 20 - 100 persons. The *dasteh* of one quarter cannot mix with the *dasteh* from another quarter (Ne`mati and Heidari) without giving cause to fighting. A *dasteh* means a group which is formed around a banner (*`alam*), under a leader who does not himself carry the banner. Usually only the lower classes participate. He who respects himself does not become a member of the dasteh."[189]

Some guilds such as the glazed pottery workers guild distinguished themselves from other groups by special banners, but mostly the banners carried by guild *dastehs* were not typical for them.[190] The different *dastehs* vied with one another in the pomp of their trappings and banners, and in their devotion to the martyred Imams, wishing to achieve public acclaim for their *dasteh*. In 1907, the most popular *dasteh* in Tehran was that of the drapers' guild (*bazzaz*).[191]

Another event in which the guilds participated was the extending of one's best wishes to the Shah or the governor on the occasion of New Year (*Nowruz*). In Kashan, for example, this practice was as follows: On the first day of the New Year the ulama (religious

187. Mirjafari 1979; Perry 2000. See in particular Appendix II.

188. Balfour 1921, 45.

189. Legatie Perzië, Letter March 4, 1891; letter March 15, 1892; van Vloten 1894, 110.

190. Van Vloten 1894, 111.

191. RMM 4, 486.

leaders) would visit the governor, on the second day the `*ommal* (government officials), on the third day the *tojjar* (merchants) and on the fourth day the leaders of the guilds and the agriculturists (*ro'asa-ye asnaf va zorra`*).[192]

I have already drawn attention to the fact that on the occasion of the *Moharram* procession that certain groups carried banners which characteristic for each of them. Apart from the example mentioned above I have found only one symbol that was peculiar to a single guild. The *hallaj* or flayers' shops were easy to recognize, because in front of these shops hung a stuffed puppet (called *pahlavan-e panbeh*). It was an old custom, dating back to the 17th century.[193]

In this connection it is interesting to take note of other customs, although these did not concern a guild symbol. The butchers were accustomed, when meat was cheap, to announce this fact by burning fat in front of their shops, to show the customers that meat was practically for the taking. The bakers had a similar custom of lighting lamps when bread was cheap.[194]

The ceremonies mentioned so far are not very convincing proof of an 'esprit de corps' among the guilds. Not only were the *Moharram* and the `*Eyd-e Qorban* ceremonies common to all Shi`a Moslems, but religious affiliation tended to come more into prominence than guild membership.

Fortunately there is information on ceremonies which were characteristic for one particular guild, which shows that at least a few had a type of social bond. The members of the sword-makers guild (*shamshir-saz*) in Isfahan convened at the grave of Asad Isfahani at Sichan. This ceremony was held in memory of Asad Isfahani on account of whose skills their guild had been exempted from taxation by Shah `Abbas I (r. 1584-1629). In this case we really have a guild showing a strong 'esprit de corps', since the craft was already dying out about 1870, but this practice was still current in 1937.[195]

Another example of a ceremony celebrated by a single guild is very interesting indeed. It is the water sprinkling festival or `*Eyd-e Abrizan*, also called *lattavi-ye mesgaran*, which was celebrated in Kashan by the coppersmiths guild (*mesgar*) up to about 1930. This festival is a great antiquity, since it seems to have been originated by the Sassanian king Peroz (r. 457-484).[196] Although originally a festival common to all Iranians it seems to have fallen into disuse after the Safavid era.

> But the tradition loving people of Kashan and Yazd continued to celebrate this custom. In Kashan it was celebrated like this: every year, on the 13th of the month of *Tir*, the coppersmiths would stop their work and that of the other artisans in the bazaar by throwing water into each other's shops. Then they went to Government House, while making merry, to congratulate the governor. There, the coppersmiths assembled around the pond and the big

192. Zarrabi 1342, 242.
193. Beyza'i 1337, 45.
194. Kosogovski 1344, 47; de Rochechouart 1867, 181.
195. Lambton 1954, 25-26.
196. Naraqi 1345, 273.

> water reservoirs and started throwing water at each other and continued to have fun. After they had received a robe of honor (*khel`at*) and presents from the governor they went in same mood to Fin, reciting poems, singing songs peculiar to their guild and clapping their hands. In Fin they remained for three days and enjoyed themselves."[197]

Furthermore, guilds showed a spirit of fellowship on the death of a guild member. "The mourning ceremonies were attended by the guild as a body and the dead man's heir escorted from the house of the deceased and installed in the premises of the bazaar."Among the butchers in Tehran a special ceremony prevailed, here a Kashmiri shawl was placed on the shoulders of the nearest relative of the deceased. This custom was also practiced by other groups.[198]

It is striking to note that for participation in the important religious ceremonies, the guild members' affiliation with darvish orders, especially the *Heydari* and *Ne`mati* orders, was more decisive than their membership of a guild. In what way were these two - guilds and darvish orders - connected and to what extent did the latter influence the former? The answer to these questions will further enlighten us with regard to the social function of the guilds. The most useful way to tackle this issue is to look for points of contact between them. Therefore, in the remaining part of this chapter I will concentrate on the linkage between guilds and the *fotovvat* organization.

Notwithstanding the prevailing idea that in Iran the guilds were identical with or organized along the lines of *fotovvat* associations we find little or no evidence at all for such a belief in either Persian or European literature.[199] The term *fotovvat* refers to a body of virtues and to an association for upholding these virtues. It moreover "denotes various movements and organizations in the urban communities of the Middle East, the study of which is made difficult by the fact, that, in the course of history they have assumed very diverse forms and because the information about these organizations and movements often appears to be irreconcilable." The *fotovvat* is often represented as being linked with the guild organizations. In the later Middle Ages a certain kind of interpenetration between the trade guilds in the Irano-Turkish territories and the *fotovvat* is undeniable. Where *fotovvat* once existed, it continued in different form, by becoming linked with the crafts, and thus, in time, became the rule of the guilds. This process occurred in all countries the Islamic Orient.[200]

This description of *fotovvat* by Cahen and Taeschner has greatly contributed to the generally held notion with regard to the situation in Iran, which was prompted by analogical reasoning rather than by facts. Studies on neighbouring countries (Ottoman Turkey, Turkestan) have led several scholars to the conclusion that the guilds in those countries were organized along the lines of *fotovvat* organizational structures as described in

197. Naraqi 1345, 274
198. Lambton 1954, 26; see also Kasravi 1319-21, vol. 2, 231.
199. Taeschner 1965, 151f.
200. Cahen and Taeschner 1965.

so-called *fotovvat-namehs*.[201] According to Taeschner, for instance, "a similar development of the *fotovvat* into a guild organisation must also have taken place in Iran during the late Middle Ages. At any rate a Persian work entitled *Fotovvatnameh-ye soltani* by Kamal al-Din Hoseyn Va`ez Kashefi points into that direction."[202] However, for this teleological argument there is no evidence to be found at all. This is strange indeed; the more so, since one would expect a strongly Shi`ite tinged *fotovvat* organization in, and consequently frequent references to it in the literature of, Shi`a Iran.

Fortunately we have some information on the prevalence of *fotovvat* associations in 19th century Iran, which gives us a better insight into the alleged guilds' role in these associations. The publication by Mahjub of material on the *Faqr-e `Ajam* was until recently the only step forward in the study of *fotovvat* in 19th century Iran.[203] A publication on the darvish order of the *Khaksar* adds some new elements which merit discussion.[204]

The *Faqr-e `Ajam* or *selseleh-ye `Ajam* was a branch of the darvish order of the *Khaksar*, or more likely, a *fotovvat* association affiliated with the *Khaksar* order.[205] Its existence probably antedates that of the foundation of the Safavid state, having its origins among the heterodox, radical Shi`a (Ghulat, Isma`ilis) groups that abounded in Iran.[206] The *Faqr-e `Ajam* association recruited the majority of its members from among the lower classes, though members of the middle and higher classes are also to be found among its adherents. Only those who were gainfully employed qualified for entrance into the *Faqr-e `Ajam* association.[207]

It would seem that towards the end of the 19th century the *Faqr-e `Ajam* were completely assimilated by the *Khaksar* order. This at least is the position taken by the *Khaksar* order as reported by Gramlich and Modarresi.[208] Mahjub, however, disputes this,[209] and although he does not quote them, he is supported in this view by two earlier observers, viz. Aubin and Lady Sheil. Aubin, writing in 1907 about the *Khaksar* and the *Faqr-e `Ajam*, considers these associations as two separate darvish orders.[210] Lady Sheil, writing some fifty years earlier, enumerates the seven darvish orders which existed in Qajar Iran, and she also names the *Khaksar* and *Faqr-e `Ajam* separately.[211]

Mahjub also seems to be right on another point about which he differs from Gramlich. According to Mahjub, the highest rank in the order of the *Faqr-e `Ajam* is that of the *`alamdar* or *saheb-e `alam*, who comes directly under the *naqib*.[212] In a note Gram-

201. Cahen and Taeschner 1965.
202. Taeschner 1979, 421 (my underlining).
203. Meier 1964, 289ff.
204. Modarresi 1358.
205. Modarresi 1358, 3; Gramlich 1965, vol. 1, 78f.
206. Mazzaoui 1972, 57; Smith Jr. 1979, 57-60, 112-113, 123, 126, 131, Moose 1987.
207. Meier 1964, 295; Aubin 1908, 242.
208. Modarresi 1358, 72; Gramlich 1965, vol. 1, 78f., vol. 2, 164, note 891.
209. Meier 1964, 207.
210. Aubin 1908, 238 f.
211. Lady Sheil 1856, 194. She mentioned the following groups: "Ajem, Khaksar, Niamaoollahee, Zahabee, Jallalee, Kemberee, and Dehree".
212. Meier 1964, 313.X

lich writes that he does not know exactly where he has to put this rank in the hierarchy of the *Khaksar* order.[213] However, Mahjub mentions the *saheb-e `alam* as being a rank of the *Khaksar* order and so does Aubin. Speaking of the *Faqr-e `Ajam,* Aubin mentions the *saheb-e `alam* (the *qotb* or pole of the order) as the highest rank, directly under the *naqib.* At that time two individuals held that rank.[214] Further the fact that a member of the *Faqr-e `Ajam* had to be gainfully employed speaks against Gramlich's contention. The *Faqr-e `Ajam,* in contrast to the *Khaksar,* did not go around begging.[215] The *Joghrafiya-ye Esfahan* states that a few of the seven darvish orders in Iran require that their members work for their living and do not become mendicants.[216] One of these orders must perforce be the *Faqr-e `Ajam.*

The *Faqr-e `Ajam* had a *fotovvat* organization and its hierarchical ranks correspond with different degrees of initiations. Its members had to learn the meaning of the mystic lore of certain 'occupations.' According to its literature this association (ideally) drew its members from 17 groups representing the 'occupations' of the 17 original 'founding members.'[217]

A few things strike us with regard to the number seventeen. Firstly, not all seventeen occupations constituted guilds. Secondly, there are seven different, partly incomplete, lists of the seventeen occupations, which do not tally with each other. The first of the preserved lists[218] of the groups constituting the *Faqr-e `Ajam* comprises the following fourteen occupations:

1. bakers (*nanva, lavash-paz*)
2. barbers (*salmani*)
3. wrestlers (*pahlavan*)
4. butchers (*qassab*)
5. pack-saddle makers (*palanduz*)
6. farriers (*na`lband*)
7. muleteers (*mokari, charpadar*)
8. watersellers (*saqqa*)
9. caravan leaders (*chavush*)
10. acrobats (*luti*)
11. patchers (*pareh-duz*)
12. darvishes
13. washers of the dead (*mordeh-shuy*)
14. eulologists of the martyrs of the Shi`a (*rowzeh-khvan*).

213. Meier 1964, 313, note 16.
214. Aubin 1908, 242.
215. Meier 1964, 294.
216. Tahvildar 1342, 86.
217. For the story of the foundation of the *Faqr-e `Ajam* see Meier 1964, 295-96.
218. Meier 1964, 295-96.

The second list[219] of fifteen items comprises the numbers 1, 2, 3, 4, 6, 7, 8, 9, 11, 12, 13, and 14 of list I as well as the following occupations:

15. darvish sheikh (*baba*)
16. sifters of grain (*bovjar*)
17. outriders (*shater-e jelowdar*).
18. thieves (*shabrow*)
19. coffee house keeper (*qahvehchi*)

The third list[220] of 12 items comprises the following numbers of lists I and II: nrs. 1, 3, 4, 6, 7, 8, 9, 10, 12, 14, 16, and 18. These three lists have all been reported by Mahjub.

The fourth list[221] has seventeen items and apart from the numbers 1, 2, 3, 4, 5, 6, 8, 12 of lists I and II comprises the following occupations:

20. blacksmiths (*ahangar*)
21. carpenters (*najjar*)
22. cobblers (*kaffash*)
23. bricklayers (*banna*)
24. cement makers (*gelkash*)
25. camel drivers (*shotordar*)
26. cotton beaters (*hallaj*)
27. stonecutters (*sangtarash*), and
28. passion play actors (*ta`ziyeh khvan*)

The fifth list[222] of sixteen items has only the following occupations of lists I to IV, viz. 2, 5, 6, 8, 12, and 23, unless we accept that the dough-stretchers (*shater-e nanva*), the *zurkhaneh* managers (*zurkhanehchi*), the ushers (*farrash*) and the stitchers (*pineh-duz*) are the same as nrs. 1, 3, 11, and 17.

List V moreover comprises the following occupations:

29. beggars (*geda*)
30. turners (*kharrat*)
31. coiners (*zarb gir*)
32. poets (*sha`er*)
33. bleachers (*gazur*), and
34. locksmiths (*chelengar*).

The sixth list[223] of seventeen items comprises the numbers 1 (*khabbaz*), 2, 5, 8, 11, 21, and 27 of lists I to IV as well as the following occupations:

35. hat makers (*kolah duz*)
36. bath attendants (*hammami*)
37. druggists (*`attar*)
38. bookbinders (*sahhaf*)
39. painters (*naqqash*)
40. retailers (*baqqal*)
41. saddlers (*sarraj*)
42. tailors (*khayyat*), and
43. tanners (*dabbagh*).

---

219. Meier 1964, 298.
220. Meier 1964, 315-16.
221. Beyza'i 1337, 25; Meier 1964, 235.
222. Janab 1303, 80.
223. Modarresi 1358, 74.

The seventh[224] and last list of 28 items comprises the numbers 1, 20, 36, 40, 41, 42, and 43 of lists I to VI as well as the following occupations:

44. cooks (*tabbakh*)	45. cloth merchants (*bazzaz*)
46. grocers (*`allaf*)	47. hired mourners (*khannaf*)
48. gold smiths (*zargar*)	49. bow makers (*kamangar*)
50. weavers (*bafandeh*)	51. dyers (*rangzir*)
52. cotton dressers (*naddaf*)	53. brickmakers (*tughul saz*)
54. physician (*hakim*)	55. governor (*hakem*)
56. headmen (*ashraf*)	57. servants (*gholam*)
58. eunuchs (*khvajeh*)	59. executioners (?) (*mir*)
60. farmers (*ra`ayat*)	61. watchmen (*pasban*)
62. diviners (*`arraf*)	63. money changers (*sarraf*)

The source of list V calls the 17 occupations mentioned by it the *asnaf-e moqaddaseh* or the blessed guilds.[225] However, it also provides us with a complete statistical overview of the guilds of Isfahan in 1924 which only mention 6 of the blessed guilds as being guilds in the usual sense of the word.[226] Moreover, the number of members of the *Faqr-e `Ajam* is significant fewer than that of the number of guild members. According to Aubin the *Faqr-e `Ajam* are "5 to 6,000, 10,000 if one adds the apprentices."[227] The number of the guilds in Tehran at that time amounted to some 40,000 members.[228]

Table 6.4: Artisan Membership of the *Faqr-e `Ajam* Dervish Order

Occupation/List Number	I	II	III	IV	V	VI	VII
1. bakers (*nanva, lavashpaz*)	X	X	X	X			X
2. barbers (*salmani*)	X	X		X	X	X	
3. wrestlers (*pahlavan*)	X	X	X	X			
4. butchers (*qassab*)	X	X	X	X			
5. pack-saddle makers (*palanduz*)	X			X	X	X	
6. farriers (*na`lband*)	X	X	X	X	X		
7. muleteers (*mokari, charpadar*)	X	X	X	X			
8. watersellers (*saqqa*)	X	X	X		X	X	
9. caravan leaders (*chavush*)	X	X	X				
10. acrobats, players (*luti*)	X		X				

224. Ivanov 1933, 12.

225. Janab 1303, 80.

226. Janab 1303, 77 f.

227. Aubin 1908, 241.

228. Based on earlier statistics the group of tradesmen and artisans represents about 12½ percent of the total population in Tehran, or in Tehran of 1907 with a population of 280,000 some 40,000 people.

Occupation/List Number	I	II	III	IV	V	VI	VII
11. patchers (*parehduz*)	X	X				X	
12. dervishes	X	X	X	X	X		
13. washers of the dead (*mordehshuy*)	X	X					
14. eulogists (*rowzehkhvan*)	X	X	X				
15. dervish sheikh (*baba*)		X					
16. sifters of grain (*bovjar*)		X	X				
17. outriders (*shater-e jelowdar*)		X					
18. thieves (*shabrow*)			X				
19. coffee house keeper (*qahvankhanehchi*)							
20. blacksmiths (*ahangar*)				X			X
21. carpenters (*najjar*)				X		X	
22. cobblers (*kaffash*)				X			
23. bricklayers (*banna*)				X	X		
24. mortar makers (*gelkash*)				X			
25. camel drivers (*shotordar*)				X			
26. cotton beaters (*hallaj*)				X			
27. stonecutters (*sangtarash*)				X		X	
28. passion play actor (*ta`ziyeh-khvan*)				X			
29. beggars (*geda*)					X		
30. turners (*kharrat*)					X		
31. coiners (*zarbgir*)					X		
32. poets (*sha`er*)					X		
33. bleachers (*gazur*)					X		
34. locksmiths (*chelengar*)					X		
35. hat makers (*kolahduz*)						X	
36. bath attendants (*hammami*)						X	X
37. druggists (*`attar*)						X	
38. bookbinders (*sahhaf*)						X	
39. painters (*naqqash*)						X	
40. grocers (*baqqal*)						X	X
41. saddlers (*sarraj*)						X	X
42. tailors (*khayyat*)						X	
43. tanners (*dabbagh*)						X	
44. cooks (*tabbakh*)							X
45. mercers (*bazzaz*)							X
46. fodder sellers (*`allaf*)							X
47. hired mourners (*khannaf*)							X
48. goldsmiths (*zargar*)							X
49. bowmakers (*kamangar*)							X

Occupation/List Number	I	II	III	IV	V	VI	VII
50. weavers (*bafandeh*)							X
51. dyers (*rangriz*)							X
52. cotton dressers (*naddaf*)							X
53. brickmakers (*tughulsaz*)							X
54. physicians (*hakim*)							X
55. governors (*hakem*)							X
56. headmen (*ashraf*)							X
57. servants/slaves (*gholam*)							X
58. eunuchs (*khvajeh*)							X
59. executioners (?) (*mir*)							X
60. farmers (*ra`ayat*)							X
61. watchmen (*pasban*)							X
62. diviners (*`arraf*)							X
63. money changers (*sarraf*)							X

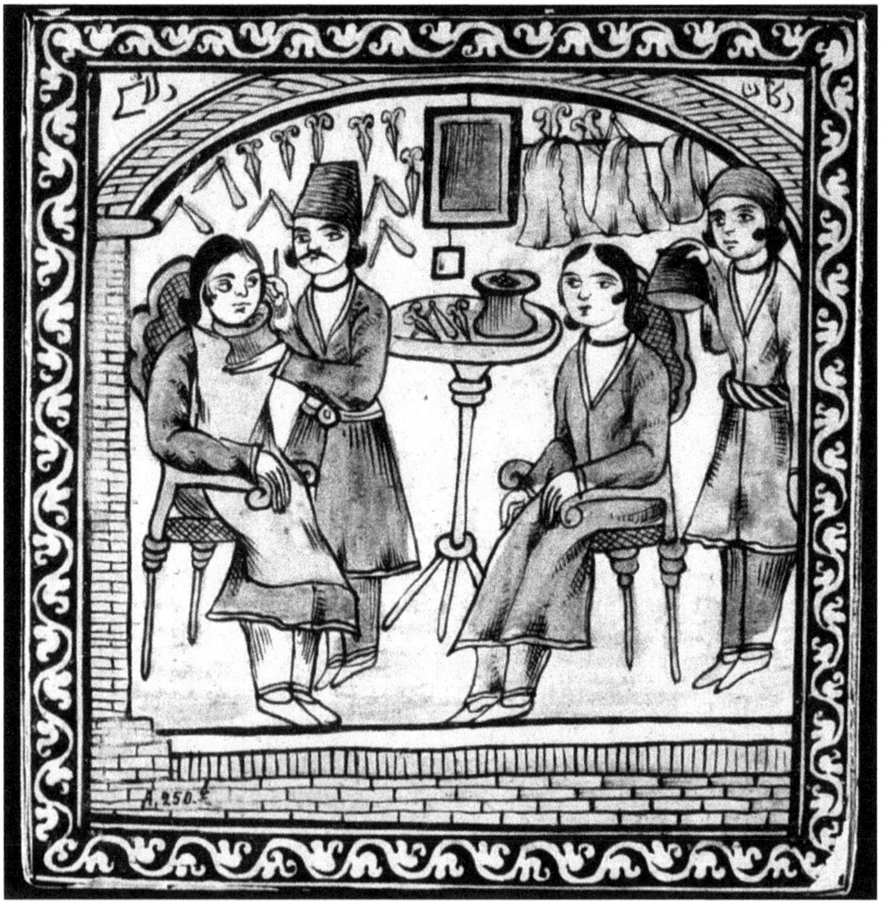

A Barber Shop

Finally, an analysis of the occupation of 34 known members of the *Faqr-e `Ajam* reveals that they were engaged in all kinds of occupations, fourteen of which do not figure at all among any of the seven lists mentioned above.[229] This means that membership of the *Faqr-e `Ajam* was not restricted to those engaged in the 17 (of whatever composition) occupations. This may be explained by the fact that the occupations are probably traditional and the number of seventeen is only symbolic, for according to other versions the number of these occupations is 18, 32, 33, or 44 instead of 17.[230]

The number of 32 in this connection is of interest. In Safavid Iran the number of royal workshops was 32.[231] This number probably had a symbolic significance as well, for the guilds in the first *Majles* (Parliament) in Iran in 1907 were also represented by 32 delegates. Each delegate being a representative for several guilds closely related to or dependent on each other.[232] According to Modarresi, in his interesting study on the *Khaksar* order 32 of the guilds in each town in Safavid Iran had to pay their taxes to the *naqib* ten days before New Year's Day (*Nowruz*). Seventeen of these guilds (mentioned in list VI) had to pay their taxes to the *naqib-e `Ajam*; the other 15 guilds paid their taxes to the *naqib-e Khaksar*.[233] Unfortunately Modarresi quotes no source for this information, so it is impossible to properly evaluate its significance and value. On one score this information would appear to be wrong, viz. the *naqib* convened the guilds in the first quarter of each year, so after and not before *Nowruz*.[234]

Modarresi's information may give credence to the belief that the *naqib* in Safavid Iran indeed initiated people into a *fotovvat* association. However, the evidence is still rather flimsy and so far is not borne out by hard evidence. Moreover, if we take the *fotovvatnameh-ye soltani*, which according to Taeschner *et alii* is proof of the existence of a *fotovvat*- guild organization in Iran we observe that this *fotovvat-nameh* gives no such indication at all, for no guilds figure among the groups mentioned by it. It is, however, interesting to note that the groups mentioned in the *fotovvatnameh-ye soltani* also figure among the *Faqr-e `Ajam*, these are the following:[235]

---

229. The following occupations do not figure among the lists mentioned above. The analysis is based on the names of the *sokhanvars* (rethoriticians), members of the *Faqr-e `Ajam* mentioned by Mahjub. 1. Peddling fruit monger (*tavvaf*), 2. rice merchant (*razzaz*), 3. servant (*khadem*), 4. dealer in second hand goods (*semsar*), 5. rice cook (*khoshkeh-paz*), 6. shopkeeper (*dokkandar*), 7. kilnman (*kuzeh-paz*), 8. bucket maker (*dalv-duz*), 9. shoe-black (*vaksi*), 10. copper smith (*mesgar*), 11. tinman (*ahankub*), 12. yoghurt seller (*mastband*), 13. dried fruit seller (*ajili*), and 14. quilt maker (*lehaf-duz*). Meier 1964, 318-19.

230. The guilds "are supposed to be '*dakhili silsila'i faqr*', i. e., participating in the sufic organisations, and are vaguely divided into eighteen trades." Ivanov 1933, 12; Modarresi 1338, 68 speaks of 44 *goruh* (groups). On the number seventeen see Melikoff 1961, 435-445.

231. Chardin 1811, vol. 5, 499; according to the Tadhkirat al-Muluk 1943, 30, there were 33 royal workshops.

232. RMM 1, 414-416.

233. Modarresi 1358, 73; On 53 he writes that it is characteristic for the 17 guilds of each town to pay their taxes to the *naqib-e shahr*! On the function of *naqib* see Floor 1973.

234. In first quarter of each year he [the *naqib*] appoints someone to convene the guild headmen of each guild. To their mutual satisfaction he fixes the bunicha of each [guild] in conformity with the Law, Right, Reason and the customs and rules of the realm." Tadhkirat al-Muluk 1943, 83.

235. Mahjub 1350; see also Savory 1969.

> The *ahl-e sokhan* and *ma`rakeh giran*, who form three groups:
>
> (1) *maddahan* (panygyrists) and *ghazal khvanan* (poetry-reciters), and *afsaneh guyan* (story-tellers).
>
> 2) The strong-arm men (*ahl-e zur*) from among the *ma`rakeh giran*, and these comprise eight groups: wrestlers, weight-lifters, (*sang giran*), wielders of the *naveh*, basket carriers (*salleh keshan*), porters (*hammalan*), mace wielders (*maghir garan*) rope dancers (*rasan bazan*), strong-men (*zurgaran*).
>
> 3) The sportsmen (*ahl-e bazi*) among the *ma`rakeh giran*, and these are three groups: jugglers (*taz bazan*), puppet players (*lo`bat bazan*), and conjurors (*hoqqeh bazan*).

Apart from the fact that the *fotovatnameh-ye soltani* refers to these groups as *ahl-e faqr* there is the interesting fact that the *naqib* in Safavid Iran "also appoints the elders of darvishes, (street) performers *ahl-i ma`arek* and so on."[236] It would seem that if the *naqib* had a function with regard to the *fotovvat* associations it would rather be in the sphere of street performers, dervishes, entertainers and the like. Such a link seems plausible in view of the fact that the supervision of the class of entertainers was divided between two officials since Timurid times.[237] One of these officials was the *naqib*, while this twofold division remained into existence till the beginning of this century.[238] This division, moreover, tallies with the one suggested by Modarresi with regard to the *Khaksar* and *Faqr-e `Ajam*.

The fact that the ranks of the hierarchy of the *Faqr-e `Ajam* are not those commonly associated with *fotovvat* organizations may not lead one to the conclusion that the *Faqr-e `Ajam* was not a *fotovvat* association. For the *Faqr-e `Ajam* had all other characteristics of such a *fotovvat* association. The veneration of the patrons (*pir*) of the 17 occupations as teachers (*morshed*) of the mystic knowledge suggests the atmosphere of the *fotovvat* association. Among the examples of *sokhanvari* presented by Mahjub figure a few verses containing the story of the creation (*ethbat*) of the art of hairdressing (*salmani*). These verses do not differ from the content of a *fotovvat-nameh* in prose.[239] Finally, Modarresi, (again without quoting his sources) states that the *naqib* taught the members of the *Faqr-e `Ajam* the fundamentals of their occupation according to the mystic lore in the form of poems and explained their meaning to them. During the session of the *naqib* with the guild headmen at *Nowruz* he would go through the question-and-answer routine common to the *fotovvat* ceremonial.[240]

During the months of Moharram, Safar, and Ramadan, members of the *Faqr-e `Ajam* staged *rowzeh-khvans* in various coffee houses and a competition in rethorics (*sokhanvari*) was held, a custom which was peculiar to the *Faqr-e `Ajam*. During those

236. Tadhkirat al-Muluk 1943, 83.

237. Tadhkirat al-Muluk 1943, 68, 83, 138-39, 149.

238. Floor 1971 a, 104.

239. Meier 1964, 315-16.

240. Modarresi 1358, 74.

events each of the 17 occupations was symbolized by a tool of trade which was nailed to the wall of the coffee house (*dar bastan beh sardam*). These symbols, banners etc., were stored for the remainder of the year in a mosque or a *takiyeh* (darvish convent) affiliated with the *Faqr-e `Ajam*.[241]

Public ceremonies show that guild members had strong ties with the dervish orders. At such festivities like the *`Eyd-e Qurban* and *Moharram* processions some guilds participated. Here, however, the town quarter and the affiliation with the *Heydari-Ne`mati* factions was the mobilizing factor. At the end of the 19th century hardly any guild groups (*dasteh*) participated in the *Moharram* processions, and only very few had banners which were typical for them.[242]

Conclusion: There does not seem to be convincing evidence to indicate that a strong bond existed among members of a guild with regard to the economic sphere of life. Guilds showed a spirit of brotherhood only when participating in socio-religious activities. But even then this spirit was focused on religious activities which they had in common with other Moslems rather than on causes peculiar to their guild. Most social activities of guild members took place within the context of dervish orders. For members of various socio-economic groups, guild members in particular, participated in *fotovvat* associations by joining for instance the *Faqr-e `Ajam*. However, there is no shred of evidence that guilds were organized along the lines of *fotovvat* organizational structures. Nor is there any evidence for the existence of initiation rites and other *fotovvat* ceremonial within the guilds. When we speak about a *fotovvat* association this term, therefore, does not refer to a guild, but to a socio-religious association affiliated with dervish orders.

V. GUILDS AND TAXATION

The payment of guild tax is one of the factors which distinguish the guilds (*asnaf*) from all other corporate groups. This tax is specific to the guilds and it is exceptional among Iranian taxes, for while all Iranian taxes are *impôts de quotité*, this particular tax is an *impôt de repartition*,[243] i.e., guilds, as opposed to all other urban groups, were treated as a corporate body for taxation purposes.[244] This peculiarity was apparently not clear to the Europeans working in Iran and therefore when their numbers grew in the latter half of the 19th century,[245] the Iranian government, for fiscal reasons, had to remind the European governments of this fact. On March 25, 1866, the Persian Iranian of Foreign Affairs sent a note to the British legation on this subject, stating that "it must be evident to Her Majesty's Legation that the taxation of wholesale merchants and of retailtraders is different and that the native shopkeepers who carry on a retail trade are subject to special taxation," and "Her Majesty's Legation will give notice to the British subjects who are engaged in

241. Meier 1964.

242. Van Vloten 1894, 110.

243. Nafiçi 1924, 132.

244. Lambton 1954, 24; Binning 1857, vol. 1, 278.

245. In 1865 there were about 50 Europeans in Tehran and in 1890 nearly 500. Curzon 1892, vol. 2, 334.

retail business to pay taxes to the Persian authorities like all other traders."[246] This statement not only proves that the last element of my definition is not superfluous; it also adds dimension and understanding to such statements as "no traders outside the guilds are liable to taxation."[247]

With these traders the whole-sale merchants (*tojjar*) are meant, who satisfy all the standards set by my definition save for the last element, the payment of guild taxes. This fact not only excludes the group of whole-sale merchants from the guilds, but also groups such as "doctors, washers of the dead, grave-diggers, singers, midwives, storytellers, wrestlers, and darvishes."[248] On the other hand it includes two important groups which are sometimes classed with the merchants, viz., the bankers (*sarraf*) and the brokers (*dallal*).[249]

The prevailing name for guild taxes in Qajar Iran is *maliyat-e senf*; we also find other terms such as *bonicheh* and *kharj* used in Tabriz and *tahmil* in Tehran. These terms refer to local usage only and are in fact synonymous with the general term *maliyat-e senf*.[250] Migeod incorrectly refers to this tax as *tamgha*, which actually means a small due (0.475 percent) collected from the merchants.[251]

Although the finance division was the most important branch of the civil administration in Qajar Iran as in the Ottoman Empire,[252] there were no established rules set by the central government for fixing the quota and collecting the guild tax.[253] Therefore the administrative methods varied locally and were generally based on the pattern already existing under the Safavid kings.[254] Allotting the quota and collecting the taxes was a task of the governors, but it was in fact delegated to one of their officers, the *kalantar*.[255] Each year the *kalantar* convoked the heads of those guilds which were not exempted from paying the guild tax. In Isfahan this took place on the first day of the month Farvardin and in Kashan sometime after *Nowruz*.[256]

Together with the heads of these guilds the *kalantar* fixed the total amount due and the proportional share to be paid by each individual guild, which in Isfahan was confirmed by the signature of one or two leading men of the guild. Whether such proceedings took place in other cities as well has not been recorded but it is probable.[257] After consulta-

246. FO 60/327, report 25 March 1886; see also Appendix III.

247. Balfour 1921, 152. Also statements like "le negociant persan ne paye pas un sou d'impot," de Gobineau, 374; de Rochechouart 1867, 176.

248. According to Lambton 1954, 25 these groups formed guilds.

249. Formally, the money changers and brokers formed guilds, as is clear from the fact their representatives were classed with the guilds in parliament. However, socially, the most influential and wealthy among them were part of the group of whole-sale merchants.

250. Greenfield 1904, 143; Brugsch 1862-63, vol. 1, 222.

251. Migeod 1990, 196; Demorgny 1913, 132.

252. Baer 1964, 74.

253. Lambton 1954, 24.

254. Lambton 1954, 24; Fasa'i 1314, vol. 2, 97.

255. Kosogovski 1344, 88; Legatie Perzië, bundel 5, letter 27 June 1893.

256. Lambton 1954, 24.

257. Lambton 1954, 24. Morier's statement that "if the kalantar's seal be not affixed to the documents which the Rayat brings forward in the time of the levy the assessment is not valid," makes it plausible that this custom also existed in Shiraz and elsewhere. Morier 1812, 235-36.

tion with the *kalantar*, each head of a guild then apportioned the amount due to be paid by his guild among the guild members, a procedure which could give cause to partiality.[258] In 1857, Binning reports for Shiraz that "this amount is divided among the tradesmen, by a mutual agreement among themselves termed boonicha-bundee, by which each man stipulates to pay so much according to their several means and prospects."[259] This consultation of the *kalantar* was the norm for guilds, who were characterized by the payment of *haqq-e bonicheh*; the quota for each guild member was fixed in consultation with and under the supervision of the *kalantar*.[260] The *kalantar* was assisted in his task to collect the guild tax by various officials.[261]

Guild tax was levied from all shopkeepers; it varied according to their location and occupation[262] and had to be levied in accordance with "the exigencies of the situation, of the province and its population."[263] This tax was not only a payment for the right to be in business,[264] but according to Curzon, guild tax could also include taxes like "ground rents of houses, the rents of caravanserais, baths, shops,[265] mills and factories." Curzon also adds, however, "these taxes are rarely exacted, and a most legitimate and profitable source of income is thus allowed to escape."[266]

In Tehran the total amount of the guild tax also included dues on coffee houses and taxes like *`eydi*, *`atassi* and some others, which are not specified.[267] Normally the amount due was apportioned uniformly over the guild members without taking their income into account.[268] Whether this rule extended to all cities in Iran is not certain. Some sources have it that "20% imposts on the profit of trade" were collected as guild tax,[269] which was more in conformity with the above spirit, in which the tax should be

258. Nafiçi 1924, 133; Balfour 1921, 152.

259. Binning 1857, vol. 1, 279.

260. Lambton 1954, 25.

261. In Tabriz the shop rent, which often included the guild tax, was collected by a *mobasher* (supervisor), while in Tehran there was a *mobasher-e asnaf* (guild supervisor). Aubin 1908, 37; see also E`temad al-Saltaneh 1306, 240; Fasa'i 1314-16, 97.

262. Legatie Perzië, bundel 5, letter 27 June 1893. Only retail traders with shops were subject to guiold tax. Hawkers did not pay guild tax. In Tabriz the drapers (*bazzaz*) forbade the whole-sale dealers (*binekdar*) to engage in the retail trade, on the grounds that the latter did not pay guild tax. Greenfield 1904, 143, n. 1.

263. Zarrabi 1342, 416.

264. Nafiçi 1924, 133.

265. In Tabriz the shopkeepers of the shops that were Government property, paid only the rent to the government, in which rent the guild tax was included. Greenfield 1904, 143, n. 1. A similar situation seems to have existed in Bandar `Abbas, considering that the rent of government-owned shops was considerably higher than the rent of those that were privately owned. Sadid al-Saltaneh 1342, 456.

266. Curzon 1892, vol. 2, 173.

267. Nafiçi 1924, 133.

268. According to a list of guild taxes for Tehran, guild tax seems to have been uniformly divided over the guild members only taking into account the location of the business, thus allowing for a difference in income. See Appendix III and also Häntzsche 1869, 133; Greenfield 1904, 143, no. 1. Moreover, one has to take into account theat the level of the guild tax depended on the negotiating skill and influence (*vaseteh*) of the guild headman and not on any established rule.

269. Curzon 1892, vol. 1, 473; Häntzsche 1869, 133.

fixed. However, they do not state in which particular city this form of taxation was followed. It probably was practiced, but apparently in a few cities only.[270] Whatever form taxation took the quota, collected legally, seems usually to have been less than this 20 percent rate. The Dutch Consul-General estimated in 1891 that the tax was not more than 10 *tumans* per person annually and probably less.[271]

The installments in which the quota had to be paid varied locally. In Isfahan, Tabriz, and Tehran the amount due was paid in twelve monthly installments,[272] but in Kashan it was due in four installments.[273] "Once in six months a meeting of all the members of the trade is called at some appointed place, when the position and standing of each individual is inquired into, and the amount that each person is to pay is determined by themselves, in such proportion as to make up the full amount due to the Government."[274] It was the task of the guild's headman to collect the quota and to pay the total sum on behalf of the guild to the governor. This was the normal practice in Kerman, Tehran and Isfahan.[275] However, another practice also existed, that of paying the governor's representative directly without the guild leader's intervention. This practice seems to have been followed in Tabriz and Isfahan by those guilds which did not have to pay the *haqq-e bonicheh*.[276] In such cases an overseer (*mobasher*) collected the guild member's allotted share each month in the bazaar.

The following exception to the rule mentioned above is interesting. According to Binning "it not unfrequently happens that the Government demands these taxes in advance; when finances are low and money required to meet expenses; and then the oostads of the trades are called on to make a certain sum, which is afterwards deducted from the amount of tax, when the proper time of payment comes around. This is called musa'ede or assistance, which is often required year after year."[277] Apart from the reason given by Binning for the existence of this practice there is the fact that the governors, who had paid a large sum in advance to the Shah for their office, were never sure for how long their office would last. Such uncertainty caused many governors to exploit their province as rapidly as possible to avoid financial disaster if they were prematurely dismissed. Whatever may have been the cause for extracting *mosa`edeh* it certainly gave the guilds leverage with the governor, which they could use to their own advantage.

For various reasons, ranging from royal whim or favor to the rational aim of helping a guild out of temporary financial difficulties, exemption from taxation could be granted to the guilds. Depending on the intention of the bestower of this privilege, the

---

270. The situation was probably as Greenfield 1904, 143, n.1. described it. "The guild tax is uniformly levied on the shops and rises up to (a maximum of) 20 percent of the (annual?) income (of the shopkeepers).

271. Legatie Perzië, bundel 5, letter 27 June 1893.

272. Actually ten installments as no collection took place during Ramazan and Moharram. Lambton 1954, 24; Aubin 1908, 37; Brugsch 1862-63, vol. 1, 222; Issawi 1971, 285.

273. Zarrabi 1342, 417.

274. Issawi 1971, 285.

275. Lambton 1954, 24-25; Issawi 1971, 285 (one of the trade together with a government official).

276. Aubin 1908, 37; Lambton 1954, 24-25.

277. Binning 1857, vol. 1, 279.

exemption was given for part or all of the taxes, for a specified period or for eternity.[278] We find many instances cited where guilds were granted such exemptions under the Qajars, as had been the practice in former times. Lambton mentions that in Isfahan the carpenters (*najjar*), the stone cutters (*sangtarash*) and the sword-makers (*shamshirsaz*) were exempt from taxation.[279] It seems that the sword-makers' exemption even dates back to the reign of Shah `Abbas I (r. 1584-1629).[280] But not only Isfahan was favored in this respect. In Kashan the bakers butchers and tanners were exempt, in Yazd the grocers in Tehran the butchers and bakers.[281]

One must realize, however, that tax exemption did not necessarily mean that a guild was free from exaction, legal or illegal, by the authorities. As in the 17th century exemption was granted in many cases, but the guilds concerned were then subject to *corvées* on demand by the government.[282] Notwithstanding the exemption, governors were wont to demand payment from the guilds and accordingly the central government had to order these governors to stop their illegal practices. But this restraint was never effective for long; even when the shah had invoked the curses of Allah on the offenders.[283]

Since the Treaty of Turkomanchay of 1828, Russian merchants, and later, when commercial treaties were concluded between Iran and other European Governments, other European merchants, also only had to pay 5 percent *ad valorem* import duties and were exempt from paying internal duties. But Europeans who came to Iran to trade or to pursue a craft did not fall under this regulation. Since the European traders and craftsmen were accustomed to tax exemption they tried under the protection of their legations to forgo paying their taxes.

In 1886 the Iranian government wanted to change this situation and sent a note to all European legations pointing out that all European retail traders and craftsmen were subject to special taxation just as their Iranian counterparts were. The legations replied that they would consent to an arrangement to be reached with the Iranian government, Russia and Great Britain. These two countries were at this time the most influential foreign powers in Iran. Thereafter the Iranian government started negotiations with the Russian government. The proposed regulation referred especially to Russian and Turkish subjects. The number of other European subjects in Iran was negligible.[284]

---

278. E`temad al-Saltaneh 1295, vol. 1, 220; Beyza'i 1337, 185.

279. Lambton 1954, 25. In Isfahan the grocers (*baqqal*) and bakers (*khabbaz*) were also exempted from taxation. E`temad al-Saltaneh 1295, vol. 2, 110.

280. Lambton 1954, 25.

281. Naraqi 1345, 251; Beyza'i 1337, 185; Kosogovski 1344, 45, 47; Greenfield 1904, 145; Forsat 1316, 490.

282. Greenfield 1904, 145.

283. Greenfield 1904, 146.

284. Legatie Perzië, bundel 5, letter 27 June 1893. The British consul-general in Tabriz wrote, "Persia offers no field for European workmen, least of all English, who are, as a rule, the most indisposed to adapt themselves to the manners and habits of other nations. Some few German have, from time to time, endeavoured to exercise their trade at Tabreez; but notwithstanding their thrifty habits and modest expectations, they seldom succeeded in gaining more than a bare livelihood." Jones 1870, 421.

Although the Russian government acknowledged that Russian and Turkish traders were in a privileged position as to taxation in Iran, they rejected the Iranian plan to incorporate foreign traders into the Iranian guilds. Finally, the Russian government agreed to the practice that foreign retail traders and craftsmen would pay taxation to the Iranian government in two yearly installments, the amount of which would be fixed by the Russian consul or by the Corps Consulaire of the Consular district. Having obtained the Russian consent to this measure the Iranian government sent notes to all other European powers, requesting them to give notice to their subjects, who were engaged in retail trade or pursued a craft, to pay taxes directly to the Iranian government. Although the European powers agreed to this measure, things did not work out very well, for the Iranian government again had to inform the European governments of their obligations on 1 June 1894.[285]

Whatever influence the two great powers of Russia and Britain may have had in Iran, it certainly did not extend to the financial administration. Even when the Iranian customs administration was reorganized by Belgian experts, this had no effect on the Iranian financial administration in general.[286] The Belgian customs officers volunteered no information, and instead of giving advice to their Iranian colleagues, they looked down upon them.[287] Therefore, "Persian finance remained tangled had there been any to tangle," Shuster, the American Treasure-General, remarked.[288]

As the financial and economic situation worsened in the latter half of the 19th century the governors became more demanding. Moreover, the rule of convening the guild chiefs to fix the quota seems to have fallen into disuse about 1890, at least in Tehran.[289] This gave cause to grave abuse and gross injustice. No one was safe from the rapacity and greed of the ruling class, as they demanded ever more money and, as we have seen, even tax exemption did not safeguard one against their exploitative practices.

Na'eb al-Saltaneh, the governor of Tehran, paid 25,000 *tumans* per annum to his father Naser al-Din Shah, being the tax from the butchers' guild. At the same time he raised guild taxes by 5000 *tumans*, all of which he put into his own pocket. All in all, in 1896, he extorted illegally from the butchers' guild as much as up to 200,000 *tumans*.[290]

Tehran, in 1921, became cognizant of the fact that the guild taxes of 60,000 *qrans* had remained fixed for a very long time. Originally, the amount was based on statistics, then long out of date. The addition of new guilds, the disappearance of old ones, increases and decreases in the size of existing guilds, had not since then been taken into account.[291] In Isfahan, for instance, the two remaining oil-mills were paying the oil-millers guild taxes,

---

285. Legatie Perzië, bundel 5, letter 27 June 1893 and bundel 4, letter 1 June 1895, see pp. 209–10.

286. Shuster 1912, 38.

287. Mostowfi n.d., 2, 408.

288. Shuster 1912, 38.

289. Balfour 1921, 152; Nafiçy 1924, 133.

290. Kosogovski 1344, 44, 46.

291. Nafiçy 1924, 133. The amount the butchers' guild, 25,000 *tumans*, in 1896 is much larger than the amount collected from the guilds in Tehran around 1921, being only 60,000 *qrans* or 6,000 *tumans*. I do not know how to explain this huge difference.

established when this guild was considerably more numerous.[292] Likewise in Tehran out of 84 guilds only some 30-odd guilds had to pay guild taxes, "while amongst those which escape are such wealthy bodies as bankers."[293]

Although the Iranian government tried to begin reforms of the financial administration following the revolution of 1906, it was not until 1921 that the first serious effort was made to reassess the fiscal contribution of the guilds, and then that was restricted to the guilds in Tehran. The new legislation, prepared by Ziya al-Din, aimed to collecting an annual amount of one million *qrans* instead of the 60,000 *qrans* previously collected. However, Ziya al-Din's cabinet fell and the draft proposals never became law.[294]

A total revision of these affairs had to wait till 1930 when Reza Shah Pahlavi, as part of his state reforms, ordered a new legislation to be designed concerning the taxation of trade. The new tax law meant that the guilds were no longer treated as corporate bodies with regard to taxation.[295] From now on the guild members were divided into income categories, paying fixed sums according to their annual income. This meant that the guilds were brought into line with other economic groups such as merchants, lawyers, doctors, etc. as to taxation. However, it did not mean the end of the guilds as a socio-economic form of organization.[296]

VI. PRICE-FIXING AND THE CONTROL OF STANDARDS OF WORKMANSHIP

Price-fixing (*tas`ir*) or rather the lack of it, is another important aspect which indicates a lack of economic solidarity and cohesion amongst guild members. The absence of price-fixing does not, however, mean that at times guilds did not exert control over their wares. Indeed they did, but the periods were usually of a short duration,[297] and were usually the result of pressure from guild leaders with already large investments in their guild, or as a result of a guild having already formed a cohesive structure within itself. However, price-fixing was never with a view to providing a reasonable minimal income to guild members.

Qajar Iran's free trade economy was not affected much by government interference. Certainly the market economy was not left completely to its own devices. The elite had large personal interests in the economy and profound power over its operation. In most cases, commodity prices were arrived at with a free rein, resulting in brisk competition. This was especially true in the bazaar, where members of the same craft or trade marketed side by side. Accordingly, consumer opportunity was fully exploited, for "a Persian does not go to a shop to buy anything without going to every other shop in the

---

292. Tahvildar 1341, 95.

293. Balfour 1921, 152.

294. Nafiçy 1924, 133.

295. Law of 1 Farvardin 1929, Bulletin 1934, 117.

296. See Floor 1975.

297. See e.g. Adams 1906, 163. "The artisans have guilds, and sometimes work in combination to regulate the price; " which seems to be a verbatim quotation of Wilson 1896, 279.

bazaar to ask whether he can get a similar article better and cheaper. Such a convenience as fixed prices, alike for all, does not exist in the Persian bazaar, and prices are generally on the ascending or descending scale, according to the merchant's estimate of his customer's wealth."[298]

The custom of haggling can be attributed to the fact that both buyer and seller had incomplete knowledge about the changes in the supply situation, due to the poor and inefficient organization of the market. Therefore, bazaar prices were often unstable and sensitive to bazaar rumors.[299] There were exceptions, however. It was part of the task of the urban governments to fix prices of products like bread, meat, wood and fodder.[300] High prices for these important products would lead to social unrest which could be very embarrassing or damaging to the authorities concerned. The chief magistrate of the city, the *kalantar,* who, as we have seen, was in charge of all affairs relating the guilds, held a meeting each month with the heads of the bakers', butchers', grocers', forage sellers' and coal sellers' guilds.[301] In consultation with the *kalantar,* the guild heads would fix the maximum price of products sold by their members. The monthly price list drawn up by them, called *tas`ir-e ajnas,*[302] was announced by *jarchi*s or public criers.[303] Beginning in 1852 the list was also published in the government newspaper in Tehran.[304]

In Tehran monthly meetings with the guild heads appear to have fallen into disuse under the governorship of Na'eb al-Saltaneh. Although Polak still attests their regularity in the fifties and sixties, these meetings were held only when demanded by public sentiment mainly in the eighties and nineties. By Kennedy's instigation (the British chargé d'affaires at Tehran) Naser al-Din Shah

> ordered that a meeting shall be held consisting of Ulemas, merchants, heads of guilds and some of the Ministers of State to discuss the question, and come to some satisfactory decision with regard to lowering the rates of bread, meat, fowl etc. H.H. [Aminu's-Sultan] remarked privately to me that, although it is satisfactory to see that H.M. does take interest in such friendly private intimations, yet as long as the administration of the guilds and the Governorship of the town remains in the band of the Naib-us-Saltaneh and his uncle Vazir Nizam no good can be expected to be derived out of such meetings. Naib-us-Saltaneh will of course preside at this meeting and he in reality, in conjunction with Vazir Nizam, is the cause of these high rates on the necessaries of life.[305]

298. Landor 1902, vol. 1, 299.
299. Sjoberg 1960, 206.
300. Aubin 1908, 37 ; Polak 1865, vol. 1, 135.
301. Aubin 1908, 37.
302. Polak 1865, vol. 1, 135.
303. Binning 1857, vol. 1, 337.
304. Mostowfi n.d., vol. 2, 18.
305. Keddie 1966, 74, see also E`temad al-Saltaneh 1345, 841.

The interest shown by the Shah worked favorably for him in two ways. Firstly, he showed his concern for his subjects, and secondly, by the participation of the religions leaders, the measures taken and the prices fixed acquired an aura of legitimacy. Both factors enhanced the Shah's position.

In spite of this government interference, guild leaders especially of the bakers' and butchers' guilds were to a great extent able to control the price of their products. The *qassab-bashi* (head of the butchers' guild) controlled the supply of stock for slaughter and thus the price of meat. It is true that the cattle owners brought their herds to the city and sold them to individual butchers, but it was the *qassab-bashi* who each day determined how many heads of cattle and sheep were to be slaughtered in the *qassab-khaneh* or abbatoir.[306] In 1895 or thereabouts, the butchers had to pay one *qran* to the government per animal thus paying tax for slaughtering.[307] The *qassab-khaneh* was situated outside the city walls. Anyone wishing to bring live animals into the city had also to pay one *qran*.[308] The object of this regulation was to make it unattractive to slaughter and sell meat illegally. It was for this purpose also that the meat in the abbatoir got a seal, so that one could discover offenders very easily.[309] The *qassab-bashi* seems to have been the contractor of the abbatoir in most cities.[310] He had to pay the rent of the abbatoir, amounting to 9,000 *tumans* yearly in Tehran in 1892.[311]

The *qassab-bashi* and the guild elders were the owners of the meat and the shops in each city. The daily supply of meat for the city was delivered by servants of the *qassab-bashi* to the butchers, who hired the shop and managed the sales. After having weighed the meat the butchers would give a receipt in return. Each night the butchers paid the money they owed for the meat to the representatives of the *qassab-bashi*.[312] A similar situation existed for the bakers' guild. Part of the supply of wheat was controlled by the government while the remainder had to be bought in the market.[313] To make greater profits in the wheat trade government officials (from the governor to the private grain owners) would form a wheat-corner and create an artificial bread shortage. One of the principal participants was invariably the *nanva-bashi* or head of the bakers' guild.[314] Only after some people had died and the mood among the population became highly explosive, i.e., when the situation in the city had become really desperate, would the government step in. The members of the wheat-corner, forewarned by the government, would sell their grain to the retail dealers who then bore the brunt of an outraged public opinion. The government ordered the prices

306. Kosogovski 1344, 44. According to Wills 1883, 299, the amount to be paid was nine pence or 5 *qrans* about 1880.

307. Kosogovski 1344, 46.

308. Kosogovski 1344, 46.

309. Kosogovski 1344, 46 ; de Rochechouart 1867, 181.

310. Kosogovski 1344, 46.

311. According to Curzon 1892, vol. 1, 299, the lease of the slaughter houses brought in an income of £2,230 per annum, being about 9,000 *tumans*. The revenue was stated by him to be 8,000 *tumans* in Ibid. vol. 2, 481 ; Kosogovski 1344, 46.

312. Kosogovski 1344, 46; Tahvildar 1342, 118.

313. See on this subject Floor 1983.

314. Shuster 1911, 171; Mostowfi n.d., vol. 2, 394 ; Algar 1969, 50.

to be lowered on penalty of the bastinado or worse. The bakers then protested that they had bought expensive wheat and could not sell their bread any cheaper, for they would then loose money. If the bakers (or butchers) refused to give in, they were flogged; sometimes a few of them were baked in their own ovens.[315]

As well as these sanguinary methods the government had other ways of lowering the price of comestibles. It could sell grain from its own stock and/or it could abrogate the monopoly of the guild.[316] In 1895, Naser al-Din Shah, under heavy pressure, gave his soldiers permission to slaughter animals in the city and to sell their meat in Tehran. This measure proved to be very effective, for in a few days the price of meat was at a third of its former level.[317] In 1916 the same measure was taken with regard to bakers, permitting everyone to bring bread into the city.[318] Unfortunately, the effect of such measures was usually of short duration. The guild concerned would pay the governor of the city some money and would obtain the repeal of the decree. The same method was used by some guilds to obtain permission from the governor - always in need of money - to fix the prices of their products themselves.[319] Another favorite price-enforcing commodity was sugar (an important element of the daily diet of the population), and several times during the Qajar period the price of sugar rose sky-high because some merchants dominated the market and fixed high minimum prices.[320] The best known example is the alleged enforcing of the sugar price by a number of merchants in Tehran in 1905. The governor of Tehran ordered them to the bastinado, and the resultant protest by the trading community and religious leaders was one of the events leading to the Revolution of 1906.[321] Other products known to be used for price manipulation were turquoises and shawls, at times more expensive in Iran than in Russia and Europe.[322]

Accompanying the guilds' general inability to fix minimum prices was the absence of any guild guarantee or control over the standard of workmanship. The absence of guild interference in this respect is yet another result of the loose organization of the guilds. This is also reflected in their apprenticeship system, which, as we have seen earlier, lacked universal criteria governing the apprenticeship training.[323]

---

315. Wills 1886, 38; Stack 1882, vol. 1, 217; Polak 1865, vol. 2, 74. Nowadays things have changed much for the better, although at times bakers are still up to their old game of cheating customers. Likewise the government penalties are less harsh but the following newspaper report is of interest: "Five bakers in Manjil near Rasht were convicted of overcharging their customers and sent to jail with shaved heads when they refused to pay fines of 1.500 rials each". Kayhan, International edition (weekly) vol. 3, no. 148, January 23, 1971, 3.

316. Mostowfi n.d., vol. 2, 43; Kosogovski 1344, 171, 172.

317. Kosogovski 1344, 47.

318. Mostowfi n.d., vol. 2, 431, 432.

319. Kosogovski 1344, 45

320. See e.g. RMM 34, 253.

321. Kasravi 1319-21, vol. 1, 82.

322. Bleibtreu 1894, 155; von Kotzebue 1819, 223.

323. See above part III. "No artizan takes a pride in excelling in his work. The laziness of the Persian character is so great that the workman can never be brought to do more than what is sufficient to earn the price of his labour." Jenner 1870, 399.

It was the government's task to supervise the maintenance of price regulations and to check the quality of products put up for sale. Since ancient times the *mohtaseb* was given the duty of checking prices, weights and measures.[324] During the 19th century this official acted under the orders of the *darugheh*, the chief of the bazaar police. In most cities the office of *mohtaseb* was abolished around 1850, and his functions were transferred to the *darugheh*. If fraudulent shopkeepers were exposed, they were fined or given the bastinado. However, for financial considerations great leniency was shown towards offenders.[325] Although Naser al-Din Shah reinstated the office of *mohtaseb* in some cities around 1860 it never regained its former importance. At all events, in Tehran the task of checking weights and measures was executed by the *nazmiyeh* or police into which force the *darugheh* with his market police had been incorporated. After the revolution of 1906 the new municipal law of 20 Rabi` al-Thani 1325 (1907) gave this responsibility to the Iranian police, although in fact the actual practice of the law remained confined to Tehran.[326]

The regulations drawn up by the local authorities regarding the quality of products concerned "comestibles, fruit, inns and teahouses, bakers, butchers etc."[327] In Isfahan regulations were laid down by the *kalantar*, for instance those enforcing cooks to preserve meat with ice; but gross neglect was shown in implementing these instructions.[328] The regulations had to be enforced regularly and for a short period thereafter they were strictly adhered to, but very soon they were neglected again.[329]

The constitution of 1906 apparently left the guilds completely unchanged.[330] In Tehran, 1910, a company was formed which had obtained the monopoly of the butcher's trade and which asked high prices for meat of inferior quality. The result was strong protest by the citizens of Tehran: "declaring that such a situation had only been possible under the absolutist [pre-constitutional] regime." Although the result of the popular demand for redress of their grievances is not known, the company probably will have been discontinued, for, as we have seen above, there were other means to obtain illicit financial benefits.[331] A new development was the creation of the Alimentation Service (*edareh-ye arzaq*) in 1916, part of the Ministry of Finance. This service had "a monopoly of the purchase and sale of grain in Tehran and adjoining provinces."[332] To maintain its regulations the service divided the city into 5 areas; each area chief was in charge of inspectors (*mofattesh*). The inspectors, one for every 6 or 7 shops, were subordinates to a chief inspector (*sar*

---

324. See on the *mohtaseb* and *darugheh*, Floor 1971 c.

325. "There are also motassibs, or inspector of markets. These men break faulty measures and scales, and seize (for their own profit) decayed or adultered provisions, or take small bribes for not doing so. Thus the offenders are reclly fined.» Wills 1886, 41,42.

326. RMM 1914, vol. 27, 232-234.

327. Polak 1865, vol. 1, 135.

328. Tahvildar 1342, 119.

329. Polak 1865, vol. 1, 135.

330. Although the levying of taxes was the most important government branch a fiscal reform of the taxation of the guilds occured only in 1926 (Law of Farvardin 1, 1929, *Bulletin* no. 1 (Janvier 1934), 17.

331. RMM 10, 255.

332. Mostowfi n.d., vol. 2, 135 ; Millspaugh 1926, 25.

mofattesh) who reported any untoward occurrences to the area chief.[333] Nevertheless, the activities by the Alimentation Services hardly affected the bakers' guild, for as late as 1923 they retained "unsanitary methods and an age-old reputation for skull-duggery."[334]

In April 1921 the Municipalty of Tehran started a Hygienic and Assistance Service charged with the prevention of illness and of unhygienic conditions in the city: Amongst other things the new municipal body supervised the trade in foodstuffs and prohibited the sale of products unfit for consomption. Their control was directed toward butchers' and the bakers' shops in particular. The apothecaries were to receive their special attention too.[335]

To summarize: The political weakness and loose organization of the guilds was reflected in their inability to agree among themselves on the setting of minimum prices. Some guilds, such as the bakers' and butchers' were sometimes able to set minimum prices because they were better organized. But these instances were only possible because government officials were partners in the deal. Moreover, these 'corners' were of short duration and were meant to make big profits quickly. Corresponding with the inability to fix prices is the fact that the guilds did not control the quality of the goods made or sold by their members. The initiative in these matters was taken by the government. Legislation was designed to protect the consumer by fixing maximum prices for necessities -to prevent social unrest - and to set forth criteria for selling and making products. The *mohtaseb* and later the *darugheh* were given the job of maintaining these regulations. Supervision was, however, lax, "so what is done by the authorities for the provisioning of the people serves the exploitation of the people rather than their benefit and profit."[336]

VII. POLITICAL FUNCTION OF THE GUILDS

At no time during the Qajar era, were the guilds able to strengthen their political or economical position by political action. Even during the periods when the traders and artisans were a power to reckon with, they failed to translate this strength into an improvement of their status. While guilds in Europe have influenced and for some time even wielded the power of city government, guilds in Iran have never done so, except during the constitutional movement (1906 - 1909). This weakness was probably due to the fact that Iranian guilds were not voluntary associations based on the assent and willingness of their members. Contrary to the situation in Europe where guilds grew into a force which has helped to build up a social structure by which they have been superseded the Iranian guilds were passive, loosely organized associations fostered and controlled by the government.[337] Iranian guilds therefore resembled the Roman *classes* rather than the European craft guilds

333. Mostowfi n.d., vol. 2, 135.
334. Millspaugh 1946, 103.
335. RMM 47, 125, 126.
336. Polak 1865, vol. 1, 135.
337. Unwin 1925, 61.

in their hey-day, being only an extension of the urban bureaucracy. This being so, they had little access to political power.

Such a development as took place in Europe was unattainable in Iran, according to Lorini. "Be it because of the political constellation, be it the lack of adequate intellectual culture among the guild members, be it because the Persian is by nature distrustful of co-operation."[338] Lorini's view is shared by de Rochechouart, who, writing 40 years earlier, is of the opinion that "co-operation above all concerned the *tojjar*, the wholesale merchants; the retail dealers and artisans have neither the opportunity nor the necessary capital to envisage an association such as meant above; for them (their association) has other advantages and ends."[339] What then were these other advantages and ends? Lambton has put it nicely as follows: "The main purposes of this gild organization were two: first individuals by their association together were more easily able to resist demands by the government. Secondly the gild organization was somewhat paradoxily encouraged by the government to facilitate its control of economic life, the collection of taxes, and the performance of corvees."[340] I wish to make the following comment on Lambton's contention.

First, Lambton presupposes that guilds were voluntary associations of traders and artisans, the natural result of structures existing in Middle Eastern society.[341] Secondly, Lambton implies that the encouragement by the government of the guild organization was a later development. I for my part do not agree with either of these implications. Guild organizations are the result of and inherent to the structure of pre-industrial society. Government in such societies lacked qualified personnel to control the activities of all the layers of society. It therefore had to waive its control of local power in favor of trusted influential representatives of such groups as tribes, village communities, cities and occupational groups, without relinquishing its right to exercise its legitimate control over these categories. Guild organization was the natural outcome of the fact that the government singled out groups for taxation and other purposes. As a result associations came into being which had their own specific interests. Whether the leaders of such groups occupied their positions because of appeal to tradition or by self-appointment is not as relevant as the fact that they were as such recognized by the government. Consequently, as the situation in Qajar Iran bears out, the fiscal and economic functions of guild organization were more important than any other function which the guilds acquired. The condition of the guilds in Qajar Iran bears witness to the fact that guild members were only associations of loosely united individuals, whose main task was to facilitate the collection of taxes and the control of economic life by the government.

As a result of their being treated by the government as corporate bodies, the guilds/tax-groups acquired specific interests as representing groups which had little or no effective access in government. Therefore the second and derived function of guild organization was "the means of defending themselves against the attempts at extortion being

338. Lorini 1900, 244.

339. De Rochechouart 1867, 177.

340. Lambton 1965, 128.

341. Lambton 1954, 20 note 2.

made upon them by Persian officials."[342] However, one must not exaggerate the political effectiveness and the power of the guilds, which were definitely non-elite groups. There is no evidence at all for Haas's contention that "the merchants and the arts and crafts are the only classes which can boast of an efficient organization. The craft guilds and merchant corporations were organizations in their own right, functioning by their own initiative and maintaining their own power and importance."[343]

Although individuals were still prone to be subject to excessive demands made by the authorities, it was only by belonging to a guild that guild members acquired some measure of security and status. Unity, however, feeble and weak its organization, makes a kind of power. It was this bargaining power which defined to what extent guild members could benefit from their association. But many of these weakly organized guilds were of no account and their members hardly benefited, since "their organization resembled rather a police regulation than a privilege."[344] For one has to bear in mind that Qajar Iran society was divided into two opposing groups, the rulers and the ruled. The loosely organized guilds could only bridge the gap existing between the rulers and the ruled, and represent their grievances to the government, through the intermediary of patron-brokers, in particular the religious leaders. Moreover the illiterate and ignorant lower classes, whose main concern was how to make a reasonable living, could not press for structural reforms in a society whose functioning they hardly understood. It is therefore not surprising to observe that concerted guild actions were controlled by their patron-brokers. These brokers always centered their demands upon their own and their followers' parochial interests. Although the political influence of the guilds was at best marginal, they had at their disposal several means of communication to get things done their way. As has been pointed out above (chapter one) the middle man role of the guild leaders was of paramount importance. By having a foot in both camps, they could bargain for conditions which were to the advantage of all parties concerned. If bargaining broke down or did not meet with success there were several lines of communication open to the guild leaders to achieve their ends. In the first place by lobbying important brokers, such as government officials and religious leaders, they could try and win support for their case against measures that had been taken. The brokers in return for the guilds' allegiance would intercede for them. If a broker had enough 'pull' he could have measures revoked or have negotiations start all over again.

As well as offering their political support, the guilds made use of other techniques, such as bribery. For example, they would step up payments to the governor, who was always in need of money, or they would present him with money presents. Na'eb al-Saltaneh, the governor of Tehran, and his deputies allowed both the butchers' and the bakers' guilds at several occasions to fix the price for their wares in exchange for a lump sum.[345] When, for instance, in 1895 the Shah gave his soldiers permission to slaughter and sell meat, in order to lower the meat price, the butchers paid the Governor of Tehran and

342. FO 60-327, report June 24, 1886.

343. Haas 1949, 104.

344. De Rochechouart 1867, 183.

345. Kosogovski 1344, 45, 60.

his mother a handsome amount of money. Then the Shah, who also got a share, forbade the soldiers to slaughter and sell meat and the price of meat rose again.[346]

But as the political situation was fluid and erratic, deals made could be unmade as easily. If the guild leaders saw no point in keeping the bargaining going and if the above mentioned techniques met with no success, they steered towards a conflict. The guilds could have recourse to what Binder calls the positive system challenging process, which is a variation of the bargaining technique.[347] The guilds in that case would either refuse to bargain any longer and to co-operate with the authorities or would start coercive actions against the government. This technique rested on the supposition that the authorities would prefer bargaining to a hold-out and a further spreading of civil disobedience. Refusal to bargain also implied delaying or refusing of pay taxes.[348] These coercive actions could be divided into several techniques, not all of which were necessarily violent. Firstly the guild could start a slander campaign, vilifying the authorities and spreading rumors. The impact of such actions could entice other groups with grievances against the authorities concerned to join in the action. Such defamation of character could lead to mobilization of the opposition and lead to the downfall of officials.[349] Another technique is the following: a dissatisfied guild starts visiting opposition leaders, thereby putting pressure on the government. When in 1913 influential leaders of the bazaar community were dissatisfied with the governments' bread policy they openly clamored for the formation of a new cabinet under the leadership of an opponent of this policy.[350] The best known technique is that of closing down the bazaar by either a particular guild and or the whole trading community. The economic life of the city would then be completely paralyzed and everybody was affected by this situation. This could lead to a highly dangerous situation since the demonstrations which the guild would stage and which were mostly led by religious leaders could easily turn into rioting. The most striking instance of this technique was in 1890/91 when religious leaders and reformists supported by the merchants and guilds challenged the government on the tobacco-concession question. The ulama forbade smoking, and pipes were broken by the population and even in the Shah's own palace nobody dared to smoke.[351] Although the guilds played an important part in this movement they did neither lead it, nor did it originate among them. The leaders were the ulama and the modernists, who each for their own reasons mobilized the dissatisfied and xenophobe bazaar community against the Shah and the foreign investors.[352] A variation of this technique was seeking sanctuary, for which the cooperation of the ulama was indispensable. As the ulama considered the granting of asylum the mainstay of their power, the guilds were always assured of at least passive cooperation. By this act the guilds severed their relation with the political authority and appealed for intercession with the religious authority.

346. Kosogovski 1344, 47.

347. Binder 1962, 275 f.

348. Kosogovski 1344, 48.

349. For examples of the use of this technique see Mostowfi n.d., vol. 2, 399; Kasravi, vol. 2, 339; Brugsch 1862, vol. 2, 332.

350. Mostowfi n.d., vol. 2, 501.

351. On this movement see Keddie 1966.

352. Keddie 1966.

The latter, of course, would act in favor of the guilds, since it enhanced their bargaining power *vis à vis* the government.

As is clear from the above, the guilds could only put pressure on the political authorities through the intermediary of brokers who had access to the government. It was these brokers rather than the guilds that had influence. The activities in which the guilds were engaged were always either controlled by these brokers or aimed at getting brokers to intercede for them.

Now we will turn to a chapter in the history of the Iranian guilds of which it has been said that guilds for a short period actually influenced local and central government, I refer to the fight for a constitution (1905-1909). As it is not my intention to discuss the ins and outs of the constitutional movement, I will only discuss those guild activities during that period which are relevant for this study.

The role played by the guilds in the constitutional movement should not be exaggerated. It is true that the movement would not have been able to achieve success if the traders and artisans had not provided their enthusiastic support. But apart from the fact that the aims of the constitutional movement went beyond the narrow confines of the guilds' interests, the guild members only provided the rank and file; the leading elements of the movement came from other quarters.[353] The wholesale merchants (*tojjar*), bankers (*sarraf*) and guilds (*asnaf*) though instrumental through their coordinated actions to obtain the Constitution and establishing Parliament, nevertheless provided mainly support to the intelligentsia in Tehran and their efforts to promote liberal ideas in the Constitutional movement. However, the guild organization alone proved to be inadequate and too loose to channel the political aspirations of their members, which militates against those authors who observe a strong organization among them.[354] Therefore, I purposely wrote 'guild members' rather than 'guilds,' for the former found an outlet for their political ideas in the *anjomans* or political clubs which mushroomed after 1906. The events leading to the revolution of 1906 culminated in the general *bast* (sanctuary) of the bazaar community and the religious leaders of Tehran. The latter went to the holy city of Qom, the former sought sanctuary on the grounds of the British Legation.[355] There each guild had its own tent; the upkeep of those present was paid by a few merchants.[356] After Mozaffar al-Din Shah (1896-1907) had granted a *Majles* or Parliament and a constitution on 5 August 1906 the guilds, amongst others, constituted *anjomans* to discuss what was to be done in the *Majles*. In Tehran alone guilds had formed seventy *anjomans*.[357] The discussions which took place reflected modernist and Islamic reformist opinions, tendencies which were also present in earlier movements, such as the tobacco régie rebellion.[358] As well as the call for modernization of the country, there was the demand for *mashru`iyyeh*, or the reinstating

353. Lambton 1963 b.

354. Haas 1949, 104.

355. Avery 1965, 124.

356. Dowlatabadi n.d., vol. 2, 72-75.

357. Lambton 1954, 29; Kasravi 1319-21, vol. 1, 226; vol. 2, 177.

358. Keddie 1966.

of Islam in its rightful place in Iranian society.[359] Besides, many bazaaris thought that the *Majles* would discuss the lowering and fixing of prices of prime necessities, thereby displaying their absence of political awareness.[360] This idea was fed by several propagandists, who promised cheaper living, for their own political ends.[361] Both the demand for *mashru`iyyeh* and the demand for cheaper living show that the guild members were mobilized because their brokers expressed the aims of the movement in Islamic terms, and in return for their support promised them immediate spoils.

It also indicates the lack of political acumen and initiative among the guilds. To strengthen their activities in support of the constitutional movement the *anjomans* of the guilds of Tehran formed a central guild council (*anjoman-e markazi-ye asnaf*).[362] Dowlatabadi, a nationalist with a religious background, was requested to become their advisor (*mo`allem*). He wrote their regulations. Each of the guild *anjomans* chose one representative, from whom twelve representatives were elected to form, together with Dowlatabadi, a kind of executive committee (*anjoman-e khass*).[363] The headquarters of the *anjoman-e asnaf* were in the Sepahsalar mosque next to the *Majles*.[364] This streamlined organization, which was joined by many provincial guild *anjomans*, enabled the guild representatives in the *Majles* to work more effectively. When the *Majles* was opened in 1907, the guilds were represented by thirty two delegates. They formed about twenty-two percent of the total number of members of the *Majles*.[365] How elections were held is not known, but the guild representatives showed a great deal of cohesion and were less divided than other groups, probably due to the organization of the *anjomans*.[366] The *anjoman-e khass* also issued a paper, called *Anjoman-e Asnaf* (Guilds Council), which was shortly thereafter changed to *Bamdad* (Aurora).[367] In other large towns the guilds also formed *anjomans*, such as in Yazd, the *hay'at-e asnaf* (guild assembly) formed by the representatives of all the guilds.[368] In Kerman the guilds, each represented by two members, constituted the *majma`-ye ettefaq-e `omumi* (general assembly). "The head of the assembly was chosen from their ranks, and generally was a member of the religious class."[369] The assembly of Kerman continued to meet until 1930.[370] In Shiraz an *anjoman-e asnafiyeh* was formed.[371]

The influence of these *anjomans* was considerable, although the situation varied per city and per year. In some cities such as Isfahan and Mashhad the religious leaders

359. Kasravi 1319-21, vol. 1, 329, 330.
360. Dowlatabad n.d., vol. 2, 84, 88.
361. Kasravi 1319-21, vol. 1, 221, 222.
362. Dowlatabadi n.d., vol. 2, 116.
363. Dowlatabadi n.d., vol. 2, 116, 117, 217.
364. Dowlatabadi n.d., vol. 2, 288; Kasravi 1319-21, vol. 2, 177.
365. Shaje`i 1344, 185-189; Kasravi 1319-21, vol. 1, 230, 231, 249.
366. Hedayat 1344, 148.
367. Dowlatabadi n.d., vol. 2, 136.
368. Lambton 1954, 29.
369. Lambton 1954, 29.
370. Lambton 1954, 29.
371. RMM 2, 554.

dominated the political arena; in other towns internecine strife prevailed.[372] In Rasht, the guilds were more progressive than the whole-sale merchants and ulama. When the guild members organized in the *Anjoman-e `Abbasi* called for abolishing guild taxes and rents from peasants, the leading Constitutionalist ulama of Rasht strongly opposed such a radical measure.[373] In spite of the existence of provincial *anjomans*, which were charged with the supervision of the administration by the governors, the popular *anjomans* often took the initiative in this respect. It is difficult to draw the line between these two (although in fact the provincial *anjoman* was an elected body, while the popular *anjoman* was a political club), for in Tabriz for instance "the provincial anjuman became in effect a popular anjuman."[374] The *anjomans* also regulated many affairs which normally would have been executed by the urban government. In Tehran for example the *anjoman-e melli* lowered the prices of prime necessities.[375] Furthermore it founded a welfare committee (*anjoman-e kheyrati*) which was charged with building an institution for disabled persons and orphans. To collect money for this purpose money boxes were erected in the streets. The money was administrated by some religious leaders.[376] The popular *anjomans* often found themselves in conflict with the provincial *anjomans*. It was their enthusiasm which made political life hectic, but kept the constitutional movement alive, and which formed the main support for the *Majles*.[377] When Mohammad `Ali Shah (1907-1909) threatened to do away with the *Majles* it was the popular *anjomans* of guilds, merchants and bankers who resisted this attempt successfully. In most cities they formed a kind of citizen's militia and in Tehran "before long 2000 men were drilling."[378] Although, the Shah scored an initial success with his coup d'état in Tehran in 1908, he experienced a set-back in Tabriz, Rasht and Isfahan.

When finally the nationalist movement won in 1909, the activities of the popular *anjomans* declined. The fact that they had no common basis or political program made itself felt now. Once their goal, the preservation of the *Majles*, had been achieved no cause for further cooperation existed. Not only did this demonstrate the lack of political co-operation among the guilds, but it also showed that such co-operation could only be achieved under the leadership of religious leaders. The short-lived political influence and experience of the guilds had not resulted in the rise of their own leaders. The intellectuals who could have provided them with both leadership and common goals were taken up by the political parties after 1909. Moreover these also acted in a traditional way and regarded the guilds only as pawns in their own political games. The elan of the movement dissipated, which was made easier because of infiltration of the *anjomans* by traditional elements who opposed reforms, after 1907.[379] Because the constitutional movement had not been able to effect other structural reforms than the grant of a constitution, in Iranian

---

372. Lambton 1963 b, 51.
373. Adamiyat 1355, 471-73; Rabino 1352, 30-40, 47-56.
374. Lambton 1963 b, 46-47.
375. Lambton 1953 b, 51.
376. Dowlatabadi n.d., vol. 2, 117.
377. Lambton 1963 b, 41.
378. Lambton 1963 b, 51, 64, 56; Kasravi 1319-21, vol. 3, 37-39 ; Appendix VI.
379. Lambton 1963 b, 50-51.

society the age old conflicts and tensions remained as strong as before.[380] In the second *Majles* (1910) that was elected, no guild representative was chosen. "The new electoral law effectively barred the guilds from political power, which during the Qajar era they were never to regain."[381] During the subsequent interval disorder, financial difficulties, Russian and British interference in internal affairs were not encouraging factors for an upsurge of the constitutional movement. The lack of tradition of independent political action made the guilds acquiesce in the situation.

After the brief interludes when artisans and traders for some time influenced local and central government, the guilds had to revert to their old means of communication. The only difference with the period before the Revolution was that after 1909 the guilds could refer their grievances to new brokers, viz. the political parties. These were quick to realize the advantage of 'representing' the bazaar community. On several occasions the opposition aligned itself with the guilds and even tried to form a united front with them.[382] The Communist party in particular exerted itself to establish control over the working class. In 1921 the Communist Party of Iran issued detailed instructions to its party branches, instructing them "to propagate the reorganization of the anjumans created in 1908 and 1909 by the workers of the same profession, the importance of which is considerable for the mobilization of the workers to waken the class spirit among them and propagate agitation among them."[383] At first the party had some success, since it couched its revolutionary propaganda in anti-British terms in conformity with the prevailing spirit amongst all Iranian classes.[384] Their main success, of course, was in Gilan where the separatist movement of Kuchek Khan was supported by large contingents of Russian-Iranian volunteers from Baku.[385] In Enzeli it appears that a kind of soviets was formed, including several kinds of artisans, but also smallholders and even large proprietors.[386]

Additionally in 1921 ten trade unions were organized in Tehran, comprising only employees. It is noteworthy that these unions either concerned employees of guilds with the *haqq-e bonicheh*, such as bakers and confectioners, or recently introduced professions, such as printers, telegraphists, postmen, shop attendants, teachers and commercial clerks, in addition to two old professions, the tailors and lacemen.[387] It appears that the total number of trade union members amounted to 8,000 persons, who, however, did not play an important role, notwithstanding the communist assertions that a demonstration by the teachers and typographers led to the downfall of the cabinet in 1922.[388] Communist influence and the formation of trade unions were stifled at birth owing to three factors. Firstly, the centralization begun by Reza Shah (1925-1941) weakened the potential

380. Lambton 1963 b, 51, 88.
381. Shaje`i 1344, 185-189; Dowlatabadi n.d., vol. 3, 151.
382. RMM 52, 139.
383. RMM 52, 148.
384. RMM 52, 148; Zabih 1969, 9.
385. Zabih 1969, 13.
386. RMM 52, 149.
387. RMM 52, 149, for details see Floor 2009 a.
388. RMM 52, 149.

of autonomous occupational organizations, be they guilds or trade unions.[389] Secondly the rigid "application of the concept of the communist revolution to a backward country like Persia and the subordination of Persian revolutionary aspirations to Soviet diplomacy disillusioned many radicals from the socialist movement."[390] Thirdly, the ties existing between the religions leaders and the artisans and traders proved to be stronger than the temporary anti-British appeal of communist propaganda.

One of the last performances of the guilds during the Qajar era was their turn-out led by the ulama, in favor of the continuing existence of the monarchy against Reza Khan's plans to found a republic in 1925.[391] Although the modernization of Iran by Reza Shah nullified the usefulness of the guilds for the government, after Reza Shah's abdication they proved to be as much alive as before.[392]

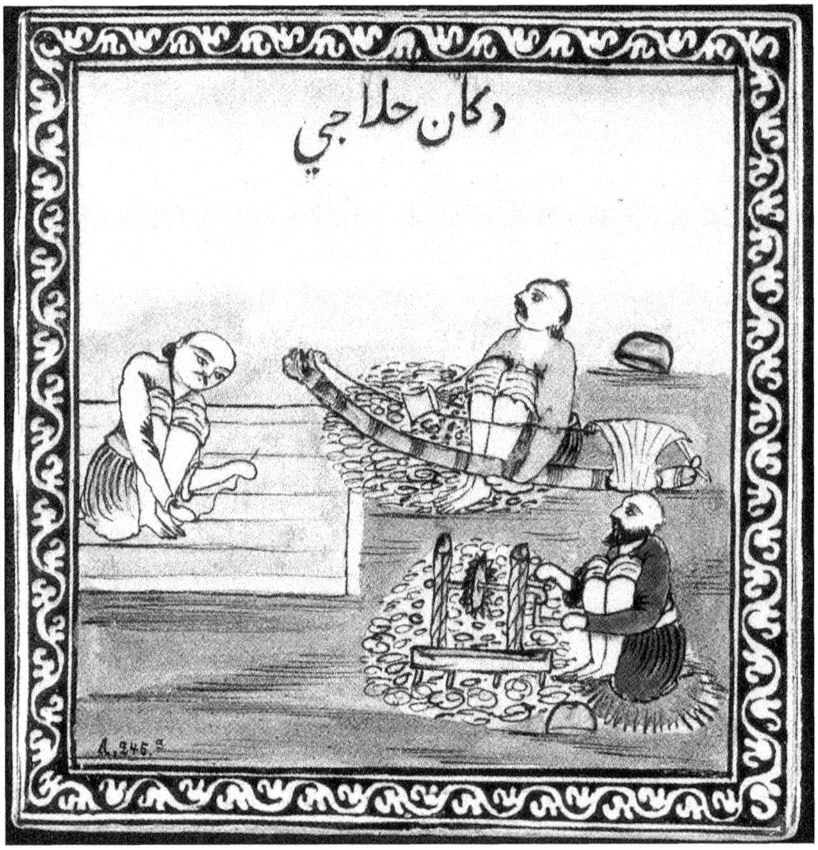

389. Lambton 1954, 30.

390. Zabih 1969, 45.

391. Mostowfi n.d., vol. 3, 594.

392. For the activities of the guilds under the reign of Mohammad Reza Shah (1941-1978), see Lambton 1954, 31; Binder 1962, 186-188, and Floor 1975.

CHAPTER SEVEN

The Guilds in Isfahan According to Tahvildar

The following pages contain the translation of an important part of the *Joghrafiya-ye Esfahan*, which was completed in 1891.[1] Its author, Mirza Hoseyn Khan, son of Mohammad Ebrahim Khan Tahvildar (the tax receiver) of Isfahan, who was a member of a local bureaucratic family that had played a significant role already in Safavid times, had an excellent knowledge of his city and province. He himself worked in the Telegraph Office, while his brothers occupied functions in the administration of the rural districts of Isfahan. One was the water bailiff (*mir ab*) of Isfahan. Mirza Hoseyn Khan Tahvildar, points out that he wished to do more than write a 'Geography of Isfahan' in the narrow sense of the word.[2] *Joghrafiya* therefore may be best translated as social geography or sociography. In this endeavor Tahvildar succeeded remarkably well, for the *Joghrafiya* represents a new trend in historiography of Iran. It belongs to the class of books that were written at the instigation of the government during the reign of Naser al-Din Shah (r. 1848-96). Such books as written by Vaziri, Zarrabi and Sadid al-Saltaneh, for example, try to give a truer picture of their city or province, their people and products than historians were wont to do up to that time. According to Kazemzadeh, "The historians of Qajar Persia were essentially chroniclers. They described day by day, year by year, either briefly or in great detail, the activities, gave dramatic even if unreliable accounts of battles and traced the intricacies of court intrigues."[3] It is true that the new genre still suffered somewhat from this enumeration syndrome, but instead of writing a chronicle they concentrated their efforts on other subjects than politics, viz. socio-economic and agricultural subjects. Of course, family biographies are not lacking, but then family was paramount in Qajar Iran.

What makes the *Joghrafiya* so interesting is that is unique in Persian literature in so far as it devotes considerable space to the guilds. The translation is the greater part of a description of the classes of people in Isfahan. I have omitted the numbers 1 to 21 and 191 to 199 from the list of groups of people, because these groups did not constitute guilds. Some of the remaining 169 groups did not constitute guilds either, but they have been retained, because they are in some way connected to the guilds.[4]

---

1. At about the same time, a German living and working in Isfahan also wrote about the guilds in Isfahan, see Höltzer 2535. For a comparative analysis of these two reports see Philipp 1984.

2. Tahvildar 1341, 9.

3. Kazemzadeh 1962, 430.

4. Höltzer 2535, 21-23 in addition lists the following crafts and trades not listed by Tahvildar: 17 rice-sellers (*razzaz*), 11 sweetmeat sellers (*halvaforush*), 20 dealers in second-hand goods (*semsar*), 186 sugar and tea sellers (*shekar va chayforush*), 40 scrubwood sellers (*tushanforush*), 60 watch-makers (*sa`atsaz*), 17 canvas makers (*lavvaf*), 14 gold and silver engravers (*talakub* and *noqrehkub*), 45 blanket makers (*lehafduz*), 25 tray makers (*sinisaz*), 7 waste silk weavers (*kajbaf*), 110 shal weavers (*shalbaf*), 46 tailors of broadcloth (*khayyat-mahutduz*), 12 male and 100 female stitchers (*suzanduzi*); 9 rice cleaners (*berenjkub*), 15 henna makers (*hennasaz*), 7 gunpower

Another factor that makes the *Joghrafiya* so interesting is that the language used by its author is quite different from the often artificial literary anguage popular in those days. The language is rather businesslike and to the point and certainly is an experiment in style, probably an attempt to write a language more akin to spoken Persian than to literary form.

The text of the *Joghrafiya* speaks for itself, while its depiction of the decline of many of the guilds has been discussed by me elsewhere.[5] I have kept the notes to a minimum and refer the reader as to technical matters concerning crafts to other publications.[6] Those who are not familiar with the urban setting of Isfahan I refer to Curzon's chapter on that city and to Gaube-Wirth's book on the bazaar of Isfahan.[7]

---

makers (*barutkub*), 3 *termeh* weavers (*termehbaf*), 17 packsaddle makers (*palanduz*); 12 comb makers (*shanehsaz*); 110 cotton carders (*hallaj*); 15 basket makers (*kepehduz*); 12 pipe-head makers (*sorkhalisaz*), 12 sheath makers (*dabehsaz*), 12 fishermen (*mahigir*), 90 hunters (*sayyad*), 12 roasted nuts sellers (*nakhudriz*), 22 milk sellers (*shirkesh*), 50 herders (*gallehdar*), 150 money lenders (*sudkhvar*), 15 yoghurt makers (*mastband*), 17 whitesmiths (*safidgar*), 32 grain cleaners (*bovjar*), 15 liver cooks (*jegarpaz*). Some of these crafts may be the same as the ones mentioned by Tahvildar under a different name, or were a part of the same head-guild. E.g., the *berenjkub* perhaps are the same as the *shal[i]andaz*, while the *halvaforush* may have been part of the guild of the *qannad*.

5. Floor 1991; Floor 1999b; Floor 2003b and Floor 2009a.

6. See Wulff 1966; Mohebbi 1996, Floor 1991b, Floor 2003a and b; Floor 2006b.

7. Curzon 1892, vol. 2, chapter 19; Gaube-Wirth 1978.

TRANSLATION

(21) Unlike olden times, heads (*kadkhoda*) and elders (*rish safid*) of the guilds (*asnaf*) are no longer noteworthy and famous and because the number of guilds has been great, it would take too much time to give a specification and a list of the names of the lesser famed. Therefore, as information about the trade, work and products of the province in every guild, a brief summary of the guilds and their products will have to do so that, at the same time, all the crafts and products of this city may be detailed.

(22) The group of *qadaq* dyers (*sabbagh-e qadak*).[8]

This is a big guild. Formerly it had many members, but now it has been halved. The members of this guild occupy very long connecting bazaars with high arched vaults, which contain 136 shops. Each shop has a site and buildings similar to a big house. The buildings are clean and pleasant. There are benches, winter and summer sleeping places, ponds, water-pools, wells, cisterns and equipment for dyeing and fulling. More than 1,500 *tumans* have been spent for the construction of some shops belonging to the head of the guild. For similar buildings in other provinces one would have to spend more than 3,000 *tumans*. Formerly most merchants and government officials who had business or were acquainted with the dignitaries of this guild came to these shops for their daily repose. Apart from these two bazaars, which are next to the *Meydan-e Naqsh-e Jahan*, there are many dyeing-houses spread out over the bazaars and the city quarters.

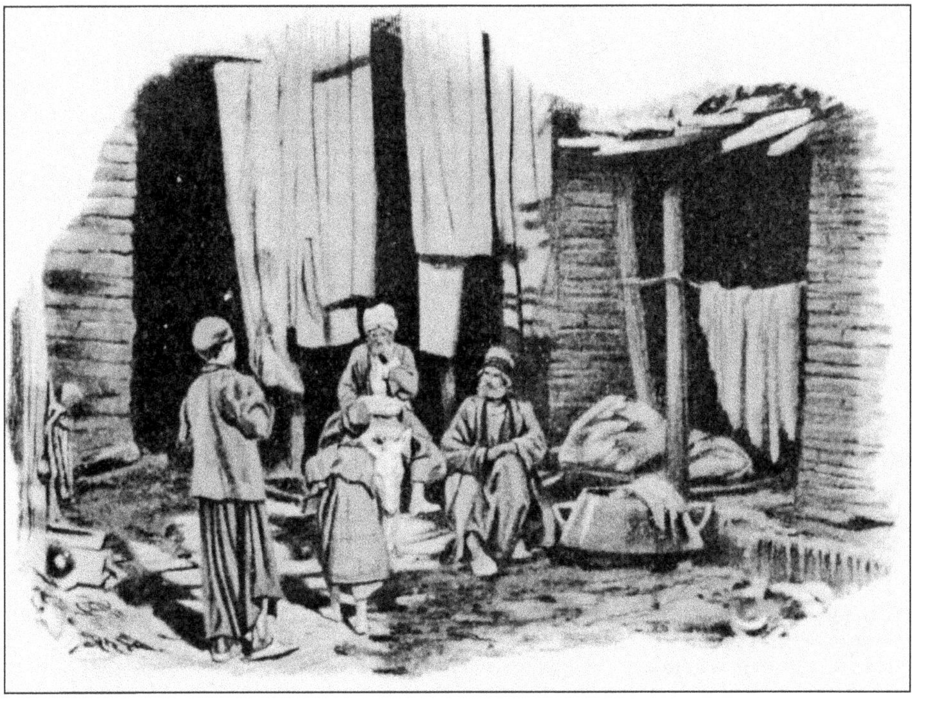

8. *Qadak* is a kind of nankeen, see Floor 1999, 186-87. The craft of the dyer is discussed by Wulff 1966, 193-94. According to Höltzer 2535, 22 there were 1456 dyers (*rangraz*) and 25 *qadak* weavers (*qadakbaf*)in Isfahan at that time.

(23) The group of the confectioners *(qannad)*.

Their number has decreased due to the decline of the trade of this guild, causing the ruin of these artisans. They have a special bazaar next to the *Meydan-e Shah* and a great number of shops in the city quarters. The confectioners of Isfahan make good sweetmeats and if there would be strong demand they would make whatever is ordered from Russian sugar better than in most provinces, but there is no such demand. What they [now] make of sugar is of average quality and suitable only for peasants and artisans, who form the greater part of their clientele. Formerly, when Isfahani sugar was in common use it was exported to other provinces. The confectioners made sugar very well and there was a difference of one-tenth with Russian sugar.[9] Now that this sugar is no longer in demand, it has become a product of inferior quality, so that even in Isfahan itself it is not used much, although loaf sugar *(qand)* was once the chief product of this guild.

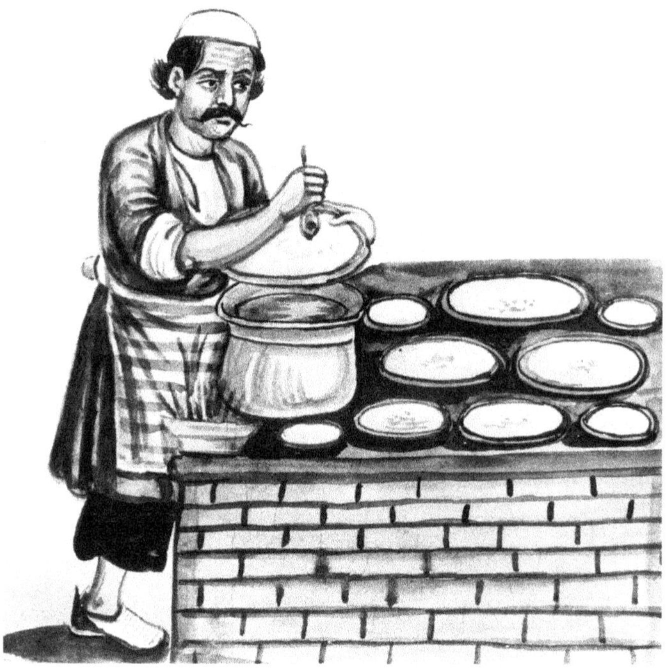

One of their best products is *gaz*, which is still in demand and which is still exported to all parts of the country. The main material for making *gaz* is manna *(gaz-e angabin)*, which is brought from the mountain passes between Fereydun and Karun. The like of Isfahani *gaz* is not found in any other country. Khvonsar, Golpeygan and Borujerd and some other towns also have *gaz*; however, none of it has the quality of the Isfahani mountain pass *gaz*. Moreover, no other province succeeds in preparing it as well as Isfahan.[10]

9. Russian sugar was the preferred sugar for Iranian customers, because it did not quickly melt in the mouth when drinking tea. Like the Russians, Irans drank tea with a piece of sugar between their teeth, see Floor 2004a, 64. Because Isfahani sugar was only slightly different from Russian sugar it was popular. For information on the making of sugar and sweetmeats see Floor 2003a, 328-70 and Wulff 1966, 300-02. According to Höltzer 2535, 22 there were 150 confectioners in Isfahan at that time.

10. On the making of *gaz* and other similar products see Floor 2003a, 370-75.

Among the confectioners there is a special *gaz* maker (*gazsaz*), who makes it better than the others.

(24) The group of the druggists (*'attar*).

Their shops are spread out over the province and are numerous.[11]

(25) The group of the textile printers (*chitsaz*).

This is a very important craft. Formerly its members formed a big group and their product was in great demand. Compared to former times it has now totally declined. From calico (*qalamkar*) they made gilt calico (*qalamzar*), a superior and more expensive form of Sadras calico.[12] Since it is no longer in demand, it is not made anymore. This guild has four connecting bazaars. One of its gates opens to the entrance of the Market Hall (*Qeysariyeh*) on the *Meydan-e Shah*. Between the bazaars, five caravanserais and smaller serais (*timchehs*) are situated, one of which is the *Saray-e Shah*. All of them are workshops of the textile printers and they comprise 284 shops, offices (*hojreh*) and manufacturies (*karkhaneh*). Their products are still used all over Iran, but European textiles have ruined their market and not even half of the original number remains.[13]

(26) The group of goldlace workers (*'alaqeh-band*).

They have one special bazaar and many separate workshops in the other bazaars and the city quarters.[14]

(27) The group of the potters (*fakhkhar*).

This guild consists of three groups. The first group has a kiln for making bricks, lime and chalk. Of this group half has not remained, compared with thirty to forty years ago. The second group has a potter's kiln. They make flacons (*tong*), jars (*kuzeh*), goblets (*qadah*), cooking pots (*dizi*), water pipes, and other vessels. This group has not diminished much compared with former times. The third group has a kiln for firing tiles. This guild has very much declined and there are only a few members left. Of the tiles that were used for [adorning] the madrasas and mosques, those that are antique, are in their own right as good as Chinese porcelain.

If there only were clients and buyers then they could make them as in former times, no, even better. For three to four years now people have been coming from Russia

11. On the druggists see Floor 2004b, 131-36. According to Höltzer 2535, 20 there were 19 druggists in Isfahan at that time.

12. Sadras, 70 km south of Chennai in the State of Tamil Nadu (India) on the Coromandel Coast, was a settlement established by the Dutch in the seventeenth century. It became a major export center of fabrics, in particular fine muslins.

13. For the decline of the indigenous textile industry in Iran see Floor 1999b and Floor 2009b. For a technical description of the craft of textile printer see Wulff 1966, 224-27 and for the fabrics see Floor 1999b, 143-48.

14. For more information on this craft see Floor 1999b, 131. According to Höltzer 2535, 22 there were 56 goldlace workers in Isfahan at that time.

to buy Iranian antique tiles. They buy all vessels and tiles they can find, if they are of good quality and antique, especially Isfahani tiles.

In Isfahan there are many beautiful madrasas and mosques that are no longer in use. Because they are religious endowments nobody is responsible for them and nobody cares for their materials. These mosques have much marble stone and very good tiles. Some people have become thieves, who gradually steal these tiles, which they sell to Russian merchants for prices ranging from three *qrans* to 5,000 *dinars* and more for a single tile. Although these madrasas and mosques are not used any longer they are still monuments of ancient art and proof of the grandeur of (our) state and country.[15]

(28) The group of the drapers (*bazzaz*).

They are numerous and their shops are distributed all over the province.[16]

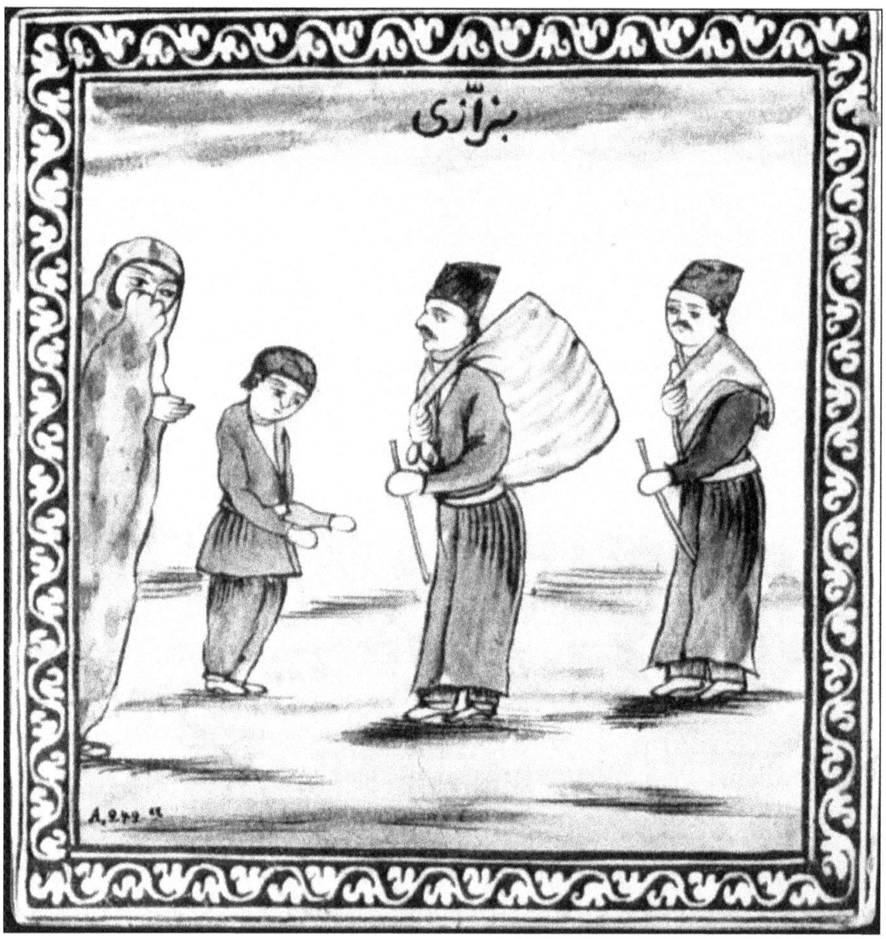

15. On the pottery craft and the theft of antique tiles see Floor 2003 a, 39-87; see further Wulff 1966, 151-71. According to Höltzer 2535, 22 there were 22 potters in Isfahan at that time.

16. According to Höltzer 2535, 20 there were 152 drapers in Isfahan at that time.

(29) The group of the hawking drapers (*bazzaz-e dowrehgerd*).

They carry drapery on their back and sell their [their wares] from house to house.

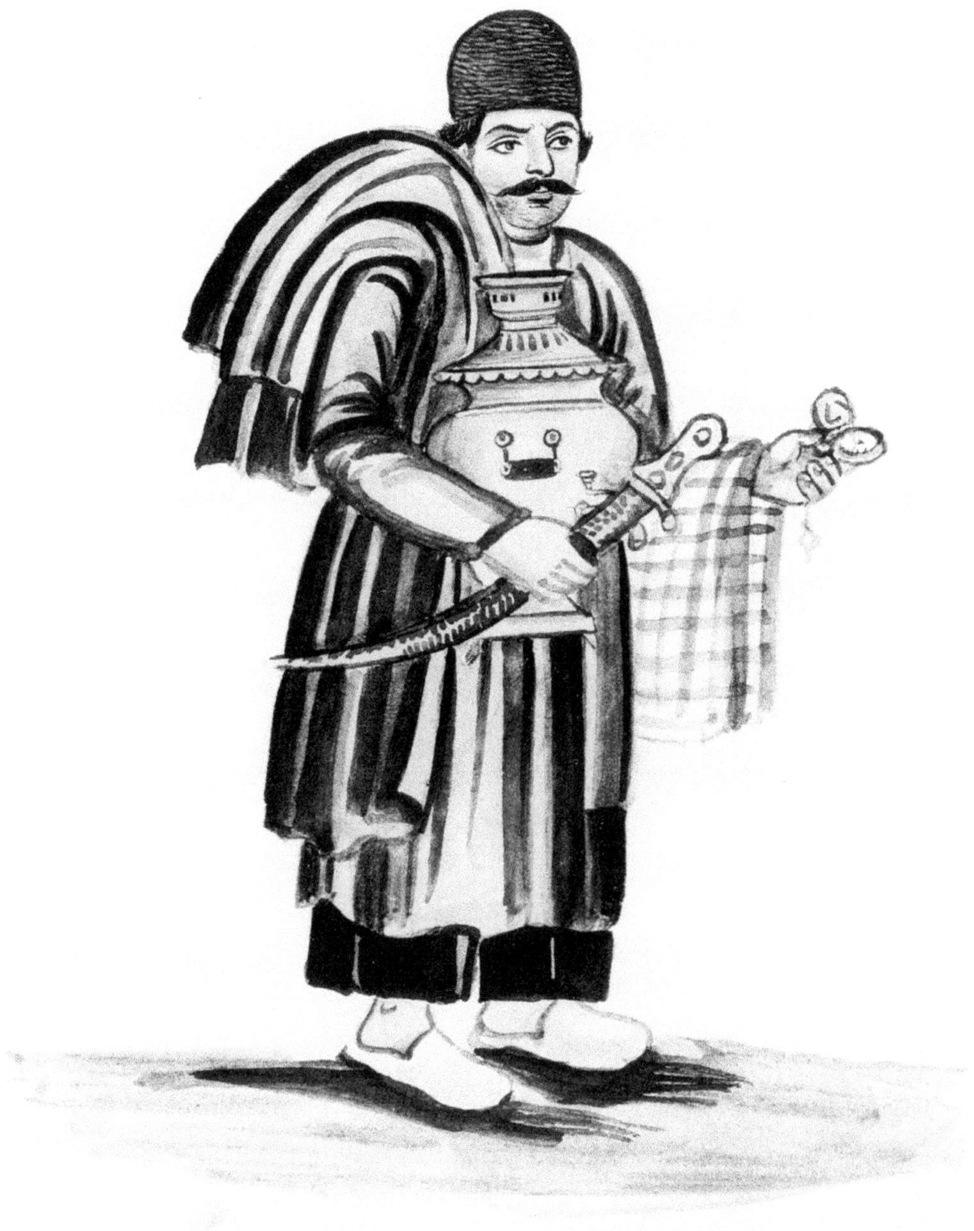

(30) The group of the blacksmiths (*haddad-e saqat* and *haddad-e khordeh*).

They form two guilds and they have one bazaar next to the *Meydan-e Shah*. The volume of their work has not much declined. Their products are iron utensils such as spades, pickaxes, plough shares, harrows, handbarrows, tripods, tongs, braziers, nails, skewers, and the like. If something has to be done with iron they do it, but other work such as casting steel (*khoshk-bandi*) is done by others.[17]

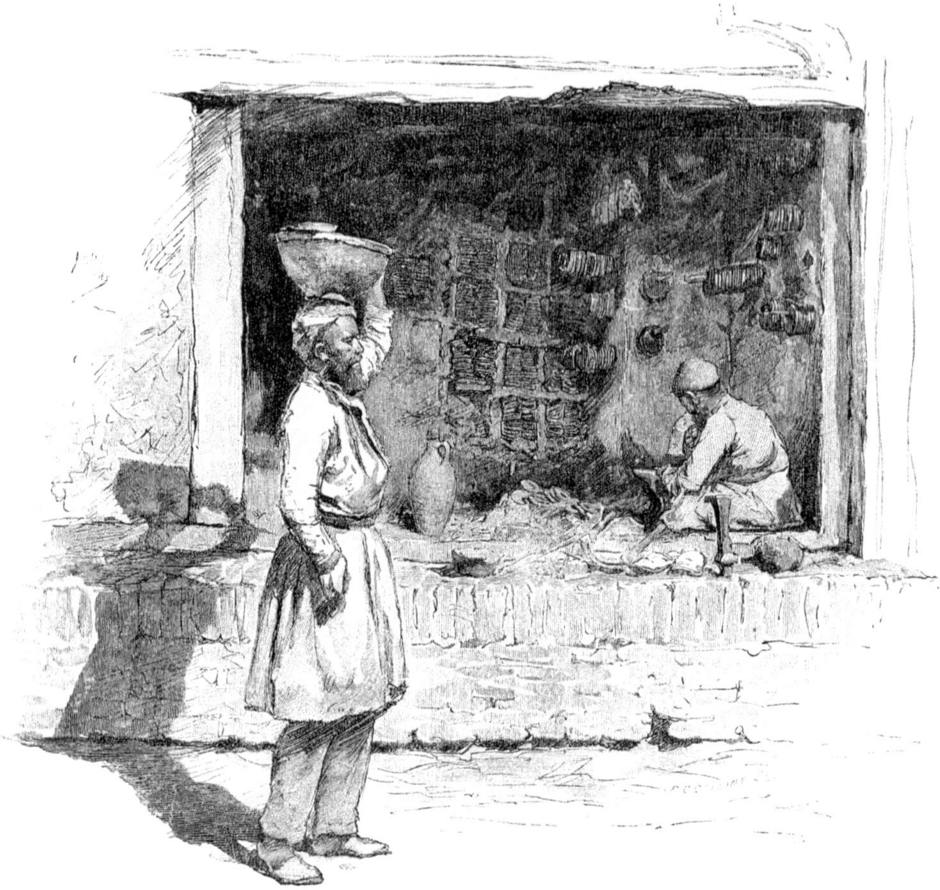

(31) The group of the hucksters (*pilehvar*).

They sell drogueries, sugar, tea and several other products to the villages in the (rural) districts and dependencies and to the the tribes.[18]

(32) The group of oil-millers (*`assar-e rowghan*).

The stone of their oil-mill is used for pressing lamp oil. Of old there have been many oil-mills in this province, now there are about one-third of them left. Formerly, all these presses were producing, but nowadays it has been deemed best to use no more than three of those remaining. These two or three oil-mills pay the guild taxes; the other oil-mills

17. On smiths see Floor 2003a, 226-31 and Wulff 1966, 48-52. According to Höltzer 2535, 22 there were 40 smiths in Isfahan at that time.

18. For more information on this trade see Floor 2003b, 62-65. According to Höltzer 2535, 21 there were 200 hucksters in Isfahan at that time.

have been closed down. The Isfahani oil-mills are notable for the size of their buildings and the solidity of the huge equipment installed, which is peculiar to them.

Oil-works of such a size and quality are not found elsewhere in Iran but in Isfahan, not even in Tehran; in such form you will not even find them abroad.

Tehran and some other cities wanted to build similar oil-works, but nothing came of it. The principal pieces of equipment needed are long, very thick and solid stones and wooden beams and very thick erect poles. The poles used here are only to be found among the 200-year old Isfahani plane trees. Stones without veins and hidden defects and of the size and weight that they have here can only be found in this province and not anywhere else, and even then only in the mountains near Ateshgah and Hematabad. [Only] in this province the foundations of the thick, high walls of the oil-mills reached the level of the ground-water built with heavy rocks, which are laid upon each other, so that they reach a height of 8 to 9 cubits (*dhar`*)[19] measured from the ground and which has become like a mountain peak. These walls are able to sustain the weight of 10,000 *man* (59 tons) of poles, stoneweights, powerful equipment, and of the impressive high arches. Wise men in olden times, who designed this type of oil-mill, made use of strong and solid lifting equipment such as pivots, cogs, beams, *bukrah* (?), screws, and *asfin* (?), whether singly or as a part of a mechanism, so that two workers each in his turn and all by himself can easily lift a pole and a stone weight with a weight of 2,000 *man* (11.8 tons) to a height of 8 cubits within half an hour.

Formerly, there were many similar oil-mills in the city and its [rural] districts. Most of them are in ruins [now] and the remains are all that is left of them. The expense and trouble taken to construct these buildings were and are not altogether without benefit. One still profits from them, especially in Isfahan, because in the villages several cereals are cultivated, which, after grinding, produce lamp-oil that is not fit for human and animal consumption. They also profit from the grass and straw, and all the other benefits that they yield for the peasant on account of their own value, fertilization of the soil, difference in irrigation needs, which are very useful and therefore they have no choice but to sow them.

These crops are amongst other things, castor beans, rape, linseed, bastard saffron, and the like, which have seeds that only can be used for making lamp-oil. The extraction of oil by boiling [the seeds] in water is only possible with difficulty and a lot of waste and is neither profitable nor easy, unless when pressed in the oil-mills, which presses these above-mentions pulses in only a short time, so that of one *kharvar* (590 kg) not more than ten *methqal* (46.9 g) of oil remains [in the crushed seeds].[20]

(33) The group of flour millers (*`assar-e ardeh*).

The group of the flour millers are those who grind sweetened sesame, fruitstones of peaches and apricot. Of this they prepare juice powder and flour for [making] *halva*. The

19. This is about 7 to 9 meters; see Floor 2008, also for other weights.

20. For the oil-millers and their products see Floor 2003a, 112-17 and Wulff 1966, 295-300. According to Höltzer 2535, 23 there were four oil-presses in Isfahan at that time.

number of people and the equipment of this group are insignificant and of no account compared with the outlay of the oil-millers.[21]

(34) The group of the sellers of roasted vetches (*hemsi*).

The sellers of roasted vetches form a large guild in Isfahan. Their product is used in the rural towns, districts and dependencies of the city itself. The twice-roasted chick-peas of the province are very good.

(35) The group of the jewelers (*hakkak*).

The jewelry of Isfahan was much in demand in former times and most of it was sold to Turkey, Egypt and India. This guild had famous masters such as Aqa Mohammad Taher and others. In this day and age they still had and have very competent masters such as Sheikh Hakkak, Hajji Mohammad Ja`far and others, who, because of the decline of trade, have remained little known.[22]

(36) The group of the turners (*kharrat*).

Apart from the middle part of the waterpipe, which is better made in Rasht in particular, turners' products are better made in Isfahan than in the rest of the country. Most of the Isfahani turners are now working in Tehran.[23]

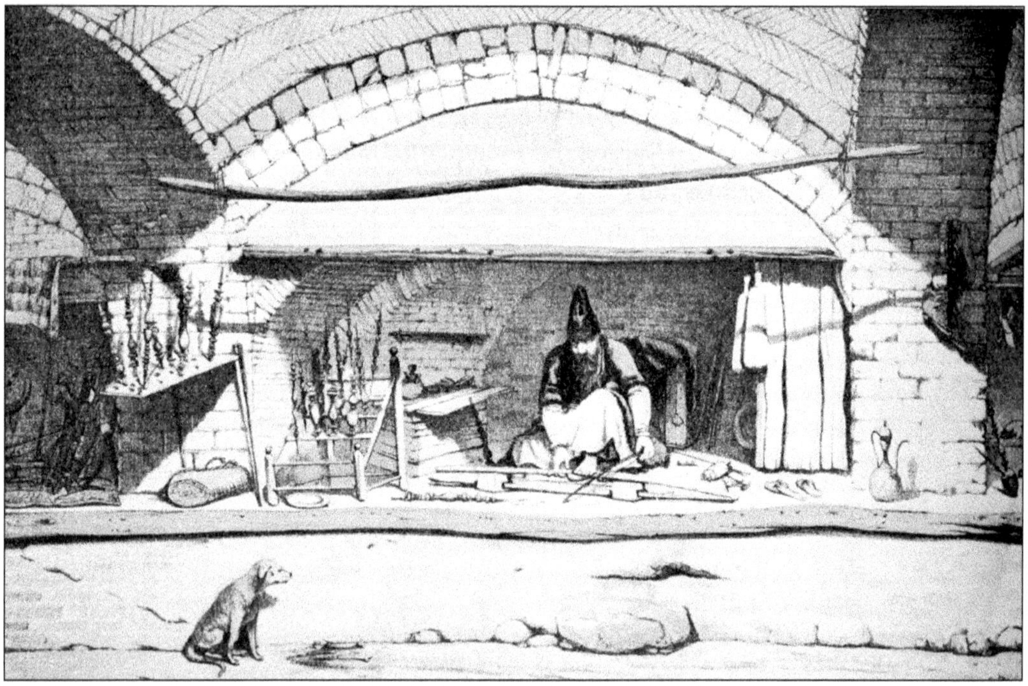

21. For more information on this craft see Wulff 1966, 300-02.

22. On the jewelers see Wulff 1966, 90-92. According to Höltzer 2535, 21 there were 5 jewelers and 11 jewelry sellers in Isfahan at that time.

23. For more information on the craft of the turners see Wulff 1966, 90-92 and Floor 2006b, 166-68. According to Höltzer 2535, 21 there were 80 turners in Isfahan at that time.

(37) The group of the silver wire drawers (*simkash*).

Formerly, when clothes of silver brocade (*naqdehduz*) and the like were much is use and items like gold lace (*golabtun*) braids and *dah-yak* cloth were much in demand, gold and silver thread were twisted together, [and then] there were many silver wire drawers; now there are only a few.[24]

(38) The group of the gold wire drawers (*zarkash*).

Formerly, when the weaving of gold brocade was important gold wire drawing was also esteemed. The gold wire drawing craft is one of the better professions of Isfahan. They have sophisticated equipment and very precise tools. The precision which they attained in former times was such that they made 1,200 cubits of gold lace from one *methqal* (4.6 g) of gold. Now the same would still be possible, if only there were customers.[25]

(39) The group of the gold brocade weavers (*zaribaf*).

Formerly, gold brocade weaving was very widespread and gold brocade was one of the high quality cloths in Iran. The elegant gold-thread clothes of the nobles and princes and the precious royal robes of honor came especially from Isfahan. It is a craft in which until now the Europeans have not been able to achieve the perfection of the Isfahan [work]. The goldbrocade, which since the time of Shah `Abbas Safavi until now has been loosing its gold, still retains its design. Master painters admit their inability to emulate this design and method and say that nowadays master painters, let alone the weavers, are not able to rival this style.

Now this guild and its craft have been ruined and fallen into disuse and its craftsmen are insignificant and its production is small. What buyers there are come from foreign countries; in Iran it is very little used indeed.[26]

(40) The group of the goldlace spinners (*golabtunduz*).

Formerly, goldlace was much in demand and the number of goldlace spinners was large; now they number only a few and their product is not much in demand.

(41) The group of the silver brocade makers (*naqdehduz*).

Formerly, silver brocade making was highly esteemed and noteworthy and many men and women were engaged in making silver brocade. First, the painters would make excellent and intriciate designs on cloth and then the silver brocade maker would sew on the designs. The old products, which have lasted until our days, are spoken off very highly. Now this craft has become very insignificant and most of the remaining artisans have gone to Tehran and Tabriz.[27]

24. For more information on this craft see Wulff 1966, 42-46.

25. For more information on this craft see Wulff 1966, 42-46.

26. For more information on this craft see Floor 1999b, 202-04. According to Höltzer 2535, 22 there were 35 gold brocade weavers in Isfahan at that time.

27. According to Höltzer 2535, 22 this was indeed a craft where women found gainful employment.

(42) The group of the crocheters (*qollabduz*).

The same description as above.

(43) The group of the bazaar tailors (*khayyat-e bazari*).

They take people's clothes into the bazaar and sew them there.

(44) The group of the bazaar stitchers (*bazariduz*).

They sew clothes for the ready-made tailors (*dukhteh-forush*).

(45) The group of the sewers of Londreh cloth (*londrehduz*).

They sew broadcloth, *barak* and the like. They are now few [in number] in Iran.

(46) The group of the hat makers (*kolahduz*).

They have a special bazaar next to the *Meydan-e Shah-e Naqsh-e Jahan*. There is little demand for their work and their guild is ruined.[28]

(47) The group of the fur hat makers (*kolichehduz*).

They sew fur hats. Formerly, their products were much in demand and they were numerous, but now they have become few.[29]

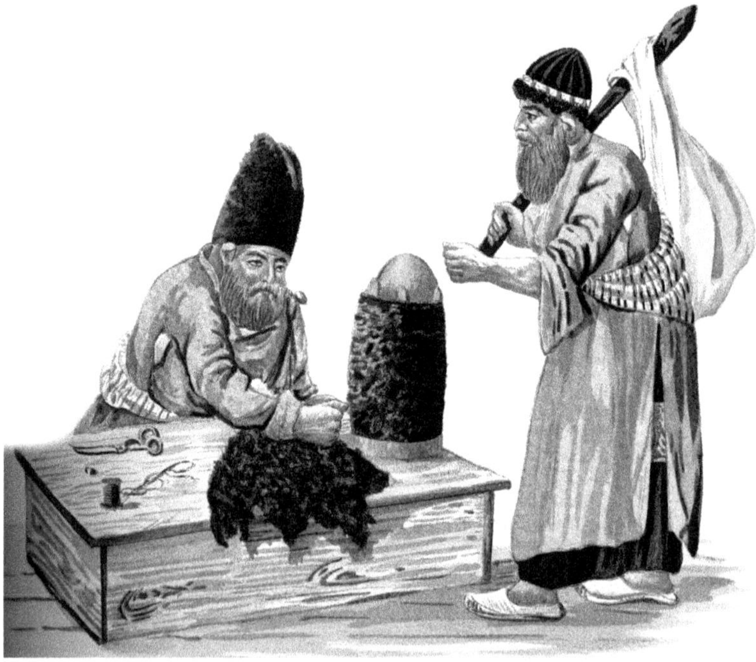

28. For more information on this craft see Wulff 1966, 24. According to Höltzer 2535, 22 there were 20 hatters (*kolahmal*) and 40 hat makers (*kolahduz*) in Isfahan at that time.

29. For more information on this craft see Floor 2003a, 394. According to Höltzer 2535, 22 there were 65 fur hat makers in Isfahan at that time.

(48) The group of the makers of silk fabrics (*khazduz*).

In this city there are no more than two men; formerly there were more.

(49) The group of fur cloak makers (*pustinduz*).

Formerly, there were many in Isfahan, who made fur cloaks from sheep skins [produced in] the province of Isfahan. They also lined dresses like watted cloaks (*kharqeh*), when it was of good quality. Now there are only a few [left].[30]

(50) The group of the makers of Georgian shoes (*gorjiduz*).

They made female Georgian shoes. Formerly the male version was in common use, but now it has fallen into disuse.

(51) The group of the makers of Russian shoes (*orosiduz*).

This is a large group and a new guild, which did not exist before.[31]

(52) The group of the makers of leather shoes (*charmiduz*).

They make leather shoes, which used to be very much in demand. Most of the mullahs and all merchants and artisans wore them. Now they are only worn by some mullahs and most merchants.[32]

(53) The group of the bootmakers (*chakmehduz*).

Formerly when soldiers wore boots and the province had many servants and many inhabitants there was much demand [for the work of] this guild, but now there is hardly any demand.[33]

(54) The group of the makers of Morocco leather shoes (*sagheriduz*).

Formerly Isfahani noblemen and women both wore Morocco leather (*sagheri*) shoes. Now little of this fashion remains.

(55) The group of the makers of Morocco leather (*sagherichi*).

They are those who turn the hides of pack and riding animals into Morocco (*sagheri*) leather.[34]

---

30. For more information on this craft see Wulff 1966, 232-33; Floor 2003a, 394.

31. According to Höltzer 2535, 22 there were 250 shoemakers (*kafshduz*) in Isfahan at that time.

32. According to Höltzer 2535, 22 there were 36 leather shoe makers (*charmsaz*) in Isfahan at that time.

33. According to Höltzer 2535, 22 there were 180 bootmakers in Isfahan at that time.

34. For more information on this and the other leather related crafts see Floor 2003 a, 389-93 and Wulff 1966, 234.

(56) The group of the embroiderers (*naqshduz*).

Formerly this guild had many members and both men and women were engaged in making embroideries. This commodity sold very well. Everything the painters designed was drawn on *qadak*, longcloth (*chalvari*), etc., and these designs were embroidered entirely with a needle, in either pure silk, in down (*kork*), or in cotton threads of different colors. The price of these embroideries varied in accordance with the material used. One piece, of the size of a man's military-style (*nezami*) trousers or equal to a women's tight undergarment, which was in common use in those days, cost from sixty to eight *riyals* up to forty *tumans* and lasts sixty to seventy years and pieces that were not much used have lasted for 200 years or longer and remained beautiful. The best were worn by the wives of the nobles, the average quality by middle class women.

This cloth had other uses too, such as on mantle shelves (*taqchehpush*), cradles, swaddling clothes, portofolios, cushions for the place of honor, packsaddles, and the like. Most of it was sold to customers in Turkey, Egypt, India, Turkestan, and Afghanistan; some was also sold to Europe.

From the time of the late Shah [Mohammad Shah, r. 1834-1848] to the present day trade had gradually declined and fallen into disuse. There were merchants known as *naqshineh-forush*, who were especially engaged in the selling and buying of this commodity. They were wealthy and formed a large group and they were all esteemed. Of their line hardly any is left, except for Hajji Hoseyn, son of the late well-known Hajji Mohammad Ebrahim and some others who are engaged in trading in other merchandise.[35]

(57) The group of the makers of one-tenth (*dah-yakduz*).

They, like the silver brocade makers, sew with silver and gold threads, which contain one-tenth of goldlace, on silken cloth and the like.[36]

(58) The group of the sequin sewers (*pulakduz*).

They sewed gold or gilt sequins onto cloth. Formerly the clothes of their royal highnesses the Princes and special royal robes of honor for the governors and others were sewn with sequins. It was also often used for women's clothes. In one way it was beneficial that this work was discontinued, for in spite of its splendor, it was not economical and did not last long. Some of the original group of the sequin sellers (*pulakforush*) and sequin sewers remain; they are now engaged in other work.[37]

(59) The group of flower sewers (*golchehduz*).

There were and [still] are are a group of men and women, who sew silk flowers onto small caps and *termeh*[38] nightcaps. This craft has now fallen into disuse and is of little account.[39]

35. For more information on this craft see Wulff 1966, 217-19 and Floor 2003a, 180-82.

36. For more information on this craft see Floor 2003a, 149.

37. See also Floor 2003a, 185.

38. A kind of figured silk.

39. For more information on this craft see Floor 2003a, 156-58.

(60) The group of face veil makers (*sokmehduz*).

They are those men and women who make the open-worked part women's face veils. Their number has remained the same as before.[40]

(61) The group of the curtain makers (*chadorduz*).

They make curtains for the sashwindows of the buildings of Isfahan, coverings for Sufi convents (*takiyeh*), tents for soldiers, curtains for the royal court and the like. This group has not been reduced in number compared with before and their number is of average proportion.[41]

(62) The group of the patchers (*parehduz*).

They repair and mend the shoes of the poor, water buckets, etc.[42]

(63) The group of saddlers (*sarraj*).

They have a special bazaar next to the *Meydan-e Shah*. They make products such as saddles and horse accouterments. Their situation is not much different from that in the past.[43]

(64) The group of the bucket makers (*dalvduz*).

They make leather butckets for wells in houses, bazaars, bath-houses, gardens and fields.[44]

(65) The group of the weavers (*nassaj*).

Formerly, when European textiles were not common, everyone, from high to low, even high government officials and some princes, wore clothes made of *qadak* (nankeen). Therefore, *qadak* of superior quality of 8 till even 30-warp (*cheleh*) was woven in Isfahan. The thread for both warp and woof was spun in Isfahan too. When the colors made by the Isfahani dyers were added to this it produced softness like *dara'i* in all its beauty. The more it was used its firmness, like dried whey, would become softer and it would become like downy broadcloth. The more it would be twisted, the woolier and shinier it would become. The poor could use one surcoat (*qaba*) for two to three years. Which European fabric does not loose its firmness and color after one time of washing? For the past few years yellow and red European fabrics, which are not sturdy, have become popular. Every time these [European] textiles had a new pattern and each one of them had the look of novelty about it, the Iranian people lost their senses and only had eyes for outward appearance. In fact, this

---

40. See for more information Wills 1883, 333-34 and Floor 2003a, 198.

41. See further Benjamin 1887, 195, 269 and Floor 2003a, 139-42. According to Höltzer 2535, 22 there were 5 curtain makers in Isfahan at that time.

42. According to Höltzer 2535, 22 there were 50 patchers in Isfahan at that time.

43. For more information on this craft see Wulff 1966, 229 and Floor 2003a, 386-87. According to Höltzer 2535, 22 there were 46 saddlers in Isfahan at that time.

44. For more information on this craft see Wulff 1966, 234

path led to ruin, but they do not realize it, especially now, that cheap sensible clothes are not sufficiently economical and longlasting.

This is the reason why the products of the weavers' guild are hardly sold. Therefore, they imitated the European style, but neglected durability [of their product] and turned to superficial prettiness. Because of its nice appearance and convenience European yarn was used for the weft of *qadak*, but these textiles turned out badly. Composed as it was of a mixture of Iranian and European style their weaving became faulty all at once. When worn it became ragged. It also lost its firmness, wooliness, and durability. The yarn-spinners became jobless and found themselves in difficult straits and misery. Russia did not buy [Iranian] textiles anymore and the Iranians lost interest in their own products. The weavers' guild was completely ruined. As a consequence everyone suffered a reverse, [each] according to his share.

At least ten percent of the guilds in this city were weavers, of which not one-fifth has remained. Almost five percent of Isfahan's needy widows, mothers of orphans, made ends meet by spinning and now are out of a job. But also other big guilds like dyers, cotton-dressers and bleachers, who were dependent on this guild, disappeared for the most part. The other classes of people also suffered from the impact of this ruin, especially the farmers, who, because there was no price-fixing[45] for cotton, suffered on account of all of their [other] crops.

Just like a few years ago, when this situation also occurred, when [demand for] cotton rose somewhat and foreigners bought it all. This caused a rise in prices of other goods and everyone profited from it. But what is the use, "it shone brightly, but it was soon over."[46] The relation between loss and profit concerns all products and individuals. Their influence it to be noticed in all things and persons to the extent of their involvement. All parts of the world are like the members of one body, having but one soul. "When misfortune has befallen one member [of the body], the other members will not go unscathed."[47] When it prospered many will share in the profit and this will be the cause of the preservation of Mankind.[48]

(66) The group of silk weavers (*sha`rbaf*).

This guild weaves silk and their work is approximately the same as that of the weavers, who use cotton. They were a large group with looms whose profits were not less than those of the weavers. What has been said about the weavers is completely applicable to them. Their products were in demand both in this country and abroad. The decline of this guild is worse than that of the other guilds, nay it has been completely ruined and there are now only a few of them left. It is said that they were very numerous in the time of the Safavid kings [r. 1501-1736] and that during the reign of the late *Khaqan* [Fath `Ali Shah, r. 1799-1834] there were 1,250 looms.

45. The government sometimes imposed prices (*tas`ir*) of certain agricultural products to facilitate the payment of taxes, which were mostly paid in kind. It then set fixed monetary conversion rates per unit of produce.

46. This is from a poem by Hafez. On the rise of textile imports see Floor 2009b.

47. This strophe is part of the most famous poem by Sa`di.

48. For more information on this craft see Wulff 1966, 199-204.

During the reign of the late king [Mohammad Shah, r. 1834-1848] there were 460 looms, in the beginning of the eternal empire 249, and now they have been reduced to twelve. The products of the abovementioned guild are: damask of several colors, *dara'i* of all qualities, [silk] fabrics [like] *halab, kurd, qasab, alicheh, shal, abrishomi,* and the like.

Formerly besides those in Iran they had customers in Turkey and Russia, but now their product is very little in demand.[49]

(67) The group of makers of head veils (*chadorshab-baf*).

They wove silk head veils and the like for women; they are a type of silk weavers.[50]

(68) The group of dark silk weavers (*meshkibaf*).

They wove the large dark-bay silk fabric (*meshki*) used by women to cover their head. Many of their products went abroad. Formerly there was not a woman in Iran who did not wear a dark-bay piece of fabric on her head. It lasted 40 to 50 years and was not without beauty and charm. Now it has fallen into disuse. This guild is also a type of silk weaver. They were very numerous, but now there are only a few and their trade is ruined.

(69) The group of the lace weavers (*jahkbaf*).

They weave women's lace from material such as *jahk, mozhegan, muj, pur-chuk,* etc. The weaving of Astarabadi and ribbons is the work of the same people who make it for [use as] bedsheet bands. Some of their products for the city's ladies have fallen into disuse and have become old-fashioned. These are now bought by the village women.

(70) The group of the string weavers (*zanjirbaf*).

They weave strings of goldlace for women's clothes.[51]

(71) The group of the loincloth weavers (*longbaf*).

They weave silk cloths used in bath-houses.

(72) The group of the weavers of *abas* (*ababaf*).

This guild was formerly a small and and an unimportant one. Now it is a big and strong guild. Their product goes to all provinces of Iran.[52]

(73) The group of weavers of *ehrami* (*ehramibaf*).

---

49. For more information on this craft see Floor 2003a, 196-97.

50. For more information on this craft see Floor 2003a, 142.

51. According to Höltzer 2535, 22 there were 27 string weavers (*zanjirsaz*) in Isfahan at that time.

52. An *aba* is a coarse cloth that serves as an overcoat. For more information on this craft see Floor 2003a, 129-30. According to Höltzer 2535, 22 there were 20 weavers of *aba*s in Isfahan at that time.

Formerly they wove very fine and long-lasting *ehrami* carpet covers. They had several looms in the city. The appearance of European and linen carpet covers ruined them reducing their capacity to two looms, which are continually inactive and idle.

(74) The group of the mat makers (*buriyabaf*).

Although quite different from the product of the silk looms it is not dull. They are [one] group that weaves mats used in mosques, and another weaves mats used in schools and homes. The floor covering of most poor people in this city consists of mats. The mat makers also weave excellent mats that are used by the rich as summer carpets.[53]

(75) The group of makers of straw packing material (*pizarbaf*).

They make slipcases for flasks and bottles as well as straw baskets and the like.

(76) The group of the bankers (*sarraf*).

This guild can be divided into two groups, both of which are numerous. They have a special bazaar in the inner wing of the *Meydan-e Shah* on the southern side, where the entire open space in front of the Market Hall plus half of the width of the *Meydan* is occupied on both sides by shops of bankers. The shops of the bankers are also numerous in the *Meydan-e Kohneh*, in the bazaars of Bidabad, Chahar Suq-e Shiraziha and in other city quarters. This guild has been and [still] is a large one. Formerly when the province was populous they all resided in Isfahan. Now half of them work in Tehran and Tabriz and in other cities. From time to time they come back to Isfahan for family visits.[54]

(77) The group of the bookbinders (*sahhaf*).

In former years, because of an abundance of development, they bound excellent books, Korans, prayerbooks, handwritten by calligraphers on *termeh* and Chinese paper and the like. Good book binding, involving such skills as arranging the text and margin on the pages, making covers, making portifolios, head bands and attractive bindings as well as other bookbinding arts, were common. Their products were much in demand and they had famous masters. For some years now the aforementioned guild has declined in importance, because handwritten books have fallen into disuse as a result of the introduction of type-set printing and lithography.[55]

(78) The group of the cotton beaters (*naddaf*).

Since the guild of the cotton beaters is dependent on that of the weavers and since the ruination of the latter, this guild has also declined proportionally.[56]

53. For more information on this craft see Wulff 1966, 219-22 and Floor 2003b, 575-76. According to Höltzer 2535, 22 there were 6 mat makers (*hasirbaf*) in Isfahan at that time.

54. On this group see chapter 4. According to Höltzer 2535, 23 there were 30 bankers in Isfahan at that time.

55. For more information on this craft see Wulff 1966, 236-38. According to Höltzer 2535, 22 there were 35 book binders in Isfahan at that time.

56. For more information on this craft see Wulff 1966, 179-82.

(79) The group of the pack-saddle makers (*akaf*).

The making of pack-saddles is dependent on the importance of agriculture as it determines the amount of work for muleteers. This guild has decreased in number, but not much.[57]

(80) The group of the tent material makers (*lavvaf*).

They twist sack-makers' thread and rope and weave wide-mouthed sacks (*galeh*), nets, bags, large woolen sacks (*joval*), saddle bags, and the like. This group has not much declined.

(81) The group of the corn chandlers (*'allaf*).

During the years of the past drought[58] they have become somewhat stronger and they still have not grown weaker as in former times. They have a long bazaar in the *Meydan-e Shah-e Naqsh-e Jahan,* where one third of the ground-level [shops with] sash-windows on both long sides of the aforementioned *Meydan* are occupied by their shops. They also have many shops spread out over the other smaller bazaars of the city quarters. Nowadays, however, their occupation does not bring them much profit.[59]

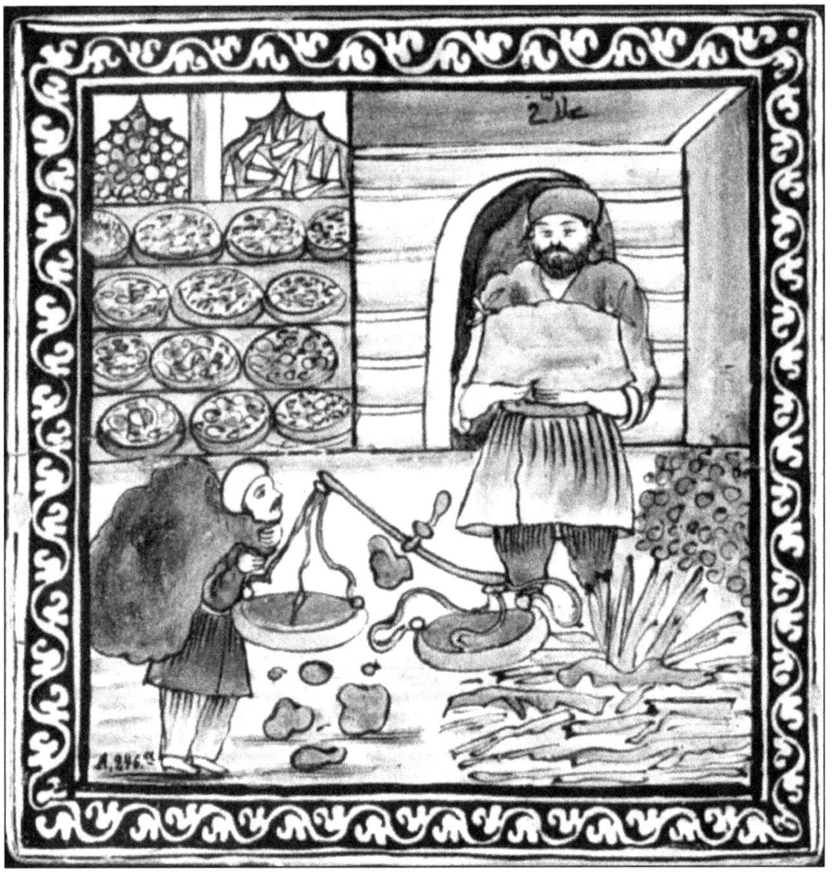

57. For more information on this craft see Wulff 1966, 234.

58. This refers to the drought of 1871-73.

59. On the food situation in the cities see Floor 1983a.

(82) The group of the makers of cotton-shoes (*rassaf*).

Formerly, when in Isfahan Russian (*orusi*) shoes were not in common use, there were many cotton-shoe sellers (*givehforsush*) and cotton-shoe makers (*givehchin*). Most nobles also wore supple cotton-shoes, mainly when amusing and diverting themselves. A pair made on order cost three *tumans* or more. It is said that the well-known Hajji Ebrahim, the former chief of the Karladan-Lenjan district, made a pair of special cotton-shoes for the late Khaqan, which weighed 12 *methqal* (55.8 g) and cost 24 *tumans*. Strachey, the ambassador,[60] took samples of this product to Europe as presents. Formerly, the Isfahani cotton-shoes were much used all over Iran, now not even one-tenth is used in this and other cities. Only a few people remain in this guild.[61]

(83) The group of the fruiterers (*tahhaf*).

They are whole-sale dealers in fruit and they rent the village gardens and orchards during harvest time. Part of the harvested fruit is sold fresh to the fruit sellers; a small part is dried and sold to the dried fruit sellers. Another part is put into storage and disposed of during the winter, making it last until after *Nowruz*. As long as the harvesting in the gardens and orchards continues, these people are engaged in the aforementioned occupation as much as their financial position permits.

(84) The group of the shoesmiths (*na`lband*).

Formerly there were more of them than there are now.[62]

(85) The group of the farriers (*na`lchigar*).

They make shoeplates; the same description as above.[63]

(86) The group of the goldsmiths (*zargar*).

They have of old a special bazaar near the *Meydan-e Shah*. Their work has diminished much compared with former times.[64]

---

60. Lieutenant Strachey, the English 'Beau Brummel', was in the suite of General John Malcolm, ambassador to Fath `Ali Shah in 1800. The Shah was so impressed with his beauty that "he composed an ode in his honour and had his picture painted in most of his palaces." Curzon 1892, vol. 1, 340.

61. For more information on this craft see Wulff 1966, 228-30; Wills 1883 190; Ibid., 1886, 134 note; Binning 1857, vol. 2, 171. According to Höltzer 2535, 22 there were 21 *giveh* makers in Isfahan at that time.

62. For more information on this craft and that of the farrier (next item) see Wulff 1966, 53-54. According to Höltzer 2535, 22 there were 30 shoesmiths in Isfahan at that time.

63. For more information on this craft and that of the shoesmith see Floor 2003a, 231-34.

64. For more information on this craft see Wulff 1966, 32-34; Wills 1883, 162, 333. According to Höltzer 2535, 21 there were 50 goldsmiths in Isfahan at that time.

(87) The group of the gold engravers (*naqqash-e zargar*).

They engrave and inlay ivory bones and fishteeth for the grips of curved daggers, mirror frames, walking stick handles, chess pieces and the like. For their inlay work they depict flowers, *butehs*, and masterly designs in an excellent way. Their mastery of fine ornamental work and of fine iron chisel work was lauded and well-known, but not any longer. The few who have remained inlay metal objects.

(88) The group of the glass makers (*shishehgar*).

They have two big manufacturies in Isfahan, which are still as active as they were in the beginning of the eternal empire.[65] They made garden glasses (*mardangi*), candle burners (*laleh*), and water pipes, which cannot be distinguished from European products with regards to elegance and beauty, when seen from a distance. They were not very much encouraged to perfect their products, which grieved them very much.[66]

(89) The group of the paper makers (*kaghadhgar*).

Of old there has been a big manufactury in Isfahan, which houses the equipment, the cisterns and the workers. Formerly, they made several kinds of paper. One was *fostoqi*, on which writing came out clearly and beautifully; it had elegance and lasted long. It was better than *fostoqi* paper made elsewhere in the country. Several books have been written on it and its beauty is self-evident.

Another kind of paper was rather thick and lasted longer than any other paper. Old decrees and sheets that have lasted to this day demonstrate this clearly.

Another kind of paper is known as *chahar baghal*. Old specimens are of a quality inferior to *termeh* paper and that what made more recently is rather impure and of lesser quality. If there were demand for it then they could make it as good and outstanding as before.

If they showed more attention and were more careful they could make it even better than in the past, such as they made for the *emameh-ye hejleh*.[67]

There was a sayyed in the time of the late king, who produced handmade paper outside the paper factory in his own house. He made very large sheets of *chahar baghal* paper, which he sold for six `*abbasis*. Such excellent paper was not to be found anywhere else. Some people preferred *khanbaleq* paper and samples of it can be found in some houses.

Finally, there is the kind of paper that is very common in this time, which is of an inferior quality. The Isfahan papermill is not doing well at present.[68]

65. Meaning since the beginning of the reign of Naser al-Din Shah in 1848.

66. For more information on this craft see Wulff 1966, 169-71 and Floor 2003a, 88-111. According to Höltzer 2535, 22 there were 15 glass makers (*shishehsaz*) in Isfahan at that time.

67. This term refers to the custom known as *hejleh bastan*, meaning that people made a paper bridal chamber (*hejleh*) for young men who had died and who had not yet been married, probably a derivative from the *Moharram* festival representation of the *hejleh-ye Qasem*.

68. For more information on this craft see Floor 2003a, 270-310. According to Höltzer 2535, 23 there was only one papermill in Isfahan at that time.

(90) The group of the locksmiths (*qoflgar*).

This is a group that makes locks. Some of them make spherical locks (*qoflha-ye qolveh*) and screw locks (*miyan-e pich*). Others make locks for jewelry boxes, caskets, and chests. Of late the products of this guild have been in greater demand than before.[69]

(91) The group of the steel workers (*foladgar*).

The make steel parts such as the top parts of water pipes, sword grips, saucers for coffee cups, belts, lampions, Koran cases, steel helmets, foot of middle parts of water pipes, iron mounting (*qobbeh*) of shields and a lot of other items. Nowadays their products are used more than before. The members of this guild were formerly few in number, now they still are not a big group, but there is a demand for their work and it is exported to Turkey and Egypt.

(92) The group of the brass workers (*davatgar*).

They are numerous. Formerly there were many of them, but nowadays their number has increased further. They have a big, long, special bazaar near the *Meydan-e Naqsh-e Jahan*. Nowadays their production has increased compared with before. They make samovars and other vessels, which do not differ much from those of foreign countries. Their products sell well and go to all provinces of Iran.[70]

(93) The group of the needle makers (*suzangar*).

This group consists of a few people; they work in five shops near the Market Hall (*Qeysari-yeh*) of the *Meydan-e Shah*. Their products are used in the city and in the rural districts.[71]

(94) The group of the knife makers (*kardgar*).

Good antique steel knives that were used in Iran were all made in Isfahan. Now their products are not much in emand. They have no customers except for the tribes and some villagers. Few remain of this guild. The greater part of their work consists in the making of ordinary knives and large chopping knives (*satur*) for butchers and cooks.[72]

(95) The group of the starch makers (*neshashtehgar*).

They make starch from wheat. Formerly there were few of them; now they still are as few [as before].[73]

---

69. For more information on this craft see Wulff 1966, 65-72.
70. For more information on this craft see Wulff 1966, 28-38.
71. For more information on this craft see Wulff 1966, 57.
72. For more information on this craft see Wulff 1966, 55-56 and Floor 2003a, 235-36.
73. For more information on this craft see Floor 2003a, 362-63.

(96) The group of the foundrymen (*rikhtehgar*).

They cast drinking cups, bells for mules and camels and some other articles in moulds. Formerly they were not very numerous and that is still the case.[74]

(97) The group of the darners (*rafugar*).

Formerly there were many of them in Isfahan, but now that *termeh* is no longer in demand there are no more than two or three men.[75]

(98) The group of coppersmiths (*mesgar*).

They are numerous and have a special, long bazaar. One side of their bazaar is connected with the *Meydan-e Shah*; the other side opens up at the *Meydan-e Chahar Howz*.

The members of this group were numerous in former times, but a number of years ago [their trade] declined and collapsed. Then, some years ago, when the [price of] cotton rose, farmers became active again and bought back the copper that they had sold before. This guild experienced a boom, which still lasts.[76]

(99) The group of the tinners (*saffar*).

This group tins new copper when it comes out of the press. Some others tin old copper.

(100) The group of embossers (*monabbatkar*).

There are [only] a few of them. They are engaged in inlay work on the exterior of vessels, utensils and gold, silver, and copper articles fashionable in Iran, Istanbul and other foreign countries, such as tea-kettles, sugar-bowls, waistbands, armlets, Koran cases, mirror-frames, copper bowls, water bottles and other items.[77]

(101) The group of the emery workers (*sonbadehkar*).

They engrave crystal, semi-vitrified porcelain, china, and gems with the buff-wheel.[78]

(102) The group of the silk workers (*abrishomkar*).

They are the silk assayers of Isfahan. They are a group of Jews who clean silk and give it to the guilds of the silk weavers, the dark-bay weavers, the lace makers and others.

74. For more information on this craft see Wulff 1966, 18-20 and Floor 2003a, 214.

75. According to Höltzer 2535, 22 there were 14 darners in Isfahan at that time.

76. For more information on this craft see Floor 2003a, 215-18. According to Höltzer 2535, 22 there were 100 coppersmiths in Isfahan at that time.

77. For more information on this craft see Wulff 1966, 25-40; Wills 1883, 189, 332. According to Höltzer 2535, 21 there were 30 engravers (*qalamzan*) in Isfahan at that time.

78. For more information on this craft see Polak 1865, vol. 2, 179.

(103) The group of the paste-board makers (*moqavasaz*).

They make pencases, mirror frames and other articles of paste-board. Formerly, the making of paste-board in Isfahan was not as good as it is now, which is clear from old papier-maché work decorated by famous painters. Because of the inferior quality of former paste-board they researched in Isfahan how to transfer drawings, so that antique drawings of old masters could be transferred onto new paste-board and [what they found] is a very good process.

(104) The group of the sword cutlers (*shamshirsaz*).

Formerly there were many of them, but now there are very few. In the beginning of this everlasting empire there was a man who made much better swords than Asad Esfahani and those made by the Indians. But as there were no buyers he discontinued his work. Nowadays they could still make good work if only there was a demand for it. [However,] there is practically no demand for their work now.[79]

(105) The group of the poniard makers (*qomehsaz*).

Formerly, the poniard and broadsword (*qaddareh*) were not very much in use in Isfahan. A number of years ago they became quite popular and a great impulse was given to the making [of poniards and broadswords]. They were well-made and almost as good as the Maragheh poniards. However, once again their market fell into a decline.[80]

(106) The group of the gunsmiths (*tofangsaz*).

Formerly there was a substantial demand in Isfahan for gunsmithing. They have a special big bazaar in Isfahan. In the time of the late Khaqan there was a master called Hoseyn; the special guns from his workshop are famous. He was better than the old renowned Russian masters. There is, for example, the gun that was made for the former governor of Isfahan, the late Hajji Soltan Mohammad Mirza. With regards to guns, Hajji Mostafa was [also] very good and people used to compare and contrast the work of Hajji Mostafa with the aforementioned gun. The work of master Hoseyn was considerably better, because of its smoothness, perfectness, polish, luster and water (*jowhar*); his work was better than a bullet and this gun was especially famous. Several other special guns were made for some noblemen and were not inferior to Hajji's work. He had apprentices who after his death turned out good work. There were and still are many other masters in Isfahan. Most of them work and do repair work in the Tehran workshops now, because of lack of work here.[81]

79. For more information on this craft see Floor 2003a, 236-47 and Khorasani 2006, 130-94.

80. For more information on this craft see Floor 2003a, 247-48 and Khorasani 2006, 212-18.

81. For more information on this craft see Floor 2003a, 249-64. According to Höltzer 2535, 22 there were 40 gunsmiths in Isfahan at that time. For technical terms used by gun-smiths see Wulff 1966, 59-61.

(106) The group of the gunhammer smiths (*chakhmaqsaz*).

There was a group of them in Isfahan when there were few European gunhammers and a lot of flint. Many good English gunhammers were brought to Iran and one cost 15,000 dinars. Master Mohammad Esfahani, the gunhammer smith, sold one for three *tumans* in the time of the late king. One has to take into account that in Europe the different parts of the gunhammer are made separately. There, the hardening of the steel of the powder horn and the hammer is done by separate groups, while in Isfahan Master Mohammad did all of this himself alone and the other masters did it in the same way. It is already many years ago that most gunhammer smiths left Isfahan for Tehran. Some chose to go to Khorasan, Kurdestan, Fars and other places. Only a few remain in their hometown. If there were a demand for their work they could still make good gunhammers. Their products are marketable in Iran only.

(108) The group of the chest makers (*sanduqsaz*).

They are a group of Isfahan that makes big and small chests in the European style. For coating they use many-colored figured tin. It is elegant, neat, and solid and much better than the latest European work.[82]

(109) The group of the jewelry box makers (*mejrisaz*).

The same description as above.[83]

(110) The group of the tin-box makers (*qutisaz*).

The same description (as above). Some sugar boxes, tea-caddies and workboxes with many compartments (*hazar bisheh*) and others are made of real plane-tree wood here. They gild and illustrate the wooden pearls with a painting brush. The surface is painted with fishglue color, saffron, and varnish, which gives [the boxes the look of] solidity and splendor, and their price is [accordingly] high.

(111) The group of the tin-smiths (*halabisaz*).

Formerly there were none in Isfahan and it was only a few years ago that they made their appearance. All of them make vessels from tin. From Isfahan this craft has spread to the rest of the country.[84]

(112) The group of the flexible water pipe-tube makers (*neypichsaz-e ghalyan*).

Formerly the flexible water pipe-tube was very much in demand in Isfahan; indeed, the flexible water pipe-tube of Isfahan and Kashan were and [still] are the most sought after all

82. According to Höltzer 2535, 22 there were 14 chest makers in Isfahan at that time.

83. According to Höltzer 2535, 22 there were 10 gold box makers in Isfahan at that time.

84. For more information on this craft see Wulff 1966, 30-31. According to Höltzer 2535, 22 there were 4 tin-smiths in Isfahan at that time.

over Iran. But of late there has not been much demand for this product and of the flexible water pipe-tube makers not even half remains.[85]

(113) The group of the chain-mail makers (*zerehsaz*).

The making of chain-mail has fallen into disuse nowadays. Some of them have remained, but are now engaged in other occupations. A few years ago, old chain-mail was collected and taken to Turkey (Islambul), because there were buyers. Here and there they still make chain-mail at home, but it is not an important guild.[86]

(114) The group of the helemet and cuirass makers (*kolah-e khod va chahar-a'inehsaz*).

Formerly they formed a large group, but in recent years [their trade] fell into disuse. But since a number of years some buyers were found in Turkey and other countries. In Isfahan some people [still] make helmets and cuirasses.[87]

(115) The group of the bowyers (*kamansaz*).

Formerly they were a group who made arrows and bow. Until the end of the reign of the late Khaqan bows were still made, but then they fell into disuse and the ancient [art of] bowyery came to an end. Of late there has been again demand for old bows, which again are sent to Turkey. There are two or three men who make new bows, which are exported.[88]

(116) The group of the scissor makers (*qeychisaz*).

They make scissors for both male and female tailoring as well as scissors for pen-cases made of iron or steel. Formerly, these had a special shape; the point was sharp and the hollow-ground blades (*miyan-e kas*) were pierced out. They were priced from two *qrans* up to two *tumans*. Nowadays they are made quite simple, without any fretwork and in shape similar to European ones. [However,] they last longer than the European ones and are sold for three to four *qrans* each. These products are marketable all over Iran and are exported to all provinces. However, only a few are [still] being made.[89]

(117) The group of mirror makers (*a'inehsaz*).

Formerly, there were many of them and they had many shops in Isfahan. The mirror glass which was brought from foreign parts, especially from Aleppo, was not mercurated and was silvered in Isfahan, put into a frame and sold. Now the guild has been reduced to four of five shops.[90]

---

85. For more information on this craft see Wulff 1966, 236. According to Höltzer 2535, 22 there were 4 flexible water pipe-tube makers in Isfahan at that time.

86. For more information on this craft see Khorasani 2006, 275-85.

87. For more information on this craft see Khorasani 2006, 284.

88. For more information on this craft see Khorasani 2006, 286-315.

89. For more information on this craft see Wulff 1966, 26, 57.

90. According to Höltzer 2535, 22 there were 21 mirror makers in Isfahan at that time.

(118) The group of the heel makers (*pashnehsaz*).

They cut leather shoe heels out of black cow horn, white ivory bones and fishteeth. This group is less numerous than in the past.[91]

(119) The group of the cutlers (*chaqusaz*).

They make knives with black bone handles for eating fruit, etc. The knives are sharp, of good quality and of an elegant form, both of cast steel and normal steel. Formerly, they made pen knives like the European ones. Since these were not of as good quality as the European knives, their production was discontinued. Before European knives came into common use they used to make steel knives in Isfahan. Their shape was like that of pen knives with a crooked point, something between a knife and a poniard with long bone handles and a short steel blade, which could not be bent.

Ahmad Esfahani was a famous cutler in Safavid times; his pen knives lasted more than 200 years. There was one Mahmud in the beginning of the reign of the late *Khaqan*. His pen knives were twins of the work of Ahmad. They were as sharp as the six to seven *tuman* European knives when [whetted] on the greekstone to make them a bit sharper and pointed, and even after having been used one or two years they did not become dull. These penknives of Ahmad and Mahmud can be found with some old calligrapher families. In the end of the reign of the late king, one or two men searched for these knives and bought the work of Ahmad and Mahmud for a high price. They collected the knives that were kept by families. It is not known what became of these knives or where they were taken. At present there is no trace of them; if they were here they could possibly be used for another 200 years. Cutlers make the same type of pen knives now, but they are not used for sharpening pens and their steel is not as well hardered as before. If there were buyers, however, they would soon be able to make them again. The ones that are made now are women's utensils, who use them to cut the hair of their eyebrows.[92]

(120) The group of the of the wood inlay workers (*khatamsaz*).

This guild used to be very numerous. That what has remained of the wood inlay (*khatam*) work of old masters on old jewelry boxes, old lecterns, chairs, mirrors, frames, doors of rooms and buildings shows their artistry. Most of the old items have been collected and taken away. On the whole, Europeans still buy some. This guild has become less important compared with former times. Their work is of inferior quality, because it not much in demand. As the situation is now, wood inlay work is only marketable in the villages of Iran and a small quantity in Turkey (Rum va Islambul). Sometimes they apply wood inlay work on chairs and tables of nobles.[93]

91. For more information on this craft see Wulff 1966, 229.

92. For more information on this craft see Wulff 1966, 55-56 and Khorasani 2006, 230.

93. For more information on this craft see Wulff 1966, 92-97; Floor 2006b, 172-73. According to Höltzer 2535, 22 there were 26 inlay workers in Isfahan at that time.

(121) The group of the street vendors (*besat andaz*).

They have many shops in the small bazaars and in the bazaars of the city quarters.

(122) The group of the rice traders (*shal andaz*).

They buy and sell dehusked rice.

(123) The group of the second hand goods dealers (*semsar*).

Formerly there were many of them in Isfahan, but they are a few now.

(124) The group of the carpenters (*najjar*).

In comparison with former times they have been halved. Because it is of simple construction and easy to make non-European work is now commonly used. As to fine ornamental work they lost some of the finesse to make it. Very solid and beautiful antique paned colored windows (*morassa` sazi*) are found in sash (*orusi*) and normal windows. The frame work (*ostekhvan-bandi*) that they make to-day does not differ that much from the old work. They have made use of modern European style for color and lacquer combination and grace of geometrical form. Nowadays their craft has increased.[94]

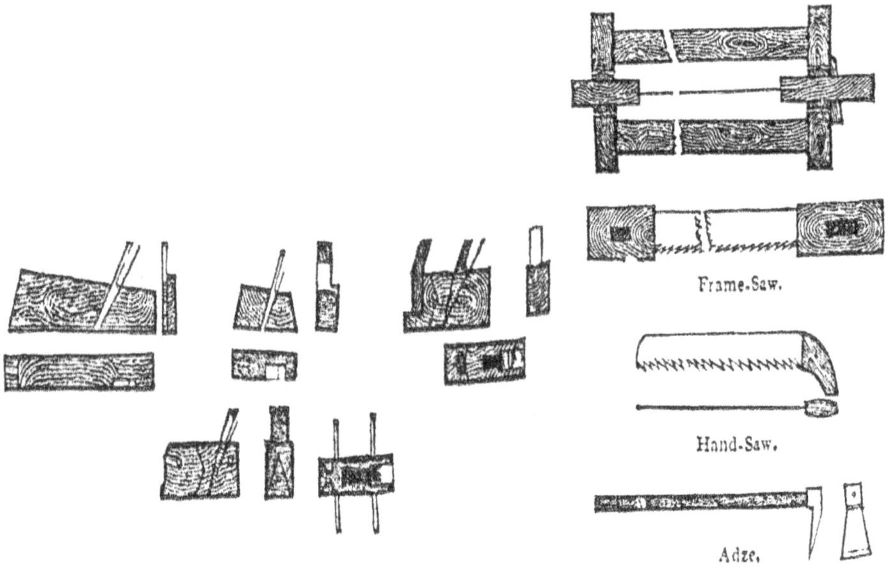

(125) The group of the stonecutters (*hajjar*).

Formerly, there were many of them; in the beginning of the everlasting empire there were still a great many of them. Now a third of them has remained. There have [always] been skilled Isfahani stone cutters, who were praised for making fine ornamental sculptures such as flower designs, strips, script cutting, etc. The good work of this craft was indicated

94. For more information on this craft see Wulff 1966, 80-85; Floor 2006b.

by the great number of workers, the many partners (*hamdast*) and the great number of masters (*sahebkar*). Now only a few are left.[95]

(126) The group of the whole-sale dealers (*bonakdar*).

They are whole-sale dealers (*sanginbari*), who sell apothecary articles and small quantities of sugar sweet meats, etc. in the passage ways of the bazaars.

(127) The group of the architects (*me`mar*).

In former times there were many of them in Isfahan, i.e., according to what has been written in the histories, this province employed 12,000 architects in Safavid times. To-day their number has been reduced to four or five men, but some of the masons, who are master, are engaged in the construction business.[96]

(128) The group of the masons (*banna*).

There are two groups. One group, that of the bricklayers, is engaged in making trenches (*shaludeh*), pisé walls, ceilings, and limestone work. The second group is that of the plaster workers (*nazukkar*). They are skilled in making stucco work, vaulting and plaster moulding. The masons of Isfahan, both in bricklaying and plaster work, were always and still are praised. The imposing nature of old and newly built houses makes this clear to intelligent people. Most of the good work is done in Isfahan itself, where space and good building materials are to be found. The master masons (*sahebkar*) are very precise and attentive to their work, using old buildings as their models. Many of the Isfahani masters have gone to other cities and have executed very slovenly work. Anyway, this group has been halved compared with ten to twenty years ago.[97]

(129) The group of the painters (*naqqash*).

This guild always had and still has a great number of people. The former and present masters of this city are famous. Their work can be found all over Iran, in European and several other countries. At present they have many famous masters.

Formerly there was a separate guild for enameling in Isfahan. They had famous masters such as Aqa `Ali, son of Aqa Baqer, the famous painter. In the art of enameling he was as honored as his father was in painting. He died at the end of the reign of the late king. At present some painters are engaged in this art. As to their painting; if they are

95. For more information on this craft see Wulff 1966, 128-30. According to Höltzer 2535, 22 there were 91 stonecutters (*sangtarash*) in Isfahan at that time.

96. According to Höltzer 2535, 22 there were 10 architects in Isfahan at that time.

97. For more information on this craft see Wulff 1966, 108-15; Benjamin 1887, 277-79; Wilson 1896, 285-86; Polak 1865, vol. 1, 50-55. According to Höltzer 2535, 23 there were 80 masons in Isfahan at that time.

commissioned they will deliver work that is as good as the work of the old masters. They make very good top parts of water pipes.[98]

(130) The group of the book gilders (*modhahheb*).

The group of the gilders used to be much bigger. All of them were well-known masters, but their number has decreased now. Those remaining are still capable and competent. From amongst two men have gone to Tehran, one of them is Mirza Mohammad Taqi and the other Aqa Mohammad Javad.

(131) The group of the polishers (*mohrehkash*).

They form a big guild. One guild glazes paper; its glazing is famous. The second one glazes calico (*qalamkar*); they are also masters of their art.[99]

(132) The group of the tray porters (*tabaqkash*).

They are people of strong build with thick and powerful necks. In this province it is their work to carry things on trays, which they put on their head. They are a type of porter (*hammal*). They have very big trays. When the trees and orchards bear fruit they go to the gardens and orchards outside the city. They carefully put fruit of good quality and delicacy, such as mulberries, apricots, peaches, nectarines, pears, and grapes, - which during transportation are liable to be damaged due to moving about and hard shocks – layer on layer on a tray and between the layers they put, leaf by leaf, fresh leaves. Among these people are skilled wrestlers, who have won laurels and have proven their strength. Especially when carrying mulberries they lift up as many as three trays. The custom and convention is thus that when carrying three very big trays full with mulberries they put a wooden frame (*payeh*) on top of the tray and then put another one on top of it. Some will even put a high stool on the third tray and put a young child upon it, while adorning the sides of the trays with roses, tulips, mirrors, and lampions. They will [even] carry as much as the weight of 70 to 80 Tabriz *man* [230-240 kg] by putting three trays on their heads. With a group of buffoons as forerunners and many rogues following they pass through the bazaars and passageways and thus will arrive blindly at the fruitseller's shop. Because of the straining exercise their health often breaks down. Sometimes it has occurred that their necks broke, so that their head dropped forward.[100]

(133) The group of carriers (*kerayehkash*).

They are people who with beasts of burden carry wares to and from bazaars and homes.

98. For more information on this craft see Floor 1999a; Ibid., 2005b. According to Höltzer 2535, 21 there were 20 painters in Isfahan at that time.

99. For more information on this craft see Floor 2003a, 281-82.

100. According to Höltzer 2535, 23 there were 27 tray porters in Isfahan at that time.

(134) The group of the knife grinders (*charkhkash*).

They form two guilds. One group is engaged in polishing and varnishing by putting newly wrought copper on the grinding bench. The second group whets sharp utensils with the wheel and makes them sharp and neat.[101]

(135) The group of the wood carvers (*qalebtarash*).

They are embossers (*monabbetkar*) who engrave flowers and butehs on wooden moulds for the calico workers (*qalamkarsaz*).[102]

(136) The group of the crystal sellers (*bolurforush*).

In former times they had many shops, but now there are only a few.[103]

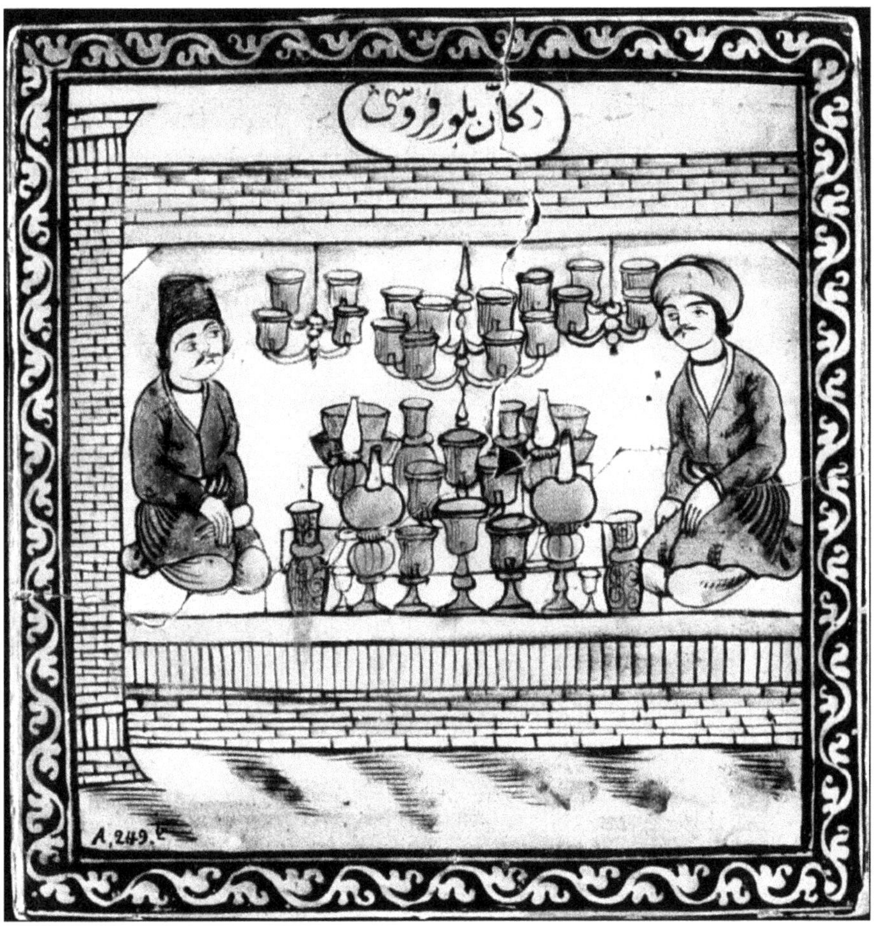

101. For more information on this craft see Floor 2003a, 266. According to Höltzer 2535, 23 there were 6 knife grinders (*charkhgar*) in Isfahan at that time.

102. For more information on this craft see Wulff 1966, 98-99.

103. According to Höltzer 2535, 20 there were 19 crystal sellers in Isfahan at that time.

(137) The group of sellers of china (*chiniforush*).

In former times there was much excellent old china porcelain, semi-vitrified porcelain, and agate available in Isfahan and its districts. Little by little needy people would bring such items to the bazaar and there was a lot of it in the shops. For years there was a brisk trade [in this commodity] for which there were customers, who exported it. Nowadays it is not selling well and there are no more than two or three shops of china sellers in Isfahan.

(138) The group of the fruit sellers (*mivehforush*).

In no other region there was and is such an abundance of fruit and fruitsellers as in this province.[104]

(139) The group of greengrocers (*sabziforush*).

There are many of them and eating vegetables is inexpensive.[105]

(140) The group of the sellers of beets and carrots (*chaghandar va zardakforush*).

They buy car loads of raw beets and carrots and store them. They sell them per load (*bar*) and per *man* (5.9. kg). The boiled-beet sellers (*labu-forush*) sell cooked beetroots and carrots.

104. According to Höltzer 2535, 20 there were 260 fruit sellers in Isfahan at that time.

105. According to Höltzer 2535, 20 there were 43 greengrocers in Isfahan at that time.

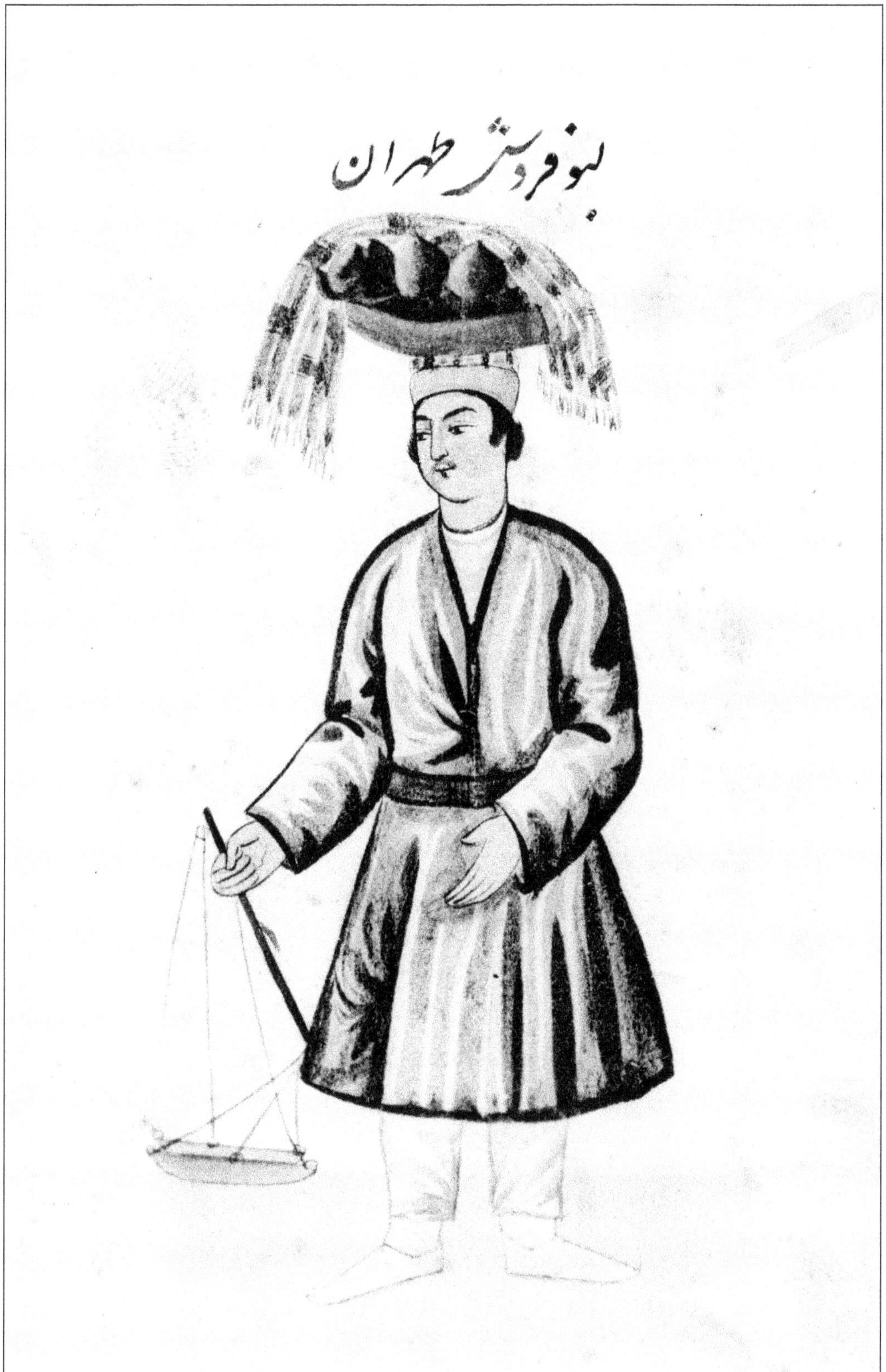

254 Vendeur de betterave cuite. - Téhéran.
Продавецъ вареной свекловицы. - Тегеранъ.

(141) The group of the sellers of dried fruit (*khoshkehbarforush*).

In Isfahan this guild is numerous.

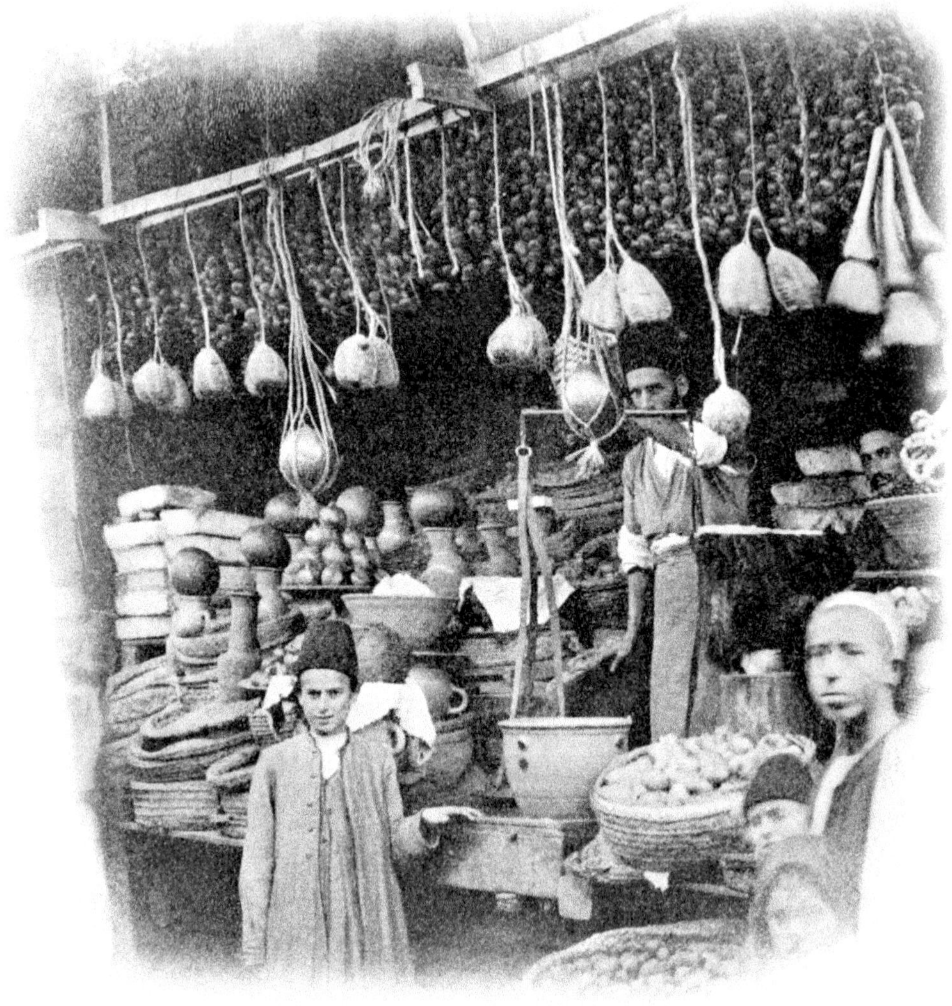

(142) The group of the old clothes sellers (*kohnehforush*).

They have a special bazaar in the *Meydan-e Shah-e Naqsh-e Jahan*. They have also many shops in the neighborhood of the *Meydan-e Kohneh* and also many shops spread out in the various bazaars and city quarters. Because of lack of money, there are many buyers (*kohnehkhar*) and sellers of old clothes up to this time in the city. God willing, they will gradually decrease in number.

(143) The group of the street vendors (*dastforush*) of the permanent market (*bazar-e modami*).

Formerly there were many, but now there are very few. Since olden times it was customary that there were markets on Wednesdays and Fridays on the *Meydan-e Kohneh* of Isfahan. Here poor, needy families brought their belongings such as clothes, coarse cloth (*palas*), vessels, utensils, tools, books, and other things, both new and old, of good and bad quality. Everything, whatever you can think of, both for men and women, is brought here and sold cheaply. The buyers also gather there these two days. On Sundays there is also a market in the *Meydan-e Jolfa-ye Esfahan*. Then Moslems who have anything suitable for Armenians go there. The rest of the week if there is need to sell something at once, they give it to the *dast-forush* to sell by going around the bazaars, or the owners themselves go to the bazaars of the Bidabad and Chahar Suq-e Shirazi quarters and sit down near the shops to sell [their wares].[106]

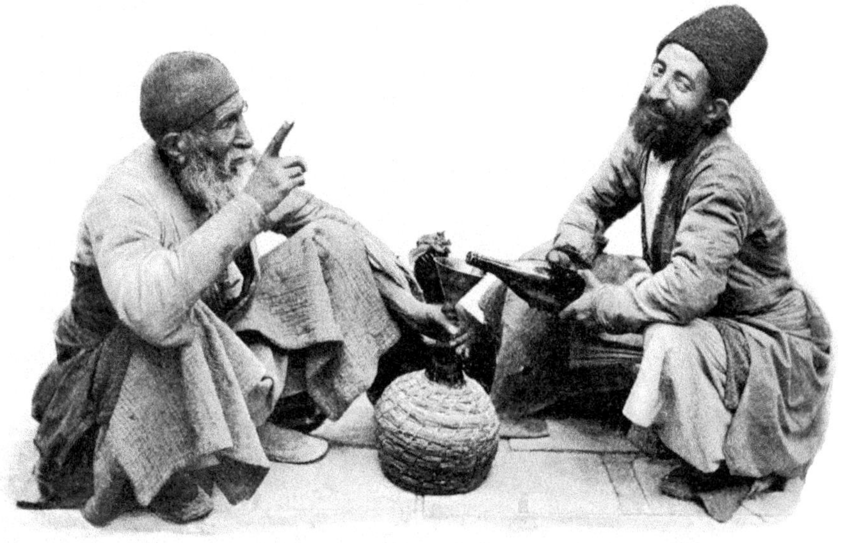

(144) The group of the tent cloth sellers (*karbasforush*).

Compared with old times there is not much difference [in its size]. In Isfahan, both inside and outside, and in some other provinces canvas is generally used for tents, pavilions, shelters, coverings, etc.[107]

106. "There is a weekly market held each Sunday in the little Maidan of Julfa; it is well attended. Raw cotton, fruit, grey shirting, chintzes and notions are sold there, and also beef for the Armenian unlike the Persian, is a beef-eater. Here, too, the Persian women hawk their cotton-yarn and buy socks, which are handknitted in Julfa by the Armenians, of wool and also of cotton. Any hardworking woman can keep herself in Julfa by knitting; the earmings barely exceed five kerans (three and nine pence) a month; but this with economy is enough to keep and cloth them." Wills 1883, 142. According to Höltzer 2535, 20 there were 65 street vendors in Isfahan at that time.

107. According to Höltzer 2535, 22 there were 120 tent cloth weavers in Isfahan at that time.

(145) The group of the tobacco sellers (*tanbakuforush*).

They form a group among the town's population.[108]

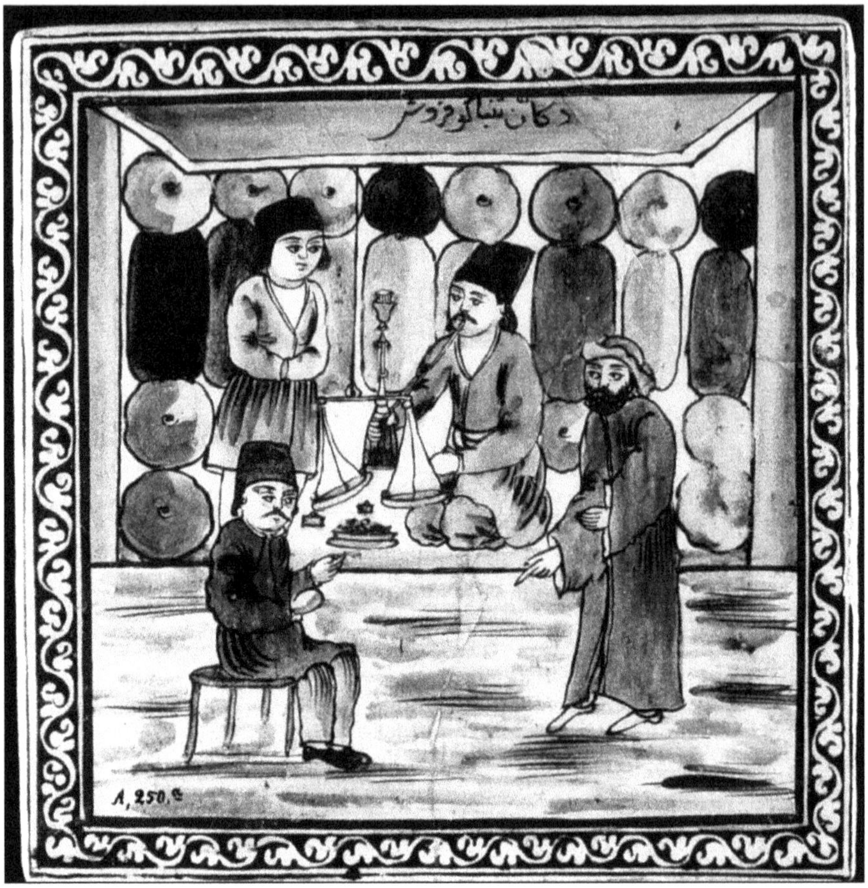

(146) The group of the opium sellers (*taryakforush*).

The opium market has now found foreign buyers and business is now rather important. The [number of the] opium shops, who sold opium in small quantities (*khordeh-forush*) for consumption in the city itself, does not differ from the old situation. The farmers and peasants themselves take care of selling raw opium (*dorosht-forush*); the merchants buy it from them per *man* (5.9 kg) and per box. After the drought [of 1871-73], this commodity has lately found its way among the people of Isfahan, because its price is not fixed (*tas`ir*). Except for taxes and revenues its effect is corruptive.[109]

(147) The group of the book sellers (*ketabforush*).

Formerly there were many in Isfahan. Now they have been reduced to two or three men who sell books only. Most of the bookbinders make a supplementary living at book selling.

108. According to Höltzer 2535, 20 there were 150 tobacco sellers in Isfahan at that time.

109. For more information on this craft see Floor 2003b, 433-60.

(148) The group of the carpet sellers (*farshforush*).

There is not much difference in [their] number with previous times, because many of their products are sold outside the province.[110]

(149) The group of the ready-made tailors (*dukhtehforush*).

They make ready-made clothes. Some of these are bought by the peasants of the rural districts and dependencies of Isfahan, [but] mostly by the Qashqa'i [tribesmen] and the Karwas Kurds. This group has not changed much in importance compared with former times.[111]

(150) The group of the sellers of jars (*kuzehforush*).

The number of their shops has not grown less compared with former times, but their sales have been halved.[112]

(151) The group of the haberdasheries (*kharraziforush*).

Compared with former times their number has very much declined. Their articles are of two kinds. First, that what is to be found in the country itself such as the articles on the detailed list [below]. With a few exceptions all of them are Isfahani products. Pen-cases, fire flints, ink, pumice stones, bath-house gloves, garment pins, chains, copper top parts of water pipes, antimony, (native) sulphur matches (*gowgerd-e fatileh*), rosaries, copper ink pots, bullets, pellets, tongs, tweezers, tinboxes for European matches, iron and copper chains, copper middle parts [for the water pipe], mirror frames, locks, tea strainers, trowels, zinc and copper rings, lead rings, glazed ink pots, zinc rings, powder horns, *qashavol* (?), tailors' scissors, top parts of the gusset, percussion cap holders, knives with bone handles, *si yak berenj tab dar kon* (?), arms of balances, hoods for hawks, funnels, sugar hammers, bridle bits, bells, iron door keys, glass beads, cheese scrapers, saws, necklaces (?) (*band gardan*), shears, screw drivers, packing needles, stucco trowels, plumb lines, *halabi-ye mashq-e atfal* (?), sharpening steel for scrapers, tin trays, zinc water bottles, copper candlesticks, bones [for nibbing pens], copper opium boxes, belts, copper tea kettles, ebony flexible water pipe hoses, ebony and other combs, copper saucers for coffee cups, kitchen knives, copper earrings, copper spoons for eating water melons, copper teaspoons, wooden

110. According to Höltzer 2535, 20 there were 11 carpet sellers in Isfahan at that time.

111. "There are several kinds of ready-made clothes (*now hazer*) (made) from every kind of fabric, both Persian and foreign. Indeed, everyone who wants (to buy) any kind of appearal of good taste, both winter and summer (fashion), can find this in several shops in the Tehran bazaar. It is not necessary to buy the material personally and bring it to the tailor and wait (for the suit)," E`temad al-Saltaneh 1306, 126. However, according to Wills, ready-made clothes were unknown. "The tailor ("khyat") in all cases makes up the materials of his clients, and ready-made clothing, or "slops", are unknown. The tailor always cuts out the coat in presence of the customer. The price for making a coat is one toman, or two or three kerans for a day's work by a master tailor. The seamstress is glad to take a less figure, and goes out to work for half a keran a day and a hot break breakfast. All sewing is invariably done with silk, which is sold by weight." Wills 1883, 191.

112. According to Höltzer 2535, 20 there were 11 jar sellers (*kasehforush*) in Isfahan at that time.

spoons for eating broth and sherbets, compasses, goldsmith's scales, barber's razors, tailors' irons, and zinc candlesticks.

Second, that what is imported from abroad [such as] percussion caps, mirrors, finger bowls, snuff boxes, needles, needle boxes, European matches, knives, scissors, sequin punches (*manganeh-ye pulak*), sexagonal buttons (?) (*tokmeh-ye shesh tarh*), all kinds of seals, European flint stones, key-rings, European *qashavols* (?), trusses, and binoculars.

The Isfahani haberdasheries have no more to offer [for sale] than this. Isfahani haberdashery items kept their ground, while in Tehran and Tabriz European articles are in the majority.

(152) The group of the opium makers (*taryakmal*).

They have become numerous in recent times.[113]

(153) The group of felt makers (*namadmal*).

Of average size.[114]

(154) The group of the brick makers (*kheshtmal*).

Their number has decreased.

(155) The group of the brokers (*dallal*).

There are four kinds. One. The cattle market brokers, who act as cattle brokers (*dallal-e chahar payan*) in the bazaar of the cattle sellers. Two. The fruit brokers (*dallal-e favakeh*), who act as fruit brokers in the bazaar of the fruit sellers. Three. The trade brokers, who act brokers for merchandise. Four. The opium brokers. Formerly there were none; they came into existence recently.[115]

113. According to Höltzer 2535, 23 there were 230 opium makers in Isfahan at that time.

114. According to Höltzer 2535, 22 there were 30 felt makers in Isfahan at that time.

115. On the brokers see also chapter three supra.

(156) The group of porters (*hammal*).

They carry merchandise etc. on their backs between the customs office, ware-houses and the bazaars.

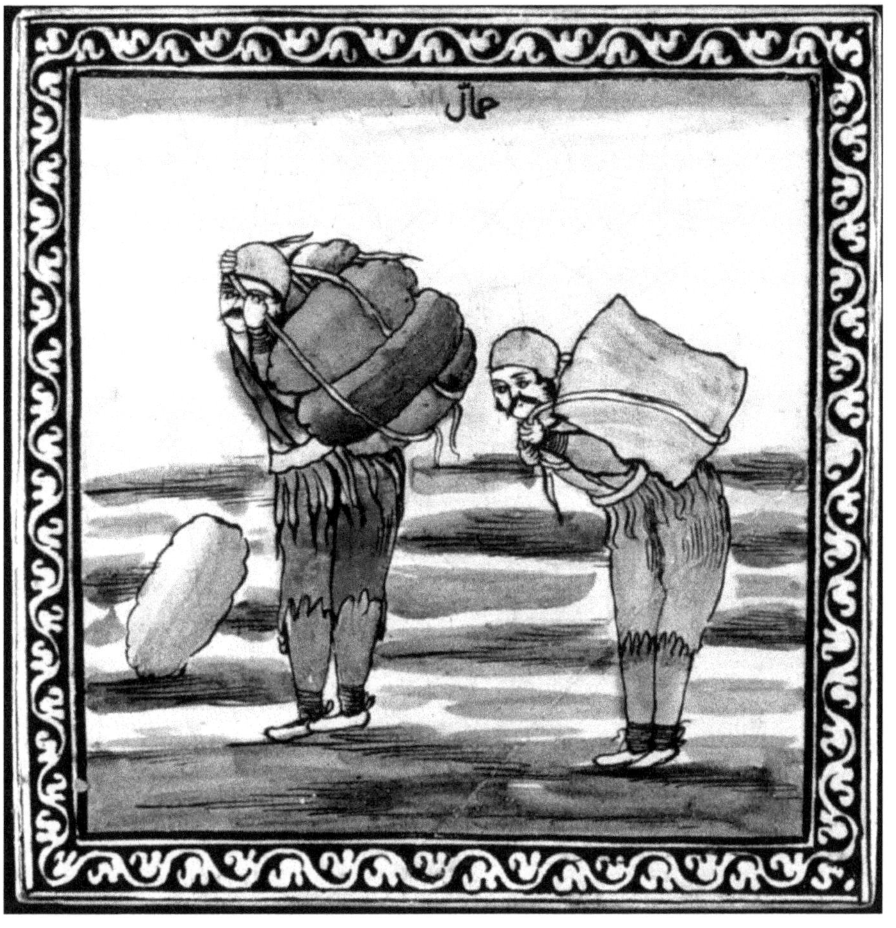

(157) The group of muleteers (*mokari*).

These are of two kinds. One. The owners of asses and mules, who work in and outside the province. Two. The camel owners, who work in the rural districts and rarely in the city.[116]

(158) The group of the bleachers (*gazur*).

They are a large group. The workers of the bleaching manufactury have one manufactury in Isfahan itself. They bleach *qadak* with many workers. There is another group formed by the workers of the textiles printers manufactury; they bring the calicoed fabrics to the banks of the river for bleaching.[117]

116. For more information on this craft see de Gobineau b, 117-19; Binning 1857, vol. 287; Aubin 1908, 304; Wills 1883, 381-82.

117. For more information on this craft see Floor 2003a, 153-55.

(159) The group of the millers (*tahhan*).

They are a group of millers other than the millers of the rural districts and dependencies, who bring the ground wheat of those parts to the city. There are many mills in this city. Some are moved by water, others by camel or donkey, some are hand or foot [mills], which are brought into rotation by human feet and hands.

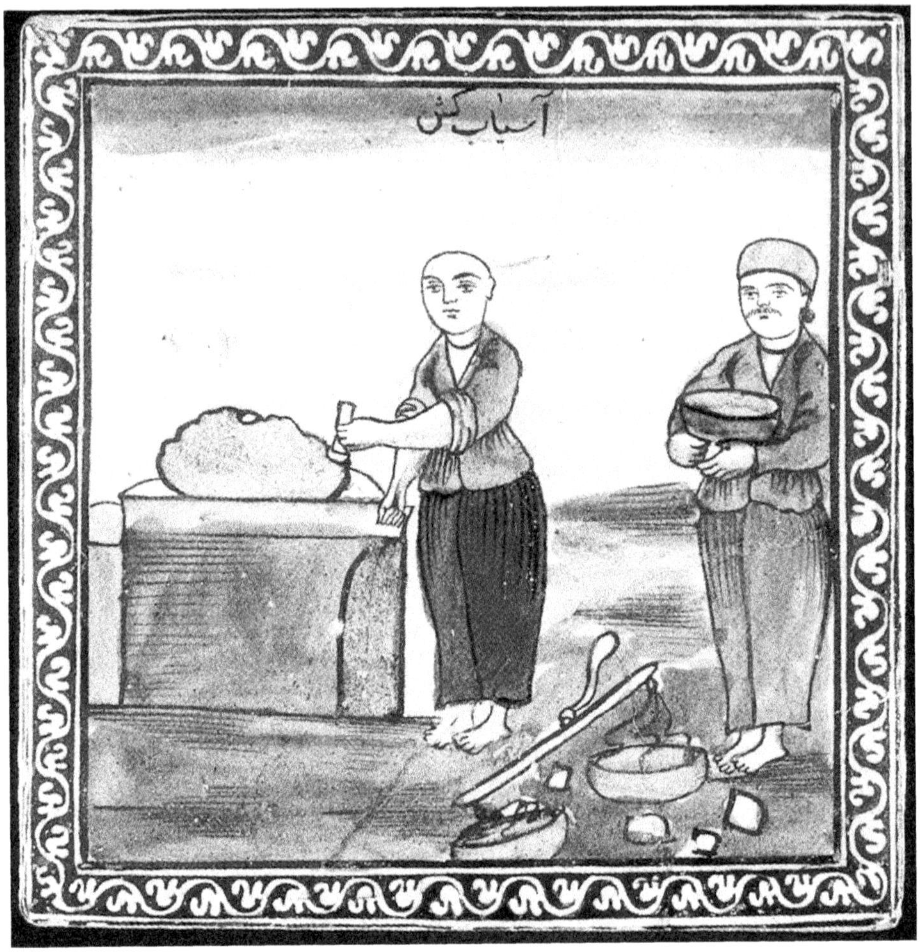

First, the water mills. Many main irrigation channels (*madi*) and streams (*nahr*) have been branched off from the river and channel a huge volume of water through the city's quarters. These mills turn constantly, but during the four months that water is at its lowest mark, the mills being dependent on the motion of water, they sometimes work and sometime they do not.

Secondly, those which are rotated by camels or donkeys are used of old especially in dry years and during the four summer months of water scarcity. There are many mills built in this city, which are rotated by camels and donkeys and are active for a third part of the year.

Thirdly, those which are moved by hand and feet. Formerly the people of this city have known times of grave adversities and siege by rebels. Most houses have hand and foot mills, so that in unsafe times wheat can be ground by hand, and there is no need to go outside [the home].[118]

(160) The group of the yarn dyers (*sabbagh-e risman*).

They are a group other than the dyers of *qadak*, who dye yarns for the weavers and tailors.

(161) The group of the silk dyers (*sabbagh-e abrishom*).

They form a separate group who dye silk. Anybody who wants the finest quality of *qadak*, which has the best color, gives it to the silk dyers.[119]

(162) The group of the tanners (*dabbagh*).

They are those who tan sheep hides. This group belongs to the slaughter-house fiscal group[120] and is dependent on the group of the butchers. The number of this guild increases whenever more sheep are slaughtered in this province. At present, compared with thirty or forty years ago, their number has decreased to half or less.[121]

(163) The group of the butchers (*qassab*).

They are, except for the flayers and the rest of the workers of the slaughter-house fiscal group, shopkeepers. Most of the aforesaid shopkeepers are the apprentices of the heads and leaders [of the guild]. Every day the latter supply meat to the butchers by weight and each day they demand its profit from the butchers. The work of the shopkeepers, who are hired workers, is not all that bad. However, masters who own shops and meat do not exist anymore as in former times.[122]

---

118. For more information on the construction of the various types of mills, see Wulff 1966, 284-89; see also Floor 2003a, 224-30. "In many houses a primitive hand-mill is used, consisting of two stones; the upper one has a grip, the lower one a slit for ejecting the flour." Polak 1865, vol. 1, 111. According to Wills 1883, 360, "Flour is generally ground in a handmill by the poor." According to Höltzer 2535, 23 there were 51 millers (*asiyaban*) in Isfahan at that time.

119. For more information on this craft see Floor 1999b, 191-95. "There is a very large dying trade carried on here. Two bazaars alone are occupied by the Guild of the Dyers. They are chciefly employed in converting white shirtings, etc. into those sombre clothes which are so affected by the Persian ladies in their outdoor costume. They also dye muslins to various tints of blue or light green, for the use of the descendants of the prophets, who use them either as a turban or a Kamar (belt)." DCR 1892 (1397), 49.

120. See Appendix I.

121. For more information on this craft see Floor 2003a, 376-86. According to Höltzer 2535, 22 there were 15 tanners in Isfahan at that time.

122. "The butchers sell by weight, and have no idea of joints; the buyer is allowed to hack of a large or small portion, and the price is the same irrespective of part. The liver, lights and kidneys, with the heart, are only eaten by the poor, while the suet is carefully removed for the candle-maker, and can be had at a higher price than meat. The huge tail of the Persian sheep is looked on as a delicacy, and a portion is allotted to each buyer. When hung outside the shops of the butchers, the carcasses are decorated with strips of Dutch foil and bunches of grass. The oxen,

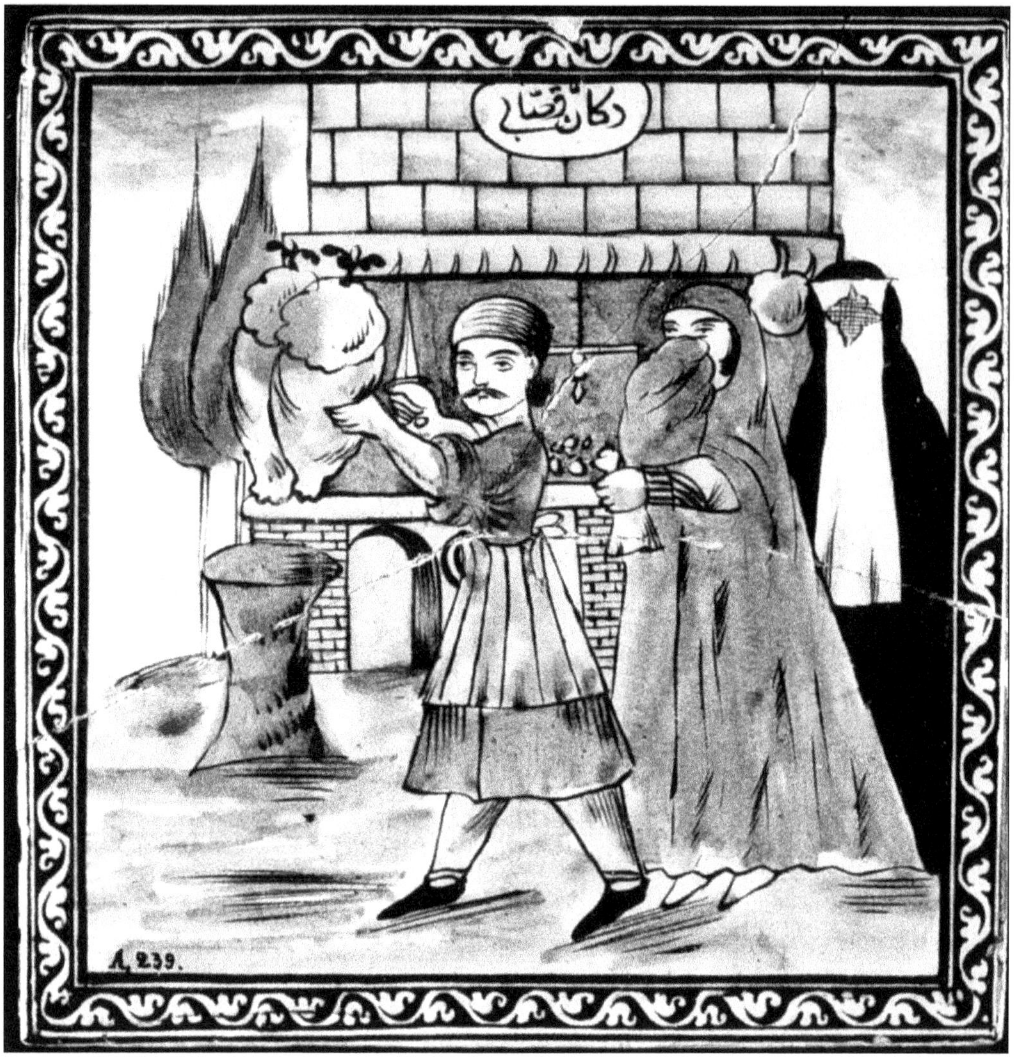

(164) The group of the candle makers (*shamma'i*).

Their importance is dependent on the importance of the butchers; at present they are ruined.[123]

being used as beasts of draught in the fields, are only slaughtered when worn out, and beef is consequently only eaten by the poor, being as a rule half the price of mutton. It is hard and indigestible, and as the Persians never hang their meat it is deservedly despised. Lamb is twice the price of mutton. Among the Christians of Julfa, however, good beef is at times to be obtained but the animals are seldom larger than Alderneys, save when buffaloe-meat is had, and this is hard and dark." Wills 1883, 299. According to Höltzer 2535, 23 there were 20 butchers in Isfahan at that time.

123. For more information on this craft see Floor 2003a, 117-34. According to Höltzer 2535, 22 there were 11 candle makers (*shamma`*) and 35 wax candle makers (*sham`saz*) in Isfahan at that time.

(165) The group of the cooked head sellers (*ravvas*).

What was said of the candle makers is applicable to the guild of the sellers of cooked heads (*kallehpaz*)[124]

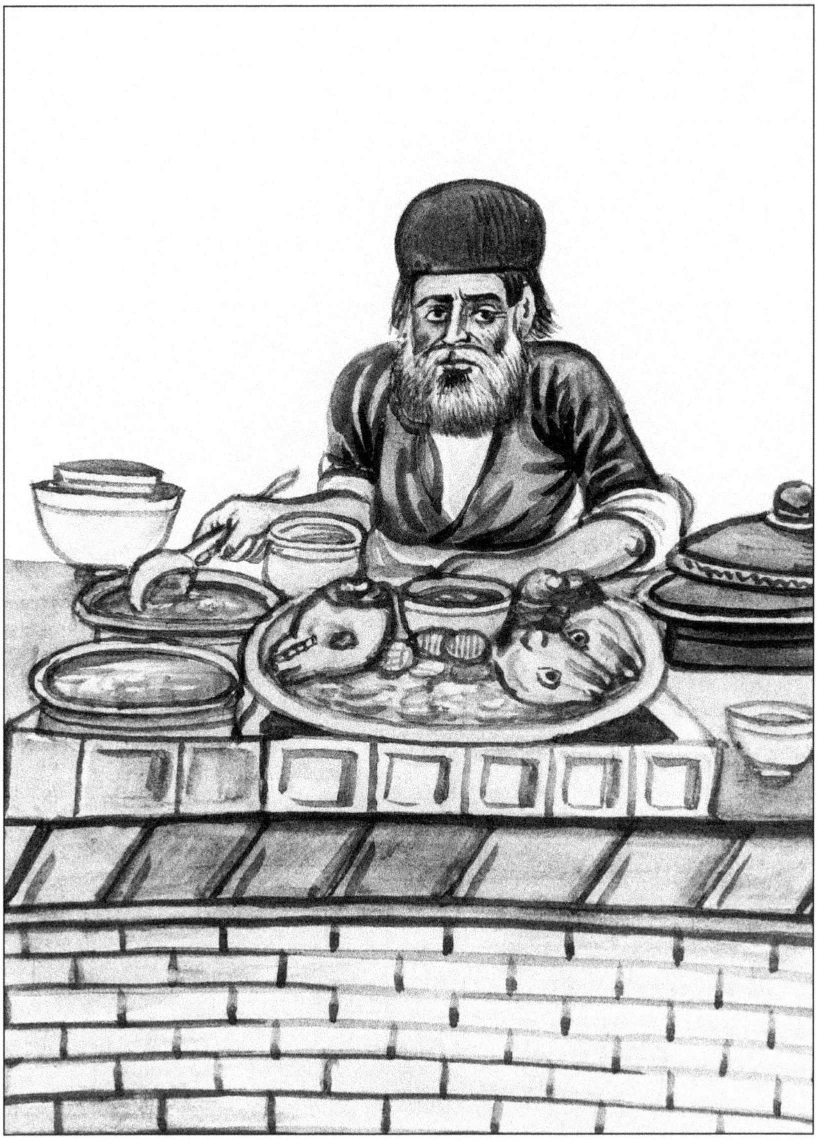

(166) The group of the grocers (*baqqal*).

This guild formerly had many members and now it still is a large guild. Their shops are spread out all over the bazaars and city quarters. Their products are all of good quality. They themselves are clean people and their shops are very spacious, well-ordered and clean. The grocery articles in the province are all good and fine and the grocers also have the

124. "The trade of the kalleh-puz, or cooker of sheep's heads and feet, is a common one; the head of sheep are slowly simmered for some twelve hours, and the liquor sold as soup; the feet, tongues and heads being retailed to peripatetic vendors." Wills 1883, 298-99. According to Höltzer 2535, 23 there were 8 sellers of cooked heads in Isfahan at that time.

knowledge of preserving the products and to keep them from spoiling. The people of this province are also very precise and meticulous; they do not care for bad quality and spoiled products.[125]

(167) The group of the bakers (*khabbaz*).

They form a group in the city consisting of shopkeepers, dough makers, dough mixers, dough formers, dough stretchers, weighers and others having to do with the city's food. Formerly, on account of the great number of inhabitants in the province, they tampered a bit with the bread, but, nowadays, because there is no price fixing and the government is well organized, bread is fine and of good quality everywhere.[126]

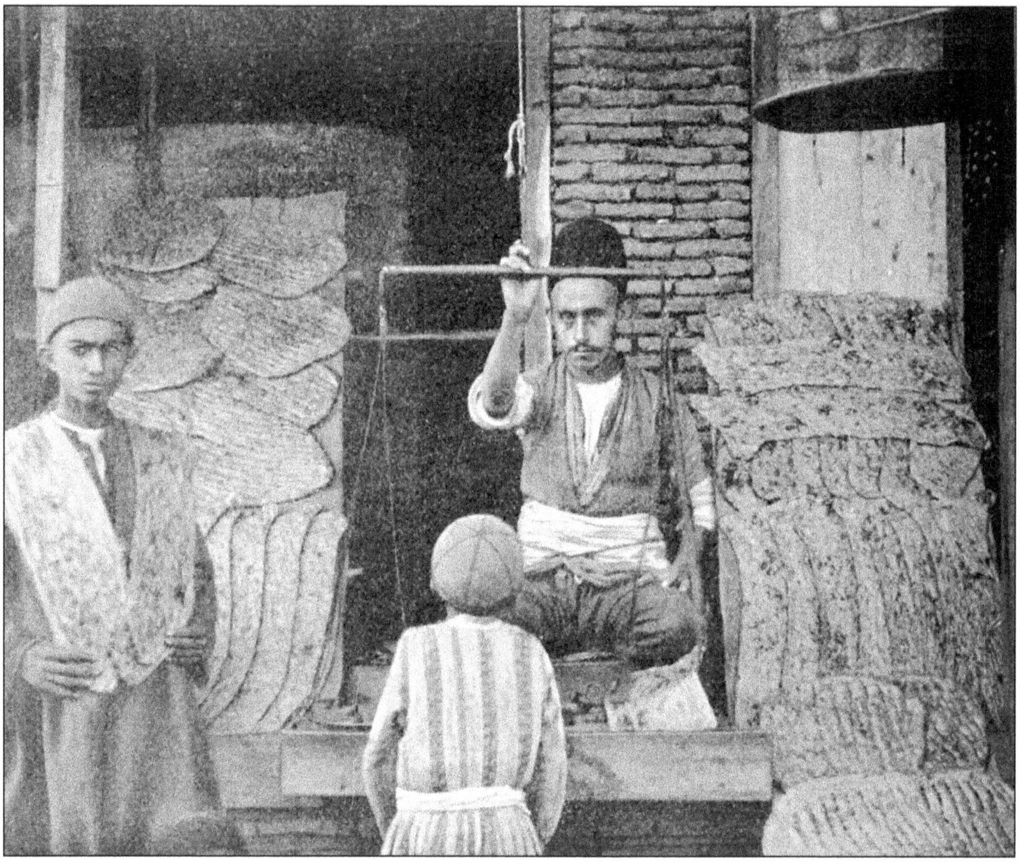

(168) The group of the kebab sellers (*kebabi*).

The kebab of the Isfahani kebab sellers has always been and [still] is good. Generally their *kebab-e luleh* is well-known. Their fatted lamb kebab (*kebab-e gusht-e bareh-ye por kardeh*)

125. For more information on this craft see Wills 1883, 190; Landor 1904, vol. 1, 307. According to Höltzer 2535, 20 there were 240 grocers in Isfahan at that time.

126. For more information on this craft see Wulff 1966, 291-95; see also Benjamin 1887, 95-96. According to Höltzer 2535, 23 there were 190 bakers in Isfahan at that time.

is not prepared as well, because they economize. At home it is roasted better than in the bazaar. The taste and delicacy of Isfahani mutton is not to be found in any other province and because sheep always get corrugated grass (*`alaf-e kerkereh*) and clover makes that their meat is tender. Sheep give birth twice annually and that is why throughout the year there is mutton and there never will be a lack of it.

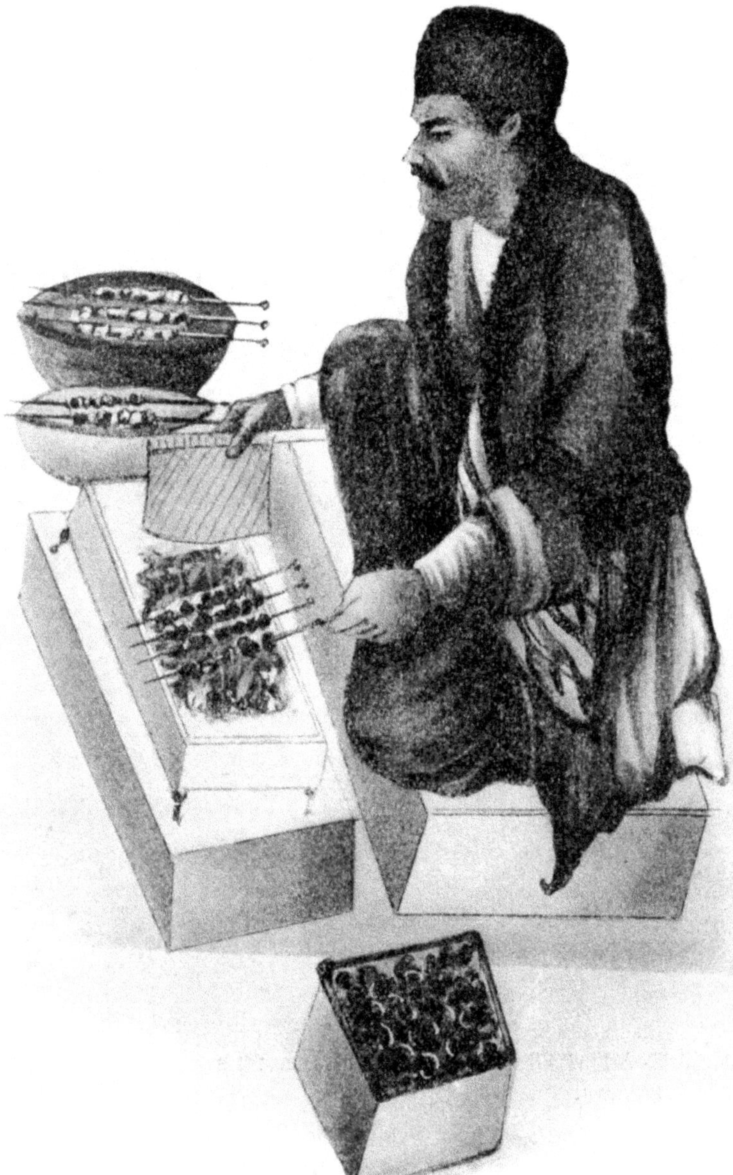

(169) The group of the cooks (*ashpaz*).

This guild consists of two groups. One group cooks *chelow* and *pelow*. Formerly, they cooked all kinds of *chelow, pelow, khoresh,* and *ash* of good quality. Since the drought [of

1871-1873] its quality has become less and it is not selling well. The other group boils and cooks [meat] (*pokht va pazi*) Since ancient times it has been regulated and recorded in the files and rules of the *kalantari* that they have to put their trays with meat on ice and have to sell it cold (*sardforush*), so that it will not be mistaken for *beryani* meat [see item 171]. The application of this regulation has become lax, so that the *beryani* sellers certainly have the right to complain.[127]

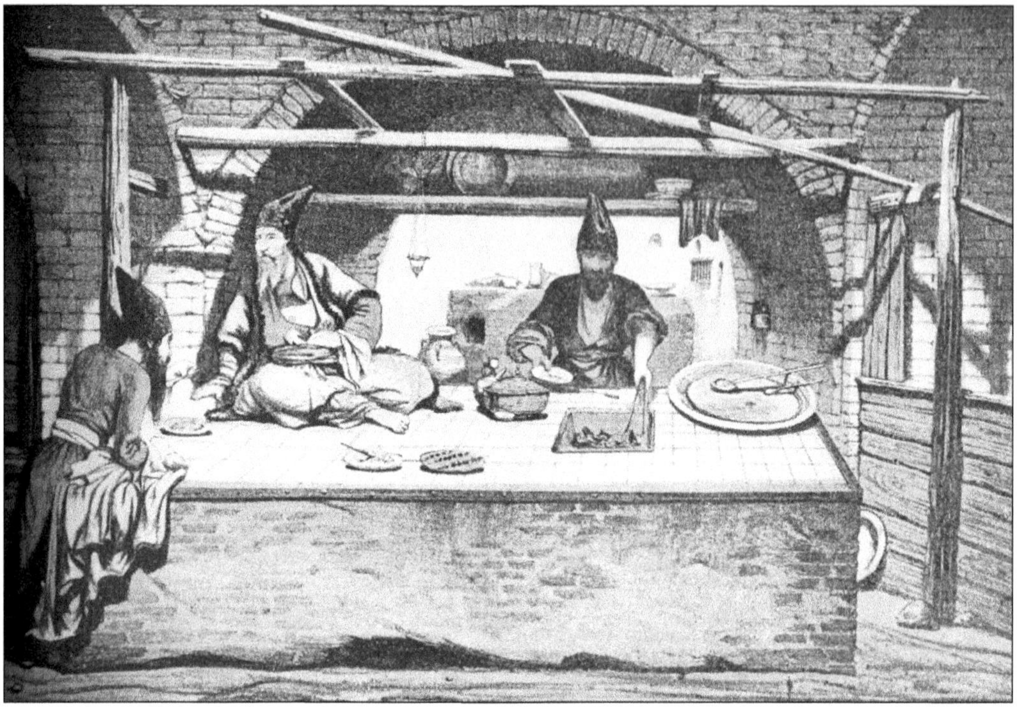

(170) The group of the juice makers (*shirehpaz*).

Apart from the existence of juice making workshops in the rural districts far from the city there are many juice making workshops in the city, who bring grapes from the neighboring villages for the making of juice and they produce good juices.[128]

(171) The group of the makers of *beryan* (*beryani*).[129]

There are several shops in Isfahan which provide the entire city with *beryan*. All their *beryan* is cooked in one manufactory. Of the cooked foods from the Isfahani bazaar it is one of the most agreeable. In Tehran they tried to make *beryan*, but it did not become very popular, let alone in the other provinces. It is not tempered with; better food for the arti-

127. For the difference between *chelow*, *pelaw* and *khoresh* and the preparation of *ash* see Polak 1865, vol. 1, 107-09. "In all cities of Persia there are cheap cook-shops. These have a good reputation, so that even people from the higher classes send for food from them." Bleibtreu 1894, 70; see also E`temad al-Saltaneh 1345, 765 and Polak 1865, vol. 1, 135-36.

128. For more information on this craft see Wulff 1966, 300-02; Floor 2003a, 364; Ibid., 2003b, 330. According to Höltzer 2535, 23 there were 14 juice makers in Isfahan at that time.

129. According to Polak 1865, vol. 1, 135 *beryan* only refers to entrails, livers and lungs.

sans and others in the bazaars is not to be found. Most families make it part of their lunch. It is something between kebab and meat boiled in water, but more delicious and digestible than those two.

The makers of *beryan* have large spacious ovens in the aforementioned workshop. Big fat sheep are hung in the oven after heating it, and a cauldron half-filled with boiling water is placed on the bottom of the oven. Then the door of the said oven is firmly closed and it is left that way from night until the next morning. When it is opened, the meat has been so heated by the vapor that the meat has come off some of the bones. Meanwhile, the broth and its fat, i.e., what has been taken out of the oven is put once more in boiling water. The result is a very thick broth. They [i.e., the makers of *beryan*] sell the broth separately from the meat, which is put on trays and sent to the shops of the *beryan* sellers, who chop it with a big knife and sell it piece by piece. Nowadays [*beryan* cooking] is tempered with; it is put into a cauldron with little water and boiled in the same oven; it is a surrogate for real *beryan*. Nevertheless, there is no better food to be found in the bazaar.

(172) The group of the porridge cooks (*halimpaz*).

They exercise this profession during the winter. During the summer they are engaged in other jobs.

(173) The group of the lentil cooks and the lentil sellers (*`adaspaz va `adasforush*).

Lentils are a kind of food which is tasty, cheap, healthy, and the daily food of the poor. The knowledge of preparing lentils in this way as it is done now is limited to one Isfahani family, who inherited this profession generation after generation and made a living of it. Others who wanted to learn this method of cooking failed, for that which they cooked was not as good and tasty. Some years ago this family went from Isfahan to Tehran and there one of the migrated Isfahani family members is still cooking lentils. This product sells well when the weather is cold. It is prepared in kettles and given to hawkers to peddle it around town.

(174) The group of the pudding makers (*ab-band*).

There are many people selling firm and starched *ferni, faludeh,* and *shir-e berenj.*[130] In former times they also prepared different types of ice cream. Now because of lack of demand the making of ice cream has fallen into disuse.

(175) The group of the water sellers (*saqqa*).

Notwithstanding the fact that in the bazaars and passage ways of the city quarters many big, beautiful, sculptured and engraved public drinking fountains can be found filled with

130. For more information on these dishes see Polak 1865, vol. 1, 109, 123; Mostowfi n.d., vol. 1, 166.

a lot of ice and that its water is given because it is a pious act there are many itinerant water sellers in the bazaars.[131]

(176) The group of the sellers of water pipes (*ghalyanforush*).

Besides being present at places likes the entrances of bath-houses, the Chahar Bagh and other recreational sites, many sellers of water pipes go around the bazaar.[132]

(177) The group of the hawking fruiterers (*tebaq besar*).

They are workers who mostly put viands, fruits and nuts on a tray on their head and go around town to sell these.

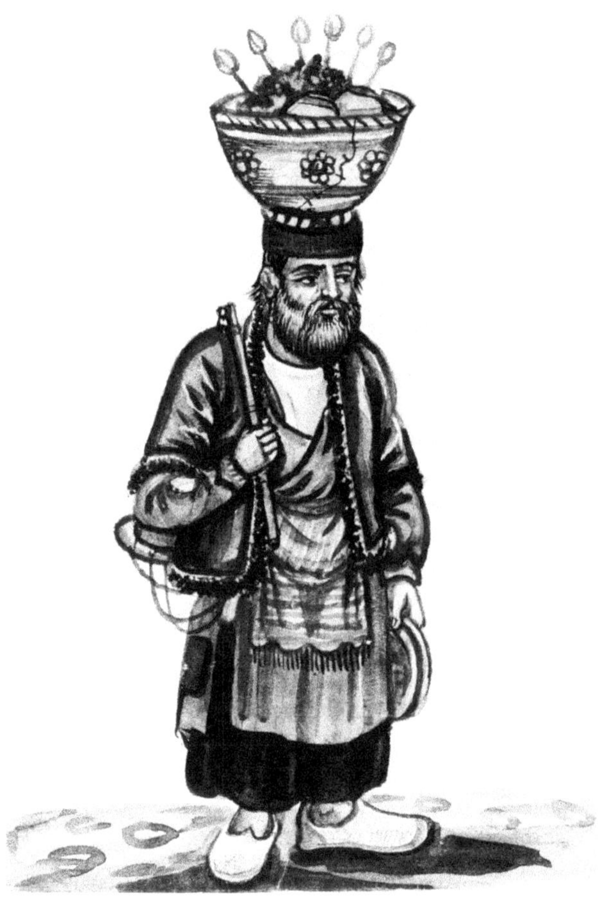

131. "The water carriers are only necessary, because the water tubes are bad and uncovered, water becomes polluted and is hardly fit to drink. The richer classes have their water brought on a mule from outside the city. For the poorer classes there is the water carrier, who, however, often sells dirty water." Polak 1865, vol. 1, 122.

132. They did not sell water pipes, but rather 'a smoke'. For more information see Floor 2002.

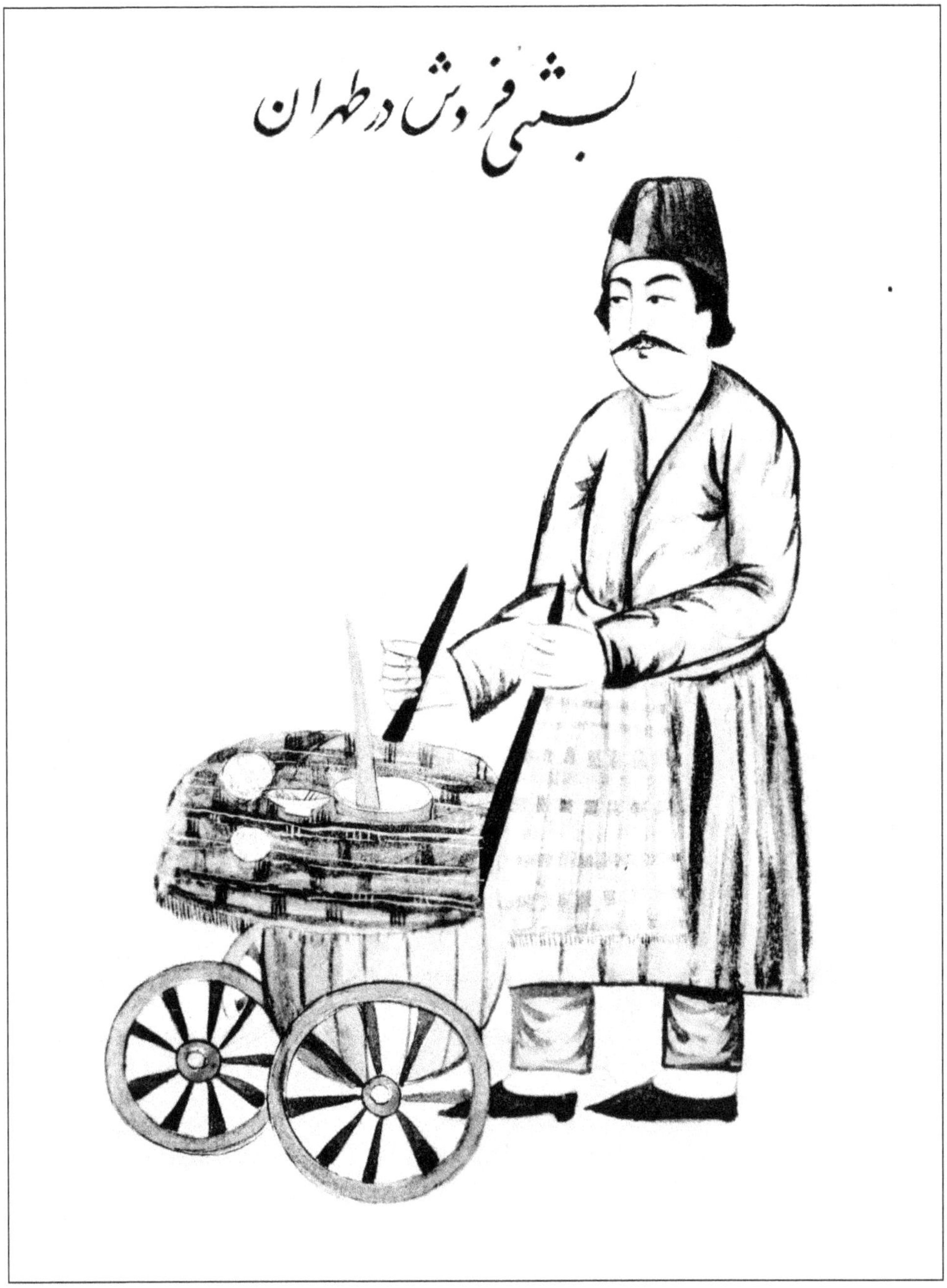

Ice Cream Vendor in Tehran

(178) The group of the itinerant tea sellers (*chayforush-e dowrehgerd*).

In this province this profession is not at all common and tea houses have not been common either. There was only one government tea house built in olden times in the middle of the *Chahar Bagh-e Kohneh*. Drinking tea has become more common in the last few years and some tea houses have been built. But people consider tea drinking in tea houses as shameful. It won't take long before they get accustomed to it and it will become popular. The importance of this trade is dependent on strangers and travelers.[133]

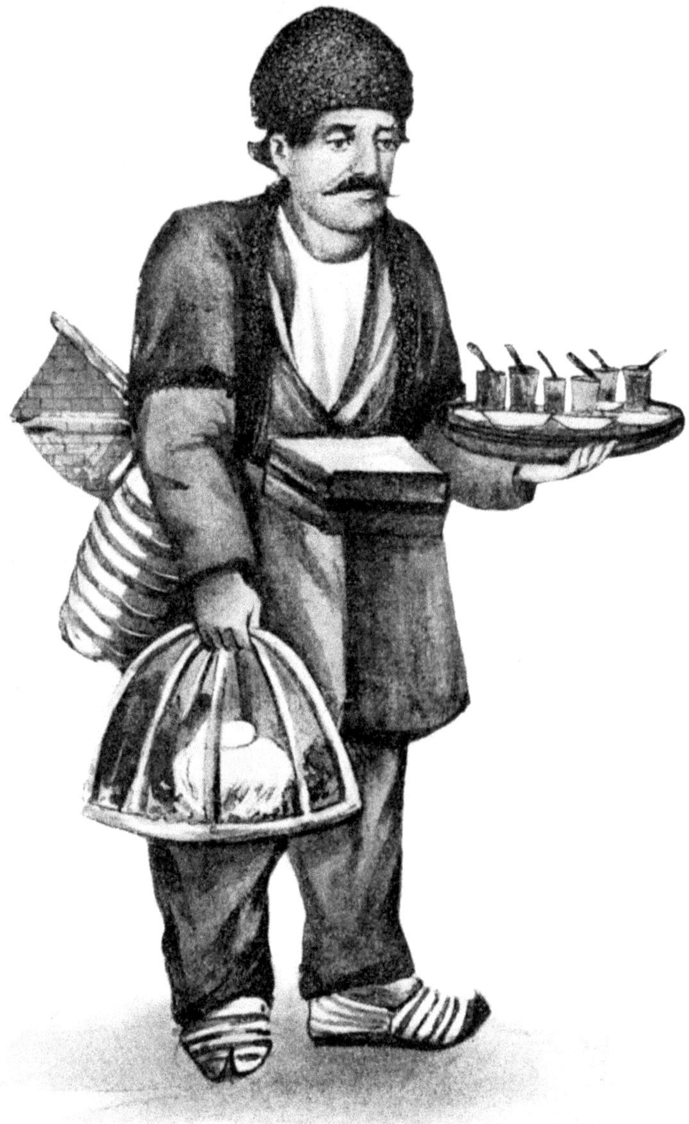

(179) The group of the itinerant grocers (*olaghdar*).

They are hucksters (*khordehforush*), who put some cereals and fruit on their donkeys and go around town.

(180) The group of the junk dealers (*`ata'i*).

133. On all tea related issues as well as on the transformation of Iran from a country of coffee drinkers into one of tea drinkers see Floor 2004a. According to Höltzer 2535, 23 there were 19 coffee-houses in Isfahan at that time.

They are a big group who dig for china in the province. They buy old horsecloth, old coarse woolen cloth, old clothes, broken china, and small glass by going from house to house in exchange for which they give needles, pins, rubber, or sharpen (implements). Of all that they collect, the broken glass and crystal is taken by the glass makers. Old clothes and coarse cloth they assort some of them are suitable for the second-hand cloth sellers and another part for the paper makers. What is rotting is used to fertilize the soil of the rice paddies.[134]

(181) The group of the twiners (*charkhtab*).

They are a group who transfer unspun silks from the skein and wind them on the twining-wheel.[135]

(182) The group of the rope and hair makers (*mutab*).

They twist ropes and sack makers' thread with jasper.

(183) The group of the gut spinners (*zehtab*).

They spin sheep guts (*rudeh*), which are used for the strings of the cotton beating bows, spinning-wheels, etc.

(184) The group of the bath-house keepers (*hammami*), clothes holders (*jamehdar*), masseurs (*dallak*) and other bath-house attendents.

The number of the group is proportional to the seventy-two working bath-houses in the city; these are all clean in accordance with their class.[136]

(185) The group of the sewer men (*kannas*).

They take waste matter from the houses to the villagers for sale as fertilizers. This group is paid by the government to do this work.[137]

(186) The group of the seed collectors (*tokhmeh bar chin*).

They collect the seeds of melons and water melons and the fruit stones of peaches from the streets and the bazaars. They dry these seeds and sell them to peasants, dried-fruit sellers and juice powder makers.

---

134. According to Höltzer 2535, 23 there were 22 junk dealers (*kohnehchin*) in Isfahan at that time.

135. For more information on this craft see Wulff 1966, 182-88.

136. For more information on this craft see Mostowfi n.d., vol. 1, 169; Polak 1865, vol. 1, 355-61; Wills 1883, 334. According to Höltzer 2535, 22-23 there were 25 masseurs and 51 bath-house keepers in Isfahan at that time.

137. For more information on this craft see Floor 2003b, 167. According to Höltzer 2535, 23 there were 150 sewer men in Isfahan at that time.

(187) The group of unskilled workers and construction workers, etc. (*`amal va banna'i va ghayro*).

In former times there was a lot construction and repair work. Many agricultural workers (*khoshneshin*) and peasants came as hired hands to the city.

(188) The group of the wood cutters (*heyzomkash*).

They form a large group, who cut wood for the shops in the bazaar and the houses in the city quarters. They have very heavy axes with sharp points and formed like the hatchet (*kaveh*) of the carpenters, but with sharp ends and curved middles. The body of the axe is made of iron and its edge of good cast steel and very sharp. The ability to cut and split hard wood with [such] an axe is restricted to Isfahan. In the other provinces they cannot wield this axe without training and exercise. The Isfahani wood cutters are known to be the best in the land.[138]

(189) The group of the gluers (*kalvehband*).

They have shops and they also hawk around town. They glue broken china and semi-vitrified porcelain.

(190) The group of the doorkeepers (*dalandar*).

There are many of them in Isfahan; every caravanserai has many doorkeepers.[139]

138. According to Höltzer 2535, 23 there were 85 wood cutters in Isfahan at that time.

139. According to Höltzer 2535, 23 there were 67 store-house keepers in Isfahan at that time.

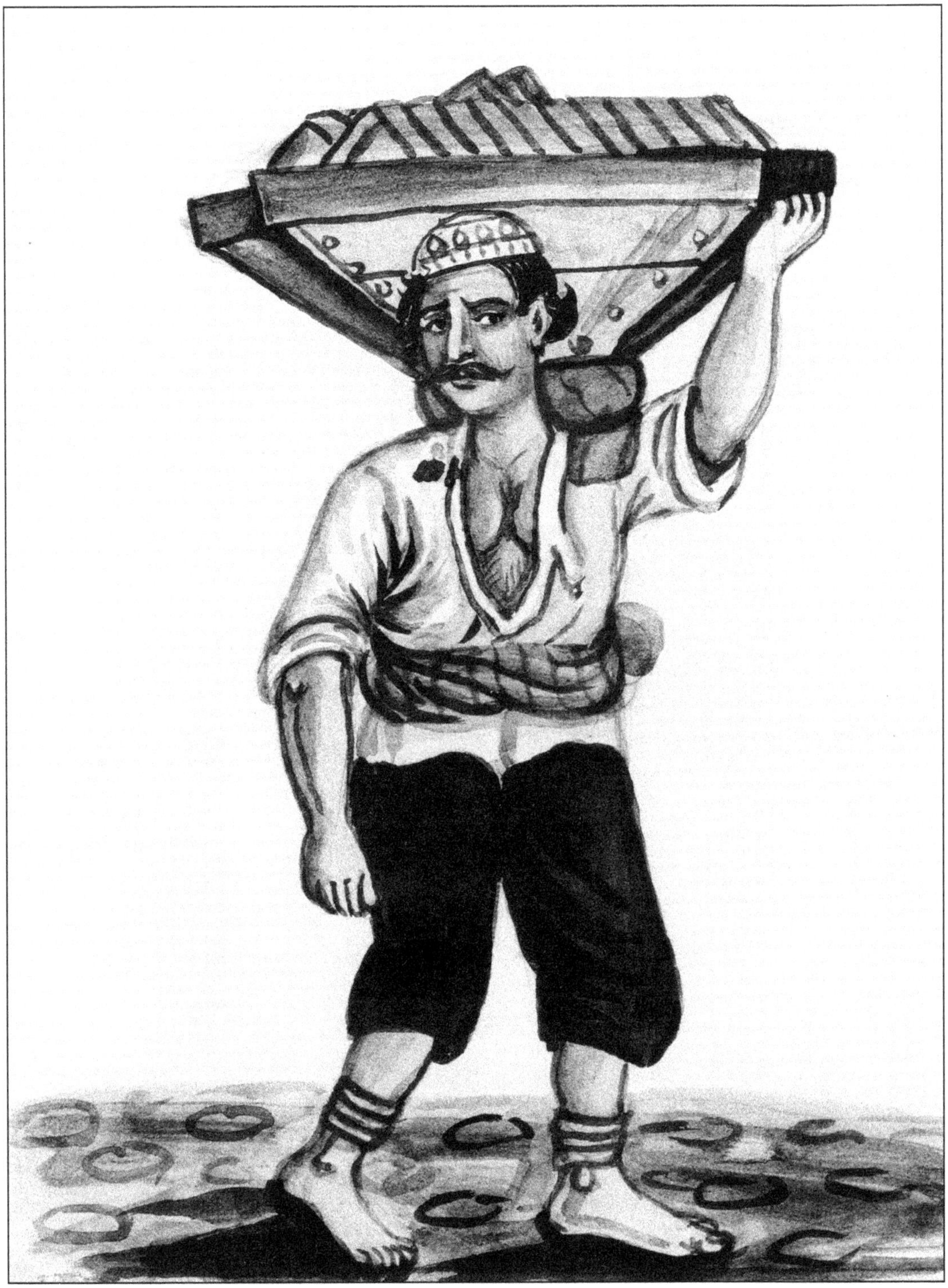

A Mason

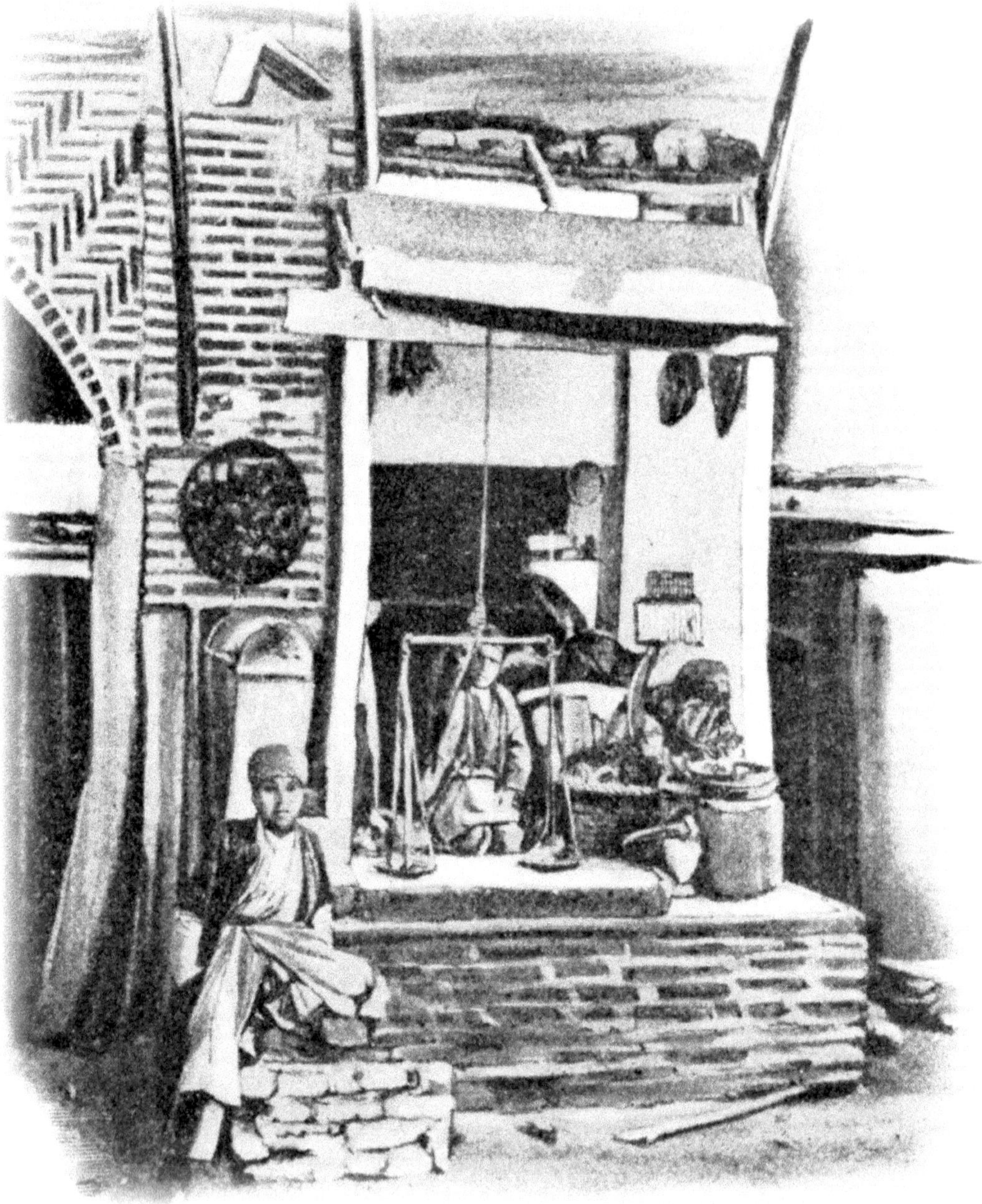

A tobacco shop

APPENDIX I

The Fiscal Categories of Isfahan.

(194) The group of controllers of the revenues and real estate administration and its staff.

(i) The customs revenues (*vojuh-e gomrok-khaneh*) are recorded in the registers at one percent. Its [staff] consists of a chief controller, an accountant, an inspector, a clerk, an assessor, a cashier, custodians, doorkeepers, road toll gatherers, and thief catchers and of each one of them there are many.

(ii) The weaving revenues (*vojuh-e nassaji*) are levied by means of the bleaching tax (*maliyat-e gazur*). Its [staff] consists of a chief controller, an inspector, a keeper of the seal, a cashier, thief catchers and others and forms a [large] group.

(iii) The guarding revenues (*vojuh-e khanbani*) are levied by means of the duties on the guarding of the caravanserais (*maliyat-e karavansaraydari*), on the weighing, and by means of duties and taxes on such goods as dried fruits, dried curd, jasper, oil, cheese, and others. The chief controller is supervisor over the staff, which consists altogether of nine sections. Each section has a section chief and a cashier, tax collectors, supervisors, etc., and they also form a large group.

(iv) The slaughter revenues (*maliyat-e dhabhi*) are levied by means of the branding tax (*maliyat-e dagh*) of the slaughter-house (*sallakh-khaneh*) and includes also guilds not subject to the slaughter-house revenues. The controller, inspector, cashier, keeper of the seal, thief catchers, and the collectors of the taxes and installments form quite a number.

(v) The Mint revenues (*vojuh-e zarrab-khaneh*) are of two kinds. The first is the assaying fee (*rosum-e mo`ayyari*), which is paid to the city's assayer and the assayer of Iran. The second are the dues paid to the government, which form a part of the provincial taxes collected by the governor, which is under a separate collector appointed by the government. For every weight of one thousand *methqals* (4.64 kg) of gold and silver a fixed tax is taken. The state and assaying fees and the pay for the staff etc. are paid out of these revenues. This is administrated by a separate inspector. All taxes, fees, salaries and expenditures are equivalent to three percent, which has been customary since ancient times and is collected in gold and silver. Also, each group of workers has a separate record. As to checking on debased or pure metal the rule has been that every piece is examined one time during the assaying process.

The Mint has seven workshops and to each workshop many workers are attached, and all of them are under the authority of the assayer.

I. The melting workingshop; here gold and silver is melted. Putting silver into crucibles and purifying gold is part of the melting process.

II. The smithery; here the ingots of gold and silver are shaped into round thin [bars].

III. The turnery; here the ready-made gold and silver having been received from the smith is pressed through holes [on a steel plate?] and ejected by rotation from the holes. The metal has now become round, flat and smooth.

IV. The punching workshop. After completion of the foregoing operations [the gold and silver] is punched here to the size and weight of gold (*ashrafis*) and silver coins (*qrans*) with the punching wheel.

V. The silver pounder workshop. Here each piece of punched [metal] is put on an anvil and is flattened with the iron smith's hammer.

VI. The minting workshop. Here the flattened [pieces] of gold and silver are put on an anvil between two coin moulds, being pounded with a hammer until they have the right imprint.

VII. The blanching workshop. Here the brass orker cleans the coins, which have become black and dirty. This ends the part [about the Mint].

(vi) The fruit revenues (*maliyat-e favakahi*) [are collected] from all fruit daily brought into the city from the villages and the rural districts. There are four bazaars for the fruit sellers at four locations in the city and all deliveries are unloaded in the bazaars beforementioned. There are brokers in the bazaar, who set the price of fruit in a reasonable manner based on the official rate of the day and sell these per load to the shopkeepers. One of the four bazaars is in the *Meydan-e Naqsh-e Jahan*, another in the *Meydan-e Kohneh*, the third in the Bidabad quarter and the fourth in the Chahar Suq-e Shiraziha quarter. Each load has a fixed tax that is collected [on the spot]. The chief controller, the clerks, and fiscal supervisors amount to a large number [of people].

(vii) The calico and the rolling shaft revenues (*vojuh-e chit va chubeh*). The calico [on which tax is levied] are prints of an inferior quality from Khvansar. It is brought from Khvansar for the lining of clothes of lesser quality. The rolling shafts are those of the dyers, which are brought to Isfahan from Azerbaijan. For these two products also a state tax has to be paid. The fixed dues are recorded by a controller and a supervisor.

(viii) The cotton market revenues (*vojuh-e bazar-e jowzqeh*). A special tax is levied on each [load of] ginned and non-ginned cotton brought into the city. There are quite a number of chief controllers, brokers, clerks, cashiers, and fiscal supervisors.

(ix) The sewerage revenues (*vojuh-e kannaseh*). There is one supervisor and the taxes are farmed.

(x) The vegetable market revenues (*vojuh-e bazar-e sabzi*) [are levied] on all vegetables brought into the city. This occurs in the same manner as in the beforementioned four bazaars where the supplies are unloaded and where the greengrocers (*sabziforushan*) buy [their products], which they carry to their own shops. [For collecting] these revenues there is also a supervisor with a staff. The state duties are recorded by them.

(xi) The Jewish poll-tax (*vojuh-e jezya-ye Yahud*). The Jewish community pays poll-tax. They had [to pay] a fixed poll-tax from the beginning of Islam until now and this revenue always has a separate supervisor.

(xii) The Armenian poll-tax (*vojuh-e jezya-ye Aramaneh*), [consists of] the weaving tax (*julaheh*) and the tax on Jolfa wines, including the *darughagi*, which all are the responsibility of the *darugheh* of Jolfa, who has several assistants.

(xiii) The real estate revenues (*vojuh-e mostaghall*) has several administrative real estate supervisors. They collect the rents of the shops, bath-houses, and of the mills in the *khaleseh-ye enteqali* estates.[1]

(xiv) The revenues of the rents of the blessed state gardens (*vojuh-e ojrat-e baghat-e mobarakat-e divani*). Apart from gardeners and head gardeners, who form a large group, there are the lease holders and tenants, who manage and administrate the state gardens and collect its taxes.

1. State lands leased to private individuals, see Floor 1999, 341-46.

APPENDIX II

The Sacrifice of the Camel Ceremony in Isfahan

(19) The groups assisting the 'shareholders' of the sacrificial camel.

If in olden times there has been [such] a custom nothing is known about it. The origin and establishment of the current practice and rules date from Safavid times. Each group and its members was, in accordance with the royal edict, entitled to the profit resulting from their activities and inherited, generation after generation, all offices and functions in connection with the aforementioned camel. In Isfahan this custom has a peculiar form and consists of:

(A) A group that accompanies the camel everywhere on its tour through the city quarters from the first day of Dhu'l-Hijja until the eve of the Day of Sacrifice [consisting of]:

(1) Two knife bearers, each with three knives of an old, valuable and strange design; also with a polishing tool and other tools and utensils.

(2) Two axe bearers, each with one engraved steel axe.

(3) One spear bearer.

(4) Two bearers with a butcher's knife.

(5) Two standard bearers.

(6) One cup bearer, who carries one large copper cup with a fretted top, which cup is engraved with Koran verses and charms on the inside and outside. The proceeds of alms, votive offerings, and presents given each day are kept in this cup. On the tenth day these are distributed among all members in conformity with the old assessment (*bonicheh*).

(7) The preacher who goes to each house and who there reads the *khotbeh* in the name of ruler-of-the-age and the *Fatehah* for the deceased relatives of the master of the house.

(8) One bridle holder. He is entrused with the accouterments of the sacrificial camel during the ten days and he leads the camel around.

(9) One group of the royal music band, with the exception of the dancers, with cymbals, drums, kettledrums, flutes, clarions and trumpets, each one of them in large number.

A strange affair that is very well known and to which all groups swear oaths to emphasize the truth of this event is [the following]: There were repeatedly conflict between the heirs of the offices beforementioned. Some of them, who in fact were not entitled to it, usurped by tricks and unscrupulous behavior the ownership of the cutting tools such as knives etc. of those who were entitled to it by right of religious and customary law. The year had not passed when this family died. As they say, 'the right returns to the rightful.' Foreign thieves who unknowingly took away these stolen tools were struck by the same affliction. Finally, the tools were returned to the original heir. God knows best.

(B) The 'shareholders' (*mochchehdaran*) of the camel. Their division is as follows;

The different parts of the body of the sacrificial animal belongs to the chief of a group (*dasteh*), according to the old royal edict, and those people who are entitled to have a part of the camel are called *mochchehdaran*.

Each 'shareholder' represents a group which has its own customs. Half of the *mochchehs* [i.e., share of the camel] belongs to the Heydaris and the other half to the Ne`matis. These two groups always have fights and quarrels and they are the cause of the strange turmoil and disturbances during the activities and tours of the groups.

The body of the camel is divided into six parts and so are the groups of the *mochchehs*, as follows: There are two groups of the Heydaris and two groups of the Ne`matis. The other two groups are formed by two very big villages in the neighborhood of Isfahan; each one belongs to one of the two parties [i.e., the Heydaris and Ne`matis]. Starting on its tour [through the city] each group with a large following and rig-out with which they flaunt each other, from among the assisting groups and others, proceeds section by section, in a regulated and well-ordered manner. Each section consists of more than one thousand men. The vanguard of the 'army' [is formed by] rogues armed with sticks, followed by well-appointed armed horsemen, then men amounted on camels, among them spearmen of the opposing army, the black clothed actors and the captives of Karbala with gilt litters and a display of a Syrian bazaar, which has been added recently. Then comes the Mir Hajj with a numerous, splendid and beautiful retinue, consisting of brass bands with timbals, trumpets, cymbals, clarions, who sit on the back of camels, *farrashes* on foot with the *chub* and *falak*,[1] armed horsemen with banners and led horses, and strings of camels with hajjis, clad in the garb of a pilgrim, their heads bare, the wrap on their shoulders; many camel litters with caravan leaders and guides in front of them. After them come the 'shareholders' dressed in special clothes and accompanied on their left and right by many servants, water carriers and men armed with shields and broadswords and by the rabble on foot. The groups of the villages also attend with three to four thousand men, all carrying musical instruments [such as] timbals, clarions, cymbals with a great many horsemen and big banners. They join with the city Heydari and Ne`mati groups. On the Day of the Sacrifice, every year in the same manner, each group sets out from its own part [of the city] to make a tour through the quarters and the bazaar until each one arrives at the *Meydan-e Naqsh-e Jahan*. In front of the gate of the `Ali Qapu palace the preacher reads the *khotbeh*.

1. Implements to give the bastinado, i.e., whipping one's bare soles.

Group after group parade past the governor of the province, who is seated on the high verandah on the front side of the `Ali Qapu. From there each group goes to the *Chahar Bagh* built by Shah `Abbas, and receives sweetmeats and gifts from the deputy-governor, who is seated on the stone marble bench in front of the Madraseh-ye Shah. From here they cross the *Si-o-Seh Cheshmeh-ye Rudkhaneh* Bridge and continue to follow the above-mentioned river until they arrive at the praying ground, which is the place of sacrifice of the camel. All the functionaries of the camel sacrifice such as the bearers of the knives and the like take care that they arrive with their different tools and utensils at the camel before their own 'shareholders.' The Isfahani spectators, who nowadays number fewer people, but formerly numbered more than fifty thousand persons, follow the camel through the *Chahar Bagh* to the praying ground. After distributing the camel's meat, all groups and spectators return via the *Hasanabad Khvaju* bridge, and come to the *Chahar Bagh* and arrive again in the *Meydan-e Naqsh-e Jahan* from there returning to their own quarters. Every year a large number of ignorant people and followers of the Anti-Christ cause a lot of ruin in this province during the feast of the Sacrifice of the Camel. The grandees and dignitaries of the province send guards to accompany the groups. At one side, the *darugheh* guards the passage ways of the quarters, where danger may occur, with a force of three hundred armed and equipped footmen. On the other side, horsemen and infantry soldiers of the government guard the flanks of the procession. Nevertheless, at the occasion of the meat distribution the different groups meet each other in the passage ways, where pushing to and fros starts disorder and the ruffians (*luti*s) given an account of themselves.

A few years ago the size of the procession and its rig-out were greatly reduced at the order of the government and since then the disorder has been reduced much indeed. Formerly, every year forty to fifty persons were wounded and at least three to four persons were killed.

APPENDIX III

Three Notes on Guild Taxes From the Persian Ministry of Foreign Affairs

From the Minister for Foreign Affairs
March 25.86

It has been reported by the authorities that some traders engaged in business do not pay any taxes to the Government, while others pay them regularly. This undoubtedly causes great loss to the public treasury.

It must be evident to Her Majesty's Legation that the taxation of wholesale merchants and of retail traders is different and that native shop keepers who carry on a retail trade are subject to special taxation and are obliged to pay it regularly to the Shah's government.

The Persian Foreign Office has the honour to send herewith for information of Her Majesty's Legation a list which has been received by the central government of Tehran defining the taxation of the different traders and has full confidence that Her Majesty's Legation will give notice to the British subjects who are engaged in retail business to pay taxes to the Persian authorities like all other traders so as to do away with the present anomalous state of affairs and that the public treasury may suffer no loss.

(Trades)	In main streets	In by streets
Shoe makers	3 = 0	1 = 10
White-shoe makers	2 = 0	2 – 0
Pad-saddle makers	6 = 0	5 = 0
Pack-saddle makers	5 = 0	-
Carpenters	8 = 0	5 = 0
Tallow chandlers	5 = 0	2 = 10
Gold smith	15	10
Black smith	1 = 0	10
Hatters	3 = 0	2 = 0
Glassware sellers	-	-
Cook houses	4 = 0	1 = 0
Kebabies	3 = 0	15
Cooks	1 = 0	15

(Trades)	In main streets	In by streets
Soup sellers	1 = 0	15
Halvajies	2 = 10	1 = 10
Treacle makers	2 = 8	1 = 10
Money changers	3 = 0	2 = 0
Oil sellers	3 = 0	1 = 10
Cotton sellers	4 = 0	3 = 0
Quilt maker	4 = 0	3 = 0
Silk dealers	3 = 0	1 = 0
Tobacco dealers	2 = 10	1 = 10
Ladies-shoe makers	5 = 0	-
Horse clothing makers	1 = 5	1 = 0
Seed dealers	4 = 0	2 = 10
Felt hat makers	10	10
Cigarette sellers	-	-
Dyers	4 = 0	2 = 0
Naphtha sellers	-	-
Tailors	-	-
Sandal sellers	3 = 0	3 = 0
Sheep head sellers	1 = 0	1 = 18
Confectioners	2 = 1	2 = 10
Shoeing smith	1 = 5	1 = 5
Poultry dealers	-	-
Looking-glass sellers	-	-
Cloth dealers	-	-
Watch makers	-	-
Painters	-	-
Drapers	5 = 10	3 = 10
Mat makers	-	-
Old cloth sellers	-	-
Grocers	1 = 10	1 = 5
Chemists	1 = 10	1 = 0

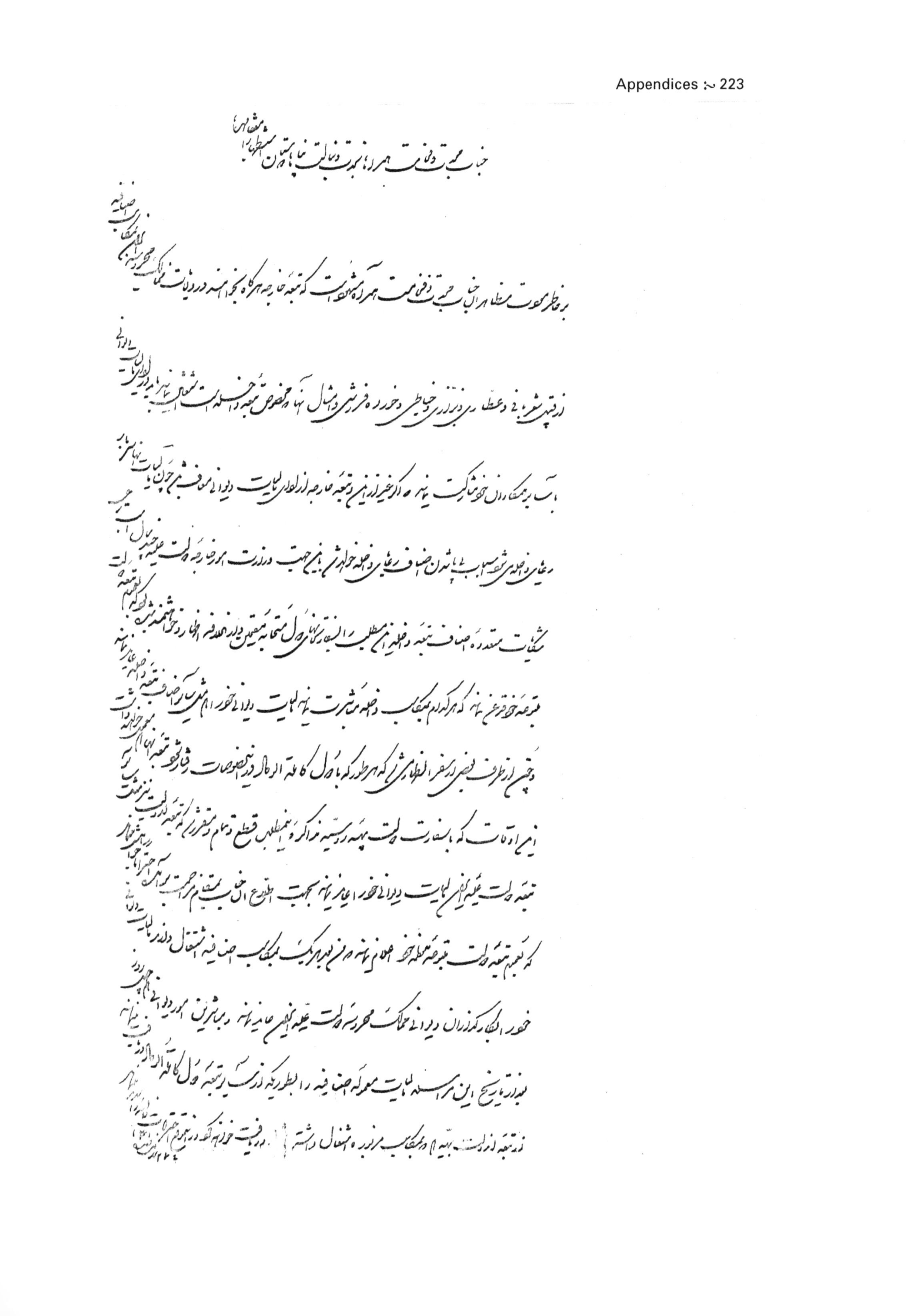

[illegible]

[illegible]

[illegible]

[illegible]

[illegible]

[illegible]

[illegible]

[illegible]

[illegible]

[illegible]

[illegible]

[illegible]

[illegible]

[illegible]

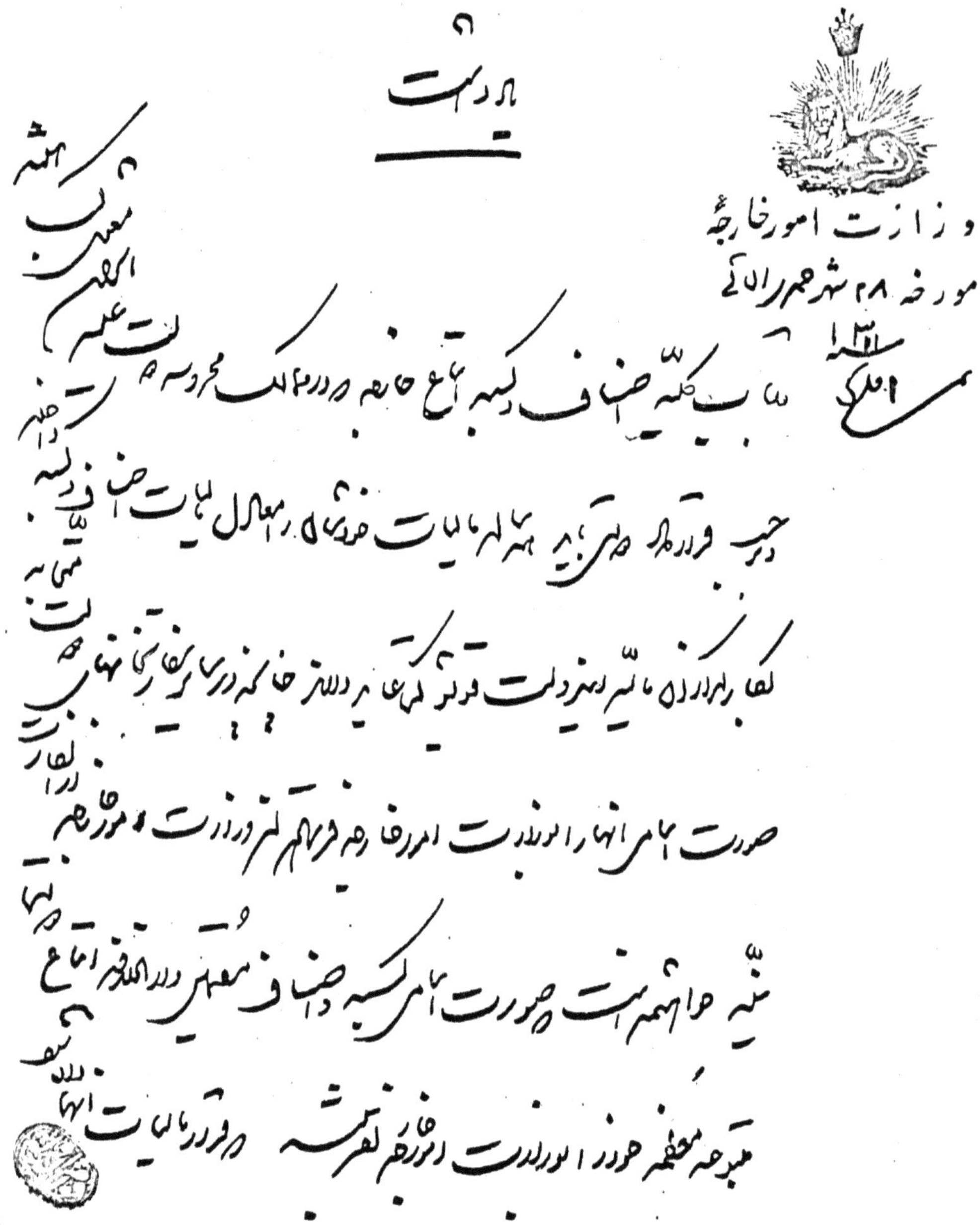
یادداشت

وزارت امور خارجه

مورخه ۲۸

APPENDIX IV

TEXT OF THE 1926 LAW ABOLISHING GUILD TAXES

قانون الغای مالیتهای صنفی و مالیات سرشماری

مصوب ۳۰ آذرماه ۱۳۰۵ شمسی

ماده اول — مجلس شورای ملی کلیه مالیاتهای صنفی را اعم از شهر و قصبات و قراء و ایلات (مطابق صورت منضمه وغیرآن بهراسم ورسم) از اول سال ۱۳۰۶ ملغی مینماید و دولت مکلف خواهد بود این مالیات را از دفاتر دولتی حذف نماید •

تبصره — وزارت مالیه مکلف است از وصول بقایا سنواتی اصناف صرفنظر نمود ومطالبه مینماید •

ماده دوم — وزارت مالیه مکلف است که مالیات سرشماری (سرانه) که از — اشخاص گرفته میشود والغای آن موکول باجرای قانون ممیزی املاک اربابی مصوبه ۲۰ دیماه / ۱۳۰۴ گردیده از ابتدای سنه ۱۳۰۶ موقوف المطالبه نموده واز دفاتر دولتی حذف کند این قانون که مشتمل به دو ماده ویك صورت ضمیمه است (۱) در — جلسه بیستم آذرماه / ۱۳۰۵ شمسی بتصویب مجلس شورای ملی رسید •

سید محمد تدین — رئیس مجلس شورای

صورت ضمیمه مذکوره در ماده اول قانون الغای مالیاتهای صنفی و سرشماری

۱ — مالیات سماکی — ۲ — کلك رانی — ۳ سوخت وتره بار ۴ — ذغال — ۵ ـ میوه وتره بار — ۶ ـ باغ میوه وبستان — ۷ ـ باغ قیس — ۸ — حمل روغن — ۹ سرب و باروت — ۱۰ — داغ کش — ۱۱ — قورخه — ۱۲ — ماشین پنبه ۱۳ — مردارکش ۱۴ — شن کش ۱۵ — رسوم کشمش ۱۶ — باج سمك ۱۷ — مالیات مازوج ۱۸ — خانات ۱۹ — عشورنیریز (تریاك — تنبا کو — کتیرا — مغز بادام وغیره) ۲۰ — اجازه تجارت ۲۱ — عیدی ۲۲ — مالیات صنف بزازرز ۲۳ — علافه بند — ۲۴ — سمسار — ۲۵ — مسگر ۲۶ —

نعلچی گر ــ ۲۷ خیاط ــ ۲۸ کماج پز ــ ۲۹ رزاز ــ ۳۰ کوزه فروش ــ ۳۱ پالان دوز ــ
۳۲ چیت ساز ــ ۳۳ شعله رنگ کن ــ ۳۴ ــ دوشاب ساز ــ ۳۵ موتاب ــ ۳۶ اطو کش ــ
۳۷ ــ نمد مال ــ ۳۸ نعلبند ــ ۳۹ چاقوساز ــ ۴۰ حلواپز ــ ۴۱ آشپز ــ ۴۲ عصار
۴۳ مالیات صنف جوراب باف ــ ۴۴ مالیات صنف شال باف ــ ۴۵ مالیات صنف فخار ــ ۴۶ ــ
مالیات صنف متفرقه ــ ۴۷ مالیات صنف آرد فروش ــ ۴۸ مالیات صنف آهنگر ــ ۴۹ مالیات صنف
کلاهدوز ــ ۵۰ مالیات صنف سراج ــ ۵۱ مالیات صنف کفشدوز ــ ۵۲ مالیات صنف چرم فروش ــ
۵۳ مالیات صنف آجیل فروش ــ ۵۴ مالیات صنف حلوائی ــ ۵۵ مالیات صنف شیره پز ــ ۵۶ ــ
مالیات صنف رواف ــ ۵۷ مالیات صنف گیوه فروش ــ ۵۸ مالیات صنف نقاش ــ ۵۹ مالیات صنف
باغبان ــ ۶۰ مالیات صنف چلنگر ــ ۶۱ مالیات صنف زرگر ــ ۶۲ مالیات صنف کلیچه ــ ۶۳ ــ
مالیات صنف صباغ ــ ۶۴ مالیات صنف خراز ــ ۶۵ مالیات صنف بلورفروش ــ ۶۶ حلاج ــ ۶۷
مالیات صنف ریسمان باف ــ ۶۸ مالیات صنف مکاری ــ ۶۹ مالیات صنف آینه ساز ــ ۷۰ ــ
مالیات صنف باروت کوب ــ ۷۱ مالیات صنف پینه دوز ــ ۷۲ مالیات صنف آسیابان ــ ۷۳ مالیات
صنف علاف ــ ۷۴ مالیات صنف قصاب ــ ۷۵ مالیات صنف طباخ ــ ۷۶ مالیات صنف شانه ساز
۷۷ ــ مالیات صنف روغنگر ــ ۷۸ ــ مالیات صنف نمد مال ــ ۷۹ مالیات صنف کفاش ــ ۸۰ ــ
مالیات صنف تخت کش ــ ۸۱ ــ مالیات صنف بقال ــ ۸۲ مالیات صنف نساج ــ ۸۳ مالیات صنف
سبزی کار ــ ۸۴ مالیات صنف تخمه فروش ــ ۸۵ مالیات صنف دباغ ــ ۸۶ مالیات صنف چرم ساز
۸۷ مالیات صنف قناد ــ ۸۸ مالیات صنف خباز ــ ۸۹ مالیات صنف طواف ــ ۹۰ مالیات صنف
ابریشمگر و گچ کوب ــ ۹۱ مالیات صنف سفید باف ــ ۹۲ مالیات صنف پنیرفروش ــ ۹۳ مالیات
صنف ریسمان فروش ــ ۹۴ مالیات صنف شماع ــ ۹۵ مالیات صنف گاوکش ــ ۹۶ مالیات صنف
ذغال فروش ــ ۹۷ مالیات صنف موج باف ــ ۹۸ مالیات صنف بنا وخشتمال ــ ۹۹ مالیات صنف
تره بارچی ــ ۱۰۰ مالیات صنف دواتگر ــ ۱۰۱ مالیات صنف قهوه چی ــ ۱۰۲ مالیات صنف
خراط ــ ۱۰۳ مالیات صنف صندوق بند ــ ۱۰۴ مالیات صنف گچکوب ــ ۱۰۵ مالیات صنف
چادری باف ــ ۱۰۶ مالیات صنف ظرف فروش ــ ۱۰۲ مالیات صنف زهتاب ــ ۸ [illegible]

۱۰۸	مالیات صنف	شمشیرگر
۱۰۹	"	تنباکوفروش
۱۱۰	"	جماعت یهود
۱۱۱	"	پاره دوز
۱۱۲	"	بنکدار
۱۱۳	"	توتون فروش
۱۱٤	"	دوافروش
۱۱٥	"	کلاه مال
۱۱٦	"	خرده فروش
۱۱۷	"	کوزه گر
۱۱۸	"	شانه بند و پیوندی
۱۱۹	"	دقاق
۱۲۰	"	لبوفروش
۱۲۱	"	ساغری ساز
۱۲۲	"	حمامی
۱۲۳	"	شیلات
۱۲٤	"	نخود بریز
۱۲٥	"	قناد وحلوائی
۱۲٦	"	بیوت الخل
۱۲۷	"	زارع
۱۲۸	"	صابون پز
۱۲۹	"	شود مال
۱۳۰	"	کبابی وجگرکی
۱۳۱	"	خرد فروش میدان
۱۳۲	"	بازار (شاید بازدار ؟)
۱۲۳	"	مجری ساز

١٣٤	ماليات صنف	نوارفروش
١٣٥	"	سبزی فروش
١٣٦	"	عطار
١٣٧	"	ابریشم تاب
١٣٨	"	خام خر
١٣٩	"	نجار
١٤٠	"	بزاز
١٤١	"	سمسار
١٤٢	"	ملکی دوز
١٤٣	"	بوریاباف
١٤٤	"	سفیدگر
١٤٥	"	پاتیل ساز
١٤٦	"	پوست دوز
١٤٧	"	گازر
١٤٨	"	سراج و کفاش
١٤٩	"	غسالخانه
١٥٠	"	شیره خانه
١٥١	"	نفت فروش
١٥٢	"	چینی بند زن
١٥٣	"	کاسه گر
١٥٤	"	آجرپز
١٥٥	"	طراح
١٥٦	"	اطاقهای کاروانسرای مسکونی تجار
١٥٧	"	سرقاطری
١٥٨	"	الاغ شماری
١٥٩	"	دکاندار
١٦٠	"	زرد چوبه کوب

١٦١	ماليات صنف	كوره پز
١٦٢	»	گيپائى
١٦٣	»	قاشق تراش
١٦٤	»	پنبه فروش
١٦٥	»	بقله فروش
١٦٦	»	داغ كرباس وغيره
١٦٧	»	كله پز
١٦٨	»	نعل بر
١٦٩	»	ساعت ساز
١٧٠	»	قبوج
١٧١	»	دلال ابريشم
١٧٢	»	مغنى
١٧٣	»	حصيرباف
١٧٤	»	سلاخ
١٧٥	»	نشاسته ساز
١٧٦	»	صباغ قدك
١٧٧	»	پالوده وبستنى فروش
١٧٨	»	سكاك
١٧٩	»	كرباس دوز
١٨٠	»	چخماق فروش
١٨١	»	دهنه گر
١٨٢	»	طايفه نياكى
١٨٣	»	خيك دوز
١٨٤	»	شيشه گر
١٨٥	»	صراف
١٨٦	»	حناساز
١٨٧	»	گرجى دوز
١٨٨	»	خرازوسقط فروش

دستمال فروش	مالیات صنف	١٨٩
قنداق ساز	"	١٩٠
میخ بر	"	١٩١
شکرقرمز	"	١٩٢
چوب فروش	"	١٩٣
کاغذ فروش	"	١٩٤
ریخته گر	"	١٩٥
نیل فروش	"	١٩٦
لباف	"	١٩٧
گله داری	"	١٩٨
عیدی گله داری	"	١٩٩
غربتی ها	"	٢٠٠
گمرک داخلی پنبه	"	٢٠١
چرخ تابی	"	٢٠٢
مراعی خلف	"	٢٠٣
خانعلی	"	٢٠٤
داروغگی	"	٢٠٥
معدن سرب	"	٢٠٦
روده تابی	"	٢٠٧
خمسگی بعنوان پنجه	"	٢٠٨
اجاره پای ستون	"	٢٠٩
پنجه علی	"	٢١٠
خاشاک برداری	"	٢١١
نظرداروغه	"	٢١٢
پوستین داروغه وغیره	"	٢١٣
ماست بند	"	٢١٤
شیرفروش	"	٢١٥
سیگاری	"	٢١٦

۲۱۷	مالیات صنف	خشکه پز
۲۱۸	"	لحاف دوز
۲۱۹	"	حکاك
۲۲۰	"	سنگ تراش
۲۲۱	"	مبل ساز
۲۲۲	"	مرغ فروش
۲۲۳	"	کتاب فروش
۲۲۴	"	صحاف
۲۲۵	"	قناویزباف
۲۲۶	"	مطابع
۲۲۷	"	تیرفروش
۲۲۸	"	عشورکوره پزی
۲۲۹	"	پول دود
۲۳۰	"	اظهارنامه کوره پزی
۲۳۱	"	پوتین دوزی
۲۳۲	"	چخماق ساز
۲۳۳	"	چهارشنبه بازار
۲۳۴	"	کرجی ولتکای سواحل کوچك وبزرگ
۲۳۵	"	دوده ودود کوره
۲۳۶	"	نمیس دوز
۲۳۷	"	چکمه دوز
۲۳۸	"	بهله دوز
۲۳۹	"	قمه ساز
۲۴۰	"	گچ پز
۲۴۱	"	تفنگ ساز
۲۴۲	"	آجیده دوزی
۲۴۳	"	گاوداری
۲۴۴	"	آب پولی

۲۴۵	مالیات صنف	احسابیه
۲۴۶	"	دلالی
۲۴۷	"	دست فروش
۲۴۸	"	بلم رانی
۲۴۹	"	قالی باف
۲۵۰	"	سنگ گچ و آهک
۲۵۱	"	اجازه سوخت کوره های آجری وگچ وآهک
۲۵۲	"	جولا
۲۵۳	"	قولك قصابی
۲۵۴	"	گرجی باف
۲۵۵	"	چوبهای مصرفی شهر
۲۵۶	"	اضطرخی
۲۵۷	"	داغ پولی
۲۵۸	"	رسوم سفره
۲۵۹	"	خانه دودی
۲۶۰	"	کدخدا پولی
۲۶۱	"	لحاف پولی
۲۶۲	"	سیرصادق پولی
۲۶۳	"	پلیه وری
۲۶۴	"	چموش دوز
۲۶۵	"	شعرباف
۲۶۶	"	حلبی ساز
۲۶۷	"	ذهابی دوز

جدول فوق مشتمل بر دویست وشصت وهفت قلم مالیات ضمیمه ماده اول قانون مالیاتهای صنفی ومالیات سرشماری بوده وصحیح است ۰م

رئیس مجلس شورای ملی ــ سید محمد تدین

APPENDIX V

Note on Hawkers

Pedlars (*dowrehforush*) abounded in the cities of Iran.[1] One might say that for every trade exercised in a fixed location there was an ambulatory variety. The itinerant petty traders hawked their wares or service at regular intervals in what would seem their own territory that had been staked out by the authorities just as is the case to-day. Many of them were known to 'their' district by their street cries.[2]

Mostowfi distinguished three classes of pedlars. In the first place there was the group that mostly sold such products as vegetables, vinegar, oil, thread, needles, rubber items, all kinds of juices, and apothecary articles. In Persian slang they were referred to as *tahhafi* or *tavvafi*. Because pedlars did not have to pay any guild tax nor shop rent they could sell their products cheaper than in the bazaar. This probably caused the Minister of Police to issue a decree in 1896 forbidding pedlars to cry their wares in the bazaars and thouroughfares. They were only permitted to hawk in those areas where people had no servants. This regulation was clearly aimed at confining them to particular areas of the city under the pretext that they were obstructing traffic with their donkeys.[3] The clients of these pedlars were mostly the lower classes. Not only were their prices low, but the men of the lower classes had no servants to shop for them, as was the case with the wealthier classes of society. According to Benjamin, however, "the upper classes and the European polulation make most of their purchases through a numerous and intelligent class of intinerant venders who carry their wares from house to house on minute donkeys."[4] His statement seems to refer only to food purchases, for Mostowfi, himself a member of the upper class, is very explicit about the lower classes being the main clients of the pedlars.

A second group of pedlars were those who bought all kinds of objects. This group was almost entirely composed of Jews, who were known as *zari yaraqha*. The few Moslems who tried their hand at this trade allegedly did not do so well. These pedlars bought articles such as brocaded silk, old trappings, to stitch in again or to get the silver out of it, cloth, gelims, felts, clothes, quilts, mattresses, and all kinds of second-hand articles.

A third group of pedlars was almost completely composed of Jews. These pedlars always went in pairs of man and wife, without crying their wares. While the women would go inside the houses the men would stay outside at the door. They mostly did business with the upper class, because they bought and sold shawls, jewelry, and gold smithery.

1. For the factual information about pedlars use has been made of Mostowfi, n.d., vol. 1, 159-65.
2. Phillot 1906, vol. 2/7, 283-85.
3. Floor 1992, 178.
4. Benjamin 1887, 81.

Mrs. Bishop calls them the "higher class of pedlars, such as those, who visit the anderuns of the rich, go in couples, with a donkey or a servant to carry their bundles."[5] In slang they were also called *zari yaraqha* like the second group, or *javaheri* (jeweler), *shal moshtari* (shawl buyer), or just *moshtari*. Notwithstanding the fact that such a Jew might be trading with a certain family for over 15 years they would never call him 'Mister" (*aqa*), but always *moshtari*.[6] They were, however, excellent businessmen and many Moslem shawl merchants (*shalforush*) or jewelers would give their wares to them to sell. If they were thus used as a *dallal* or broker for selling a shawl they had to give a ring as security, whose value was twice that of the shawl. Thus this badly treated group was discriminated against even in their own trade.

---

5. Bishop 1891, vol. 1, 261.

6. "Jews that buy old clothes, broken or discarded articles, when hailed are styled mulla or khwaja." Phillot 1906, vol. 2/7, 285, note 1.

APPENDIX VI

JOINT DECLARATION BY THE *Anjomans* OF THE MERCHANTS, GUILDS AND BANKERS CONCERNING THE NEED TO PROTECT THE CONSTITUTION AND PARLIAMENT (14 JUNE 1908)

۱۴ ج ۱ (اخطار از طرف انجمن مرکزی تجار) ۱۳۲۶

(و انجمن مرکزی عموم اصناف وصرافان طهران)

چون هروقت مامات بهر قصد صحیحی اقدام نمائیم مفسدین و مستبدین بطور دیکر در انظار عوام مطالب حقرا الباس باطل پوشانیده واذهان عامه را مشوب مینمایند بدین جهة انجمن مرکزی تجار و مرکزی عموم اصناف وصرافان مطالب حقه خودرا که باعث تعطیل عمومی در تمام ایران کشته وامروز باقتضای وطن پرستی ما اهالی طهران هم در دارالخلافه غیر از تعطیل تکلیفی نداشته ونداریم ذیلا خدمت برادران وطن عزیز عرضه میداریم که راه اشتباه کاری مفسدین بدینواسطه مسدود باشد اولا تا در مملکت مشروطه حفظ مواد قانون مشروطیت علی ماهو حقه نشود جان و مال وشرف و ناموس مردم مسلماً محفوظ نخواهد بود ومملکت روز بروز خراب و از اهلش آسایش مرتفع خواهد شد و دراین صورت کم کم اجانب را اسباب ازدیاد طمع در مملکت شده ودر صدد تصرفات مالکانه برمی آیند مخصوصاً تجار وکسبه الان دو سال است بواسطهٔ انقلابات مستبدین در داخلهٔ ممالك ایران چه خسارتها که کشیده وچه ضررها که ندیده اند وباین ترتیب ممکن نیست بتوانند مشغول بکسب وکار خود شوند مگر بعد از تحصیل اطمینان کامل در اجرای قانون مشروطیت وحفظ مواد قانونیه آن ثانیاً تمام افراد اهالی یعنی اشخاص متدین هریك در انجمنهای متعدده قسم یاد نموده اند که در حفظ اساس مشروطیت ومجلس شورای ملی وقوانین موضوعه آن در بذل جان ومال لدی الاقتضا مضایقه ننمایند وامروز برحسب اسلامیت خودمان می بینیم که چندین ماده از قانون اساسی نقض شده واکر ساکت باشیم کذشته از آنکه تمام مواد قانون اساسی در بوتهٔ اجمال خواهد ماند بقسمی هم که خورده ایم خیانت وخلاف نموده ایم لهذا باکمال نجابت وارامی تعطیل عمومی نموده تا جبران موادیکه از قانون اساسی نقض شده بشود واجتماعی هم که در مسجد سپهسالار چند روز قبل شد، بود بجهة همین مطالب بوده محض امتثال امر مجلس مقدس خارج شده ولی محال است تااین دو مطالب که مطالب کلی در ضمن آن مندرج است بانجام نرسد مشغول بکار وکسب بشویم و برادران وطنی را هم بوجدان انسانیت خود محول میداریم

(انجمن مرکزی تجار) (انجمن مرکزی عموم اصناف) (انجمن صرافان)

Déclaration de la corporation centrale des commerçants des gens de metier et des changeurs.

Ceux qui poursuivent un but personnel et qui ne visent que leurs interêts individuel tâchent toujours de falsifier et de mal interprêter chaque élan de patriotisme que cette nation donne. Il nous obligent donc de faire connaître à nos confrères les raisons justifiées pour lesquelles nous fermons nos magasins et nous provoquons une interruption des affaires en général.

1° Dans un pays constitutionnel, si les clauses de la constitution ne sont pas remplies, le desordre et le trouble s'y propagent à tel point qu'ils donnent lieu à l'intervention étrangère. – Il y a environ deux ans que les ennemies de la liberté ne font que troubler le pays et ils ne laissent pas un moment de tranquilité pour le peuple. Les dommages

et les sacrifices qu'ils lui ont imp
sont incalculables.

Notre patience est à bout et
nous est impossible de pouvoir
reprendre nos affaires jusqu'à ce
qu'il y ait une assurance formelle
que les clauses de la constitution se
dans l'avenir strictement observées

2° Tous les membres de corp
rations nationales ont prêté serme
de n'épargnier ni leur fortune n
leur sangs pour le maintien de la
constitution et du Conseil Nationa
et de veiller à l'exécution des loi
constitutionnelles.

Nous considerons, aujourd
que certaines clauses de notre consti
tion sont abolies et les apparan
nous font croire que l'on a l
tention de les suspendre toutes.
Nous ne pouvons donc travailler,
nous discontinuons forcément e

calmement nos affaires jusqu'à
ce qu'il y ait une réparation aux préju
portés aux clauses de notre constitution.

Nous avons quitté il y a quelque
jours la mosquée de Sepahsalar pour
obéir aux ordres du parlement et n
restons ferme dans notre décision de
ne pas laisser annuler nos droits.

(s) "La corporation centrale"

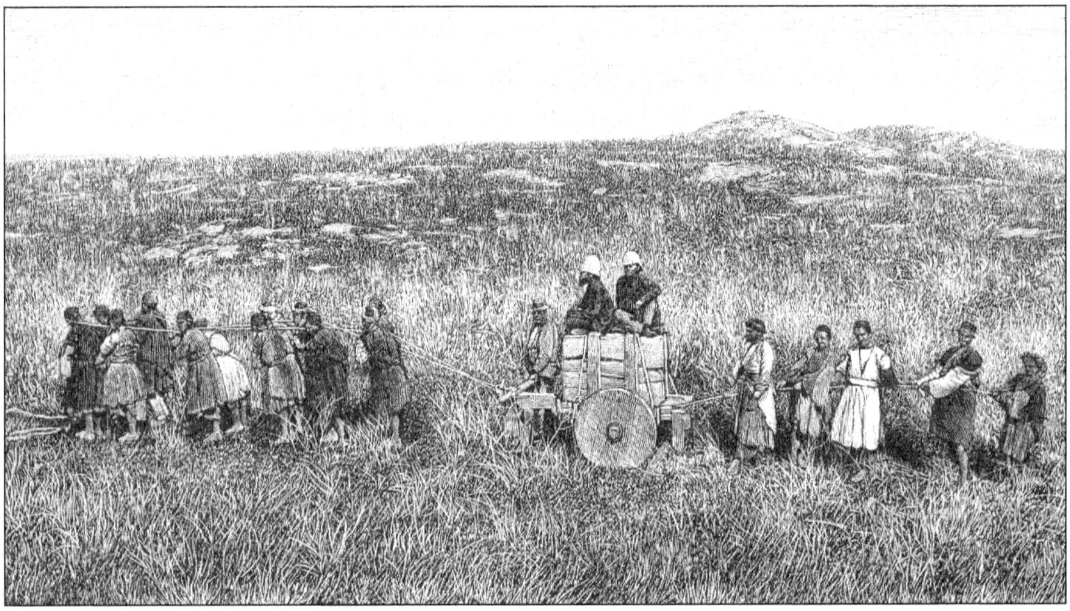

Hauling treasure from Susa to the Persian Gulf

BIBLIOGRAPHY

Abbot, K. E. 1855. "Geographical Notes taken during a journey in Persia in 1849-50," *JRGS* 25, pp. 1-78.

Abdullaev, A. 1963. *Promyshlennost i Zarozhdenie Rabochecego Klassa v kontse XIX nachala XX*. Baku: Nauka.

———. 1968. *Formirovanie Rabochego Klass Iran*. Baku: Nauka.

Adamec L. ed. 1981. *Historical Gazetteer of Iran*, 4 vols. Graz.

Adamiyyat, Fereydun. 1348/1969. *Amir Kabir va Iran*. Tehran: Amir Kabir.

———. 1351/1972. *Andisheh-ye Taraqqi va Hokumat-e Qanun-e `Asr-e Sepahsalar*. Tehran.

———. 1355/1976. *Ideyolozhi-ye nahzat-e mashrutiyat-e Iran*. Tehran.

Adamiyyat, Fereydun & Natiq, Homa. 1356/1977 *Afkar-e ejtema`i va siyasi va eqtisadi dar athar-e montasher nashodeh-ye dowran-e Qajar*. Tehran: Amir Kabir.

Adams, Isaac. 1906. *Persia by a Persian*. London.

Adib al-Molk, `Abdol-`Ali. 1349/1970. *Dafe` al-Ghorur*. ed. Iraj Afshar. Tehran.

Afshar, Iraj. 1349/1970. *Savad va Bayad*. 2 vols. Tehran: Dehkhoda.

Afzal al-Molk Kermani. 1396/1976. *Tarikh va Joghrafiya-ye Qom*. ed. Hoseyn Modarresi Tabataba'i. Qom.

Afzal al-Molk, Gholam Hoseyn 1361/1982. *Afzal al-Tavarikh* ed. Mansureh Ettehadiyeh and Sirus Sa`vandiyan. Tehran.

Algar, H. 1969. *Religion and State in Iran 1785-1906*. Berkeley: University of California Press.

Amanat, Abbas. ed. 1983. *Cities & Trade: Consul Abbott on the Economy and Society of Iran 1847-1866*. London: Ithaca.

Amanat , Abbas. 1989. *Resurrection and Revival. The Making of the Babi Movement in Iran, 1844-1850*. Ithaca/London: Cornell.

Amar-e Dar al-Khelafeh Tehran 1368 edited by Sirus Sa`dvandiyan and Mansureh Ettehadiyeh (Nezam-Mafi) Tehran.

Amin al-Dowleh, Mirza `Ali Khan. 1339/1960. *Khaterat-e siyasi.* ed. Hafez Farmanfarma'iyan Tehran: Ketabha-ye Iran.

Amir-Khizi, Esma`il. 1339/1960. *Qiyam-e Adharbayjan va Sattar Khan.* Tabriz: Ketabforushi Tehran.

AP or *Accounts and Papers*, Government of Great Britain, Parliamentary Papers.

Arasteh, R. 1961 a. "The character, organization and social role of the lutis (javanmardan) in the traditional Iranian society of the 19th century." *Journal of the Economic and Social History of the Orient*, 4, 47-52.

———. 1961 b. "The social life of the Zurkhana (House of Strength) in Iranian urban communities during the 19th century." *Der Islam* 37, pp. 47-52.

———. 1962. *Education and Social Awakening in Iran.* Leiden : Brill.

Ardakani, Hoseyn Mahbubi. 1353/1974. *Tarikh-e mo'assasat-e tamaddoni-ye jadid dar Iran.* 2 vols. Tehran: Daneshgah.

Asaf, Mohammad Hashem. 1348/1969. *Rostam al-Tavarikh.* ed. Mohammad Moshiri. Tehran.

Ashraf, Ahmad. 1970. "Historical Obstacles to the Development of a Bourgeoisie in Iran." In: Studies in the Economic History of the Middle East edited by ed. M.A. Cook. Oxford: Oxford Univ. Press.

———. 1359/1980. *Mavane`-ye tarikhi-ye roshd-i sarmayehdari dar Iran.* Tehran: Payam.

Aubin, E. 1908. *La Perse d'aujourd'hui.* Paris: Armand Colin.

Avery, P. 1965. *Modern Iran.* London : Benn.

Baer, G. 1964. *Egyptian Guilds in Modern Times.* Jerusalem: Israel Oriental Society.

Bahar, Malek al-Sho`ara. 1357/1978. *Tarikh-e mokhtasar-e ahzab-e siyasi-ye Iran.* Tehran: Amir Kabir, 2nd edition.

Bailey, F. G. 1969. *Strategems and Spoils.* Oxford.

Bairoch. P. 1976. *Urban unemployment in Developing Countries.* Geneva: ILO.

Bakhash, Shaul. 1978. *Iran: Bureaucracy & Reform under the Qajars: 1858-1896.* London: Ithaca.

Balfour, J. 1921. *Recent Happenings in Persia.* London: Blackwood and Sons.

Barth, F. 1956. *Nomads of South Persia.* London: Allen & Unwin.

Basset, J. 1887. *Persia, the Land of the Imams.* New York: Charles Scribners Sons.

Bélanger, Ch. 1838. *Voyage aux Indes-Orientales.* 2 vols. Paris.

Benjamin, S.G.W. 1887. *Persia and the Persians.* London: John Murray.

Berichte über Handel und Industrie. 1910 Band 14, Heft 7, Juni.

Beyza'i, D. 1344/1965. *Namayesh dar Iran*. Tehran: Kaviyan.

Beyza'i, Hoseyn Partav-e. 1377/1958. *Tarikh-e Varzesh-e Bastani-ye Iran*. Tehran: Heydari.

Bharier, J. 1971. *The Economic Development of Iran: 1900-1970*. Oxford: Oxford Univ. Press.

Binder, L. 1962. *Iran, Political Development in a Changing Society*. Berkeley: California Univ. Press.

Binning, R. M. B. 1857. *A Journal of Two Years in Persia, Ceylon, etc.* 2 vols. London.

Birch, A. H. 1964. *Representative and Responsible Government*. London.

Bishop, Mrs. 1891. *Journeys in Persia and Kurdistan*. 2 vols. London: John Murray.

Blau, E. 1858. *Commercielle Zustände Persiens*. Berlin: Hofbuchdruckerei (N. v. Decker).

Bleibtreu, J. 1894. *Persien, das Land der Sonne und des Löwen*. Freiburg in Breisgau: Herder.

Bratislaw, A. C. 1923. "Turbulent Tabriz," *Blackwood's Magazine*, 37-59.

Bricteux, A. 1930. *Les comédies de Malkolm Khan*. Liège-Paris: Droz.

Browne, E. G. 1889. *A Year Amongst the Persians*. London: A. & C. Black.

———. 1909. *The Persian Revolution*. Cambridge. Cambridge UP.

Brugsch, H. 1862. *Reise der Königlichen Preussischen Gesandschaft nach Persien (1860-1861)*. 2 vols. Leipzig : Hinrichs.

———. 1886. *Im Lande der Sonne und des Löwen*. Leipzig.

Buckingham, J.S. 1830. *Travels in Assyria, Media and Persia*. London: Henry Colburn. 2 vols.

Buhse, F. A. 1860. *Aufzählung der auf einer Reise durch Persien gesammelten Pflanzen nebst einleitendem Reiseberichte*. Moskou.

Cahen, C. 1958 and 1959. "Mouvements populaires et autonomisme urbain dans l'Asie Musulmane du Moyen Age." *Arabica* 5, 225-250; 6, 233-265.

———. 1960. "Reflexion sur l' usage du mot féodalité," *Journal of Economic Social History of Orient* 3, 2-20.

———. 1970. "Y-a-t-il des corporations professionelles dans le monde musulmane classique?" in Hourani and Stern, *The Islamic City*, 51-64.

Cahen, C. and Taeschner, F. 1965. "Futuwwa." *Encyclopeadia of Islam*, vol. 2.

Chaqueri, C. 1972. *Historical Documents of the Labour Movement in Iran*. vol. 4. Avetis Mikailian (Sultanzade) Selected Writings. Florence: Mazdak.

Chardin, Jean. 1811. *Voyages du Chevalier Chardin en Perse etc.* ed. L. Langlès, 10 vols. Paris: Le Normant.

Clawson, Patrick. 1993. "Knitting Iran Together: The Land Transport Revolution 1920-1940," *Iranian Studies* 26, 235-50.

Cole, Juan. 1985. "Shi`i Clerics in Iran and Iran, 1722-1780: The Akhbari-Usuli Conflict Reconsidered," *Iranian Studies* 18, 3-34.

———. 1989. "Ideology, Ethics and Philosophical Discourse in Eighteenth Century Iran" *Iranian Studies* 22, 7-34.

Commercial Reports, no. 20, Tabriz, 1872-73; Commercial Reports, no. 241. UK Government.

Couldborn, R. 1956. ed. *Feudalism in History*. Princeton: Princeton UP.

Curzon, G. 1892. *Persia and the Persian Question*. 2 vols. London: Longmans, Green & Co.

d'Erp, Baron. 1893 "Rapport concernant l'établissement d'une sucrerie en Perse." Bruxelles.

De Fournaux, G. 1897. "L'industrie, le Commerce et l'Agriculture en Perse." *Societé géographique commerciale de Bordeaux*. Bulletin de deuxième série, 1-33.

De Gobineau, A. 1907a. *Les réligions et philosophies de l'Asie Centrale*. 5th. ed. 2 vols. Paris: G. Crés et Cie.

———. 1907b *Trois Ans en Asie (1855-1858)*. Paris: Bernard Grasset.

De Lacy O'Brien, H. 1873. *Banking in Persia*. London.

Demorgny, G. 1913. *Essai sur l'administration de la Perse*. Paris: Ernest Leroux.

Denis, A. 1843. "Question de Perse. Affaire de Kerbela." *Revue de l'Orient*. I, 129-42.

De Penisse, Comte. 1867. *La Russie, la Perse, l'Inde. Souvenirs de Voyage. 1865-1866*. Paris: Jouaust.

De Rochechouart, J. M. 1867. *Souvenir d'un voyage en Perse*. Paris: Challamel Ainé.

DCR or Diplomatic and Consular Deports, Government of Great Britain, Parliamentary Papers:

(a) Miscellaneous Series no. 590, "Report on the Trade and General Condition of the City and Province of Kermanshah," by Mr. H. L. Rabino.(cited as DCR 590).

(b) Annual Series: DCR no. 33,1878; DCR no. 241, Tabriz, 1886; DCR no. 445, Tabriz, 1888; DCR, no. 976, Mashad, 1892; DCR, no. 1376, Isfahan, 1892-93; DCR. no. 1474, Shiraz, 1894; DCR no. 1662, Isfahan, 1894-95; DCR no. 1671 Isfahan, 1895; DCR no. 1953, Isfahan, 1879; DCR no. 2346, Persian Gulf, 1898; DCR. no. 3032, 1903, Kerman; DCR no. 3724, 1906, Khorassan; DCR, no. 3748, Yazd, 1905-06; DCR no. 3923, Isfahan, 1906; DCR no. 3885, Bandar Abbas, 1907; DCR no. 4397, Bushire, 1908-09; DCR no. 4179, Bushire, 1909; DCR no. 4365, Kermanshah, 1908-09; DCR no. 4379, Bushire, 1909-10; DCR no. 4559, Kermanshah, 1910; DCR no. 4606, Bushire, 1911; DCR no. 4838, Isfahan, 1911; DCR 5003, 1912, Bushire; DCR, no. 5048, Yazd, 1912; DCR, no. 5093, Bushire, 1913; DCR no. 5254, Isfahan, 1912; DCR, no. 6254, Isfahan, 1913.

Dhabihi, Masih. 1348/1969. *Astarabadnameh*. Tehran: Iran Farhang Zamin.

Donboli, `Abd al-Razzaq. 1351/1972. *Ma'ather-e Soltaniyeh*. ed. Gholam Hoseyn Sadri Afshar. Tehran: Ebn Sina.

Dowlatabadi, Yahya. n.d. *Hayat-e Yahya*. 4 vols. Tehran: Ebn Sina.

Drouville, G. 1819. *Voyage en Perse fait en 1812 et 1813*. 2 vols. Paris: Pluchart.

Du Mans, R. 1890. *Estat de la Perse en 1660*. ed. Ch. Schefer. Paris : Ernest Leroux.

Dunlop, H. 1912. *Perzië, Voorheen en Thans*. Haarlem: De Erven F. Bohn.

Dupré, A. 1818. *Voyage en Perse*. 2 vols., Paris: Dentu.

Eastwick, E. B. 1864. *Journal of a Diplomate's three years' residence in Persia*. 2 vols. London: Smith, Elder & Co.

Ebn Bazzaz Ardabili. 1373/1994. *Sefvat al-Safa* ed. GholamReza Tabataba'i-Majd. Tabriz.

Edwards, A. C. 1949. *The Persian Carpet, a survey of the carpet weaving industry of Persia*. London: Duckworth.

Entner, Marvin L. 1956. *Russo-Persian Commercial Relations, 1828-1914*. Gainsville: Univ. of Florida Press.

Eqbal, `Abbas. 1327. "Hojjat al-Eslam Hajj Seyyed Mohammad Mohammad Baqer Shafti," *Yadgar* 5 (10), 28-43.

Eskandar Beg Torkoman. 1334/1965. *Tarikh-e `Alamara-ye `Abbasi*. ed. Iraj Afshar. Tehran: Amir Kabir.

E`temad al-Saltaneh, Mirza Mohammad Hasan Khan (Sani` al-Dowleh). 1306/1889. *Ketab al-Ma`ather va'l-Athar*. Tehran (lithograph).

———. 1294-96/1877-80. *Mer'at al-Boldan*. 4 vols. Tehran (lithograph).

———. 1298-1300/1880-83. *Montazam-e Naseri*. 3 vols. Tehran (lithograph).

———. 1301-03/1884-86. *Matla` al-Shams*. 3 vols. Tehran 1301-03 (lithograph).

———. 1345/1967. *Ruznameh-ye Khaterat*. ed. Iraj Afshar. Tehran: Amir Kabir.

———. 1357/1978. *Sadr al-Tavarikh*. ed. Mohammad Moshiri. Tehran.

Ettehadiyeh, Mansureh. 1361/1982. *Maramnamehha va Nezamnamehha-ye Ahzab-e siyasi-ye Iran dar dovvomin dowreh-ye Majles-e shura-ye melli*. Tehran: Tarikh.

Farmanfarmayan, Hafez. 1968. "The Forces of Modernization in Nineteenth Century Iran." In: *Beginnings of Modernization in the Middle East*, 119-154 edited by W.R. Polk & R.L. Chambers, Chicago: Univ. Chicago Press.

Fasa'i, Hajj Mirza Hasan. 1314-16/1894-96. *Farsnameh-ye Naseri*. 2 vols. Tehran (lithograph).

Fatah. M. K 1926. *The Economic Position of Persia*. New York.

Fekete, L. 1955. *Die Siyaqat-Schrift in der türkischen Finanzverwaltung* 2 vols. Budapest.

Feuvrier, J. B. 1900. *Trois ans à la Cour de Perse*. Paris: F. Juven.

Fischel, J. 1950. "The Jews of Persia." *Jewish Social Studies* 12, 119-160.

Floor, Willem. 1971a. "The Lutis, a social phenomenon in Qajar Persia." *Die Welt des Islams*, 13, 103-120.

———. 1971b. "The office of kalantar in Qajar Persia." *Journal of the Economic and Social History of the Orient*, 14, 253-68.

———. 1971c. "The market police in Qajar Persia, the office of darugha-yi bazar and muhtasib." *die Welt des Islams*, 13,212-29.

———. 1972. "The police in Qajar Iran." *Zeitschrift der Deutschen Morgenländische Gesellschaft*, 123, 293-315.

———. 1973. "Two communications". *Zeitschrift der Deutschen Morgenländische Gesellschaft* 123, 97-81.

———. 1975. "The Guilds in Iran - an Overview from the earliest Beginnings till 1972" *Zeitschrift der Deutschen Morgenländische Gesellschaft* 125, 99-116.

———. 1976. "The merchants (*tujjar*) in Qajar Iran." *Zeitschrift der Deutschen Morgenländische Gesellschaft*, 126, 101-135.

———. 1977. "Bankruptcy in Qajar Iran." *Zeitschrift der Deutschen Morgenländische Gesellschaft* 127, 61-76.

———. 1979. "The bankers (*sarraf*) in Qajar Iran." *Zeitschrift der Deutschen Morgenländische Gesellschaft* 129, 263-81.

———. 1980. "Das Amt des Muhtasib im Iran - zur Kontrolle der Oeffentlichen Moral in der Iranischen Geschichte", in: K.Greussing & J-H. Grevemeyer (eds.), *Revolution in Iran und Afghanistan*, Mardomnameh - Jahrbuch zur Geschichte und Gesellschaft des Mittleren Orients. Berlin.

———. 1981. "The Political Role of the Lutis in Iran," In: *Modern Iran, the Dialectics of Continuity and Change*, edited by M.E. Bonine and N.R. Keddie, 83-95. Albany: SUNY.

———. 1983a. "The creation of the food administration in Iran." *Iranian Studies*, 16, 199-227.

———. 1983 b. "Hotz Versus Muhammad Shafi`: A Case Study In Commercial Litigation In Qajar Iran, 1888-1894," *IJMES* 15 (1983), pp. 185-209.

———. 1983 c. "Change and development in the judicial system of Qajar Iran (1800-1925)," ed. Edmund Bosworth and Carole Hillenbrand (Edinburgh 1983) 113-47.

———. 1984a. "Guilds and Futuvvat in Iran," *Zeitschrift der Deutschen Morgenländische Gesellschaft* 134, 106-114.

———. 1984b. *Industrialization in Iran 1900-1941*. Durham Centre for Middle Eastern and Islamic Studies, Occasional Paper No 23.

———. 1985 a. *Labour Unions, Law & Conditions In Iran: 1900-1941*, Durham : Centre for Middle Eastern & Islamic Studies.

———. 1985 b. "The office of muhtasib in Iran." *Iranian Studies*. 18, 53-74.

———. 1987. "Asnaf," *Encyclopedia Iranica*.

———. 1366/1987. *Jostarha'i az tarikh-e ejtema`i-ye Iran dar `asr-e Qajar*. Tehran: Tus. Translated by Abu'l-Qasem Serri.

———. 1991. "Traditional handicrafts and modern industry in Iran: 1800-1914." *Zeitschrift der Deutschen Morgenländische Gesellschaft* 141, pp. 317-52.

———. 1992. "Les premières règles de police urbaine à Téhéran," in *Téhéran Capitale bicentinaire* eds. C. Adle and B. Hourcade (Paris-Tehran), 173-98.

———. 1999a. *A Fiscal History of Iran in the Safavid and Qajar Periods*. (New York: Bibliotheca Persica).

———. 1999b. *The Persian Textile Industry, Its Products and Their Use (1500-1925)*. Paris: L'Harmattan.

———. 1999c. "Art (Naqqashi) and artists (Naqqashan) in Qajar Persia," *Muqarnas* 16, 129-58.

———. 2001. "The Economic Role of the Ulama in Qajar Persia," in Linda Walbridge ed. *The Most Learned of the Shi`a*. New York: OUP, pp. 53-81.

———. 2002. "The Art of Smoking in Iran and other uses of tobacco," in *Iranian Studies* 35, 47-86.

———. 2003 a. *The Traditional Crafts of Qajar Iran*. Costa Mesa: Mazda.

———. 2003 b. *Agriculture in Qajar Iran*. Washington, DC: MAGE.

———. 2004a. "Tea Consumption and Imports in Qajar Iran," *Studia Iranica* 33, 47-111.

———. 2004b. Public Health in Qajar Iran Washington DC: MAGE.

———. 2005a. *The History of Theater in Iran*. Washington DC: MAGE.

———. 2005b. *Wall Paintings in Qajar Iran* Costa Mesa: Mazda

———. 2006 a. *The Persian Gulf. A Political and Economic History of Five Port Cities, 1500-1730*. Washington DC: MAGE.

———. 2006 b. "The Woodworking Craft and Its Products in Iran," *Muqarnas* 23, 159-89.

———. 2008. "Weights and Measures in Qajar Iran," *Studia Iranica* 37, 57-115.

———. 2009a. *Labor and Industry in Iran. 1850-1941*. Washington DC: MAGE.

———. 2009b. *The Imports of Textiles Into Qajar Iran* Costa Mesa: Mazda.

Floyer, Ernest Ayscoghe. 1882. *Unexplored Baluchistan*. London.

Forbes, Frederick. 1844. "Route from Turbat Haideri, in Khorasan, to the river Heri Rud, on the borders of Sistan," *JRGS* 14, pp. 145-92.

FO (Foreign Office) Files. Public Record Office, London (transcripts of Crown copy-right records in the PRO appear by permission of Her Majesty's Stationary Office).

Forsat, Mirza Aqa Forsat Hoseyni Shirazi. 1316/1898. *Ketab-e `Ajam*, Tehran (lithograph).

Frank, C. 1926. "Über den schiitischen Mudschtahid," *Islamica* 2, 171-92.

Fraser, J. B. 1825. *Narrative of a Journey into Khorassan*. London: Longman, Rees, Orme, Brown, and Green.

———. 1826. *Travels and Adventures in the Persian Provinces on the banks of the Caspian Sea*. London: Longman, Rees, Orme, Brown, and Green.

———. 1842. *An Historical and Descriptive Account of Persia*. New York.

Gasteiger Khan, Albert. 1881. *Von Teheran nach Beludschistan*. Innsbruck.

Gaube, Heinz and Wirth, Eugen. 1978. *Der Bazar von Isfahan* Wiesbaden: Reichert.

Ghaffari. 1361/1982. *Khaterat va Asnad-e Mohammad `Ali Ghaffari*. eds. Mansureh Ettehadiyeh (Nezam Mafi) and Sirus Sa`vandiyan. Tehran.

Gibb H. A. R & Bowen H. 1956. *Islamic Society and the West*. 2 vols. Oxford: Oxford UP.

Gibb, H. A. R. 1966. "The evolution of government in early Islam", In *Studies on the Civilization of Islam* by H.A.R. Gibb, 34-46 edited by S. Shaw and W.R. Polk. London: Routledge & Kegan Paul.

Gilbar, Gad. 1976. "Demographic Developments in Late Qajar Persia, 1870-1906." *Asian and African Studies* 11, 125-56.

———. 1978. "The Persian Economy in the mid-19th century." *Welt des Islams* 29, 177-211.

———. 1983. "Trends in the development of prices in late Qajar Iran 1870-1906," *Iranian Studies* 16.

Gleadowe-Newcomen, A. H. 1905. *Commercial Mission to South-Eastern Persia during 1904-05*. Calcutta: Government Press.

Goitein, S. D. 1966. *Studies in Islamic History and Institutions*. Leiden: Brill.

Goldsmid, F. 1876. *Eastern Persia, an account of the Persian Boundary Commission, 1870-72*. 2 vols. London: MacMillan & Co.

Golriz, M. A. 1326/1947. *Minudar ya Bab al-Jennah-ye Qazvin*. Tehran: Daneshgah.

Golzari, Mas`ud ed. 2535/1976. *Safarnameh-ye Astarabad va Mazandaran va Gilan*. Tehran.

Gordon, T. E. 1896. *Persia Revisited*. London: Edward Arnold.

Gramlich, F. 1965. *Die schiitischen Derwischorden Persiens*. 3 vols. Wiesbaden: Franz Steiner.

Greenfield, J. 1904. *Die Verfassung des Persischen Staates*. Berlin: Franz Vahlen.

———. 1906. "Das Handelsrecht, einschliesslich das Obligationen und Pfandrechtes, das Urkundearecht, Konkursrecht und das Fremdenrecht von Persien" In *Die Handelsgesetze des Erdbals*, Band VI. Berlin: R. v. Decker.

Gurney, D. 1983. " A Qajar Household and Its Estates," *Iranian Studies* 16, 137-76.

Ha'eri. A. H. 1977. *Shi'ism and Constitutionalism in Iran*. Leiden: Brill.

Hakimian, Hassan. 1985. "Wage Labour and Migration: Persian Workers in Southern Russia, 1880-1914," *The International Journal of Middle East Studies*, vol. 17, no 4, November.

Hall, E. T. 1966. *The Silent Language*. Fawcett Premier Book.

Häntzsche, J. C. 1866. "Spezial Statistik von Persien." *Zeitschrift f. Erdkunde* Berlin, 429-450.

Hedayat, Mehdiqoli. 1344/1965. *Khaterat va Khatarat*. Tehran : Zavvar.

Höltzer, Ernst. 2535/1977. *Persien vor 113 Jahren*. Tehran.

Horst, H. 1964. *Die Staatsverwaltung der Grosseljuqen und Khorazmshahs (1083-1231)*. Wiesbaden: Franz Steiner.

Houtum-Schindler, Albert. 1881. "Reisen in südlichen Persien 1879," *Zeitschrift der Gesellschaft für Erdkunde zu Berlin* 16, pp. 312-31.

———. 1896. *Eastern Irak*. London.

———. 1911. "Persia", *Encyclopedia Brittanica* 10th ed.

Hume-Griffith, M. E. 1909. *Behind The Veil In Persia And Turkish Arabia*. London.

Hurewitz, J. C. 1956. *Diplomacy in the Near and Middle East, A Documentary Record 1535-1914*. New York.

Ibn Battutta. 1962. *The Travels of Ibn Battutta*. Translated by H. A. R. Gibb. 4 vols. Cambridge: Cambridge UP/Hakluyt Society.

Issawi, C. 1971. *The Economic History of Iran 1800-1914*. Chicago: Chicago UP.

Ivanov, M. S. 1356/1977. *Tarikh-e Novin-e Iran*. Stockholm: Hezb-e Tudeh-ye Iran.

Ivanov, W. 1933. *Divan of Khaki Khorasani*. Bombay Islamic Research Association.

Jaberi Ansari, Hajji Mirza Hasan Khan Sheikh. 1322/1944. *Tarikh-e Isfahan*. Isfahan: Hoseyn `Emadzadeh.

Jamalzadeh, Mohammad `Ali. 1335/1916. *Ganj- e Shayegan*. Berlin: Kaveh.

Janab, Aqa Mir Sayyed `Ali. 1303/1924. *Ketab al-Esfahan*. Isfahan (lithograph).

Jaubert, P. A. 1821. *Voyage en Arménie et en Perse*. Paris: Pélicien et Nepveu.

Javadi, Shafi`. 1350/1971. *Tabriz va Peyramun*. Tabriz.

Jenner, George. 1870. "Report by Mr. Jenner on the Condition of the Working Classes in Persia," AP 32 (LXVIII), 396-400.

Jones, Henry L. 1870. "Report by Consul-General Jones on the Condition of the Indstrial Classes in Tabreez," AP 32 (LXVIII), 417-22.

Juvaini, `Ata-Malik. 1958. *The History of the World Conqueror.* translated by J. A. Boyle. Manchester: Manchester UP.

Kashefi Sabzevari, Mowlana Hoseyn Va'ez. 1350/1971. *Fotovvatnameh-ye Soltani.* ed. Mahjub, Mohammad Ja`far. Tehran: Bonyad-e Fahang-e Iran.

Kasravi, Ahmad. 1319-21/1940-43. *Tarikh-e Mashruteh-ye Iran.* 3 vols. Tehran: Peyman.

Kazemzadeh, F. 1962. "Iranian Histiography," in B. Lewis and P.M. Holt eds. *Historians of the Middle East.* London.

Kaye, J. W. 1921. *The Life and Correspondence of Major-General Sir John Malcolm.* 2 vols. London.

Kazem Beg, "Bab et les Babis." 1866. *Journal Asiatique* VII, 329-84, 457-522; VIII, 196-252, 357-400, 473-507.

Kazemzadeh, F. 1968. *Russia and Britain in Persia, 1864-1914.* Yale UP

Keddie, N. R. 1950. *Historical Obstacles to Agrarian Change in Iran.* Claremont.

———. 1966. *Religion and Rebellion in Iran.* London: Cass.

———. 1969. "The Roots of the Ulama's Power in Modern Iran," *Studia Islamica* 29, 31-53.

Keyhan, Mas`ud. 1311. *Jografiya-ye mofassal-e Iran.* Tehran.

Khorasani, Manouchehr Moshragh. 2006. *Arms and Armor from Iran. The Bronze Age to the End of the Qajar Period* Tübingen: Legat.

Kosogovski, V. A. 1344/1965. *Khaterat-e Kolonel Kasakufski.* Translated by `Abbasqoli Halabi. Tehran: Ketabha-ye Simorgh.

Kotzebue, M. von. 1819. *Narrative of a Journey into Persia.* London.

Kuznetsova. N. A. 1358/1978. *Owza`-ye Siyasi va Eqtesadi - Ejtema`i-ye Iran [Ocherki novoi istorii Irana xix- nachalo xx vv,* Moscow 1978] tr. Sirus Izadi. Tehran.

Lady Sheil. 1856. *Glimpses of Persian Life.* London: John Murray.

Lambton. A. K. S. 1954. *Islamic Society In Persia.* London.

———. 1958. "Secret Societies and the Persian revolution of 1905-1906," *St. Anthony's Papers* no. 4.

_———. 1961. "Persian Society under the Qajars," *Journal of the Royal Central Asian Society* 48, 123-139.

_———. 1963a. "The Office of kalantar under the Safawids and Afshars." In *Mélanges d'Orientalisme offerts à Henri Massé,* 206-18. Tehran: Daneshgah.

———. 1963b. "Persian Political Societies, 1906-11." *St. Anthony's Papers,* 16.

———. 1965. "The Merchant in Mediaeval Islam", In *A Locust's Leg, Studies in Honour of S.E. Taqizadeh*, edited by W.B. Henning and E. Yarshater. London : Percy Lund, Humphries & Co.

———. 1970. "Persian Trade Under the early Qajars." In: *Islam and the Trade of Asia*, 215-44 edited by D.S. Richards. Oxford: Cassirer & Univ. Pennsylvania Press.

Landor, A.H.S. 1902. *Across Coveted Lands*. 2 vols. London : Charles Scribners Sons.

Layard, Sir A. 1894. *Early Adventures in Persia*. London: John Murray.

Legatie Perzië, Algemeen Rijks Archief (National Archives), the Hague, the Netherlands.

Legatie Perzië II, Letter August 17, 1907. When I consulted this letter it was kept in Record Group B 993, Ministerie van Buitenlandse Zaken, den Haag (the Netherlands). Meanwhile, I have learnt that these records have been transferred to the Algemeen Rijks Archief around 1990, probably to record group Legatie Perzië.

Lenczowski. G. 1968. *Russia and the West in Iran*. New York: Greenwood Press.

Lewis, Bernard. 1937. "The Islamic Guilds." *Economic History Review* 8, 20-37.

Litvak, Meir. 1990. "Continuity and Change in the Ulama Population of Najaf and Karbala, 1791-1904: A Socio-Demographic Study," *Iranian Studies* 23, pp. 31-60.

Lorimer, J.G. 1908. *Gazetteer of the Persian Gulf*. 5 vols. Calcutta: Government Printing.

Lorini, E. 1900. La *Persia economica contemporeana e la sua questione monetaria*. Rome: Ermanno Loescher.

Ma`ani, Ahmad Golchin. 1347/1968. *Shahr-e ashub dar she`r-e farsi*. Tehran: Amir Kabir.

Mafi 1361/1982. *Khaterat va Asnad-e Hoseyn Qoli Khan Nezam al-Molk Nezam al-Saltaneh Mafi* 2 vols. ed. Ma`sumeh Nezam-Mafi and Sirus Sa`dvandiyan. Tehran.

Mahjub, Mohammad. 1337/1958. "Sokhanvari." *Sokhan*, 9, nrs. 6, 7, 8; translated by Meier 1964.

Majd al-Islam Kermani, Ahmad. 1350/1971. *Tarikh-e enqelab-e mashrutiyyat-e Iran*. 2 vols. ed. Mahmud Khalilpur. Isfahan: Daneshgah.

———. 1351/1972. *Tarikh-e Enhelal-e Majles*. ed. Mahmud Khalilpur Isfahan: Daneshgah.

Malcolm, John. 1820. *The History of Persia from the early period to the present time*. 2 vols. London: John Murray.

Malekzadeh, M. 1328-38. *Tarikh-e enqelab-e mashrutiyat-e Iran*, Tehran: Soqrat. 6 vols.

Massé, H. 1938. *Croyances et Coutumes Persanes*. 2 vols., Paris: Maisonneuve.

Massignon, L. 1920. "Les corps de métiers et la cité islamique." *Revue Internationale de Sociologie* 28, 473-89.

———. 1927. "Sinf" in *Encyclopeadia of Islam*, vol. 7.

Mazzaoui, M.M.1972. *The Origins of the Safawids*. Wiesbaden: Franz Steiner.

Mehrabadi, Abu'l-Qsem Rafi`. 1367. *Ateshkadeh-ye Ardestan*. 3 vols. Tehran.

Meier, F. and Gramlich, R. 1961. "Drei moderne Texte zum Persischen Wettreden," *ZDMG* 23, 289-327.

Melikoff, Irene. 1961. "Nombres symboliques dans la littérature épico-réligieuse des Turcs d Anatolie." *Journal Asiatique*, 435-445.

Migeod, Heinz-Georg. 1959. "Die Lutis. Ein Ferment des städtischen Lebens in Persien." *JESHO* 2, 82-91.

———.1990. *Die persische Gesellschaft under Nasiru'd-Din Shah* (1848-96). Berlin: Klaus Schwarz.

Mignan, R. 1839. *A winter journey through Russia, the Caucasian Alps and Georgia*. 2 vols. London.

Miller, W. G. 1969. "Political organization in Iran." *Middle East Journal* 2, 159-67.

Millspaugh, A.C. 1926. *The Financial and Economic Situation of Persia*, 1926. New York.

———. 1925. *The American Task in Persia*. New York: The Century.

Minorsky, V. 1921. "Notes sur la secte des Ahle-haqq." *R.M.M.* vols. XL (1920), pp. 20-97 and XLV (1921), pp. 205-302.

Mirjafari, Hossein. 1979. "The Haydari-Ni`mati Conflicts in Iran." *Iranian Studies* 12, 134-162.

Modarresi, Nur al-Din Chahardehi. 1358/1979. *Khaksar va Ahl-e Haqq*. n. p.

Modarresi-ye `Alam, Ma`sum `Alishah. 1338/1959. *Ganjineh-ye Owliya*. Tehran.

Molkara, `Abbas Mirza. 1325/1946. *Sharh-e Hal*. ed. `Abbas Eqbal. Tehran: Babak.

Monthly Labour Review 1946. US Government.

Moose, Matti. 1987. *Extremist Shiites*. Syracuse: Syracuse UP.

Morgan, J. de 1905. *Histoire et Travaux de la Délégation en Perse*. Paris.

Morier, James. 1812. *A Journey through Persia etc. in the years 1808 and 1809*. London: Longman, Hurst, Reese, Orme and Browne.

———. 1818. *A Second Journey through Persia. London*: Longman, Hurst, Reese, Orme and Browne.

Moser, Henri. 1885. *A Travers l'Asie Centrale*. Paris: Plon.

Mo'taman, `Ali. 1348/1969. *Rahnama ya Tarikh va Towsif-e Darbar-e Velayatmadar-e Razavi*. Tehran.

Mostowfi, `Abdollah. n.d. *Sharh-e Zendegani-ye man*. Tehran: Zavvar, 2nd edition.

Mounsey, A. H. 1872. *A Journey through the Caucasus and the interior of Persia*. London: Smith, Elder & Co.

Müller, H. 1966. *Studien zum persischen Passionsspiel*. Freiburg.

Najm al-Molk, Hajj `Abdol-Ghaffar. 1341/1962. *Safarnameh-ye Khuzestan*. ed. Mohammad Dabirsiyaqi. Tehran.

Naficy, H. 1924. *L'impôt et la vie économique et sociale en Iran*. Paris.

Naraqi, Ehsan. 1345/1966. *Tarikh-e Ejtema`i-ye Kashan*. Tehran: Daneshgah.

Neligan, A.R. 1926. "Public health in Persia." *The Lancet* 20 March, 635-39.

Nizam al-Mulk 1960. *The Book of Government or Rules for Kings*. Translated by Hubert Darke. London: Routledge & Kegan Paul.

Olmer, U. 1906. "L'Industrie Persane," *Nouvelles Archives des Missions Scientifiques et Littéraires*, 16, 1-110.

Olson, William J. 1980. "The Mazandaran Development Project and Haji Mohammad Hasan," In *Towards a Modern Iran*, 38-55. edited by Elie Kedourie & Sylvia G. Haim. London.

Orsolle, E. 1885. *Le Caucase et la Perse*. Paris: Plon, Nourrit & Co.

Ossetrov V. 1922. "Rabochee professional'noe dvizhenie v Persii," *Novii Vostok*, 2.

Pakdaman, Naser. 1353/1974. "Najm al-Dowleh va Resaleh-ye Nofus-e Tehran," *Farhang Iran Zamin*, 324-347.

Perkins, J. 1843. *A Residence of Eight Years in Persia*. Andover: Allen, Morrill & Wardell.

Perry, John R. 2000. "Toward a Theory of Iranian Urban Moieties: the Haydariyyah and Ni`matiyyah Revisited." *Iranian Studies* 32, 51-70.

Philliot, D.C. 1906. "Some lullabies and topical songs collected in Persia. Fair samples of those composed and sung by the lutis (strolling player. buffoon)." *Journal of the Asiatic Society of Bombay*, vol. 1, 41-53.

———. 1907. "A note on Sign-, Gesture-, Code- and Secret language etc. amongst the Persians." *Journal of the Asiatic Society of Bombay*, vol. 2, 619-22.

Phillip, Thomas. 1984. "Isfahan 1881-1891: a close-up view of guilds and production," *Iranian Studies* 27/4, 391-411.

Pigulevskaia. N. V. 1346/1967. *Tarikh-e Iran az dowran-e bastan ta saddeh-ye hejdahom*. Translated from the Russian by Karim Keshavarz. 2 vols. Tehran: Daneshgah.

Polak, E. J. 1861. "Über die Communicationsmittel, die Sicherheit des Eigenthums und der Reisenden, und über Asyle in Persien." *Mitteilungen der Kais.-Kgl. Geographischen Gesellschaft*, 40-64.

———. 1865. *Persien, das Land und seine Bewohner*. 2 vols. Leipzig: F.A. Brockhaus.

Qazvini, Mohammad Shafi`. 1370/1991. *Qanun-e Qazvini*. Ed. Iraj Afshar. Tehran: Talayeh.

Rabino, J. 1892. "Banking in Persia." *Journal of the Institute of Bankers*, 1-56.

Rabino, H. L. 1914. "Les sports au Guilan." *R.M.M.* 26, 97-112.

———. 1352/1973. *Mashruteh-ye Gilan*. Resht: Ta`ati. Edited by M. Roshan. Tehran: Tahhuri.

Radimsky, W. 1909. *Industrie und Gewerbe Verhältnisse im Persien*. Wien.

Rafi`, `Abd al-Rafi` Haqiqat. 1352/1973. *Tarikh-e Semnan*. Tehran: Farmandari-ye Koll-e Semnan.

Ra'in, Ema`il. 2536/1977. *Hoquqbegiran-e inglis dar Iran*. Tehran: Javidan.

Rashid al-Din. 1940. *Tarikh-e Mobarak-e Ghazani*. ed. Karl Jahn. London: Luzac.

Ravasani, S. n.d. *Sowjetrepublik Gilan. Die sozialistischen Bewegung in Iran seit Ende des 19 Jhdt bis 1922*. Berlin: Basis.

RO or *Revue de l'Orient*, Paris.

RMM or *Revue du Monde Musulman*, Paris

Rich, C.J. 1836. *Narrative of a residence in Koordistan etc*. 2 vols. London: James Duncan.

Roemer, H. R. 1952. *Staatsschreiben der Timuridenzeit*. Wiesbaden: Steiner.

Ronall, J. 1969. "The Beginnings of Modern Banking in Iran." In *Wissenschaft und Technik* edited by K.-H. Mangold. Munich.

Rumlu, Hasan. 1934. *Ahsan al-Tavarikh*. translated by C. N. Seddon 2 vols. Baroda.

Saba, Mohsen. 1971. "A note on Lebas al-Taqva." *Tahqiqat-e eqtesadi* 8, no. 21, 103-06.

Sadid al-Saltaneh, Mohammad `Ali. 1342/1963. *Bandar `Abbas va Khalij-e Fars*. Tehran: Ebn Sina.

Safa'i, Ebrahim. 1344/1965. *Rahbaran-e mashruteh*. Tehran.

Safiniya, R. 1307/1928. *Kelid-e Esteqlali-ye gomroki-ye Iran*. Tehran: Ferdousi.

Savory, R. M. 1969. "Communication." *Der Islam* 38, 161-165.

Sayyah, Hajj. 1346/1967. *Khaterat-e Hajj Sayyah*. ed. Hamid Sayyah. Tehran.

Schwartz, Benjamin. 1942. *Letters from Persia, written by Charles and Edward Burgess 1828-1855*. New York: Public Library.

Seidov, R.A. 1974. *Iranskaja Burzhuazja v kontse XIX nachala XX veka*. Moscow: Nauka.

Sepehr, Lesan al-Molk. 1808. *Tarikh-e Dar al-Saltaneh-ye Tabriz*. Tehran (litho).

Setareh-ye Sorkh 7, April 8 1960 (published in Germany).

Shaje`i, Zahra. 1344/1965. *Namayandegan-e Majles-e Shura-ye Melli dar bist va yek dowreh-ye qanungodhari*. Tehran: Daneshgah.

Shakeri, Ramazan `Ali. 1346/1967. *Joghrafiya-ye Tarikhi-ye Quchan*. Mashhad.

Shamim, `Ali. 1342/1963. *Asghar Iran dar dowreh-ye saltanat-e Qajar*. Tehran: Ebn Sina.

Sepsis, A. 1844. "Perse. Quelques mots sur l'état réligieux actuel de la Perse." *Revue de l'Orient*, III, 97-114.

Shuster, W. M. 1911. *The Strangling of Persia*. New York: The Century Comp.

Sirjani, Sa`idi ed. 1361/1982. *Vaqaye`-ye Ettefaqiyeh - gozareshha-ye khafiyeh-nevisan-e englis*. Tehran.

Sjoberg, G. 1960. *The Pre-Industrial City*. Glencoe: Univ. of Illinois Press.

Smith, E. & Dwight, H. G. O. 1834. *Missionary Researches in Armenia*. London.

Smith Jr, J. Masson. 1979. *The History of the Sardabar Dynasty 1336-1381 AD and its sources*. The Hague: Mouton.

Smith, Sydney. 1870. "Report by Major Smith, Assistant Resident at Bushire on the Condition of the Working Classes in Bushire", *AP* 32 (LXVIII), 400-04.

Southgate, H. 1840. *Narrative of a Tour through Armenia, Kurdistan, Persia and Mesopotamia*. 2 vols. New York.

Stack, E. 1882. *Six Months in Persia*. 2 vols. New York : Putnam.

Stern, S.M. 1970. "The Constitution of the Islamic City." In *The Islamic City*, 25-50 edited by A.H. Hourani and S.M. Stern, Oxford: Cassirer.

Stirling, Eddward 1991. *The Journals of Edward Stirling in Persia and Afghanistan 1828-1829*. ed. Jonathan L. Lee Naples.

Stolze F. & Andreas, F.C. 1885. "Die Handelsverhältnisse Persiens." In *Petermanns Mitteilungen* Erg.-Band. 17, no. 77.

Stuart, Lt. Col. 1854. *Journal of a Residence in Northern Persia*. London.

Sykes, Sir Percy M. *Ten Thousand Miles* (London, 1902).

Sykes, Ella 1910. *Persia and Its People*. London.

Tadhkirat al-Muluk 1943. edited and translated by V. Minorky. London: Luzac.

Taeschner, Franz. 1965. "Fotuvat, eine gemeinschaftbildende Idee im mitteralterlichen Orient und ihre verschiedenen Erscheinungsformen." *Schweizerisches Archiv für Volkskunde* 52, 122-158.

———. 1979. *Zünfte and Bruderschaften im Islam*. Zürich.

Tahvildar, Mirza Mohammad Hoseyn Khan. 1341/1962. *Joghrafiya-ye Isfahan*. Ed. M. Setudeh. Tehran: Daneshgah.

Tehran Municipality. 1310/1931. *Second Statistical Yearbook of the City of Tehran, 1925-29*. Tehran: Majles, or Baladiyeh-ye Tehran (Servis-e Ma`aref va Ehsa'iyeh va Nashiriyat), *Dovvomin Salnameh-ye Ehsa'iyeh-ye Shahr-e Tehran* Tehran.

Temple, B. 1922. *Report on the Trade and Transport Conditions in Persia to January 1922*. London: HMSO.

Thompson, R.F. 1864. "Report [on the trade of Persia]." UK Government, Parliamentary Paper, *Accounts and Papers* 30-2, LXI 2 (3392).

Thorning, H. 1913. *Beiträge zur Kenntnis des islamischen Vereinswesens*. Berlin.

Unwin, G. 1925. *The Guilds and Companies of London*. London.

Vambery, A. 1884. *His life and adventures*. London.

———. 1867. *Meine Wanderungen und Erlebnisse in Persien*. Pesht.

Van Vloten, M.G. 1894. "Les Drapeaux en Usage à la Fête de Husein à Téhéran." *Internationales Archiv für Ethnographie* 5, 105-111.

Vaziri, Ahmad `Ali Khan. 1346/1967. *Joghrafiya-ye Kerman*. ed. Bastani Parizi, Tehran: Farhang Iran Zamin.

Verslag van bevindingen omtrent den Staat van Zaken te Bender Bushire, Ternate 30/12/1877, unfoliated. Dossier B 93, Archives Ministerie van Buitenlandse Zaken, den Haag, the Netherlands. Transferred to the National Archives.

Von Kotzebue, M. 1819. *Narrative of a Journey into Persia etc. in the year 1817.* London.

Waring, E. Scott. 1807. *A Tour to Sheeraz by the Route of Kazroon and Feerozabad.* London: T. Cadell and W. Davies.

Weber, M. 1925. *Wirtschaft und Gesellschaft*. 2nd ed. Tübingen.

Wilber, D.N. 1963. *Contemporary Iran*. London.

Wills, C. J. 1886. *Persia As It Is*. London.

———. 1883. *In the Land of the Lion and the Sun*. London: Ward, Lock and Bowden.

Wilson, S.G. 1896. *Persian Life and Customs*. New York: Fleming H. Revell.

Wilson. Arnold. 1942. *South West Persia. Letters and Diary of a Young Political Officer 1907-1*. London: Oxford UP.

Wirth, E. 1976. *Der Orienteppich und Europsa Ein Beitrag zu den vielfälltigen Aspekten west-ostlicher Kulturkontakte und Wirtschaftsbeziehungen*. Erlangen (Erlanger Geographischis Arbeiten 37).

Wulff, H.E. 1966. *The Traditional Crafts of Persia*. Cambridge : MIT

Yate, C. E. 1900. *Khurasan and Seistan*. London/Edinburgh: Blackwood and Sons.

Zabih, S. 1969. The Communist Movement in Iran. Berkeley : California UP.

Zarrabi, `Abd ol-Rahman. 1342/ 1963. *Tarikh-e Kashan*. ed. Iraj Afshar. Tehran: Ebn Sina.

INDEX

N

O

T

U

V

W

Y

Z

www.ingramcontent.com/pod-product-compliance
Ingram Content Group UK Ltd.
Pitfield, Milton Keynes, MK11 3LW, UK
UKHW051459290926
15471UKWH00008B/1289

9 781933 823317